Other Books by Kasma Loha-unchit

It Rains Fishes: Legends, Traditions, and the Joys of Thai Cooking

DANCING SHRIMP

Favorite Thai Recipes for Seafood

Kasma Loha-unchit

Simon & Schuster

New York London Toronto Sydney Singapore

SIMON & SCHUSTER
Rockefeller Center
1230 Avenue of the Americas
New York, NY 10020

SIMON & SCHUSTER and colophon are registered trademarks
of Simon & Schuster, Inc.

Book design by Ellen R. Sasahara

Illustrations by Toby Goodenough

Manufactured in the United States of America

10 9 8 7 6 5 4 3 2 1

Library of Congress Cataloging-in-Publication Data
Loha-unchit, Kasma.
    Dancing shrimp : favorite Thai recipes for seafood / Kasma Loha-unchit.
      p.   cm.
    Includes index.
    1. Cookery (Seafood)   2. Cookery, Thai.   I. Title
TX747.L64 2000
641.6*92'09593—dc21
        00-041268

ISBN 0-684-86272-7

To my husband, Michael,
for his loving support
and his inspiring love of seafood!

ACKNOWLEDGMENTS

WHEN I FIRST STARTED OFFERING THAI COOKING CLASSES MANY, MANY years ago, I did not have written recipes to hand out to my students. I had learned from my mother to work intuitively with the ingredients at hand, tasting and making adjustments as necessary in the process of creating dishes to please the palate, and this creative style was what I wished to impart to those who came to my classes. It didn't take long before I discovered that, in the fast-paced, modern American society into which I had transplanted myself, the oral and sensory tradition of working with food had all but become lost, replaced by confident reliance on the precise measurements and instructions given on the printed pages of cookbooks.

Realizing how busy people were and how little time they had to devote to learning a foreign cuisine, I set out on the painstaking task of measuring every shake of sauce from a bottle, every dollop of paste from a jar, and every pile of chopped ingredients, handful of herbs, and sprinkling of spice that I so casually added to the pot and pan as I cooked. My students helped me and I learned from them how to write recipes and give instructions in the clear language that even complete novices in the kitchen could understand. I knew I had succeeded when beginners who admitted they had never cooked anything in their lives and didn't even know how to go about boiling a pot of water, much less an egg, could within a few weeks confidently entertain friends to a Thai food feast!

Looking back, I have a lot for which to be grateful to all the patient students who came through my kitchen over the past sixteen years, especially those in the early years who encouraged me to teach more classes and expand the range of what I offered. I am also thankful to those who persisted in urging me to write books on what I taught. There are too many of them to name, but I would like to give special acknowledgment to Eleanor Hopewell, who helped me start the intermediate and advanced level classes, and Gary Campbell, who kept after me to write books.

I deeply appreciate all my wonderful advanced students who over the past decade gave their loyal support and tested with great satisfaction many of the recipes that are now finally being published herein. As for those recipes specially developed for *Dancing Shrimp*, I wish to thank many devoted recipe testers, including Curt Chamberlain, Mike Ledesma, Melinda Blau, Cynthia Juenemann, Jeff Lichtman, Donna Allen, Mark Torresan, Daryl Ansel, John McHugh, Richard Ostreicher, and Bruce Carter.

Sincere thanks also go to my caring agent, Judith Weber; my neighbor, Marie Simmons, who introduced me to her; and my editor, Janice Easton, with whom it has been a pleasure to work. Above all, I owe a world of thanks to my loving husband, Michael Babcock, without whose unfailing support, refreshing sense of humor, and eager assistance this book would not have been born. He was also the recipe tester extraordinaire, producing exquisite seafood dinners nightly from *Dancing Shrimp* recipes through the entire summer when I was too busy writing the text for the book and had little time to cook.

CONTENTS

Introduction: The Story of Dancing Shrimp   13

1   Thai Cooking Basics   17

2   A Seafood Culture   25

3   Preserved Foods and Flavoring Ingredients
    from the Sea   33

4   Ingredients and Tips for Selection and
    Preparation   49

5   Techniques and Equipment   75

6   Fish   91

7   Crustaceans   167

8   Mollusks   229

Appendix: Thai Markets Throughout
    the United States   285

Index   289

DANCING SHRIMP

INTRODUCTION

THE STORY OF DANCING SHRIMP

As everyone knows, seafood is best when it is very, very fresh. Judging by the lively activity that takes place in the fresh fish markets found in America's major international districts, Asians can be most particular about this. These markets offer a wide selection of live fish swimming about in large aquarium tanks, next to long counters displaying a profusion of colorful, sparklingly fresh seafood laid out on ice. There is no glass case over the counters to separate you from the  fish, allowing you to touch, smell, peek under the gills, and make the best selection for the occasion—just as you would when buying fruits and vegetables. Many cities even boast Asian seafood restaurants with fish tanks from which diners can make their pick and be assured that their choices are truly fresh.

The scene is not much different from the open market stalls in the Orient, a culture shock to the Westerner unaccustomed to crowded shops with wet floors and drippy counters, fishmongers wearing rubber boots with net in hand to scoop up whichever fish, crab, or geoduck you desire. Right before your eyes, your choice is scaled, gutted, and cleaned, and, within a few short minutes, ready to be taken home to cook for dinner. To some of my cooking students, a visit to a live fish market in the local Chinatown is like taking a trip overseas.

But even this level of freshness pales in comparison to the freshest seafood dish I've ever had the pleasure of eating. It was at a food stall along the banks of the infamous Mekong River on the northeastern border of Thailand. The Mekong flows from its headwaters deep inside China through mainland Southeast Asia on its way to the South China Sea, and, for some 450 miles, it is the natural boundary separating Thailand from Laos.

To local people living near the river, the Mekong is famous for its giant catfish, some as large as a great white shark, but the seafood dish I had was made with something very tiny—a minute freshwater shrimp no larger than a hummingbird feather. This shrimp is transparent and, though hard to see, it thrives in such abundance that running a fine cloth net through the water is sure to yield a handsome catch.

My two traveling companions (a Thai and a visiting American) and I happened upon the rural food stalls on a high bank overlooking the point where the Mekong first meets the Thai border. There is no town there, just a few rudimentary stalls set up on the scenic overlook to serve passing travelers.

We were tired from a full morning of exploration in the mountainous country south of there, and were hungry for some of the good, spicy food for which the mom-and-pop food stalls in the northeast are famous. My Thai friend, Ong, who did the driving, pulled over to the vista point and proclaimed that we must have lunch at one of the stalls there, known for their *dancing shrimp* (*gkoong dten*).

Dancing shrimp is the name of a Thai dish in which very fresh raw shrimp is served with a very spicy, garlicky, and limy sauce. Because people in northeastern Thailand and neighboring areas of Laos have a liking for raw foods spicily laced with chillies and seasonings and served with fresh herbs, vegetables, and steamed sticky rice, some food enthusiasts have opined that sushi, so identified with Japanese cuisine, might have originated here. What with the texture of the rice, the ritual of rolling it with the hand and eating it with raw meats, fish, and vegetables and spices, the idea sounds quite plausible to me.

We found ourselves a quiet spot with a good view of the river in the shade of an open-sided bamboo shelter. Sitting on the ground on woven straw mats at a low table, my American friend, Jack, found this experience reminiscent of Japanese restaurants in which he had dined in the past. We placed our order with the smiling host—of course, we must have the barbecued chicken, green papaya salad, and steamed sticky rice, staple foods of the northeastern (*Isahn*) region. Add to these the specialty of the area: crisp batter-fried shrimp cakes and *dancing shrimp*.

No sooner had we ordered than our host hurried down a sloping path to the river's edge and pulled out of the water a net that we assumed was filled with shrimp, and brought it to the cooking area under a distant bamboo shelter. Distracted by the beautiful views and conversation about our morning adventures, we lost track until dish after dish of scrumptious food started to show up at our table. The barbecued chicken and green papaya salad were excellent—only *Isahn* folk can make them taste so good! The shrimp cakes were divine, with a rich taste and delicious crunch, the light batter barely disguising the tiny shrimp. Then, out came our host with a small but deep plate covered with another overturned plate. Incredibly, we could hear a sharp and insistent "ping, ping, ping" coming from inside the two metal plates.

Jack had a look of disbelief on his face. Ong gave instructions: "Get your spoon ready. I will lift the top plate just enough for you to scoop a spoonful. Then don't wait, just stuff whatever you get into your mouth and enjoy!" Sure enough, the shrimp were dancing and jumping like we had never seen before when devouring *dancing shrimp*. The shrimp danced in our mouths, down our throats, and into our bodies.

Although this may sound barbaric to some, the experience was actually surprisingly enlightening. We felt the shrimp become us—we were the vehicle through which their spirit would carry on in the world. We didn't feel that we were eating them alive, taking away their life. Instead, we felt their life continuing on within us, that they happily became part of us. They danced in us and made us dance with life. I was reminded of the teaching that "energy never dies; it is only transformed," and, because something must die (whether this be animal or vegetable) in order that we may live, may we be worthy to carry on the spirit that has sacrificed its life for our nourishment at every meal.

But please don't think of this book as being about eating live and raw foods, rather, it is a celebration of the life that food gives us. It is about the importance of the freshness of food, the care and respect in handling and preparation, and about adding the living flavors of Southeast Asia to *your* life. It is about a culture: a way of life in a part of the world where food has meaning far beyond its physical dimensions. May our food dance with the spirit of the life from which it came.

1

THAI COOKING BASICS

THAI COOKING IS AN ART, NOT A PRECISE SCIENCE OF MEASUREMENTS. To learn any art well, it is helpful to have a good working knowledge of the basics and an openness to explore possibilities inspired by the guiding principles.

Just as there are primary colors that our eyes can see, there are primary flavors that our taste buds are able to discern. From three primary colors, a skilled visual artist can generate an infinite array of colors in differing shades and hues, and arrange them in special ways to evoke particular emotions. A good cook, on the other hand, has at her disposal five primary flavors, which she can blend in diverse ways to create unlimited flavor combinations to satisfy a broad range of preferences.

The first two primary flavors—salty and sweet—are universally known and used in all the world's cuisines. The third—sour—flavors Western cuisine to some degree, but not nearly to the extent it is used in Thai cuisine. Thai people love the sour flavor nearly as much as salty and sweet, and are not shy about liberally dousing a wide range of dishes, from salads and soups to curries and sauces for main course dishes, with the sharp sour of fresh lime juice, white vinegar, and the juice extract from a sour fruit, tamarind.

The fourth, which groups the hot, spicy, and pungent flavors, is an underexplored variable in most Western cuisines, but plays a sensational starring role in the signature dishes of Thai cuisine. The fifth—the bitter—is perhaps the most misunderstood flavor in Western cultures, frequently conjuring up unfavorable connotations of bitter medicine. Again, like the sour and spicy, the bitter flavor is cherished in Thai cuisine and presents itself in the numerous herbs, roots, and bitter vegetables, which not only serve as flavoring ingredients, but as main features in finished dishes.

Various kinds of ginger, for instance, lend both the pungent, spicy flavor and the bitter. Many aromatic herbs impart not only a delightful fragrance but add a bitter background taste as well. Try chewing on lemon grass, galanga, kaffir lime peel, cilantro, and other common Thai culinary herbs by themselves and see for yourself. Add to these the forest of vegetables, including bitter melons and eggplants, edible leaves and flower buds from trees and shrubs, and a host of biting herbs that frequently appear on the dinner table to accompany spicy dipping sauces and incendiary curries.

Because Thai cooking uses all five primary flavors, derived from an extensive range of ingredients and preparation techniques, it gives the uninhibited cook immense opportunities to create an extraordinary array of distinctive dishes, from pleasantly mild to intensely spicy. Many bold and contrasting combinations contradict the ground rules of Western cooking, which is what makes Thai food so refreshing and intriguing to the awakening Western tongue.

Since they come from a multitude of sources, flavoring ingredients bestow their own unique characteristics. The various foods with which they are cooked also contribute their own flavors and textures, much like different papers and canvases take on colors in their own special ways. In addition, methods of preparation and cooking techniques add their influences to the outcome.

The wide range of variables makes Thai cooking exciting and Thai food both a simple and complex blend of invigorating flavors. All this may sound overwhelming to a beginner in Thai cooking, but it really isn't. Recipes serve as guidelines and following them should yield satisfactory results. As you become more experienced and have learned the nuances of flavor balances, you will be in the position to add your own personal touches to custom tailor dishes to suit your own palate and those of guests you serve.

Principles of Flavor Harmony

When working with strong flavors, like strong colors, it is important to keep them in balance with other flavors, so that one does not overpower the other and cover up the more subtle flavors. Sharp sours, fiery spiciness, and cutting bitterness can make peace and share the stage without conflict. Here is where the art of Thai cooking lies: the creation of flavor harmonies that bring together seemingly disparate flavors and integrate them into a unique and magnificent whole.

Your own cooking experience may have already revealed to you that the salty and sweet flavors balance each other. If something is too sweet, add a little salt; if it is too salty, add a little sugar. Taking this a step further, both the sweet and salty flavors balance the sour. For instance, if a dipping sauce is much too sour, determine first whether you can taste a salty flavor. If not, add a little salt (or fish sauce if the recipe uses fish sauce as the salty ingredient).

When the sauce tastes equally salty and sour, the addition of a little sweet often helps pull these two flavors together, so that they do not stand alone as separate ingredients, but embrace each other as partners. At the same time, this will enable you to taste their distinctive sources, as well as the flavors of other ingredients that may be in the sauce. Therefore, instead of just sour, you may now notice that the sauce is limy, garlicky if there is garlic in it, and may even taste hotter than before, since you are better able to taste the flavor of the chillies swimming in it. The sweet flavor, on the other hand, is also known to mellow the heat of chillies but, usually, it tightens flavors first until you are able to taste a very faint sweetness at the back of your tongue. The harmony of the sauce peaks at this point, and any further additions of sugar mellows the heat as well as the sour and salty flavors.

When working with strong sour, salty, and hot flavors, the sweet flavor serves an important balancing function. It harmonizes the disparate flavors, pulling them together into a whole greater than the sum of its parts, opening up doorways for your taste buds to taste the multidimensional flavors of all the ingredients in the dish. The fresh bouquet of aromatic herbs, unique textural taste of vegetables, and the delicately sweet and luscious flavors of fresh seafood come through the strongly flavored sauce to the foreground and are not smothered by it. At the same time, the bitterness of pungent roots and roasted spices takes a seat in the background, adding its own virtues like bass in an orchestra.

Strong sour flavors, especially, benefit greatly from the balancing role of sweet. Frequently, a significant amount of sugar is required in order to bring this about. Just a small pinch may have little effect, and sometimes may even muddy up the waters, as if it has not yet convinced the strong players to cooperate. Keep adding a little more sugar until the faintest sweetness is noticeable at the back of your tongue. At this point, sugar is no longer needed as a peacemaker, but comes to the fore for its own sake, to be an equal player with the rest of the team. Whether more sugar should be added depends on whether the sweet component is an important feature of a particular savory dish. Its role varies from dish to dish, and on the taste preference of the partakers of the meal.

Of course, not all Thai dishes contain all five flavors in their full intensity. Some are actually rather plain and simple, using one or two flavor ingredients; others are in between. The Thai love for variety and harmony is reflected in the balance of dishes in a meal. A typical meal, consisting of five dishes, would usually have one, or at most two, intensely hot dishes, accompanied by one or two of medium spiciness, and the remaining mild and bland. If there is a sharply sour salad or soup, the rest of the dishes are not likely to contain a sour flavor that would clash with it. If a rich curry is on the menu, the accompanying dishes can be expected to be light, and coconut milk will not be used in any of them, and so on. In short, not only should flavors be in harmony within a dish, all the dishes in a meal should be in harmony with one another.

Cooking to Taste

Learning how to balance and harmonize flavors is particularly important when working with a foreign cuisine in which the available flavor ingredients can vary considerably from batch to batch or brand to brand. Fresh ingredients, such as herbs, chillies, and vegetables, as well as various kinds of seafood, can differ, depending on how fresh they are, where they are grown or raised, and how they are packed for transit and stored. Produce of tropical origins will likely be less full flavored when grown in temperate zones; seafood that has been frozen or aged can be expected to be less than optimal in both taste and texture.

One brand of fish sauce may be saltier and fishier than another, and palm sugar can vary in levels of sweetness, as it is a natural sugar that is not highly processed. Tamarind juice, too, may differ in degrees of sourness, depending on how thick or thin it is made. Chillies are notorious for inconsistency from batch to batch, although they outwardly look the same and are called by the same name.

Since ingredients can vary considerably, it is important to make adjustments in the quantity used to bring about the optimal flavor balance in each dish. Therefore, do not follow recipes religiously but, rather, cook to taste. Remember that recipes serve as guidelines; they cannot speak for variances in the quality of ingredients that are available in different locales. They also cannot speak for your particular taste preference, so, cut down on the amount of chillies if you can't take the heat and the amount of lime juice if you don't like sharp, sour flavors. Use more garlic and basil if you are a garlic and basil lover, less if you find them too strong for your taste, and so on.

Many recipes in this book give a suggested range of amounts to use of particular ingredients. Start out with the lower end and work your way up if you like it hotter, saltier, sweeter, or more sour. Taste as you go along, until you have developed a sense of how to work intuitively with the ingredients in the form in which they are available in your community. If you are comparatively new to Thai food, you may find the lower end of the range too much for you to take; on the other hand, if you have spent a lot of time in Thailand and love the intensity of food you've had there, the upper end of the range may fall short of where your preference lies. Play around until you get the combination of flavors most suited to your palate.

If a finished dish you make from a recipe tastes off, or as if something is missing, simple balancing will usually help perk up the particular batch of ingredients you used. Frequently, a sprinkle of good-quality fish sauce will take care of the problem. If the food is salty enough, see if it could benefit from a little sweetness; if you can taste all the ingredients but they just do not seem to be blended very well, a little bit of sugar will often help. Go through the suggestions in the previous section and try to ascertain what is needed to fix the dish. Most Thai dishes are rescuable if you are adept at balancing flavors.

Thai people do not eat seafood dishes by themselves, but as accompaniments to plain steamed rice. Therefore, we usually make the dishes saltier and spicier than to taste, so that when they are served over unflavored rice, they do not become bland and lose their punch. Because our meals consist of rice as the main food, with several accompanying nonrice dishes, we consume smaller amounts of each protein dish than our Western counterparts would. Western-style meals are the opposite of ours, as they place a protein dish as the main course and relegate rice (if served) a secondary role as a side dish.

Especially with highly flavored, spicy dishes, a pound of seafood goes a long way toward feeding an entire Thai family. The number of servings for the recipes in this book are generous servings for multicourse Thai-style dining, taking into account the spiciness of the dishes, which would encourage more rice to be eaten. For Western-style dining with fewer courses and a preference for more protein, make adjustments accordingly—allowing six to eight ounces of seafood per person, or more for whole fish with head and tail still attached.

Thai Food *Is* Fusion Food

Today, there is apparent confusion among some Western chefs who borrow ingredients commonly used in Southeast Asian cooking to create their own blend of East-West cuisine, frequently referred to as *fusion* food. Little do they realize that many of the ingredients are not native to that region of the world, but have come from someplace else, including the Americas.

I am amused whenever I see a bottled sauce, or item on a Western menu, being described as "Thai," just because it contains peanuts or a peanut sauce, but does not reflect the flavor balance that makes Thai cuisine what it is. Peanuts really are more American than Thai, since one of the world's largest producers and consumers of peanuts is the United States.

The ubiquitous peanut really has an interesting history: Its origins can be traced way back to South America, where it is believed to have been a prime staple food for millennia before the arrival of the Spanish explorers in the fifteenth century. Grave sites of the ancient Incas have been found to contain peanut-shaped urns, solid gold peanut necklaces and ornaments, and jars filled with peanuts to provide the dead with food in the afterlife. Peanuts likely played an important ceremonial role, since some ceremonial sites were covered with their shells.

When the New World was discovered, so to speak, the peanut was being widely cultivated as far north as Mexico. The Spanish took it back with them to Spain, where it is still grown, and later they and the Portuguese transplanted it to Africa and Asia. In many parts of tropical Africa, the peanut quickly integrated into the culture, and the peanut plant came to be regarded as one of several sacred plants that possess a soul. From Africa, the peanut returned across the Atlantic into North America when Africans were brought over as slaves to work the southern plantations. Its easy culture made it an inexpensive, nutritious food for the poor in the South, and it was consumed by soldiers during the Civil War; when peanut butter was invented in the United States in the late nineteenth century, it became just as popular across the country as it is today.

In Asia, the peanut was introduced into India and China (now two of the world's largest growers) in the sixteenth century, where it was immediately recognized for its nutritional value and good taste. It quickly became a major source of inexpensive protein and oil to feed the masses—its importance approaching that of the soybean in China. In fact, the peanut became so inseparable from Chinese food culture that, when it spread from there southward into Southeast Asia, it came to be known as *Chinese bean* in the languages of Malaysia and Indonesia, two of Asia's large producers and consumers. As most people who have spent sufficient time in Thailand would tell you, relatively few dishes in Thai cuisine use peanuts, and spicy peanut sauces really have their origin in the Indonesian archipelago.

Although chillies are a beloved Thai ingredient and used intensively, they, too, are not native to the region, but were introduced from the Americas. Thai cuisine cannot even lay claim to its most essential flavoring ingredient, fish sauce, which really has roots in Mediterranean cuisine. The ancient Romans cherished this salty extract of anchovies, which they called *garum* (or *liquamen*), and enhanced a wide variety of dishes with its flavor and aroma. In addition to these notable examples, there are numerous other foreign ingredients, as well as styles of cooking, that have been absorbed into the cuisines of Southeast Asia. Thai food is already *fusion food* and is what it is not because of the individual ingredients, but because of the particular flavor balances that set the cuisine apart.

Owing to the country's auspicious location and her people's openness, Thai cuisine has seen tremendous changes over the past few centuries. During the sixteenth and seventeenth centuries, booming international maritime trade brought a host of flavor ingredients and cooking styles from around the world, many of which made their way into Thai cooking via the nobility.

On their long, circuitous journey, merchant ships sailing between India, the Spice Islands of the Indonesian archipelago, and China would stop at the fabled ports of Ayuthaya in the kingdom then known as Siam. Ayuthaya was an amphibious city, situated on an island formed by the confluence of three rivers and, in its heyday, supported a population of over one million, most of whom lived on houseboats along the rivers and their many tributaries. It was a glittering, very cosmopolitan, and international city, described by some awed travelers as even more glorious than the London and Paris of its day.

More than forty nationalities at one time or another resided here, many occupying their own quarters in the city with their own docks. They brought with them ways of cooking from their homeland. Those involved in international commerce traded the spices and foodstuffs they carried on their ships, so there was a great exchange of culinary delights, and many new and unusual ingredients found their way into Siamese kitchens to be given a distinctly new identity.

It was during this period that chillies were introduced into Asia, brought from the New World by the Portuguese. It took no time for them to be adopted, and their extensive use continued through the centuries so that, now, they are inseparable from Thai cuisine. Prior to their arrival, the spiciest ingredient used in Thai cooking was pepper, in the form of white, black, and green peppercorns, introduced by Indian immigrants in earlier times. Ironically, it was black pepper that led to the discovery of chillies by the Old World, as Christopher Columbus sailed west in search for a shorter route to India to obtain this spice treasured in the European cooking of his day. On that voyage, Columbus did not land in India, though he called the people there *Indians*, and did not find black pepper, though he called the fiery chillies there *peppers*. The rest is history.

Aside from the lucrative international maritime trade, spices and other flavor ingredients came in through age-old overland trade routes between the Far and Near East. Migration of diverse ethnic cultures at different times in history brought lasting culinary contributions as these peoples settled and became assimilated into the kingdom of Thailand's populace. Despite numerous foreign influences, Thai cooking developed on a course that firmly established itself as a distinct cuisine, with its own unique combinations and balance of flavors. This development closely reflects the nature of the Thai people themselves, whose easygoing ways and adaptability to outside ideas combine with their resilient independent identity. Since the birth of the nation, Thai people have retained a special ability to hold on to their own unique, independent identity, even as they accept and integrate foreign elements into their culture.

Thai cuisine continues to evolve today, as the Thai love for variety challenges innovative chefs to experiment with ever-new ingredients from around the world, blending them with native herbs and spices to create dishes that still retain a quintessential Thainess. The cooking of ethnic minorities and of neighboring countries continues to exert tremendous influences, as will be evident in many of the recipes in this book. A large number of the ingredients covered in the chapters 3 and 4 have roots outside Southeast Asia, but have become fully assimilated into Thai cuisine and are indispensable in creating the flavor balances that are uniquely Thai.

2

A SEAFOOD CULTURE

THE SCINTILLATING LIGHT OF THE EARLY MORNING DANCES ON THE rippling waves as they gently lap upon the shore. Another day is dawning on a quiet stretch of the gulf coast.

Nimble feet move swiftly to and fro, into the water and out, as if dancing in rhythm with the waves. They sink into soft wet sand, then rise into cool morning air, before sinking again into sand and sea. Sun-darkened hands grasp onto rope and net as muscled arms stretch and pull. Wrinkled skin on bare feet betray this lively spirit, who's been up and about long before dawn's first light.

Side by side with next of kin, the fisherman weaves in and out, working his way up the sandy stretch: casting, pulling, emptying, folding, and casting yet again. Silhouettes in the distance down the shore dance along like shadows in step, as neighbors from the village work for their morning's catch. Faint sounds of voices talking, singing, humming, laughing, drift by from time to time, carried by the soft sea breezes. Soon, the first glimpse of the waking sun will greet the villagers from beyond the misty horizon.

Little fishes flip and flop as the cast net is drawn out of nutrient-rich waters. Into buckets and baskets they go, soon to be gutted and cleaned for the fisherman's kitchen, for markets near or far, or for drying racks to preserve them for monsoon days when swelling seas keep even the bravest soul safely home.

Beyond the shore, small wooden boats are rowed from spot to spot, and lines are dropped in hopes of hooking bigger fish. Nets strung on wooden hoops scoop up smaller fare swimming close to the water's surface during this cool time of morning. Further out, long-tail boats chug about, setting and collecting traps for squid, cuttlefish, and crustaceans. These dangle from recycled-plastic-bottle floats, each marked by a pole topped with a colorful flag. Men and women—old, middle-aged, and young—all help out, whether on shore or in boats off shore, in carving out a living from the sea.

From beyond the horizon, larger fishing boats will soon appear, returning from an early morning's catch, or a full night's excursion out to sea. At the village pier, different boats prepare to leave, loading nets and ice in oversized coolers for a day's journey to harvest other species of nature's bounty.

Come evening, when the sand and shallow waters, warmed by the hot tropical sun, cool, activity resumes along the shore. Men, women, and children, armed with sticks and woven baskets, wade ankle deep in clear, dark waters, as if taking a leisurely stroll, gathering clams.

The day's activities witnessed on this quiet stretch of coastline are repeated on numberless other stretches of Thailand's long sunrise coast—from its eastern border with Cambodia, across the eastern seaboard, then curving south down the peninsula, until the Gulf of Thailand opens into the South China Sea and beyond. These western shores of the mighty Pacific, with warm equatorial waters, are a rich haven for abundant varieties of marine life.

Across the narrow southern peninsula lies yet another shore, Thailand's sunset coast, on the enchanting Andaman Sea. Here, on the eastern shores of the Indian Ocean, can be found dazzling beaches, punctuated here and there by dramatic limestone karsts; mangrove swamps, spawning grounds of precious marine resources; and countless idyllic islands, islets, and rocky outcroppings, surrounded by extensive reefs and eerie underwater caves, home to innumerable species of fish, crustaceans, and mollusks. Here, deeper waters and a current different from that of the Pacific brings a differing mix of marine life, giving the country an extraordinary range of wonderful seafood to serve up at the dinner table and to export to seafood-loving cultures around the world.

"Fish Bridges"

While most of the catch of small fishing villages scattered along the kingdom's two extensive coastlines are consumed locally, fleets of large trawlers work the deeper waters of both oceans, bringing in their mammoth hauls to large fish piers in major seaport towns. These piers are aptly called "fish bridges" (*sapahn bplah*), bridges over which marine life crosses from their watery world into the world of human consumption. These bridges are entry points from which thousands of tons of seafood are packed daily into refrigerated trucks and sped to city markets and processing houses, where they are prepared and frozen or canned for shipment to markets abroad.

In contrast to the quaint fishing scenes, the fish bridges are a bustling madhouse from early morning when the first trawlers arrive, continuing on for hours until the last fish from the last boat is sold. Frenzied activity is the norm, as millions of fish are unloaded, sorted, and hastily moved through chaotic crowds of haggling buyers and sellers, finally to be repacked with ice and loaded onto cars and trucks. Agents for wholesalers, distributors, export houses, canning factories, large retailers, and restaurants arrive early, staking their spots so that they don't miss out on any opportunity to strike their deals for the day. Big money will change hands and savvy agents stand to make a hefty sum with their shrewd bargaining skills.

Fish are unloaded huge barrel by barrel, overflowing case by case, and dumped onto concrete floors of the sheltered piers. Mountainous heaps of small fish are purchased by the lot and hauled off to processing houses. Less overwhelming mounds are sorted out by type and size, the larger and more prized fishes lying mostly single file on the floor. Price tags with large numbers written on cardboard are placed alongside each of the sorted piles. Here and there between large groupings can even be found some rather small batches, with maybe half a dozen or so fish of the same type and size—clearly suitable for small-market vendors, who provide an assortment of varieties for their customers, or small restaurants.

On the outer fringes of the fish piers, small groups of women and men sit in corners cleaning fish for particular agents and wholesalers. Their experience shows as they excavate enormous mountains with great agility—scaling, gutting, filleting, and whatever else they have been contracted to do. The cleaned fish are then loaded onto waiting refrigerated trucks and rushed off to market, processing house, or packaging plant. Of course, the big mounds of guts, heads, tails, fins, and bones left behind are not thrown out but are, in turn, sold to be processed into animal feed and fertilizer.

Besides fish harvested from the sea, fish and shrimp farms along both coasts yield a tremendous added tonnage, making Thailand one of the world's premier exporters of frozen seafood products. Large rectangular ponds dug in flatlands near the shore are filled with water pumped in from the sea. In these aerated pools are raised some of the world's best tiger prawns—so lusciously succulent, plump, tasty, and sweet. Most of them will end up on dinner tables in faraway lands.

The Birth of *Seafood*

With coastal waters so abundantly endowed, it would seem that fresh fish, crustaceans, and mollusks from the sea would naturally have constituted a major source of food for the Thai people since time immemorial. Actually, the mass consumption of fresh marine creatures is a relatively recent development in the country's seven-hundred-year history, and in world history.

In fact, the word *seafood* was not even coined until the nineteenth century—by Americans—to group in one word all edible marine creatures, including fish, crustaceans, and mollusks. Initially, the English adamantly objected to this all-inclusive word to describe such a vast array of marine life but, in the end, the word caught on, and, by the close of World War II, it had become widely accepted. Like other languages, the Thai word for seafood, *ah-hahn talay*, most probably came from a literal translation of the American term, although it was not clear when this was first adopted.

Prior to the development of technology which made ice readily available, the consumption of fresh seafood was by necessity limited to populations in coastal towns and to seafood caught in waters in close proximity to shoreline (that is, shallow-water fish, mostly smaller varieties), which must be served the same day in order to be fresh. Because seafood spoiled rapidly without ice and refrigeration, especially in the tropics, most fish caught far out at sea were salted, dried, or pickled to pre-

serve them from spoiling during the hours that it would take fishing boats to return to shore. Keeping them alive in tanks of cool seawater would be an alternative, but it was far from practical in terms of labor, space, equipment required, and cost.

For centuries, the preservation of food by salting, drying, pickling, or smoking was commonplace in cultures worldwide, and was applied not only to seafood, but also to meats and vegetables. Well-known examples that come to mind include salt-cured and smoked ham, beef jerky, corned beef, salt cod, preserved anchovies, pickled herring, and smoked salmon. In Thailand, a wide variety of seafood had, for generations, been preserved by salting, drying, and pickling. Many of these traditional seafood products continue to be staple foods and indispensable flavoring ingredients in today's Thai kitchen. Among them are fish sauce, shrimp paste, dried shrimp and cuttlefish, salted and pickled crab and clams, and various kinds of salted, dried, and pickled fish.

It was not until the eighteenth century that ice was first made, and it took until the following century for the icebox to come into widespread use. The refrigerator made its debut in the second decade of the twentieth century, replacing the icebox in fairly recent history. The advent of the icebox, followed later by refrigeration units, made it possible for fishing vessels to keep their catch of ocean fish fresh until they reached retail markets, restaurants, and home kitchens. It was around this time when fresh seafood first became readily available, not just in coastal areas but also to inland population centers, that the word *seafood* was born in America—a country in which private capital made possible the rapid application of advances in technology to create a new breed of fishing vessels, railroad and trucking units, and supermarket counters.

Ice was imported into Thailand for the first time during the reign of King Rama V, in the latter part of the nineteenth century. This was followed soon after by the establishment of domestic ice-production factories. Due to their high cost, refrigerators remained a luxury until the last few decades of the previous millennium, during which the Thai fishery industry expanded dramatically, and emerged as a significant supplier of frozen seafood products to the world.

A Fish and Rice Culture

Although the consumption of fresh seafood is a relatively new development, fish has long been one of the most important sources of food for the Thai people and is inseparable from Thai culture, because Thailand, along with her neighbors in much of Southeast Asia, sits on a very fertile drainage basin and, for centuries, the vast network of rivers and waterways has blessed the people of the region with a wealth of freshwater fish, as well as freshwater crustaceans and mollusks.

Since the kingdom's early years, the daily meals of the people throughout the country have consisted of rice and fish. Fish as a food is second only to rice. It is said that both come with the water; therefore, they belong together as an indivisible pair. To eat rice is to eat fish, and, by *fish*, what is meant is freshwater fish from the rivers, streams, canals, ponds, lakes, and flooded fields during the rainy season.

An inscription on stone dating back seven hundred years to the days of Sukhothai, not long after the kingdom was founded, spoke of fish and rice, and how the abundance of these two natural resources was a measurement of the happiness of the people and the prosperity of the land. ". . . In the water there is fish, in the fields there is rice. . . ." This famous line from the ancient inscription is still a standard by which rural people measure their contentment with their easygoing lifestyle. To some degree, it still describes the abundance of the land, an abundance that is water based, and the water comes freely each year with the monsoons.

Thailand essentially has two main seasons of approximately equal length—the wet season and the dry season. Every year, when the rains come in their full glory following months of dry weather, the rivers and canals overflow their banks, flooding the fields. It is at this time that farmers work the fields, planting their main crop of rice. When they are done working in the fields, the villagers band together and go out to wherever there is water to catch fish. This family and village activity is engaged in with great merriment. The season of working the fields is the time when water flows in freely. With the water comes fish, and, wherever the water goes, the fish goes. The villagers catch enough fish to eat fresh and to dry, salt, pickle, and preserve for the remainder of the year.

I still recall with great fondness my own childhood experiences with fish that flow in with the monsoon waters. Whenever a big downpour brought flash floods, my brothers and I wasted no time rushing out into our front yard, and even onto the streets, with our buckets to catch fish. The water was clear and fish were everywhere, even in the smallest puddles! Those excitement- and fun-filled days are forever engraved in my memory, and in the memories of many others of my generation, and those before us.

For centuries prior to the days of modern development in the second half of the twentieth century, the inland waters of Thailand and other Southeast Asian countries were indeed blessed by extraordinary abundance. By some accounts, this region was known to be one of the world's richest grounds for freshwater fish. There were countless varieties, too numerous to name, some very specific to particular streams and wetlands. Foreign explorers who pioneered their way into the region could not help but marvel at this natural bounty in the journals they kept and the letters they sent home to families and associates. Among them was Marco Polo, who described the freshwater fish here as among "the best in the world."

Much of the abundance can be explained by the lay of the land and its fertility. The innumerable rivers and waterways that flow through the region are surrounded on both banks by vast fertile flatlands and alluvial plains with natural contours and dips. During the heavy rains of the monsoon season, when the rivers flood their banks, nutrients from the surrounding land are washed into the water, providing a bountiful supply of food. The time of high water, from May through October, naturally coincides with the spawning season for most varieties of freshwater fish found here.

Fish, fish eggs, and fry flow with the water over the flooded flatlands and grow quickly in the nutrient-rich waters. Later in the season, when the water recedes, they become trapped in temporary ponds and waterholes, or in year-round lakes, where they fatten to a good-eating size. These temporary pools provide a welcome source of food and fishing entertainment for villagers until the pools gradually dry up toward the middle of the dry season, some not too long before the next rains begin.

During the early part of the dry season, when the weather is cool, the fish are fattest and richest tasting after months of endless feasting. This coincides with the time of year when new-crop rice, harvested following the monsoon season, is ready for eating. Hence, the common saying "new rice, fat fish" tells people the time for good eating and prosperity has arrived—a time for rejoicing in the bountiful harvest of both their favorite foods. The saying is extended to mean whatever is new is just right, much like the fullness and bliss a newlywed couple experiences.

Numerous other sayings and proverbs using fish as a metaphor reflect the importance of fish in Thai culture. "Dig pond, lure fish" is one especially rooted in the natural abundance that flows in freely with the monsoon waters. Instead of digging ponds to stock with fish, villagers who live in the flatlands dig ponds to attract fish from nearby rivers and other natural bodies of water to swim in with the flooding waters. This saying is extended to refer to concocted schemes that fool or entice gullible people.

Of course, in many parts of Thailand today, ponds dug for fish must be stocked with baby fry purchased elsewhere. The overwhelming abundance of freshwater life that once existed has dwindled with the coming of modern development, which has seen many dams built, drying up countless streams and wetlands that in the past supported bountiful water life, and brought industrialization to poison major rivers and their tributaries with untreated toxic discharges.

The destruction of habitat has meant the extinction of innumerable species of delicious freshwater fish, and the remaining varieties in natural bodies of water are being threatened. With the Thai love for the taste of freshwater fish, a growing aquaculture business has sprung up to ensure the supply of fish. Most of the freshwater fish sold in city markets today is farm raised. As expertise in aquaculture increases, it is hoped that many threatened species will be added to the numbers farmed.

Thai fish aficionados, however, insist that farm-raised fish are not half as tasty as those that grow naturally on nutrients in running waters, and make special trips into the countryside to savor the delectable flavors of wild fish, especially during the season of "new rice, fat fish." If you should happen into Thailand during the beautiful months of December, January, and February, join them in the countryside for an unforgettable feast, which may forever change your opinion about freshwater fish.

While modernization has brought about a decline in the abundance of freshwater fish, it has, on the other hand, greatly increased the availability of marine fish, which, in urban areas, has replaced many freshwater varieties. Because freshwater and saltwater fish, crustaceans, and mollusks cook up similarly, *seafood* will be used in the remainder of this book to include all freshwater species. Many traditional recipes for freshwater fish will likewise be applied to saltwater varieties.

Fish and Rice: A Healthy Diet

A growing body of research points to the healthful properties of seafood, especially fish, making the traditional Thai diet of rice and fish appear more and more appealing to people concerned about fat intake and calories. The Thai way of dining, in which plain, unseasoned, no-fat-added, steamed rice is the centerpiece of the meal, with the nonrice dishes as accompaniments, cuts down further on

calories. Furthermore, because much Thai food is spicy, smaller quantities of the highly flavored protein dishes are eaten. There are also plenty of nutritional benefits to be gained from the herbs, spices, and other ingredients liberally used in Thai cooking.

Seafood is an excellent source of complete protein, which is easily digestible, making nutrients readily available to the body. Compared to meat and poultry, seafood is significantly lower in fat and calories; this includes oily fish with a relatively high fat content. Seafood is also rich in iodine, calcium, phosphorus, iron, zinc, potassium, and B vitamins, especially niacin, pantothenic acid, B_6, and B_{12}. Moreover, the fat in fish is a *good* fat, containing essential omega-3 fatty acids, recognized by medical experts as fundamental in maintaining good health. These fats play a role in keeping arteries clear, and also benefit the central nervous system.

In addition to the healthfulness of seafood, the many fresh herbs used in Thai cooking contribute nutritional benefits and healing qualities. For instance, chillies and garlic—two generously used flavoring ingredients—are known for their antioxidant properties, which help neutralize damaging free radicals before they can harm healthy cells. Each has become the focus of studies addressing the most critical health concerns of modern times—heart disease, cancer, and immune dysfunction.

High in vitamin C, chillies have been known through the ages to benefit the circulatory system—cleaning the blood of undesirable cholesterol, keeping the blood vessels supple and healthy, improving circulation and, thereby, increasing the supply of nutrients and oxygen to the cells of the body. Garlic, on the other hand, has been shown to reduce total cholesterol levels by gobbling bad LDL cholesterol and increasing good HDL levels. Besides chillies and garlic, numerous other herbs have healing properties.

The Thai diet, therefore, combines the goodness of seafood and beneficial herbs in grain-based meals. I hope the recipes, information, and ideas contained in this book not only enable you to make delicious Thai seafood dishes, but inspire you to incorporate more seafood into your daily diet.

3

PRESERVED FOODS AND FLAVORING INGREDIENTS FROM THE SEA

THE RICH WATERS OF THE TWO OCEANS THAT LAP THAILAND'S SHORES yield a bountiful supply of fish, crustaceans, and mollusks. Much of the catch is salted, dried in the sun, smoked, pickled, fermented into seasoning sauces and pastes, and preserved in other ways. This was especially essential in the days before refrigeration, and still is among many small fishing villages where modern amenities have not made their advances. These preserved seafoods are not only eaten as main courses with rice during days off from fishing, they are also used extensively as flavoring ingredients, adding a taste of the sea to each meal.

Even with the use of refrigeration becoming increasingly entrenched in urban areas, making fresh and frozen seafood easily available for daily consumption, much of the catch continues to be preserved in the traditional ways. The flavors of preserved seafood, which have become so familiar to the Thai palate and definitively given the cuisines of the region their distinctive character, are nothing like that of fresh seafood, just as sundried tomatoes and raisins are not the same as fresh tomatoes and grapes. Preserved seafood products, therefore, continue to be prized as food in themselves and as flavoring ingredients integral to Thai cuisine. At the same time, they continue to be important sources of high protein foods for rural population during times of year when freshwater life is scarce, and inclement weather keeps fishing boats home from stormy seas.

This chapter will cover the most common preserved seafood products that are widely consumed either as main sources of food in themselves or as seasonings and flavoring ingredients in Thai cooking.

Fish Sauce
(Nahm Bplah)

The single most important flavoring ingredient in Thai cooking is none other than fish sauce, a clear, reddish brown liquid made from fish fresh from the sea. Used like salt in Western cooking and soy sauce in Chinese cooking, good-quality fish sauce imparts a distinct aroma and flavor all its own. It is indispensable in the Thai kitchen; Thai food wouldn't be quite the same without it. Fish sauce complements seafood dishes especially well and is used in just about every recipe in this book.

Called *nahm bplah*, literally "fish water," genuine fish sauce is the water, or juice, in the flesh of fish, extracted in the process of prolonged salting and fermentation. It is high in protein (as much as 10 percent), and the protein is a complete one, containing all the essential amino acids that the body requires for growth and regeneration. Top-quality fish sauce also contains a rich supply of B vitamins, particularly B_{12}, pantothenic acid, riboflavin, and niacin. Other beneficial nutrients include calcium, phosphorous, iodine, and iron.

Because good fish sauce adds a delicious dimension to Thai food, it is important to know how to select from the myriad brands sold in Asian markets. Just as there are many grades of olive oil that can make a big difference in the quality of the Italian dishes you cook, there are many grades of fish sauce that can make your Thai dishes vary from simply acceptable to exceptionally flavorful. Unlike olive oil, however, even top-grade fish sauce is quite inexpensive and affordable. A standard twenty-four-fluid-ounce bottle of premium quality fish sauce costs under three dollars in Asian markets. Therefore, it is good to know how it is made, what makes for different grades, and what characteristics to look for in making your choices from among the many brands available in the markets near you.

Though most fish sauce today is made from saltwater fish, it can also be made with small freshwater fish, as was done extensively in the past before pollution and dams drastically reduced the once-plentiful supply of freshwater fish. A limited quantity is still produced in a few areas in the vast, wet flatlands of Thailand's central region, which is traversed by several major river systems and an endless maze of canals.

Whether freshwater or saltwater, fish used for making fish sauce are usually small ones that otherwise would have little value for consumption. Among the most common marine fish used are anchovies and a few related species of schooling fish, from two to five inches in length, found in bountiful supply in the rich gulf waters. Varieties of larger fish, such as mackerel and sardines, also make good fish sauce but, because they are relatively more expensive due to their value as a food fish, they are seldom used in the commercial production of fish sauce.

For fish sauce to develop a pleasant, fragrant aroma and taste, the fish must be very fresh. As soon as fishing boats return with their catch, the fish are rinsed and drained, then mixed with sea salt—two to three parts fish to one part salt by weight. Large earthenware jars, or concrete vats, with a layer of salt on the bottom, are filled with fish and topped with another layer of salt. A woven bamboo mat is placed over the fish and weighted down with heavy rocks to keep the fish from floating when their juices are extracted by the salt and fermentation process.

The jars are covered and left in a sunny location for nine to eighteen months. From time to time, they are uncovered to air out and to let the fish be exposed to direct, hot sunshine, which helps digest them and turn them into fluid. The periodic sunning, in addition to a long fermentation period, produces a fish sauce of superior quality, giving it a fragrant aroma and a clear, reddish-brown color.

After enough months have passed, the liquid is removed from the jars through a spigot on the bottom of the jars, or by siphoning. Any sediment is strained out with a clean cloth. The filtered fish sauce is then ready for bottling. The finished product is 100 percent, top-grade, genuine fish sauce.

Second- and third-grade fish sauces are made by covering these fish remains with salt water, letting the mixture sit for two to three months more, then filtering again before bottling. Finally, the final fish remains are boiled with salt water, then strained and discarded, to produce the lowest-grade fish sauce. Because flavor is substantially reduced with each fermentation, top-grade fish sauce is frequently added to the lower grades to improve their flavor.

Since natural fish sauce requires time to make as well as very fresh fish, substantial investment is necessary for large-scale production. This has resulted in the proliferation of a number of less-than-pure products. Some are made by hydrolysis, in which some kind of enzyme or acid is added to hasten fermentation, while others are made by diluting natural or hydrolyzed fish sauce with salt water flavored and colored with sugar, caramel, monosodium glutamate (m.s.g.), and other natural or artificial flavorings and coloring.

How can you tell which brands are good? Check the labels, though the certification of quality awarded by Thailand's Commerce Department is not always translated into English. Ingredient lists and nutritional analyses cannot always be relied upon either.

Short of being able to decipher or trust the labels, look for fish sauce with a clear, reddish brown color, like the color of good whiskey, without any sediment. If the color is a dark or muddy brown, the sauce is likely to be either a lower grade, or one that is not properly or naturally fermented; it may also have been sitting on the shelf a bit too long. After a bottle of fish sauce has been opened, it may darken in color (as it is exposed to air) without losing much flavor for some time, but, when salt crystals or grit begin to form at the bottom of your bottle of fish sauce, it is time to throw it out and buy a new one.

Good fish sauce has a pleasant aroma of the sea, not an overwhelming smelly fishiness, and it should not be overly salty. If the bottle you have been using makes the dishes you cook taste too fishy, try a new brand. My favorite brands from among those available near my home in California are Golden Boy and *Tra Chang* (meaning "weighing scale"). The former is favored by my students for its endearing label, showing a baby boy sitting on a globe, cradling a bottle on the left arm with right thumb up. Both are excellent, adding a superb flavor to Thai dishes.

Reasonably good are the Squid, Anchovy, and *Tiparos* brands, though some of my students find the last a bit fishy; also try the premium Vietnamese Three Crabs brand. Since the degree of saltiness varies from brand to brand, make adjustments as necessary in your cooking, adding just enough to salt the food to your liking.

Fish sauce does not require refrigeration after it is opened unless you will be using it very infrequently. Store with the lid snapped shut in a cool place in your cupboard. It will keep indefinitely.

Shrimp Paste
(Gkabpi)

As with fish sauce, no true Thai kitchen is quite complete without *gkabpi*—the dense, dark purplish and grayish brown, fermented shrimp paste with an intensely pungent odor, which most Westerners find overpowering and even repulsive. If you think that fish sauce is quite enough and no way are you ever going to be talked into eating this rotten-smelling stuff, think again. Just about every delicious Thai curry you've ever had has *gkabpi* as a vital component; this strong character blends beautifully with the robust flavors of chillies, garlic, fragrant spices, pungent roots, and aromatic herbs to make each curry a delightful whole. In addition, there are many spicy soups, salads, sauces and stir-fries that would not be the same without its essence.

In one form or another, *gkabpi* makes its mark in just about every Thai meal and, especially among villagers in the Thai countryside, there is hardly one that would be complete without some kind of *nahm prik* (hot-and-spicy dipping sauces for vegetables and fish) in which this shrimpy paste simply shines. A favorite *nahm prik* is named after it (*nahm prik gkabpi*), since it is the primary ingredient; accompanying pan-fried, local gulf mackerel (*bplah too*) and raw, blanched, and egg-dipped-and-fried vegetables, this humble food of peasant origins undisputedly constitutes one of Thailand's favorite foods, and is popular among both poor and rich. In fact, when one of Thailand's beauties won an international beauty pageant, her answer to the question "What's your favorite food?" delighted Thais around the country when she without hesitation named this combination of *nahm prik*, mackerel, and vegetables (*nahm prik bplah too*, recipe on page 139).

Like fish sauce, *gkabpi* is rich in protein, B vitamins, calcium, and iodine. Also, like fish sauce, not all *gkabpi* is the same and can vary quite a bit in color, aroma, and quality. Though much of it is rather smelly, reminding one of rotting shrimp, the fresher and higher grades can actually have a pleasant, albeit strong, aroma. Some of the best can be found in the bustling markets and roadside stalls of several seaside towns known for their seafood products; each chance I get to vacation on the southern coast back home, I can't resist picking up a supply for my kitchen. When I run short, the two I favor from among brands imported into America are: *Pantainorasingh* and *Tra Chang* (also of fish-sauce fame). Both have a distinct smoky aroma, reminiscent of roasted shrimp and, when combined with other robust Thai ingredients, a little bit of the concentrated paste goes a long way to adding a whole lot of delicious shrimpy flavor.

Unlike fish sauce, shrimp paste is still mostly made by fishing families in villages along the coast, then sold to market vendors for resale to consumers, or to middlemen and distributors, who package them in containers with their brand names on them. Because each area has its own way of making shrimp paste, the product collected from families and villages in the same vicinity tends to share similar qualities. *Gkabpi*, therefore, becomes known by its province or village.

My husband and I once visited a small village known for the quality of its *gkabpi*, made from minuscule white shrimp, known as *keuy*, smaller even than a housefly. Fishing boats leave for sea in the morning and return in late afternoon with their catch. The sleepy village suddenly awakens, as the shrimp are unloaded, rinsed, laid out to drain before salting (approximately one cup sea salt to two pounds shrimp), then filled into earthenware jars overnight.

The next morning, they are spread out on plastic or fiberglass mats on the ground next to the fishermen's simple wooden homes to dry in the hot tropical sun. Late in the day, they are gathered and re-stored in the jars for the night, to be laid out again the next day when the sun burns hot. This goes on for three or more days, until the shrimp disintegrate and dry from pink to a dark purplish brown. When the shrimp are no longer recognizable and completely turned into dense paste, the *gkabpi* is ready for use and is returned to the earthen jars until an agent comes by to collect it. The shrimp paste gathered from all the families in the village is mounded into enormous, colorful, plastic tubs, each weighing several hundred kilograms when filled. If properly dried, the paste can keep for several months without refrigeration.

To make *gkabpi* from larger shrimp, the shrimp are allowed to ferment for a few days in the earthen jars to soften their shells before placing out to dry in the sun. The drying takes longer, the number of days or weeks depending on the size of the shrimp. During the drying stage, partially decomposed shrimp are periodically put through a grinder, or pounded in a large mortar, then placed out to dry further until they become a fine paste and develop the dark, finished color.

The agent keeps the different grades made from different kinds of shrimp in separate, color-coded tubs. Even though we were surrounded by huge mounds of paste, several tons in all, we were amazed that we barely noticed the stench of fermenting shrimp unless we put our noses right up close to the paste. That day, we bought a few kilograms of the best grade from the village to give as gifts to family and friends for a mere pittance; stalls along the major highway nearby sell the same grade for double the price and, by the time it makes its way into Bangkok, the price would have climbed a lot more.

Similar pastes made from shrimp are also used in the cooking of southern China and other Southeast Asian countries. These can vary from light pinkish gray and very moist, fluidlike sauces in jars to dark chocolate-brown, firmly compressed blocks. The kind used for Thai cooking leans toward the latter. Since other Asian cultures use shrimp paste differently in their cooking and prefer different strengths, it is best to purchase a product from Thailand for use in Thai dishes.

Gkabpi from Thailand usually comes packaged in small plastic containers, labeled as *shrimp paste*, and listing shrimp and salt as the only two ingredients. Most brands cover the top of the paste with a layer of wax to seal in freshness; remove before using. When refrigerated after opening, it will keep indefinitely. Because different batches vary in saltiness and shrimpiness, make adjustments as necessary in the recipes that call for it.

Dried Shrimp
(Gkoong Haeng)

Used both as a food in itself and as a flavoring ingredient, dried shrimp comes in different sizes and grades. Generally, the larger the size, the higher the price. The better grades are mildly salted and have an appealing pinkish and orangish tinge and a fragrant aroma. Those made from shrimp from tropical waters usually are stronger in flavor than shrimp from colder, temperate seas. For flavoring purposes, which call for the dried shrimp to be ground or chopped, the smaller sizes will suffice.

Good-quality dried shrimp can stand on its own as a protein food. It can be snacked on as dried jerky, or made into salads in the same way in which fresh shrimp is often used. A common salad served with rice porridge for breakfast combines dried shrimp with finely slivered ginger, sliced shallots, garlic and chillies, fresh lime juice, fish sauce, and a touch of sugar to pull together the varied flavors (see recipe). Sometimes, fried or roasted peanuts or cashews are added to give the salad a richer taste. For a crispy edge and a roasted fragrance, the dried shrimp can also be fried in oil or toasted in a dry pan ahead of time.

Dried Shrimp and Ginger Salad
(Yâm Gkoong Haeng)

½ cup good-quality medium-size dried shrimp
¼ cup finely slivered ginger
¼ cup sliced shallots or onion
2 to 3 cloves garlic, thinly sliced into oval pieces
4 to 6 Thai chillies (*prik kee noo*), cut into thin rounds
1 to 2 tsp. fish sauce (*nahm bplah*), to taste

Juice of ½ to 1 lime, to taste
½ to 1 tsp. sugar, to taste

Toss all the ingredients together. Adjust the salty, sour, and sweet flavors to your liking.
Serve with plain rice porridge.

Serves 6 in a multicourse family-style meal.

More frequently, dried shrimp serves an important role as a flavoring ingredient in many Thai dishes. It is crushed, chopped, ground, or used whole, to season a wide range of soups, salads, stir-fries, dipping sauces, fillings and toppings for appetizers and snack foods, and noodle dishes. It is also used as a base for certain kinds of chilli pastes that in turn flavor a host of other dishes. Moreover, it is an essential ingredient in numerous dry or preserved, ready-for-serving spicy mixtures (*nahm prik*), which are delicious accompaniments to plain steamed rice.

If the stores near you do not carry good-quality dried shrimp, you can easily make your own with a little bit of time. Start out with small, fresh shrimp. Rinse and drain well. Boil the shrimp with sea salt and water in a pot placed over medium heat until the water has completely evaporated—for each pound of shrimp, use one teaspoon of sea salt and half a cup of water. Spread the cooked shrimp on a rack and dry in the hot sun for several days until they are thoroughly dried, or spread on a cookie sheet and place in an oven at the lowest setting for several hours until they are completely dried through. Rub off the remaining shells. If properly dried, the shrimp keep for three to four months in an airtight container in a cool, dry place in the pantry, or refrigerate to retain freshness of flavor.

For dishes that call for ground dried shrimp, grind the whole shrimp to a fine powder in a clean coffee grinder or blender, or pound in a heavy mortar. Since grinding fluffs up the dense, dehydrated shrimp, start out with less whole dried shrimp to make the amount of ground dried shrimp you need. For instance, if a recipe calls for two tablespoons of the ground stuff, start out with about half that amount in whole dried shrimp. Dried shrimp is also available already ground in small jars labeled "shrimp powder," which usually has ground dried chillies mixed in. Grinding your own from good-quality dried shrimp generally yields fresher-tasting results.

Roasted Chilli Paste
(Nahm Prik Pow)

One of the most commonly used seafood-based chilli pastes in Thai cooking is *nahm prik pow* or, literally, "roasted chilli paste." It is most frequently made with dried shrimp and *gk-abpi* shrimp paste, but there are also versions made with dried fish instead of shrimp.

In this paste, a ground mixture of roasted and fried ingredients, including plenty of dried red-hot chillies, dried shrimp or dried fish, shrimp paste, garlic, and shallots, is seasoned with fish sauce, tamarind, and palm sugar and cooked together in oil into a thick, well-blended paste with a very dark, burnt red color. Against a fragrant backdrop of roasted flavors, the paste is hot and shrimpy, as well as sweet and tangy, complimenting seafood dishes especially well.

Nahm prik pow is used to flavor soups, including the popular hot-and-sour prawn soup; stir-fries with seafood, meats, or vegetables; noodle dishes; dipping sauces; and dressings for salads. Its sweetness also makes it a likable ready-to-use spread to put on toast, crackers, or shrimp chips for a quick snack.

Two good brands of prepackaged roasted chilli paste are available in Southeast Asian markets— *Pantainorasingh* (labeled as "chilli paste with soya bean oil") in eight-ounce and sixteen-ounce glass jars, and *Mae Ploy* ("chilli in oil") in fourteen-ounce plastic tubs. The first comes in a choice of hot, medium, and mild; skip over the mild as it lacks the fragrance of roasted chillies—the primary ingredient that gives the paste its name. Since the combination of flavors and level of hotness and sweetness can vary considerably from brand to brand, make adjustments as necessary in cooking with recipes in this book to flavor dishes to your liking.

If imported roasted chilli paste is not readily available where you live, you can make your own supply with the recipe on page 175. In fact, if all the roasting is done properly and only the freshest and best-quality ingredients are used, your homemade paste may turn out more fragrant and tasty than any of the store-bought brands. Whether homemade or store-bought, the paste keeps well for a few months when refrigerated in a sealed container.

Oyster Sauce
(Nahm Mân Hoi)

Borrowed from the Chinese, this richly flavored, dark brown sauce made from oysters with salt and water, thickened with cornstarch, and color-enhanced with caramel or burnt sugar, is extensively used as a seasoning for stir-fried vegetable, meat, seafood, and noodle dishes.

An excellent product from Thailand depicts on the front of the label a plump woman stir-frying while shaking sauce from a bottle into the wok. Underneath her are the words *Mae Krua*, which means "mother of the kitchen," the Thai way of referring to a female cook. (A male cook is called *paw krua*, "father of the kitchen.") On either side of her are pictures of oysters. This brand is quite flavorful and is available in small, medium, and large bottles, the largest holding twenty fluid ounces. Another tasty brand is the Healthy Boy brand, but it is not widely distributed in America.

Both these Thai brands of oyster sauce taste noticeably different from Chinese brands available in American Chinatowns. They are comparatively less salty, have a more pronounced oyster flavor, and do not contain monosodium glutamate (m.s.g.). In fact, many of my students have switched to one of these Thai brands even for their Chinese cooking.

When refrigerated after opening, oyster sauce keeps for up to one year.

Sun-Dried, Salted, and Smoke-Dried Fish
(Bplah Haeng/Kem/Gkrawb)

Among the most prevalent of preserved seafood are dried and salted fish, most of which are consumed as main protein foods, especially among poorer segments of the population throughout Asia. A visit to any well-stocked Oriental supermarket will expose you to innumerable varieties, from very small whole anchovies to sizeable chunks from fish as large as giant king mackerel. Their strong fishy flavors may take unaccustomed Western palates some getting used to, but there are many fine-tasting varieties well worth acquiring a taste for.

Some fish are both salted and dried, others are just dried. Depending on the size of the fish or thickness of the fillets, the latter may simply be fried until crispy, or soaked to reconstitute before cooking. Of those that are also salted, some are heavily salted, others only mildly so; some are completely dried and stiff while others are semimoist and pliable. Small, whole anchovies, which are salted and dried, are usually deep-fried until crispy and eaten with rice porridge for breakfast, either plain, or tossed with crushed, roasted dried chillies and lime juice.

In Thailand, many kinds of freshwater fish are mildly salted and partially sun-dried, usually for just one day in the hot tropical sun. Because there's still moisture inside the fish, they can spoil if not refrigerated or hung in a well-ventilated area. Such "single sun" fish (*bplah daed diow*) are excellent simply fried until their edges are crispy all around.

Two varieties of tasty, partially sun-dried, salted fish are now imported from Thailand, available wrapped in heavy plastic in the refrigeration units of many well-stocked Southeast Asian markets. They are pilot fish (a member of the good-eating gouramy fish family) and mudfish (also called serpent-head fish). Both are very popular staple foods enjoyed by Thai people, especially in the central region.

Pilot fish (*bplah salit*) is small and fries to a crisp with the crunchy fins and tail eaten along with the delicious flesh. Because it has been salted, rinse first, or soak for a few minutes, to remove the salt on the surface of the fish before pan-frying in hot oil until well browned and crispy. Serve by itself with plain steamed rice, or with a chilli dipping sauce. Or, debone the flesh from the fried fish and toss with sliced shallots, chillies, mint leaves, cilantro, and lime juice to make a salad for a multicourse Thai meal.

The larger mudfish (*bplah chon*) is a favorite freshwater fish; usually the one- to two-pound size is used for drying. Because the center bone has been removed and the flesh on either side spread out like a butterfly, the dried fish looks circular, as if two different fish have been joined. Roast the fish whole over medium-hot charcoals, or cut into bite-size pieces and fry in hot oil. Its denser flesh makes it chewier than the smaller pilot fish. Serve plain with rice, or dipped in bottled *Sriracha* chilli sauce.

Another category of dried fish treasured in Thailand and Cambodia is crisped, smoke-dried fish (*bplah gkrawb*), which are only mildly salted, or not at all. Freshwater fish, especially the smaller varieties, are placed in a smoker fueled by coconut husks and hardwood chips and smoked for many hours or days over very low heat until they are completely dried and crispy. Often the fish are first partially dried in the sun, or by roasting over wood coals at very low heat for several hours before being placed in the smoker. A distinct characteristic of Thai smoke-dried fish is its crispiness, which is possible to attain with most freshwater fish; saltwater fish, with only a few exceptions, turn hard rather than crispy when dried the same way with smoke.

The wonderful fragrance and superb flavor and texture of crisped, smoke-dried fish make them a highly prized delicacy in Thailand. Because of the dwindling supplies of freshwater fish, demand far exceeds supply, turning them into an expensive commodity, unlike other preserved fish products. Restaurants snatch up a big chunk of the supply and use them sparingly in spicy salads, incendiary soups, and hot, dry curries. The next time you visit Thailand, do look for smoke-dried fish (*bplah gkrawb*) dishes on the menus of Bangkok's fine restaurants.

Among highly salted fish, my personal favorite is salted mackerel. If you like preserved anchovies, you will most likely fall for salted mackerel, too. Look for narrow oval steaks of salted king mackerel either vacuum-packed in plastic and refrigerated, or stuffed in glass jars covered with oil. Pan-fry in a small amount of oil for a couple of minutes on both sides until well browned and flaky. Drain from oil and sprinkle with thinly sliced shallots, thin rounds of Thai chillies, and fresh lime juice. Because it is very salty, only a small bit of the mackerel is mixed and eaten with plain steamed rice. My mother and I share a fondness for salted mackerel and just a tiny piece can help us polish off a big pot of rice, and feel very satisfied!

Salted mackerel is also used as a flavoring ingredient, as in the Chinese steamed, chopped pork with salted fish. Use it as you would salted anchovies. It makes a particularly tasty flavoring for stir-fried Asian broccoli, or broccoli rabe (recipe below). Flake the flesh of pan-fried salted mackerel and toss with the greens. Instead of salted mackerel, small pieces of fried, dried salted mudfish may also be used.

When working with any kind of dried and salted fish, beware of the strong fishy odors likely to be released during cooking, especially frying. Make sure there is plenty of ventilation in the kitchen to disperse the lingering fumes.

Asian Broccoli with Salted Mackerel
(Ka-nah Bplah Kem)

1 bunch Asian or Chinese broccoli
¼ cup peanut oil
1 small piece (about 2 oz.) salted mackerel
10 cloves garlic, chopped finely
3 to 4 Tbs. Thai oyster sauce
2 to 3 tsp. fish sauce (*nahm bplah*), to taste

Starting from the stem end, cut Asian broccoli at a very sharp angle, ½ inch apart, to make pieces about 1½ inches long. Peel the bottom of the larger, more fibrous stems before cutting. For pieces with leaves attached, cut the leaves into 2-inch segments. Do not make it a point to detach the leaves from the stems; there should be pieces of stem with some leaf attached. Keep the pieces from the bottom half of the stems separate from the leafier upper half.

Heat 2 tablespoons oil in a wok over medium-high heat until it begins to smoke. Fry the salted mackerel in the oil for 2 to 3 minutes on each side until well browned. Remove from wok.

Increase heat to high and swirl in the remaining oil. When it is smoking hot, add the chopped garlic; stir for 10 to 15 seconds, then toss in the bottom stem pieces. Stir-fry 30 seconds to 1 minute before adding the leafy pieces. Continue to stir-fry until the leaves have mostly wilted. Sprinkle with oyster sauce and 1 teaspoon fish sauce, stir, and mix well. Break the mackerel into small chunks and toss in with the vegetable. Stir-fry a little while longer until the broccoli is tender but still crisp, and a vibrant green color. Taste and add more fish sauce as needed to the desired saltiness. Stir well and transfer to a serving dish.

Serves 6 with rice and other dishes in a shared family-style meal.

Notes and Pointers:

A very nutritious bitter-green vegetable readily available from most Oriental produce markets, Asian or Chinese broccoli has insignificant flower buds and is prized for its deep green leaves and firm, crisp stems.

Select a bunch with small tender stems. If the stems are large, the bottom half may need to be peeled to remove the tough fibers. Cutting the stems at a very sharp, slanted angle helps break up the fibers that run the length of the stalks, giving them a more tender texture. The sauce can also penetrate the vegetable better through the longer cut that exposes the interior of the stems.

If the bunch of broccoli you have is not very young and may be tough, you may need to add a couple of tablespoons of water during the stir-fry to help the vegetable cook. The broccoli may also be blanched for a few seconds in lightly salted boiling water and drained before tossing into the wok to stir-fry.

Fermented or Pickled Fish
(Bplah Daek, Bplah Rah)

Fermented freshwater fish (also called *pickled fish*) belongs among the world's aged and preserved foods that are at once disgustingly foul smelling, yet remarkably tasty (to people with a palate for strongly pungent foods). Available in jars in just about every Southeast Asian market, it is a cherished staple food in much of that region of the Far East.

In Thailand, fermented fish (*bplah daek* in northeastern Thailand, *bplah rah* in the rest of the country) lies at the heart of northeastern culture, especially in the provinces along the Mekong River and its numerous tributaries. Interestingly, this is also the part of the country known for its consumption of raw foods, including meats, fish, and other freshwater life.

Since ancient times, making *bplah daek* has been a communal affair during the fishing season, and hardly a day goes by when fermented fish does not touch villagers' lives in some way. More frequently than not, the day begins and ends with it in a wide array of delectable dishes. On special occasions, such as a wedding, special birthday celebration, or house-blessing ceremony, visiting extended family and friends who have traveled from afar are frequently rewarded with jars of the fish to take home. Some families are known for their outstanding homemade *bplah daek,* so being given such a gift is regarded as a special honor.

Fermented fish is made by salting cleaned fresh fish, then stuffing them tightly into vats or earthenware jars and letting them ferment for several days. The resulting water is drained and the fish rinsed before coating with either rice husks, or ground roasted rice, and salt. They are repacked tightly into vats or jars and permitted to ferment for six months to a year.

Fermented fish is consumed both as a main food in itself, or used as a flavoring ingredient in spicy salads, soups, curries, stewed dishes, and dipping sauces. Generally, the kind made from small fish, like gouramy, is used for flavoring: The fish is chopped and simmered in water, the flavored liquid strained and used. The flesh may also be removed from the bones and cooked in with the dishes it is to flavor.

Larger, meaty fish, such as tilapia and serpent-head fish (or mudfish, *bplah chon*) are fried whole or in large pieces, dressed with herbs, seasonings, and chillies, and served as a main dish—a delicacy in the northeast.

The repugnant stench of fermented fish dissipates with cooking. Usually the smaller the fish, the more repulsive the odor, though most of my cooking students, Asians included, find any kind to be beyond reasonable limits of tolerance for them to handle in their kitchen. I have, therefore, avoided northeastern-influenced seafood dishes flavored with fermented fish in this book, or substituted it with the more benign *gkabpi* shrimp paste.

If you are bold, have a liking for pungent preserved foods, and are curious about giving this treasured food of Southeast Asia a try, look for big chunks of fish tightly stuffed in glass jars, surrounded by a caramel-colored sauce made with ground roasted rice. A good product from Thailand, the Double Golden Elephant brand, identifies it in English as "Fish Sauce," listing the ingredients as mudfish, rice, and salt. It comes in one-pound jars. The fish should have an appealing appearance and the thick sauce an appetizing color that is evenly brown from top to bottom. The jar and lid should also look clean and new, without any substance oozing through the seal.

Rinse the fish, dredge in flour, and fry in plenty of hot oil until well browned. Make sure there is good ventilation in your kitchen as the oil will smoke and foam. Drain from oil and sprinkle with sliced shallots, chopped Thai chillies, thin rounds of lemon grass, finely slivered kaffir lime leaves, and fresh lime juice before serving. Although sometimes referred to as pickled fish, it does not have a sour flavor like most pickled foods, but tastes more like salted fish, with its own distinct aroma.

The fried fermented fish may also be crumbled and added to spicy dishes, including green papaya salad, pungent stews, and robustly flavored seafood dishes. Because it is salty, cut back on fish sauce or salt in those recipes.

Dried Squid and Cuttlefish
(Bplah Meuk Haeng)

The shallow waters of the Gulf of Thailand are home to millions of squid and cuttlefish, which quickly breed to fill the vacuum whenever huge netfuls of their kind are pulled out of the sea. (Cuttlefish look like round-bodied squid; their flesh is thicker but has a similar texture and taste to squid.) Most of them end up on wire racks or strung on lines to dry in the sun, later to be shipped around the country and world. Japan is one of the big buyers, turning the squid and cuttlefish into tasty snacks.

If you've traveled around Thailand, you might have noticed the ubiquitous sidewalk vendors, who display neatly strung rows of dried squid above their pushcarts. These squid are roasted on charcoal braziers, releasing a wonderfully fragrant aroma irresistible to many passers-by. They are then rolled through hand-cranked presses to tenderize. Though still quite tough, they are snacked on like chewy jerky, each chew releasing a sweet, salty, and pungent flavor of the sea. Sometimes the pressed, roasted squid are coated with flavorings, such as chillies, salt (or fish sauce), and sugar, or are eaten dipped in a hot-sweet-and-sour sauce as desired.

Dried squid and cuttlefish are available in large and small sizes from most Asian markets. The smaller sizes are generally more tender and roast to a crisp. Hold them with tongs and pass back and forth directly over the flame of a gas burner, or over hot charcoals, until they blister, curl, and char lightly. When cooled, they develop a crispy edge. Break and tear into bite-size pieces and snack on plain, or dipped in a sweet-and-sour chilli sauce. Or toss with herbs and seasonings to make a salad. Small dried squid and cuttlefish also fry to a crisp for a richer taste; tear first into small pieces before frying in plenty of hot oil.

Dried squid and cuttlefish can also be reconstituted by soaking in cool tap water for a day, or overnight, then used for cooking. They swell to a few times their original size. Remove the purplish membrane and soak in clean water for another hour. Reconstituted, they can be used the same way as fresh squid in stir-fried dishes and seafood soups, and are frequently cooked with fresh squid. Because their texture is firmer and crisper than the fresh, score the thick flesh of large squid or cuttlefish an eighth to a quarter inch apart in a crisscross pattern before cooking to tenderize.

Some people say the flavor and texture of dried squid and cuttlefish, whether roasted dry, or cooked after reconstituting, are an acquired taste. They certainly aren't anything like their fresh counterparts.

Short of drying completely, squid are sometimes laid on wire racks in the hot tropical sun for only one day before being used for cooking. A delicious Thai preparation, called "single sun" squid (*meuk ∂ae∂ ∂iow*), fries such partially sun-dried squid in hot oil and serves them with a sweet-and-sour chilli dipping sauce. The rays of the sun add an exquisite, full-bodied flavor to mild-tasting squid that I find absolutely heavenly! One great place to eat such squid is Sunee, a family-run, open-air, beachside restaurant next to Pranburi marina and a small squid-fishing village on a quiet stretch of the gulf coast. My cooking students who have traveled with me to Thailand find the "solar" squid here truly unforgettable!

Salted Crab

(Bpoo Kem)

In my childhood days, I was fascinated by the myriad moving, darting, and crawling creatures inhabiting the edge of the pond that wrapped around two sides of my family's property. Among them were these small black crabs, no larger than a small Louisiana crayfish; they would scurry through the rushes and sometimes venture across the wide expanse of our lawn to the hedges at the edge of our neighbor's pond. Their strange sideways movement always caught my curiosity but, whenever I approached one, it would come to a complete halt, raising its front pincers up toward me, its alarmed eyes protruding out from their sockets and moving side to side to study me closely. I had even come across ones that would foam around their mouths. A bit too ominous for a small child to touch!

These small freshwater crabs are found in great numbers in and around ricefields and flatlands turned into wetlands during the rainy season. Though they do not have much meat, they are caught and fermented in salt water, making a briny crab sauce for seasoning. The best part, though, are the crabs themselves, which are cut up into chunks shell and all, and added to salads, including the delicious salted crab green papaya salad (*som ∂tam bpoo kem*) —to this day my favorite rendition of this popular national dish. They are also cooked in saucy dishes to lend their flavor, and make a wonderful sauce with chopped pork, shrimp, and coconut cream for serving with crisp vegetables, aromatic herbs, and rice (see recipe).

Since other Southeast Asian cultures also delight in the flavor of salted crabs, these small black crustaceans can occasionally be found among the unusual offerings of ethnic markets located near areas where large concentrations of Southeast Asians have settled. Look for them in small plastic pouches or containers in a refrigeration unit.

Salted Crab Coconut Cream Sauce

(Loen Bpoo Kem)

6 small salted crabs
2 cups coconut cream
¼ lb. ground pork
¼ lb. fresh shrimp, shelled and chopped finely
¼ cup tamarind juice, the thickness of fruit concentrate
¼ cup palm or coconut sugar
Sea salt as needed to taste
2 small shallots, quartered lengthwise and sliced thinly crosswise
1 red or orange serrano pepper, cut into fine slivers with seeds
1 green serrano pepper, cut into fine slivers with seeds
4 red and green Thai chillies (*prik kee noo*), cut into 2 segments
Assortment of fresh firm and crisp vegetables, such as green or long beans, snap
    peas, cauliflower, and cucumber; and sprigs of leafy aromatic herbs, such as
    mint and basil

Pull off back shells of salted crabs and discard. Remove gills and cut each crab into four pieces, each piece with a few legs attached to a body part. Rinse and drain.

Heat coconut cream in a saucepan over medium heat until smooth. Spoon out 2 tablespoons and reserve for later use. Add ground pork and chopped shrimp, stirring to break into small bits as they cook. When most of the pork has lost its raw pink color, add crab pieces and return to a boil. Season sauce to taste with palm sugar and tamarind.

Simmer uncovered for 10 to 15 minutes. Taste and, if it is not salty or sweet enough, add a little salt and palm sugar. Stir in the sliced shallots and red and green serrano peppers. Return to a boil, stir, and transfer to a sauce dish. Let cool for 10 to 15 minutes. Top with reserved coconut cream and garnish with Thai chillies.

Arrange vegetables on a platter and serve with the salted crab coconut sauce. The sauce may also be eaten with plain steamed rice. Suck on the crab pieces for a burst of salty crab flavor.

Serves 8 to 10 in a multicourse family-style meal.

Notes and Pointers:

Dip the vegetables and herbs into the sauce to eat, or place a few pieces at a time on the side of your dinner plate and spoon a little sauce over them. Dip and nibble as you desire, rather than serve it as a course.

The sauce may also be spooned a small amount at a time onto a little bit of rice and eaten to clear the palate after spicy bites from other dishes in the meal.

In addition to mint and basil, many other kinds of leafy aromatic herbs and strong-tasting vegetables found in Southeast Asian markets are delicious with this sauce, such as polygonum (called *rau ram* by the Vietnamese), sawleaf coriander (oblong leaves with serrated edges), rice-paddy herb (rows of very small green leaves growing up soft, light green stems), lemon mint, and edible chrysanthemum leaves. Bitter and astringent vegetables like bitter melon (warty, oblong squash) and fresh banana blossom also make good accompaniments, as the sauce softens their strong bite. Look for these unusual produce in Asian markets near you and give them a try, or substitute strong-tasting salad greens, such as arugula, radicchio, endive, sorrel, and parsley.

If you wish to try the exotic banana blossom, it is available from time to time during the warmer months in Southeast Asian markets. The outer layers are a rich purplish-red color, but the best parts for eating are the light ivory leaves in the center. Because the sap can blacken the heart and leaves, soak in salted water immediately after cutting. Banana blossom has an unpleasant astringent bite (an acquired taste) when eaten by itself, but this disappears when accompanied by the creamy sauce — a very unusual experience!

Shrimp Butter and Crab Butter Pastes
(Mân Gkoong, Mân Bpoo)

Seasoned pastes made from the golden buttery substance in the heads of shrimp and inside the shells of crabs are traditional foodstuffs of the southern region of Thailand, where most provinces border the sea. They are popularly eaten by mixing with hot steamed rice at the dinner table, along with sliced shallots, cut-up Thai chillies, fish sauce, and a squeeze of fresh lime juice. Fresh vegetables, such as cucumbers, long beans, and small Thai eggplants are served alongside. The pastes are also commonly used to impart a rich seafood flavor to fried rice, noodle, stir-fried vegetable, and seafood dishes.

Available in seven-ounce jars, both shrimp and crab pastes are among the staple products carried by Southeast Asian markets, labeled "shrimp (or crab) paste with soya bean oil." Besides the butter from the crustaceans, these bottled pastes also contain chopped pieces of shrimp or crabmeat, garlic, white pepper, cilantro roots, soybean oil, fish sauce, and sugar. Kaffir lime leaves and large pieces of lemon grass are frequently stewed with the shrimp and crab butter and other ingredients, but are pulled out and discarded before bottling.

Most shrimp and crab pastes today are made from by-products of the burgeoning fishery industry, which exports a tremendous tonnage of dried shrimp, frozen headless shrimp, crab claws, and shelled crab worldwide each year.

4

INGREDIENTS AND TIPS
FOR SELECTION AND
PREPARATION

INGREDIENTS FOR THAI SEAFOOD COOKERY ARE NUMEROUS AND
diverse. Many are exotic and unfamiliar to American home cooks new to
Southeast Asian cooking. In the following summary, I hope to acquaint you
with them and the different forms in which they come. In addition, I have included tips that you may find useful on selection, preparation, substitution,
and storage. The list is by no means an exhaustive commentary on all the ingredients used in Thai cooking, but covers those that are used in the recipes
in this book.

Aside from the ingredients covered in this chapter, chapter 3, "Preserved
Foods and Flavoring Ingredients from the Sea," discusses many common
seafood products (including a few recipes), some of which are not used in the
recipes comprising the heart of the book.

If you live in or near a major metropolitan area with a diverse ethnic population, you should have no trouble finding most of the ingredients in the
following list. Look for markets that cater to Southeast Asians in the international district or in the local Chinatown. Some Southeast Asian markets may
be located by themselves in particular neighborhoods; so if you see a store
with a name that looks Asian, stop and check it out. If there are Thai restaurants in your area, ask the staff to point you in the right direction.

If you live in an area with few or no ethnic markets, you may have to depend on mail-order sources to locate your Thai cooking ingredients. To help
you out, a list of markets in various metropolitan areas, including a few online
markets, is included in the appendix. Many of these markets will be more
than glad to ship supplies to you, so don't hesitate to call and inquire.

Alphabetical List of Ingredients

Banana leaves (*bai dtong*): The large, lovely green and shiny leaves of the banana plant are thick, tough, and pliable, making them useful for wrapping foods for roasting or grilling, for shaping into leaf cups to hold foods for steaming, or simply for lining serving platters to add a decorative touch. In addition to the function they serve, they also impart a pleasant aroma to the foods cooked in them, but are not themselves eaten.

Banana leaves are imported from a few Southeast Asian countries in pound-size frozen packages; because they have not been cleaned before packaging, rinse or wipe with a damp towel to remove the sap and powdery substance that naturally coats the leaves. Freshly cut banana leaves need to be softened with heat to make them pliable—simply pass the leaves closely over a hot burner or charcoal pit until they become limp and flexible.

Because banana leaves have ribs that tear easily horizontally but not vertically, crisscross the ribs of two pieces of leaf stacked one on top of the other when wrapping foods for cooking. This prevents the leaf packet from splitting and food spilling out during cooking.

Basil: Two varieties of the lusciously fragrant herb basil generously enhance Thai seafood dishes. The first and most prolifically used is a tropical strain of sweet basil, frequently referred to in American Asian markets as *Thai basil (bai horapa)*, although it is also common in the cuisines of Vietnam, Laos, and Cambodia. Thai basil has lush, deep-green leaves, purplish flower buds and stems, and carries anise overtones to its sweet basil scent. It is added by the big handfuls in whole leaves, to green and red curries and spicy stir-fried dishes; sprigs of it regularly appear with other herbs on vegetable platters to be nibbled on with spicy salads and chilli dips. The flower buds are also edible, adding a wonderful floral bouquet.

Thai sweet basil is readily available in most Southeast Asian markets and can be grown easily in an herb garden in summer. Many nurseries carry the seedlings, and seeds for an improved strain called Siamese Queen can be acquired through several gourmet vegetable seed catalogues.

Also extensively used and even more deliciously perfumed, is *holy* or *sacred basil (bai gkaprow)*, often called *hot basil* because of its peppery taste, especially when very fresh, along with a hint of mint and cloves. Since its exotic flavor becomes fully released with cooking, it is not eaten raw, but added in generous amounts to stir-fried dishes and some spicy soups. Holy basil is so called because it is a sacred herb in India, where it frequently is planted around Hindu shrines.

There are two kinds of holy basil: The more exuberantly flavored red holy basil has dark green leaves with reddish purple stems and a purplish cast on the younger leaves; the milder white has medium-green leaves with very light green, almost white, stems. The leaves of both varieties are smaller than Thai sweet basil, and are slightly hairy and jagged around the edges. They are fragile and do not keep as well as Thai basil, wilting and losing their aroma easily and therefore should be used within a few days of purchasing. Keep the leaves dry by wrapping with paper towels before placing in a plastic bag in the refrigerator. Wet leaves turn black and rot quickly.

Decidedly tropical and requiring more heat to grow than Thai basil, holy basil is not as readily available and, in many cases, has to be flown in from Hawaii. It is worth seeking as its unique flavor is heavenly, making it the beloved basil among Thai people. It gives several of the seafood dishes in this book their magical qualities. Look for it in Thai/Cambodian stores and during the warm summer months at farmer's markets with Southeast Asian stalls. Try growing it if you cannot locate a supply near you; seeds are available from a few seed catalogues (see appendix)—select the variety known as *sacred purple basil* for best flavor. Substitute with Thai sweet basil if you must.

Although holy basil is sometimes available in dried form, this is not an acceptable substitute by itself as its aromatic oils are lost through drying—use only in combination with a fresh basil. For best flavor in stir-fried dishes, reconstitute the dried basil by soaking in cool tap water, pull off and discard the twiggy stems that do not soften, and toss into the stir-fry with fresh Thai basil.

Bean thread noodles (*woon sen*): These slippery noodles are sometimes called cellophane noodles or glass noodles since they become almost transparent when softened in water. They are made from mung beans, which, because of their green hull, are sometimes called "green beans," hence, the dried, stringy noodles are most often labeled as "green bean thread" or "green bean vermicelli." Not all brands are good; those that don't have an elasticity of texture and tend to fall apart and get mushy easily are usually not made of pure mung bean flour. A good and widely available brand is *Lungkow*, which has two circling dragons as its logo. It comes in small (1.7 ounce) and medium (3.5 ounce) packages.

Bitter melon (*mara*): There are several different varieties of this light- to dark-green, fleshy, oblong squash, ranging in size from no longer than two inches to as long as a foot. They all share a peculiar warty-looking surface, with irregular ridges and bumps running their entire length. As the name suggests, bitter melon is indeed bitter due

to the high concentration of quinine it contains. In addition, it is rich in iron, beta-carotene, calcium, potassium, phosphorus, and vitamins B and C, making it one of the most nutritious vegetables around. In fact, modern science has discovered compounds in this melon that can be used in the treatment of diabetes, cancer, and HIV infections.

More mature, lighter green melons are generally less bitter. In Thai cuisine, bitter melon is frequently eaten raw or lightly blanched as an accompaniment to either strongly pungent or creamy dipping sauces, both of which temper its bitterness. It also accompanies many spicy salads and finds its way into intensely flavored curries. Bitter melon is an acquired taste for the many Americans who are not accustomed to bitter vegetables, but those who have developed a taste for it, as they have for highly spiced foods, treasure the extra dimension of flavor and nutrition it contributes to their meals. My husband, for one, loves it and couldn't walk past a pile in an Asian market without snatching up a few.

Black pepper, black peppercorns (*prik tai dâm*): See *pepper*.

Black soy sauce (*si-ew dâm*): See *soy sauce*.

Black vinegar (*jek choew*): See *vinegar*.

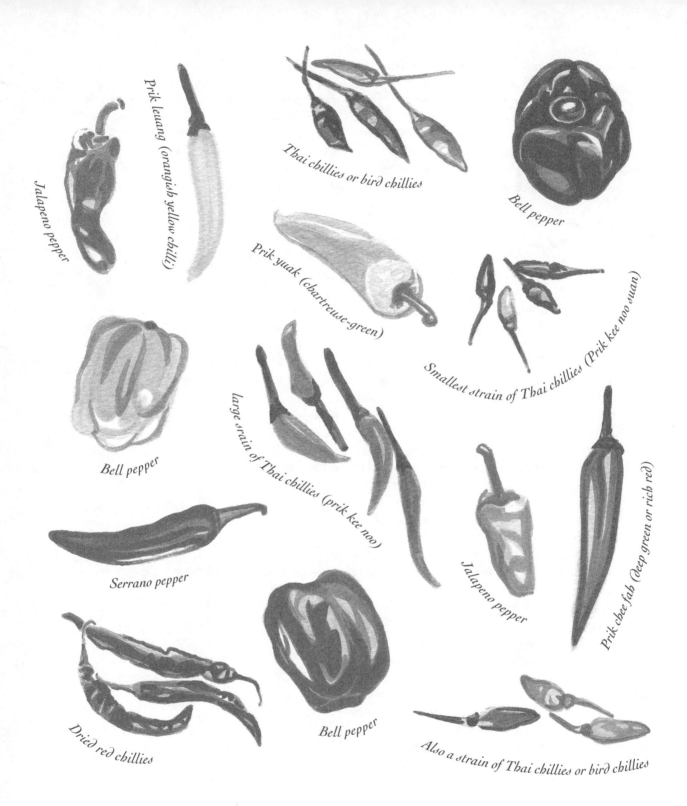

Jalapeno pepper

Prik leuang (orangish yellow chilli)

Thai chillies or bird chillies

Bell pepper

Prik yuak (chartreuse-green)

Smallest strain of Thai chillies (Prik kee noo suan)

Bell pepper

large strain of Thai chillies (prik kee noo)

Jalapeno pepper

Prik chee fah (deep green or rich red)

Serrano pepper

Dried red chillies

Bell pepper

Also a strain of Thai chillies or bird chillies

Cashews (*med mamuang himapahn*): Raw whole cashews are sold in small bags in Asian markets, or in bulk in natural-food stores. Cook them as they are needed for a fresher, richer, and nuttier flavor. They may be dry-roasted in a pan on the stove, or in the oven (see *peanuts*); or fried in oil over low heat until they brown all the way through. Cashews are an important crop of southern Thailand, and the freshly fried nuts are frequently sprinkled on salads.

Chillies (*prik*): Of the numerous varieties used in Thailand, only one is now widely grown in America. Called *prik kee noo* or, literally, "mouse dropping chilli" (its small size and irregular, slender shape give it the appearance of the rodent's excrement), this member of the bird chilli (or spur chilli) family is indisputably a Thai favorite. Its sharp bite and spicy aroma are integral to our cuisine, and because we use it with such unrestrained vigor, it has come to be known here as *Thai chilli*. Cut-up rounds of *prik kee noo* swimming in fish sauce appear regularly as the salt and pepper at the Thai dinner table. Never remove the seeds from this skinny chilli; after all, it is mainly a bag of seeds held together by a thin skin.

There are different strains of Thai chillies, with the smallest, *prik kee noo suan*, being the hottest and best loved of all. This tiny half-inch mouse, however, is rarely seen here; most frequently, Thai chillies come larger, averaging one and a half inches long, and a little milder, though still quite intense for unaccustomed Western palates. They are slender and pointed at the tip, with a bumpy feel from the protruding seeds tightly packed inside. Flavor varies slightly with different stages of maturity but, whether green, red, or yellowish orange, they pack a strong punch that lingers in your mouth, intensifying with each bite. This, however, depends on the batch, as chillies grown in cooler climates develop less heat. Buy a mixture of red and green if you can, to add a range of lovely color and delicious chilli flavor to your Thai dishes.

Red Thai chillies also come sun-dried to give a different flavor dimension. Roast them in a dry pan on the stove with frequent stirring, until they turn dark red and lightly charred, then grind and toss into salads, soups, sauces, and curry pastes, to lend a fragrant aroma and roasted flavor. When roasting chillies, add a pinch or two of salt to help keep down the irritating chilli fumes; make sure there is plenty of ventilation and take care not to burn them.

Dried Thai chillies (*prik kee noo haeng*) are also fried whole to a dark red color, with the stem still attached; the glistening, crisped pods make a pretty garnish and are a delight to chew on, imparting a searing, deeply smoky, piquant taste. Dried Thai chillies are available from most markets that carry Thai ingredients; they are small, skinny, and usually more crinkly in appearance than other dried red chillies. Fresh red Thai chillies can be easily dried in the sun, or on a plate in a well-ventilated area.

Three other varieties of chillies common in Thai cooking are: *prik chee fah*, which come dark green and rich red; *prik leuang*, in a lovely shade of orangish yellow; and *prik yuak*, in chartreuse green. Not as hot as *prik kee noo*, these peppers enhance foods with their own particular flavors. The first two are similar in size, shape, flavor, and hotness to serrano peppers, which I have substituted for them in the recipes in this book. Fresh red cayenne peppers also make a good substitute. The third is a larger and milder chilli and can be replaced by jalapeno, fresno, or yellow wax peppers. Fresno peppers are normally sold red and ripe; though mild and sweet, their pleasant flavor goes well with other Thai ingredients, making them a good substitute for less iron-plated palates.

In many recipes, orange and red hot peppers are called for to add the reddish color and sweeter chilli flavor associated with the dishes; but if you cannot find any ripe peppers, please do not skip over these recipes, but feel free to substitute any fresh hot pepper. Or, look for pickled, whole red Thai chillies imported from Thailand in sixteen-ounce jars. A very good brand is the Buddha brand labeled "pickled hot chilli."

When a recipe calls for *dried red chillies* or large dried red chillies (*prik haeng*) without specifying Thai chillies, use the larger two- to three-inch-long variety. They are readily available in small cellophane bags and are imported from Thailand. Dried cayenne peppers, dried Sichuan red chillies, or dried Japanese red chillies may be substituted. Do not use the large varieties of dried Mexican peppers that are mild and sweet.

Because chillies can vary in intensity from batch to batch and taste preferences, too, can differ considerably, use your own discretion in deciding how many to use. Start with the lower end of the scale (or below if you are an unmistaken wimp) and work your way up. Your tolerance for spicy heat may increase over time as you acquire a taste for the addicting chillies. Be aware that the hotness in chillies is not water soluble, but oil soluble; so milk, coconut milk, or any creamy food or drink will more quickly douse the fire in your mouth than will water or beer. The acidity in lemon, lime, and orange juices, as well as certain wines, also works well. Best of all is to eat lots more rice along with mild dishes and sauces in the meal.

Chillies give an essential piquant flavor to Thai food. If you are not able to find any of the chillies mentioned here, substitute any hot peppers you can find. If you are deprived of fresh hot peppers of any kind where you live and cannot find the pickled Thai chillies, substitute reconstituted dried red chillies softened by soaking in water—cut off the stem tip before covering with water for faster results.

Thai cooks seldom remove seeds from fresh chillies; do so only if you cannot take the heat, but be careful not to touch the interior of the chillies with unprotected hands! If your hands burn, soak in vinegar or lime juice, then wash a few times with a cream-based soap. Dried chillies are sometimes deseeded, since the seeds hold little flavor; this way, more of the flavorful pods can be used until the desired heat level is reached. To deseed dried chillies without getting your hands hot, cut the stem end to open them up, hold them with opening faced down, gently squeeze the pods, and tap out the seeds.

Chinese celery (*keun chai*): Unlike its mild, pale green, and large-stalked Western cousin, Asian celery has slender, dark green, leafy stems, and a robust aroma and pungent flavor with a slightly bitter aftertaste. It is used more as an herb, like cilantro, than as a vegetable to munch on by itself. If you are not able to find any, substitute the tender leaves of regular American celery.

Cilantro (*pak chee*): Also known as "coriander" and "Chinese parsley," cilantro is the most widely used leafy aromatic herb. In Thai cooking, the whole plant is valued, from the tender leaves to the firm roots. The sweetly scented leaves are tossed into soups at the last minute (cooking dissipates the refreshing flavor) and eaten raw in salads; sprigs serve as the ubiquitous garnish; and roots and bottom stems get smashed and added to soup stocks and stews, or minced and reduced with other herbs to make curry and chilli pastes. (See *coriander* for a discussion of the seeds.)

Cilantro root (*rahk pak chee*) has a deep, earthy flavor lacking in the leaves and stems, and is an important Thai flavoring ingredient. Pounded with garlic and white peppercorns, it makes a fragrant and peppery basic seasoning mix. Unfortunately, cilantro usually comes with its roots already cut off. Look for whole cilantro plants with roots at farmer's markets with ethnic Southeast Asian stalls or grow your own but, if you must, the bottom stems substitute well in seafood dishes. If you are able to find cilantro with roots, rinse them well and use the roots along with an inch of the bottom stems to which they are attached. Store extra roots in a zipper bag in the freezer; clean and let dry before freezing.

Coconut (*maprao*): The coconut palm is one of the most useful of all trees in the tropics, providing not only food but raw materials for making all sorts of useful furnishings, household supplies, and even recreational equipment. The fruit or nut is eaten at different stages of development; for the recipes in this book we are primarily interested in the flesh of the mature coconut, which is shredded and roasted to add a rich, nutty flavor to certain dishes and pressed to make coconut milk and cream for curries and soups.

For the handful of recipes that call for roasted shredded coconut, it is not essential to go through the laborious process of removing the flesh from a fresh whole coconut. Simply use the dried, unsweetened shredded coconut sold in well-stocked Asian markets, natural-food stores, or gourmet supermarkets. Make sure it has not been sweetened. Store leftovers in an airtight jar or plastic bag in a cool place.

To roast, spread the shredded coconut in a dry pan over moderate heat. Stir frequently until the coconut turns a rich and even golden brown and is very fragrant. Remove from pan and set aside to cool before using. Roasted coconut shreds keep for a couple of months in a sealed jar.

For a discussion on coconut cream and milk, see the following entry. Aside from the food value of the fruit, the coconut palm yields a sweet sap for making sugar (see *palm sugar*) and tender, edible shoots (unopened new leaves atop the palm, called "palm heart") which make a delectable crisp vegetable.

Coconut milk/cream (*gkati*): Coconut milk is not the juice found inside a coconut but the diluted cream pressed out from the thick, white flesh of a well-matured coconut.

To make coconut milk, finely grated coconut meat is steeped in hot water until it is cool enough to handle. It is then squeezed until dry; the white fluid is strained to remove all the pulp. When allowed to sit for a while, the *coconut cream* (*hua gkati*) rises to the top. Commercially, coconut cream is obtained by pressing grated coconut flesh by itself without water, using specialized, heavy machinery.

More hot water is added to the pulp and the process is then repeated to yield a lighter fluid, or *coconut milk* (*nahm gkati*). Frequently, a third pressing is done to obtain a *light coconut milk* (*hahng gkati*), which is used for stewing meats or for thinning coconut milk to make a coconut soup or a light curry. An average mature coconut yields about one cup of coconut cream and one to two cups of coconut milk, depending on how light a milk is desired.

For most working American families with limited time to cook, making fresh coconut milk from scratch from a whole coconut is too laborious a process, especially when canned or bottled unsweetened coconut milk can easily be substituted.

Not all brands of canned coconut milk are good. Some actually can be downright foul tasting. Try a number of different brands to find the one most to your liking. Good coconut milk has a clean, white color and tastes rich, creamy, and mildly sweet with the essence of coconut. It should also have a complexity and depth of flavor that keeps you intrigued, and not leave an unpleasant aftertaste. As is true with other kinds of natural cream that have not been artificially homogenized, natural coconut cream will rise to the top and separate from the heavier water component.

Good brands of coconut milk, therefore, will have thick cream floating on top of the can while the milk on the bottom will be much more watery. The cream usually coagulates in cool weather, or when refrigerated. Brands with milk that looks homogenized tend to have an artificial taste, because of additives introduced to make the cream homogenize, or excess processing that changes the nature of the cream. My two preferred brands are *Chao Koh* in fourteen-ounce cans, and *Mae Ploy* in nineteen-ounce cans. The latter is the richest and creamiest of brands I have tried; *Chao Koh,* while lighter, has a delicate, sweet natural flavor. Beware of lookalike cans of inferior brands. Both are carried by most Southeast Asian markets.

For recipes requiring coconut cream, do not shake the can before opening; spoon out the thick cream on top. On hot days, refrigerate the can so that the cream will harden and can be easily separated from the lighter milk.

I do not recommend canned "light coconut milk," it has little flavor, if any. Usually, some kind of flour has been added to make it look thicker and whiter than it really is, although this is not made known on the listing of ingredients. Better results can be obtained by thinning a good-quality, creamy coconut milk with water or cooking liquids to the lightness desired.

If you are concerned about the saturated fat content in coconut milk, know that this saturated fat has been shown in many independent studies to be a good saturated fat, easily metabolized to give your body quick energy. Contrary to popular myth, it does not transform into bad cholesterol to clog arteries. In fact, cultures around the world that depend on coconut as their main source of fat have been found to be free of heart disease. The principle fatty acid in coconut milk is lauric acid, which is the same fat found in abundance in mother's milk and known to promote normal brain development and contribute to healthy bones. It also has important anticarcinogenic and antipathogenic properties and is less likely to cause weight gain than polyunsaturated oils. The potent antiviral, antifungal, and antimicrobial effects of coconut oil have implicated it in the treatment of both AIDS and candida. Whatever bad things you may have heard or read about coconut milk have not stood up to the scrutiny of unbiased food scientists; however, the goodness of coconut milk has not been given equal press because of intensive lobbying against it by the powerful vegetable oil industry. Southeast Asians, meanwhile, have been staying healthy for generations with coconut an integral part of their diet.

Coconut milk should be refrigerated once the can is opened. It keeps for a couple of days to one week. I do not recommend freezing coconut milk as this increases the likelihood of its curdling when it is next used in cooking, unless you are just warming it through without boiling.

Be careful not to buy sweetened coconut milk for Thai cooking. As for powdered coconut milk or the waxy, condensed blocks requiring dilution with water, I do not recommend them, unless you are going backpacking and just can't do without your Thai curry!

Coconut milk is the base of most Thai curries. Contrary to Western ideas of working with cream, to make the curry sauce, coconut cream is first reduced over fairly high heat to break down the cream and allow the oil to separate. The curry paste is then added and fried in the coconut oil until all the herb and spice flavors are released and blended, before the rest of the coconut milk is added to make the sauce. Finished Thai curries will have a thin layer of oil floating on top of the sauce. This oil picks up the color of the curries—bright red for red curry, glistening green for green curry, and so on—giving them a lovely appearance rather than a dull, whitish sameness. The color serves as a reminder of their true nature—spicy hot from red and green chillies and not creamy and bland.

Coconut sugar (*nahm dtahn maprao*): See *palm sugar.*

Coriander seeds (*loog pak chee*): The seeds of the cilantro or coriander plant are used mainly for making curry pastes, chilli pastes for stir-frying, rich dipping sauces, and marinades for grilled foods. They are ground plain, or roasted first on a dry pan over the stove before grinding for a stronger scent and toasted flavor. Always buy whole seeds rather than pre-ground coriander, as spices lose their flavor and fragrance quickly after they are pulverized. Store in an airtight jar in a cool, dark place in the cupboard. Roast the seeds only as you need them.

Thai coriander seeds are smaller than the Western variety, and are more sweetly perfumed and fuller flavored, but if you are not able to find them in the Asian markets near you, substitute the commonly available seeds. See *cilantro* for a discussion of the plant itself.

Cumin (*mellet yira*): This spice is sometimes erroneously called fennel or caraway in Thailand, perhaps because the first Western translators were not familiar with it, and mistook it for the other two because of their similar appearance. Therefore, if you should find a package of seeds in a Thai market labeled "fennel," it is most likely cumin.

Cumin is used primarily in curry pastes, some marinades, and a few Indian-influenced dishes. It is normally used in combination with coriander seeds, either roasted first for more aroma, or plain for more subtle flavoring. Because it is not a primary flavor in Thai cooking and can be overpowering, take care not to overuse it.

Roast cumin seeds in a dry pan over low to medium heat, shaking the pan frequently to roll the seeds around until they are aromatic and a darker shade of brown. If the pan is too hot, the seeds will pop; reduce heat accordingly. Do not burn, as this will add a bitter taste. Since spices lose flavor and fragrance quickly after they are ground, always buy whole cumin seeds, and grind them yourself when needed. Store in an airtight jar in a cool, dark place in the cupboard. Roast the seeds only as you need them.

Curries (*gkaeng ped*): Curry making is a way of cooking introduced into Southeast Asia by Indian immigrants over the past several centuries. While dry aromatic spices from seeds, dried roots, and bark figure prominently in Indian curries, they are used sparingly in Thai curries. (Incidentally, yellow curry powder is only one of many spice blends used in making curries.) Instead, fresh herbs, roots, stems, leaves, bulbs, and vegetables constitute the essential ingredients, making Thai curries refreshingly herbal, robustly pungent, lusciously tangy, and distinctively Southeast Asian.

There are dozens of different curries in Thai cuisine, each a unique combination of herbs, spices, and preparation techniques that enhance the tastes and textures of particular foods. Some curry pastes are fairly simple; most are complex symphonies of tantalizing flavors. Most have at their core lemon grass, galanga, kaffir lime peel, garlic, shallots, and shrimp paste. To them are added innumerable other herbs, roots, seeds, and spices in varying proportions to create almost endless combinations.

The two most common curries are *red curry* (*gkaeng ped*) and *green curry* (*gkaeng kiow wahn*); because of their fresh herbal flavors, they go quite well with seafood. Red curry paste is used not only in making the saucy curry known in many American Thai restaurants, but also in dried wok-tossed curries called *pad ped* (literally, spicy stir-fry) and steamed or grilled custardlike curries called *haw moek*. Both are very popular in Thailand and are exceptional ways to cook seafood (recipes for them are included in this book). While *haw moek* is exquisitely rich with coconut cream and eggs, *pad ped* is light and intensely spicy, as the seafood or meats are tossed in a hot wok with a little oil, the curry paste, a profusion of fresh aromatics, and little or no coconut cream.

Red curry paste is red from red chillies, usually in dried form or a mixture of fresh and dried, giving the curries made with it a fiery red color. Green curry, on the other hand, has a greenish tint from the fresh green chillies and leaves it contains. Green curry paste is a relatively simple paste, made mainly from fresh herbs, whereas red curry paste comes in a number of permutations ranging from simple to complex.

Prepackaged green and red curry pastes come in tin cans, plastic pouches, plastic containers, and glass jars in a number of different sizes and brands of varying quality. My two preferred brands are *Mae Ploy* and *Mae Anong*, the first having both a saltier and hotter bite. I find them to be fresher tasting and to have a greater depth of flavor than pastes that come in tin cans, mainly because the process of canning destroys some of the more subtle flavors. Both are readily available in Southeast Asian markets. Gourmet grocery stores that carry a wide selection of international foods may sell small jars of specially bottled and labeled pastes suited to milder Western palates.

Curry pastes keep indefinitely in the refrigerator; once opened, they gradually lose freshness of flavor. Keep the containers well sealed and always use a clean spoon to dish out the amount you need.

Because none of the prepackaged pastes compare with the fresh flavors of homemade curry pastes, I have included a number of recipes with instructions on how to make your own curry or chilli pastes. Some of these pastes are fairly easy to make and produce wonderfully delicious curries. Curry pastes can be made a day or two ahead of time, allowing the flavors to mingle, marry, and peak; although they keep for weeks in the refrigerator (the salt, chillies and garlic preserve them naturally), use them fairly soon before the flavors dissipate, losing the advantage of freshness that makes them superior to store-bought pastes.

Most Thai curries are made with coconut milk, but there are a number of very spicy, souplike dishes without coconut milk, which we also call curries. Among them are jungle curry (*gkaeng bpah*) and sour curry (*gkaeng som*). Although brothy like soup, they are served more like curries—spooned over and eaten with plain rice.

Curry powder (*pong gkaree*): The yellow curry powder with which most Americans are familiar is not used to make curries in Thai cuisine, but is used as a spice blend in combination with other Thai ingredients to flavor Indian-influenced sauces and marinades, and a few stir-fried dishes. Use any good-quality Madras curry powder.

Dried red chillies (*prik haeng*): See *chillies.*

Dried shredded coconut (*maprao kood*): See *coconut.*

Dried shrimp (*gkoong haeng*): See page 38.

Dried Thai chillies (*prik kee noo haeng*): See *chillies.*

Eggplants (*makeua*): Whereas chillies have roots in the New World, eggplants are indigenous to Southeast Asia and are that region's contribution to the world. A walk in any market in Thailand reveals numerous varieties, from tiny pea-sized eggplants to long slender ones and large ovals. They come in different colors—white, yellow, lavender, bright and deep purples, varying shades of green, some variegated, some not, others a mixture of green variegated with purplish tints, and so on. Their flavor and texture vary, too, just like the many varieties of tomatoes have their own characteristics.

The two used in recipes in this book are the so-called *Thai eggplant* (*makeua bprawh*) and *pea eggplant* (*makeua puang*). The first is small, round, and tomato-shaped, looking much like a tomatillo or a large cherry tomato, and comes in a number of different colors, though by far the most common is variegated green—dark and shiny green on top, dribbling down in an interesting pattern to meet a uniform light green wash on the bottom. It is seedy, has a mild flavor and crisp texture when eaten raw with spicy salads and dips, and is wonderful cooked in curries and stir-fried with hot chilli pastes and seafood.

Pea eggplant is even smaller, and looks like a pea, as it is round and of similar size, in a dull medium green. It grows in a bunch, similar to grapes, on woody stems, but is firm and hard when raw. Its strong bitter bite mellows when softened by cooking, adding a depth of flavor to curries and spicy soups. Pea eggplant is also added raw to pungent dipping sauces and is frequently stir-fried, along with Thai eggplant, in hot and spicy dishes, to be chewed for a burst of bitter flavor to temper the fiery heat of chillies and accompany fragrant herbs.

Thai eggplant is becoming more readily available during the warm summer months in major metropolitan areas with sizeable Southeast Asian populations. Pea eggplant, on the other hand, is still a novelty in most areas, making rare appearances in ethnic markets and farmer's markets attended by Southeast Asian growers. If you are not able to find either, substitute Chinese, Japanese, or other kinds of eggplant for Thai eggplant; there is really no substitute for pea eggplant, but toss in some fresh peas in its place just for appearance's sake.

Fermented soybean sauce (*dtow jiow*): See *soybean sauce.*

Fish sauce (*nahm bplah*): See page 34.

Fried garlic (*gkratiem jiow*): See *garlic.*

Fried shallots (*hawm jiow*): See *shallots.*

Galanga or galangal (*kah*): This robustly pungent member of the ginger family is the primary ginger used in Thai cooking and is, therefore, sometimes referred to as *Siamese ginger.* It is also called *greater galanga* (there is a very different relative called *lesser galanga,* see *rhizome*) and *laos root.* Fresh galanga has an ivory or very pale yellow color and its growing tips are tinged pink, much like young ginger. Denser, firmer, and even more knobby than

common ginger, this rhizome is also rounder, marked with concentric rings a half-inch apart, and has no skin to be peeled. Tasting nothing like ginger, its hotter and sharper bite combines with a tangy, spicy flavor which, to some people, is reminiscent of hot mustard. To others, it tastes medicinal and, indeed, it is.

Like other members of the ginger family used in Thai cooking, galanga's pungent spiciness freshens the taste of seafood, making it a valued herb in seafood salads and soups. For salads, slice the root as thinly as possible, then stack several slices at a time and cut into very fine slivers; for soups, thin slices are simmered to flavor the broth. Galanga is also an essential ingredient in most Thai curries, and is chopped and pounded to a paste with other paste ingredients.

When buying galanga, select a young rhizome that is as light in color as possible with pinkish shoots and few or no brown spots. Avoid large, fat roots, as these can be very hard and woody, making them almost impossible to cut. Sometimes a piece will be tender at the tips and woody further down; save the tender end for salads and use the more fibrous section for seafood soups. Store fresh galanga wrapped with a paper towel inside a plastic bag in the refrigerator; it will keep for two to three weeks.

If you are not able to find fresh galanga, frozen roots imported from Thailand are available in most Southeast Asian markets. These roots may have an orangish brown color, because they are a slightly different variety, but they are the next best thing to fresh. For pounded chilli and curry pastes, the frozen roots grown in the tropics give a fuller range of flavors than the fresh ones grown in temperate zones.

Galanga is also sold in slices packed in brine in glass jars; rinse before use. (Beware of jars confusingly labeled as "galanga" or "galingale," that actually contain the slender, finger-shaped "lesser galanga.") It is most commonly available in dried woody pieces in plastic bags. The dried form is acceptable for soups (use about one-third to one-half of the quantity called for in fresh slices), but lacks the fresh flavor required for seafood salads, in which case, fresh ginger can be substituted. The dried pieces come in handy for recipes that require ground, roasted galanga.

Avoid the powdered kind unless you are not able to find fresh, frozen, bottled, or dried pieces.

If you live in a frost-free area, try growing galanga to assure yourself a continual supply. Buy a very fresh rhizome with unbruised pinkish shoots and plant shallowly in moist, well-drained soil. Like ginger, it grows into a lovely tropical plant for the garden, producing sweetly fragrant, white orchidlike flowers atop lush four-foot stems over many weeks in late summer and autumn. It grows very vigorously once established.

Garlic (*gkratiem*): This infamous member of the onion family finds its way into just about every savory Thai dish, giving the background flavor that enriches all sorts of dishes, from mild to extra spicy. It is crushed, chopped, and minced for stir-fried dishes; pounded to paste for curry pastes and hot-and-sour sauces and salad dressings; roasted and mashed to add a mild, sweet flavor and smoky dimension to chilli sauces; and sliced, chopped, and fried to make crispy garlic and garlic oil to flavor soups, salads, and noodle dishes. It is also pickled to nibble on in whole cloves with appetizers and snacks.

For *fried garlic* (*gkratiem jiow*) and *garlic oil* (*nahm mân gkratiem*), chop the garlic evenly, not too fine or too coarse, or slice into thin ovals, and fry in hot oil over medium-high heat, stirring frequently, to a uniform golden brown. Use both fried garlic pieces and oil. For recipes that call only for fried garlic pieces, strain them from the oil with a fine, wire-mesh skimmer. Reserve the wonderfully fragrant, garlic-infused oil for stir-frying. Fried garlic is available prepackaged in plastic containers from Asian markets. Choose a brand with garlic pieces that are loose and crispy rather than lumped together in a soggy wad. A fairly good product is made by the Joo Lee Trading Co. of Malaysia, labeled simply "Fried Garlic," but it really is very easy to make your own for a fresher flavor.

To roast garlic, cut the root tip off of each clove, but leave on the skin. Place on a pan in a hot oven (450° F), and roast until they are soft and slightly charred (about ten minutes). Do not brush with oil. Garlic cloves may also be roasted on a dry pan over a burner set at medium heat, turning frequently until softened through. Cutting off the root tip before roasting prevents the garlic cloves from popping and making a sticky mess in your oven or on your stove. Squeeze the softened garlic out from their skin and add to dishes for a pleasing smoky flavor. In Thailand, garlic cloves are usually roasted in charcoal braziers, giving them an even smokier flavor.

Sold in most Southeast Asian markets, *pickled garlic* (*gkratiem dong*) from Thailand comes in glass jars in whole heads and has a pleasant sweet-and-sour taste. Peel off the fibrous skin to prepare cloves for nibbling.

The amount of garlic to use in a recipe is not critical, since much of Thai food is highly flavored with many other ingredients. If you like it, use more; if not, cut back. Because clove size can vary considerably, depending on the variety and whether the clove comes from the outside or inside of the bulb, here is a rough guide: An average head has about sixteen to twenty cloves and yields approximately a quarter cup finely chopped garlic; four to five cloves chop into roughly one tablespoon. Asian garlic, similar to the variety grown in Thailand, generally has smaller cloves with papery-thin skin and can simply be smashed up and added to dishes, skin and all; double or triple the number of cloves to make up for their size.

Ginger (*king*): Although the ginger family is large, with some four hundred members growing wild in tropical Asia, there is only one that is universally known and sold as ginger root. Mature ginger is knobby and has a light, beige-brown papery skin that can be easily scraped off (even with a spoon) before being cut into fine matchstick slivers for salads, stir-fries, steamed and braised dishes, and soups; it can also be cut unpeeled into large slices and bruised with a cleaver to be used as a soup stock ingredient. In seafood cookery, ginger serves an essential role, as its pungent spiciness freshens the taste of fish.

Purchase only firm, heavy rhizomes without wrinkles, that are not too big around to assure that they are still tender and have not become fibrous at the core. If you have a choice, select the more knobby, dull- and rough-skinned variety over the prettier, smooth and shiny-skinned kind, as it is a special low-fiber ginger with good flavor. Fresh ginger keeps for a few weeks in the refrigerator; wrapping with a paper towel before placing in a plastic bag extends storage, as the paper absorbs moisture and keeps the surface of the rhizome dry to prevent mold growth. Since it is readily available in most grocery stores, there is no reason to freeze ginger, as freezing alters its flavor. Never substitute powdered ginger.

Ginger is also available during the growing season in its young form, recognizable by its skinless, pale yellow or cream color and pinkish shoots. *Young ginger* (*king awn*) is tender, juicy, and mild in flavor, making it pleasant for eating raw and for pickling. *Pickled ginger* (*king dong*) from Thailand is available in pink slices, or in beige matchstick slivers packed in glass jars. It usually has a slightly sweet taste, and is often nibbled on as an accompaniment to appetizers and snacks.

Gold Mountain seasoning sauce (*sawd poo kow tong*): Made from soybeans, this seasoning sauce from Thailand has a flavor reminiscent of *Maggi* sauce, a Swiss product that has become widely adopted by Asians. It can be used like a light soy sauce to add a different flavor dimension to certain dishes. Substitute Maggi sauce for recipes in this book.

Green curry paste (*gkaeng kiow wahn*): See *curries*.

Green mango (*mamuang dip*): Most Westerners know mango only as the lusciously sweet and juicy, red or golden fruit eaten when fully ripened and soft, but, in Southeast Asia, we eat just as many of these fruits in their young, green, immature state, when their seeds are not yet fully developed and their flesh still white, crisp, and very tart. They make wonderful sour salads, especially for serving with fried fish.

Green mangoes are available at a premium in America; frequently, they are not the best as they are a bit too close to maturity, even when their peel is still thoroughly green. Select the smallest and firmest in the batch for that extra-special tart flavor and crisp, chewy texture. In Thailand, small fruits thinned from trees, or those that drop from trees in nature's course of self-thinning, are collected and sold in markets.

If you can't find green mangoes, substitute tart green apples (for example, Granny Smith); sprinkle fresh lime juice over julienned strips for a sharper sour flavor. Peel both green mangoes and green apples before julienning.

Green onions (*dton hawm*): These are the same as "spring onions" or "scallions," and are commonly available in any American supermarket.

Green peppercorns (*prik tai awn*): See *pepper*.

Holy basil (*bai gkaprow*): See *basil*.

Kaffir lime (*magkrood*): A profusely fragrant tropical citrus, kaffir lime is indispensable in Thai cooking and cannot be substituted with other kinds of citrus. The valued parts are the *leaves* (*bai magkrood*) and the *peel* (*pew magkrood*), or zest, of the limes. The juice is also aromatic, but is not generally used in cooking, since its perfumy quality can overpower light, sour dishes. Both leaves and peel are available fresh, frozen or dried.

The dark green leaves come in double form—a pointed top leaf joined to a more rounded bottom leaf. They impart not only a sweet, lemony scent but a wondrous flavor of their own to soups, salads, curries, and stir-fried dishes. For watery, simmered dishes, the leaves are bruised and added whole; for dry dishes, they are cut into very fine hairlike slivers. To sliver, stack a few leaves at a time and cut at a slanted angle with a sharp knife, or use scissors. The ribs of the leaves need not be removed before slivering, except for those of the few unusually large leaves that have stiff ribs; shaving off the bottom part of these ribs with a knife usually suffices.

The dark green limes have irregular bumpy surfaces and, in the tropics, can grow larger than the common American lime, though they usually are much smaller when grown in temperate zones. Their peel is even more richly perfumed than the leaves, with an exotic flavor unlike that of any other citrus. Along with lemon grass and galanga, kaffir lime peel is a foundation ingredient in most Thai curries, giving a complexity of flavor that distinguishes them from Indian curries.

If substituting the dried forms, use the dried leaves like bay leaves in watery simmered dishes; for dry dishes, soak in warm water to reconstitute before slivering. The dried peel needs to be soaked to soften before chopping and pounding with a heavy mortar and pestle to reduce to paste. I find the dried peel imported from Thailand to have a richer dimension of flavor than the peel from limes grown in California. If you are not able to find the peel fresh or dried, substitute equal parts of fresh lime zest and minced kaffir lime leaves.

Because kaffir lime is such an essential Thai flavoring ingredient, and both fresh leaves and lime peel are sometimes hard to find, it is worth growing your own bush. Ask your local nursery to get you one, or order directly from Four Winds Growers (see source list in appendix). If possible, start with a better-established five-gallon size. If you do not live in a frostfree area, grow it in a planter that you can wheel indoors for the winter. During the warm months, give it plenty of water, citrus fertilizer, and sunshine. Prune to a bushy shape and, when established, harvest leaves in the summer to freeze for the cold months when growth slows. Sealed in a plastic bag, both leaves and limes freeze well, and will keep for a year or more. If you are not ambitious about making your own curry pastes, keep the bush from fruiting too heavily at the expense of leaf production.

Krachai (*gkrachai*): See *rhizome*.

Lemon grass (*dtakrai*): Related to citronella, this bulbous, grayish-green tropical grass is a favored herb in Southeast Asian cuisines, where its delicate, lemony essence permeates a wide assortment of dishes. In Thai cooking, lemon grass is used most frequently to flavor soups, salads, and curries.

Lemon grass is a very fibrous grass and comes in long, slender stalks about a foot long, normally with its coarse, flat, grassy blades already cut off. Choose thick, light green stalks that feel firm all along their length, and that are not dried out and wilted. They usually require further trimming before they can be used. Cut off the woody root tip of each stalk until the purplish rings begin to show. Remove the loose, dry outer layer(s) and use only the faintly colored, dense, inner stalk that holds together when cut into shorter segments or into concentric rings. Usually, the top third of the stalk is dry and fibrous and, if so, should be trimmed off.

For soups and simmered dishes, cut the trimmed stalk at a very sharp angle into inch-long pieces, exposing its fragrant interior. Smash with the flat blade of a cleaver or heavy knife to bruise and release the aromatic oils before adding to these dishes. For salads, cut with a sharp knife into very thin rounds, breaking up the fibers that run the length of the stalk. When slicing, if the outer layer seems fibrous, peel it off before proceeding. Such thinly sliced rounds of the inner stalk can be easily chewed with other salad ingredients for a refreshing burst of lemony herb flavor.

For curries, cut the stalk into thin rounds before pounding in a stone mortar to reduce to paste. Although lemon grass appears dry when you are slicing it, when crushed, you will see that it really is quite moist. Crushing breaks the juice sacs in the fibers and releases the aromatic oils that make lemon grass so special.

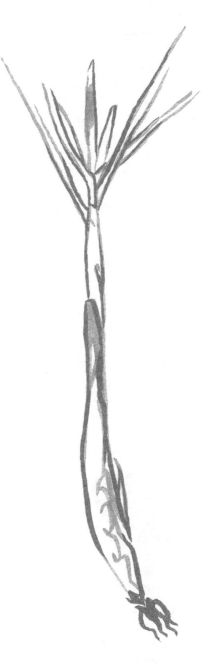

Lemon grass is now widely available all over the country, and can even be found in some chain supermarkets, so there is no reason to use the inferior dry or powdered kinds. Its mild, delicate, but yet exotic, flavor has made this tropical herb popular in East–West cuisines. Lemon grass can be easily grown in any frost-free area, or in a planter to bring indoors in winter; it is not particular about soil as long as it gets plenty of moisture. Root a stalk by submerging the root end in a glass of water, or insert directly into damp soil and keep well watered. One stalk easily multiplies into fifty in no time, and forms a large clump. Lemon grass grown in cool-weather areas tends to be grassier, with smaller and shorter stalks tinted a deep purplish green.

Wrap well in plastic before storing in the refrigerator to keep the stalks from drying out. Depending on how fresh the stalks are when bought, they can keep for one to three weeks.

If you must substitute dry lemon grass, simmer in water to make stock for soups, and soak in warm water to soften a little before chopping and pounding in a mortar to make a chilli or curry paste. Since the powdered kind is not a good substitute, and the dried pieces do not soften enough to chew, skip lemon grass entirely in salads that require thinly sliced rounds.

Light soy sauce (*si-ew kao*): See *soy sauce*.

Limes (*manao*): Limes, not lemons, are the main citrus that gives the sharp sour and zesty flavor that Thai people so love. The larger, thick-skinned, yellow lemon is a temperate climate citrus and does not grow in tropical Thailand. There is, however, confusion in the use of English terminology among Thai people, and limes are erroneously referred to as lemons in Thailand. (The Thai word for lime is *manao*.) Perhaps the reason is that the first Westerners to translate local language into English did not know what limes were and called them lemons since they are sour like lemons. As a result, *lemon* has stuck and *lime* does not exist in Thai people's English vocabulary; therefore, in present-day recipe exchanges with English-speaking peoples, the mistaken term *lemon* may be used.

Limes do have a much more intensely sour and zesty flavor than lemons and, although the latter may be substituted, the results definitely lack the vigor that limes give to Thai dishes. So, use fresh limes whenever possible, but avoid the presqueezed or bottled varieties, which lack freshness of flavor.

Thai limes are smaller than American limes, but are packed with flavor and juice. They are also a little sweeter and rather similar to Key limes. When using the larger American limes, I frequently need to add a little sugar to invigorate their flavor to approximate Thai limes. Because limes can vary in degree of sourness, as well as juiciness, the best thing to do when working with a recipe calling for lime juice is to go by taste. Often, it is not the amount you use, as some juicy limes may lack the intensity of flavor that other dryer limes may possess. With cooked dishes, add lime juice toward the end of cooking, since the fresh flavor of lime and its sourness can simmer away; exceptions are cooked dishes in which it is a background flavor.

When buying limes, select ones with smooth, shiny skin and a good weight for their size. They should not be hard—there should be some give when squeezed to indicate ripeness and juiciness. To get more juice out of your limes, roll them on a hard surface, applying pressure to break the juice sacs. Some people say zapping them in the microwave oven for a few seconds helps; others let the limes sit in hot water for a few minutes to soften.

Limestone water (*nahm bpoon daeng*): A natural mineral water made with red limestone is widely used in batters for fried foods and pastries as a key ingredient that promotes crispiness. It is also used to crisp cucumbers for pickling and vegetables for salads.

To make limestone water, empty the contents of a small container of red limestone, available from Thai and Southeast Asian markets, into a two-quart jar and fill with water. Cover jar tightly with a lid and shake to dissolve the limestone. Let stand one to one and a half hours, or until the water has almost cleared. Use the very faintly pink water with fine particles of suspended limestone dust in the recipes that require this crisping agent.

Store the limestone and water remaining in the jar unrefrigerated in the pantry, adding more water and shaking the jar about an hour or so before it is needed again. One package of red limestone will last you a very long time; it keeps indefinitely. Discard when the solids completely settle in less than half an hour, indicating that the remaining particles are too coarse.

Red limestone is also a main ingredient used in betel nut chewing among traditional Southeast Asians unwilling to give up the practice of this once very popular pastime throughout China and Asia. As the alkalinity of the limestone paste neutralizes the acids in the mouth, the chemical compounds of the areca nut (erroneously called "betel nut") are easily absorbed into the bloodstream, producing the desired stimulating effect to the nervous system. Now discouraged due to dental health concerns, betel nut chewing used to be a social activity and daily ritual engaged in by people of all classes of society, similar to tea time in England.

Maggi seasoning sauce (*sawd magkee*): A product of Switzerland, this seasoning sauce, made of hydrolyzed peanut and corn proteins, has found its way into some Thai kitchens, where it is used to add an extra dimension to particular sauces. It also frequently appears on the dining table to sprinkle over fried eggs in Western-style breakfasts. Gold Mountain seasoning sauce, a Thai product made from soybeans, has a similar taste and can be substituted.

Mint (*bai saranae*): The refreshing coolness of mint leaves contrasts beautifully with the hot and limy dressings for seafood salads. In Thai cooking, a small-leaf variety of tropical spearmint is almost always used fresh and uncooked; it is similar to and can be substituted with the common mint used in Western countries.

Morning glory (*pak boong*): Also called "water spinach," "water convolvulus," "swamp cabbage," "ong choi" (Cantonese Chinese), and "kang kung" (Indonesian), this favorite vegetable of Southeast Asians has lovely morning-glorylike flowers that are white with lavender centers, but it is not a close relation to the inedible, broad-leaved garden variety. The narrow, pointed, deep green leaves are attached to long, fleshy, light green hollow stems.

In Thai cuisine, morning glory is eaten both cooked and raw. It is stir-fried with garlic and chillies as a main vegetable dish, cooked with other foods in curries and spicy soups, or served on vegetable platters, either raw or lightly blanched, accompanying spicy salads and pungent dipping sauces. It is sold in large bunches, since it reduces down to a third or less of its mass when cooked. Choose a bunch with tender, skinny stems. Snap the stems in between leaves into short segments; do not separate leaves from stems as they will lump into a wad when cooked. General rule of thumb: Use the stems up to an inch below the last good leaf unless they are very skinny and tender, in which case the entire stem may be used.

Morning glory is fragile and cannot keep beyond a couple of days in the refrigerator. Wrap well in plastic bags, as the leaves wilt easily.

Oil (*nahm mân*): My preferred cooking oil is *peanut oil* (*nahm mân tua*), because it is a stable oil with a high smoking point. This means it can be heated to high temperatures for long periods of time without burning and breaking down, making it invaluable for stir-frying and deep-fat frying. When used for deep-frying, it sears the outside of foods quickly and does not penetrate them, giving them a light crispy edge; as a result, less oil ends up being used and foods fried with it are not greasy. In fact, if the oil is heated properly before beginning frying, you will frequently have almost the same amount remaining in the wok or fryer when you have finished cooking as when you started.

Recent research pointing to the healthful benefits of peanut oil gives further reason to choose it for cooking. Studies showed that diets using this polyunsaturated oil led to an increase in the level of good cholesterol in the blood while, at the same time, reducing the level of bad cholesterol.

Since peanut oil is stable and does not easily break down, oil remaining from deep-frying usually stays clean, clear, and fresh-tasting for two or more weeks, and can be reused. I keep the used oil in a bowl covered with a plate near my stove, using it whenever I need oil for stir-frying. Sometimes, the oil imparts a delicious shrimpy flavor to stir-fried vegetables if it has been used before to fry shrimp. I save oil from frying fish only for fish dishes. Refrigerating used oil from deep-frying is not recommended, because of the risk of water droplets condensing into the oil, making unpleasant splattering inevitable when next used. Peanut oil can be reused for deep-frying a few times within a two- to three-week period, after which it should be thrown out. In any event, when the oil smells and tastes old, or looks very dark and no longer clear, it is time to get rid of it.

A very good brand of peanut oil now widely available in Asian markets is Lion and Globe, imported from Hong Kong. If you do not like its nutty flavor, less expensive and more neutral-tasting peanut oils are also available, such as the Panther brand. Store cooking oil in a cool, dark place in the cupboard; make sure the lid is snapped tightly shut.

If you are allergic to peanuts, substitute corn, safflower, or sunflower oils, which produce satisfactory results in stir-frying and deep-frying. Many vegetable and salad oils do not do well when heated to high temperatures—they break down, adding an unpleasant, greasy taste. Since they cannot hold high temperatures, foods fried in such oils do not sear properly and absorb a lot of oil, wreaking havoc in your body and giving fried foods a bad reputation.

The oil pressed from sesame seeds is a flavored oil that is not meant to be used as a general-purpose cooking oil, but as a seasoning. *Sesame oil* (*nahm mân nga*) is used in Thai cooking infrequently, mostly in dishes that are Chinese influenced. It is sprinkled in small amounts to lend its highly fragrant, nutty flavor to sauces and marinades and, since it can burn easily if heated over high temperatures, is added to stir-fried foods toward the end of cooking. When buying sesame oil, read the label carefully, as many brands are not pure, but a mixture of sesame oil with other oils, like soybean oil. My personal preference is for black sesame oil because of its more intense aroma and depth of flavor; use a toasted sesame oil for an extra-special toasted flavor.

Olive oil, another flavored oil, is not recommended for Thai cooking.

Oyster sauce (*nahm mân hoi*): See page 40.

Palm sugar (*nahm dtahn bpeep/buk*) and **coconut sugar** (*nahm dtahn maprao*): Although the names are used interchangeably, palm sugar and coconut sugar are not the same. One comes from the palmyra or sugar palm, and the other from coconut palm. Both are produced from the sweet, watery sap that drips from cut flower buds. The sap is collected each morning and boiled in huge woks on the plantations until a sticky sugar remains. This is whipped and dropped in lumps on cellophane, or poured into containers. Because it is not highly processed like brown sugar, the color, consistency, flavor, and level of sweetness can vary from batch to batch, even within the same brand.

The color can be as light as creamy beige and as dark as rich caramel brown, and the consistency soft and gooey, or rock hard, depending on how long the sap was reduced. Palm sugar usually has a darker color, a more fragrant smoky aroma, and a more complex flavor than coconut sugar, though sometimes additives are mixed in to lighten its color. Palm sugar may also be labeled coconut sugar and vice versa. So, it is best to buy your sugar by sight and feel (squeeze the plastic container to ascertain its consistency) than by its label. If you have a choice, select a soft, rich brown sugar; if not, any kind is better than none.

A soft sugar makes it easier to spoon out and use, but more often than not, coconut and palm sugars come in hard, crystallized chunks which keep better. If so, it is best to cut and peel back the plastic container, place the lump in a bag and hammer it into small crystals for ease of usage. Some people add water and melt the sugar in the microwave; however, this often increases the likelihood of spoilage, reducing its otherwise indefinite shelf life. Neither coconut nor palm sugar needs to be refrigerated, but if it is soft and moist, take care to keep it away from heat and exposure to air which may encourage mold growth. If mold begins to appear on the sugar, remove the top half to one inch; the remainder of the dense sugar may still be fine.

In Asian markets, palm and coconut sugars are available in plastic containers or plastic bags of various sizes and also in tin cans. Although they are used primarily for making sweets and desserts, their creamy, caramel-like sweetness also enhances the flavor of curries and rich sauces for savory dishes. Since the degree of sweetness may vary from batch to batch, add enough "to taste." Substitute with brown sugar only if you absolutely cannot find either. For sweetening light dishes, granulated sugar is preferred over palm or coconut sugar.

Peanut oil (*nahm mân tua*): See *oil*.

Peanuts (*tua lisong*): Shelled and skinned raw peanuts are sold in small bags in Asian markets. Dry-roast them yourself for a fresher, richer, and more nutty flavor. This may be done on a dry pan on top of the stove over low to medium heat, stirring frequently until they are a rich, even, golden brown; or in a 325° F oven, turning from time to time to roast evenly. Do not use too high a heat, which browns the surface only, while the core remains raw. Cool first before chopping, crushing with a mortar and pestle, or grinding in the food processor.

Store-bought unsalted, dry-roasted peanuts may be used in recipes calling for roasted peanuts.

Pea eggplants (*makeua puang*): See *eggplants*.

Pepper, peppercorns (*prik tai*): The berries of a tropical vine native to India, peppercorns are used in different stages of ripeness. When young and green, they are soft, highly aromatic, and mildly hot. Short segments of stems with rows of small green berries clinging are tossed into spicy stir-fried dishes, dry curries, dipping sauces, and intensely flavored soups. They are chewed on for a refreshing burst of flavor. Occasionally, sprigs of these young green peppercorns (*prik tai awn*) can be found in frozen bags in Thai markets, although freezing would have turned them black; also look for them packed in brine in stout glass jars. Some gourmet grocery stores carry loose green peppercorns in small, skinny glass jars, which taste much the same.

As the green berries mature, they start to turn pink and red. If picked at this time and dried in the sun, the outer covering turns black and shrivels, giving *black pep-*

percorns (*prik tai dâm*) their characteristic look. When permitted to fully ripen on the vine, the berries turn bright red; they are picked and placed in a moist place, or are submerged in a solution for a few days, then their skin is rubbed off to yield round whitish seeds called *white peppercorns* (*prik tai, prik tai kao*). White peppercorns are not uniformly white but a mixture of greys and off whites, until they are put through a bleaching process that produces the evenly white peppercorns sold in supermarkets. Because bleaching also leaches out some of the flavor, use the less uniformly white peppercorns available from Asian markets and specialty stores if you wish a more fragrant aroma and spicier flavor. Likewise, the much whiter white pepper powder sold in supermarkets is less flavorful than the speckled grey powder imported from Thailand and other Far Eastern countries. White pepper is the popular form in which pepper is used in Thai cuisine. Green peppercorns are also prevalent, while black pepper is used to a much lesser degree.

For a refreshingly aromatic peppery taste, grind your own pepper when you need it. Use a pepper mill, mortar and pestle, or, if you are grinding a large amount, a clean coffee grinder designated solely for grinding dry spices. Preground pepper loses aroma and flavor over time. Buy powdered pepper for seasoning dishes that require only a subtle pepper flavor, such as mild stir-fried dishes.

Preserved Tianjin vegetables (*dtang chai*): Originating in China, this preserved, shredded cabbage with salt and garlic has become a common flavoring ingredient for soups and noodle dishes. Although it is also made in Thailand, I prefer the depth of flavor of the original product from China, which comes in a squat, brown crock in most Asian markets. A Thai brand comes in a container of the same shape made of clear plastic. Because *dtang chai* is very concentrated in flavor and saltiness, use only a small amount at a time. Keeps indefinitely in a cool place in the pantry; no need to refrigerate.

Pickled garlic (*gkratiem dong*): See *garlic*.

Pickled ginger (*king dong*): See *ginger*.

Pickled salted plum (*buay dong*): A very sour and salty preserved plum, pickled with vinegar and salt, is used for making plum sauce for fried foods and for flavoring Chinese-influenced steamed fish dishes. The small, cherry-sized plums are packed in brine in small glass jars, either labeled "pickled plum" or "salted plum." If you are not able to find them in a Thai market, look in Chinese grocery stores. A widely available brand is Koon Chun, imported from Hong Kong. A newer product appearing in many markets is Shan Tou. The Japanese also use a similar type of sour-and-salty plums, called *umeboshi*, which are sold already drained from the brine, and can be substituted.

Polygonum (*pak pai*): A sweetly perfumed and tangy herb, its Thai name literally means "bamboo herb" because it resembles a miniature bamboo. It is mainly eaten fresh, appearing on vegetable and herb platters accompanying spicy minced meat or seafood salads. Also loved by the Vietnamese who call it *rau ram*, look for it in Vietnamese markets that carry a profusion of aromatic herbs.

Red curry paste (*gkaeng ped*): See *curries*.

Rhizome (*gkrachai*): Although it has come to be called in English by a broad name, *gkrachai* (also *kachai*) is not just any rhizome, but a very specific kind, with its own distinctive piquant flavor and tangy fragrance that cannot be mistaken for other members of the ginger family to which it belongs. Known also as *lesser ginger, lesser galanga,* and *Chinese key,* this root is comprised of a cluster of long, slender, orangish brown fingers joined to an insignificant, knobby, gingerlike rhizome. Because its exuberant aromatic quality freshens the taste of seafood, it is used primarily in seafood dishes. The fingers are cut into fine slivers and tossed, along with other fragrant herbs, into hot-and-spicy seafood stir-fries, curries, and incendiary soups.

Rhizome is rarely available fresh in the United States, but is imported from Thailand in frozen pouches found in Southeast Asian markets. It also comes pickled or packed in brine in glass jars, rinse and soak a few minutes to wash away the brine before using; or dried slivers in plastic

bags, soak in water to reconstitute. I recently saw jars of this long, skinny rhizome labeled simply "galanga" or "galingale"; so take care not to confuse it with the totally different "greater galanga" (see *galanga*). The frozen roots yield far better results that come closest to fresh and should be used whenever possible but, if you have to substitute dried pieces, use only half the amount called for. Soak in warm water to reconstitute; they won't soften quite enough to chew on, but will flavor stir-fries, and can be chopped to pound into curry paste.

Rice flour (*bpaeng kao jao*): Milled from regular rice, this white flour is primarily used for making cakes and desserts. It is also used to thicken coconut milk to a rich, smooth, and creamy consistency. Readily available in most Asian markets, do not confuse it with glutinous rice flour. Many supermarkets also carry rice flour in small boxes or bags.

Rice vinegar: See *vinegars*.

Rice wine (*lao jeen*): A mild cooking wine called Shao Hsing, made by fermenting glutinous rice, adds a delicate fragrance and gives depth of flavor to Chinese-influenced dishes. A dry sherry can be substituted, although any Chinese grocery store should stock this inexpensive item. Do not confuse with rice wine vinegar.

Roasted chilli paste (*nahm prik pow*): See page 39.

Roasted rice powder (*kao kua*): Available from some Southeast Asian markets, roasted rice powder is simply white rice that has been dry-roasted until the grains turn a rich brown color, then ground to make a fine tan powder. Tossed into spicy salads, it adds a pleasant toasted fragrance and flavor while, at the same time, absorbs juices to keep the salads dry. Ground roasted rice is popularly used in very spicy northeastern-style salads.

If you are not able to find the packaged powder, make your own by roasting white rice in a dry pan, preferably cast iron, over low to medium heat, stirring frequently, to evenly brown into a rich dark color. This takes ten to fifteen minutes. If the grains are browning too quickly or unevenly, the heat is too high; lower accordingly. Slow roasting yields a more fragrant and less gritty result, as the grains brown not only on the outside, but cook through to the interior. The grains do pick up a lot of heat, so let them cool before grinding to a fine powder in a clean coffee grinder. Hot rice can melt the plastic lid of your grinder.

I prefer using white glutinous rice to regular white rice for roasting, because it is more porous, cooks through easier, and yields a less gritty powder. Roasted rice powder keeps for up to a year in an airtight jar in a cool place in the pantry.

Salt (*gkleua*): Sea salt is preferred for Thai cooking. Common table salt has an artificial, chemical aftertaste and should be avoided. Kosher salt can be substituted but, since it has a less salty taste, use more of it to approximate the saltiness of sea salt.

Salted black beans (*dtow see*): Used in dishes with a distinct Chinese origin, these salty, preserved black beans come as soft, loose, dry beans in most Chinese and Southeast Asian markets. For the recipes in this book, use the dried variety, not the mixed flavored sauces in jars in which salted black beans are but one of several ingredients.

Salted soybean sauce: See *soybean sauce*.

Sawleaf coriander (*pak chee farang*): Also called "sawtooth coriander," "sawtooth herb," or "long leaf coriander," the Thai name for this tasty, aromatic herb simply means "foreign coriander," suggesting origins outside the region. The slender, dark green leaves are serrated, and approximately one-half-inch wide by two to three inches long; they look and grow a lot like the basal leaves of Shasta daisies. With a succulent taste reminiscent of cilantro, these leaves are used in soups in much the same way, and are also nibbled on fresh along with spicy salads. Still a novelty in America, look for this special herb in large Vietnamese markets.

Seafood stock (*nahm soop ah-hahn talay*): Simple seafood stock can be made with shrimp and crab shells, fish bones, fish heads, and other seafood parts (excluding viscera) that otherwise would be discarded. Add to boiling water along with a few slices of ginger, crushed cloves of garlic, and crushed cilantro roots or stems, then reduce heat and simmer for fifteen to twenty minutes. Save the water used for blanching seafood for salads to make stock; it will add an even sweeter seafood flavor. Because seafood stock does not keep well unless it is frozen, make it as it is needed, or no more than a few days ahead of time.

Sesame oil (*nahm mân ngah*): See *oil*.

Sesame seeds (*ngah*): Used mainly in Chinese-influenced dishes, the small white seeds are toasted and sprinkled on certain dishes to add a toasted, nutty taste.

Shallots (*hawm daeng*): The preferred onions for Thai cooking are red shallots; they are purplish red in color and are smaller than the orangish brown shallots sold in American markets, which may also be used. Although larger varieties, such as yellow onions, are grown in Thailand, most of them are exported and relatively few find their way into Thai dishes. Shallots give a greater depth of flavor when chopped and pounded to make curry and chilli pastes; on the other hand, when eaten raw in salads, they are sweet and mild, leaving much less of a lingering aftertaste or onion breath. Their size can vary considerably but, because the amount used for most dishes is not critical, make your own rough estimate on how many to use based on the size of the shallots you bought (if they are large and are in double sections, count them as two, and so forth). Thai people use red shallots very generously and, like garlic, shallots are a fundamental ingredient.

For some curries and chilli pastes, shallots are roasted to give a smoky dimension. This may be done by placing them with their skin still on in a very hot toaster oven (450° F), or in a dry pan over a burner set at medium heat. Cut the root tip off first to keep them from bursting when heated. Roast until softened all the way through and slightly charred on the outside. This may take fifteen to twenty minutes. When roasting in a dry pan over the stove, turn them frequently. In Thailand, shallots are usually roasted in the charcoal brazier, which adds a much more pronounced smoky flavor.

Shallots are also fried into brown, crispy pieces to sprinkle on salads and garnish finished dishes. Fry thin slices in plenty of oil (enough to submerge the pieces) in a wok or small pan until they turn golden brown. Because Western shallots contain more moisture than Thai red shallots, they should be fried over low heat for a prolonged period of time (twenty minutes or longer) to allow the slices to dry before they brown. This ensures that the pieces turn crispy after they are drained and cooled. When fried at high temperatures, the pieces brown quickly but are likely to be soggy and greasy. When crisped properly, the shallot pieces absorb little oil and should not taste greasy. For Western shallots, I find that slicing them crosswise into rings tend to produce more evenly crisped shallots than slicing lengthwise.

While frying, stir only occasionally until the pieces begin to turn color, then stir frequently to evenly brown to a rich shade. They will shrink to a third or less of their original mass. Drain through a fine wire-mesh strainer balanced over a bowl to catch the remaining oil. Reserve this fragrant oil to add a delicious flavor to your stir-fried dishes.

To reduce frying time, shallot slices may first be dried in a dehydrator, very low oven, or on a rack in the sun. If making your own crispy fried shallots seems too much trouble, look for packaged products in Asian markets. The pieces should be loose and sound crispy when the container is tapped. A fairly good product now readily available is imported from Malaysia, packed for the Rockman Company, Inc., and is simply labeled "Fried Onion."

Shrimp paste (*gkabpi*): See page 36.

Soybean sauce (*dtow jiow*): Made from whole fermented soybeans, this intensely salty and pungent sauce adds a delicious flavor to sauces in Chinese-influenced dishes. There are two distinct varieties: light brown (*dtow jiow kao*) and dark brown (*dtow jiow dâm*), the latter being more strongly flavored; it should be used sparingly.

A good product from Thailand is the Healthy Boy brand's Soy Bean Paste, in tall bottles, now carried by many Southeast Asian markets. Another recommended product is Yeo's Salted Soy Beans from Malaysia in jars. Soybean sauces do not need to be refrigerated and keep indefinitely in the cupboard.

Soy sauce (*si-ew*): Brewed from fermented soybeans with wheat, salt, and water, soy sauce originated in China more than 2,500 years ago. Its extensive use in Southeast Asian dishes is a testament to the pervasive Chinese influence on the region's cuisines. There are numerous varieties, differing in color, flavor, saltiness, and sweetness. Three distinct kinds are used in this book's recipes: dark soy sauce, light or thin soy sauce, and black soy sauce.

The common soy sauce familiar to most Americans and sold in most supermarkets is *dark soy sauce* (*hua si-ew*), with Kikkoman being the best-known. It is very dark brown and has a pronounced soy sauce flavor that is richer, sweeter, and less salty than light soy sauce. Since it has been brewed for a longer period of time, it also has a greater depth of flavor. When a recipe does not specify what kind of soy sauce to use, use this kind.

Buy only soy sauce that has been naturally brewed or naturally fermented. Superior, naturally brewed, dark soy sauces have a reddish tint and an appetizing fragrance. On the other hand, inferior products made by hydrolysis rather than natural fermentation have an opaque, muddy brown color; a strong, unpleasant chemical aroma; and an artificial flavor with an acrid, often bitter, aftertaste. An excellent brand imported from Taiwan now widely available in Oriental markets is Kimlan, which comes in a number of grades with varying prices. Its premium Super Special soy sauce is superb, in addition to being low sodium, and is well worth the high price.

The second kind of soy sauce is *light* or *thin soy sauce* (*si-ew kao*), which is noticeably lighter in color than dark soy sauce and thinner in consistency. Mild and delicate in flavor, it salts without clashing with or overpowering subtle flavors. This is the kind most commonly used in Chinese and Chinese-influenced Southeast Asian dishes. It comes closest to a vegetarian substitute for fish sauce. There are a number of different brands with varying flavors and levels of saltiness to choose from in Asian markets. The thin soy sauce with the dragonfly logo and the Healthy Boy brand's soy sauce, imported from Thailand, have subtle, but pleasant, flavors and a medium-brown color similar to fish sauce. Kikkoman also makes a good-quality light soy sauce. Do not confuse this kind of soy sauce with low-sodium and tamari soy sauces.

The third kind of soy sauce used in this book is *black soy sauce* (*si-ew dâm*). It is very dark, almost black, in color and as thick as light syrup in consistency. Its flavor is sweet, almost like molasses. A good black soy is made by the Kwong Hung Seng Company of Thailand, with the dragonfly logo on the label. Because this company makes three different kinds of soy sauces bottled in the same kind of bottles, make sure the label in front or back identifies it as black soy sauce. The other two soy sauces they make are thin soy sauce and sweet soy sauce, which is much sweeter and thicker than black soy sauce and used for other purposes. If you are unable to find black soy sauce, substitute a mixture of equal parts dark soy sauce and either palm sugar or blackstrap molasses.

None of these sauces need to be refrigerated, and will keep indefinitely in a cool place in your cupboard.

***Sriracha* chilli sauce** (*prik Sriracha, sawd prik*): This smooth, orangish red sauce with a consistency similar to light ketchup originated in the coastal province of Sriracha on the eastern seaboard of Thailand. Because the waters off Sriracha are known to be shark infested, a well-known brand of this imported sauce has a shark as its logo. The sauce comes in different degrees of hotness, the hottest usually sporting a "strong" sticker near the lid; there is also a "medium," which is as mild as you should use for the recipes in this book.

Sriracha chilli sauce is sometimes referred to as Thai Tabasco sauce, but it really is unlike Tabasco, being less vinegary, sweeter, and more garlicky. It is, however, used at the table similarly to Tabasco sauce to add quick heat and chilli flavor to finished dishes; it is also used in cooking. The same formula for *Sriracha* sauce is now made in California; the domestic version comes in a plastic squeeze bottle, labeled *Tuong Ot Sriracha*. It frequently appears on the table of Vietnamese restaurants and noodle houses. It is widely distributed and is quite good. Refrigerate to keep fresh.

Sticky rice (*kao niow*): Also known as glutinous rice or sweet rice, this starchy grain is steamed dry after prolonged soaking to yield a sticky, chewy texture. Steamed sticky rice is the staple food of northern and northeastern Thailand, where it replaces the regular steamed rice of the central region. Use medium- to long-grain glutinous rice, not the round short-grain variety, for Thai-style meals.

Soak the opaque white grains in plenty of water for four hours or more. The grains will absorb water and grow in size. Then, drain and steam without any water for about one-half hour. For less than two cups of rice, steam in a dry dish on the rack of a stacked steamer; for more than two cups, use the special sticky rice steamer available from Southeast Asian markets—a woven, hatlike bamboo basket that fits over a pot that has a collar shaped somewhat like a spittoon.

Tamarind (*ma-kahm*): The reddish brown, curved seed pods of a lovely tropical tree hold several large seeds encased by moist, sticky, dark brown flesh that varies from very sweet to very sour. The latter is used as one of the primary souring agents in Thai cooking, imparting a delicious fruity tartness to soups, salads, stir-fries, and sauces. Although imported, fresh tamarind pods can often be found in Southeast Asian markets, much of them are sweet tamarind (*makahm wahn*), which may not have even the slightest hint of sourness. It is a delicacy that is snacked on like fresh fruit.

If you are able to find sour tamarind pods, break open the brittle pods and remove the moist flesh from the strings that hold them in place. Remove the seeds and use the meat to make tamarind water or juice. To get consistent results in cooking, it is best to purchase tamarind in compressed blocks wrapped in clear plastic wrap, labeled simply *tamarind,* or *wet tamarind* (which is a direct translation of the Thai term for this form of cooking tamarind, *makahm bpiak*). Most already have seeds and strings removed. Occasionally, I have come across compressed tamarind that is labeled "candy" although the sole ingredient listed is tamarind; this is done to avoid the necessity of having to include the nutritional analysis required of imported food products.

Simply break off a chunk and place in a bowl with a small amount of water. Work the tamarind with your fingers, mushing the soft parts until they melt into the water to make a thick, reddish brown fluid, which in Thai is called *tamarind water* (*nahm makahm bpiak*). Because of its appearance, I have chosen to call the resulting fluid *tamarind juice.* When all the soft parts have dissolved, gather up the remaining pulp with your fingers, squeeze dry, and discard. Making tamarind juice with your fingers works best, as mashing with a spoon or fork does not do as efficient a job in dissolving the soft pulp and will either take more time or waste a lot of tamarind; and straining through a sieve only makes a mess that requires more time to clean. If you are making a large quantity, adding hot water to the tamarind and letting it soften for a few minutes before working with your fingers will help speed the process.

How much tamarind to use for a given volume of water depends on whether there are seeds and how much soft pulp there is in the chunk. Start out with one tablespoon to one-quarter cup water. If the fluid becomes too thick, add a little more water; if the fluid is thin, add more tamarind. For most dishes, you want to have a fluid the consistency of fruit concentrate. If it is too thin and runny, it can dilute flavors and introduce unwanted liquid to dry dishes, such as salads, while at the same time, add too little of the desired sour flavor.

Premixed, ready-to-use tamarind water in containers is available from most Southeast Asian markets; however, it is not as fresh tasting as homemade, and tends to have a very dark, unappetizing color. Once opened, it must be refrigerated and, even so, can spoil after a couple of weeks. On the other hand, the compressed tamarind block does not need to be refrigerated; wrap well in plastic and store in an airtight container in a cool place in your pantry. It lasts indefinitely. If you make a large batch of tamarind juice, keep it no more than a week in the refrigerator as it may start to ferment after that.

When buying tamarind, squeeze the package and select one that is as soft as possible and has a pleasing dark reddish brown color.

Tapioca flour or starch (*bpaeng mân*): A fine, velvety white powder made from cassava or manioc root, tapioca flour or starch imparts a wonderfully light, crispy texture when used to coat foods for frying. Its sticky quality makes it adhere easily to the moist surface of fish, drying it, thereby eliminating likelihood of splattering from surface moisture. Because it does not wash out into the oil like other kinds of flour, the oil stays relatively clean of burnt bits of flour, and can be reused with good results. Tapioca starch also helps chopped ingredients in a marinade stick to the foods that are to be fried. Coat foods lightly as too thick a layer can result in a gooey texture when a sauce is later spooned over the fried foods.

Tapioca starch is also used as a thickener for sauces and marinades. It has a tenderizing quality and gives a velvety coating to certain foods. Cornstarch may be substituted, but it does not do as good a job and has a tendency to lump. There is really no reason to substitute since tapioca starch is readily available in most Asian markets in fourteen- to sixteen-ounce bags. Do not confuse the flour or starch with the tiny, round tapioca pearls and quick-cooking tapioca crystals, both of which are for making tapioca pudding.

Thai basil, Thai sweet basil (*bai horapa*): See *basil*.

Thai chillies (*prik kee noo*): See *chillies*.

Thai eggplants (*makeua bprawh*): See *eggplants*.

Thin soy sauce (*si-ew kao*): See *soy sauce*.

Turmeric (*kamin*): Unlike other members of the ginger family used in Thai cooking, fresh turmeric is pleasantly mild and does not have a sharp bite. On the other hand, it has a very loud color—deep orange inside an orange-tinged, beige-brown skin. When added to foods, its carrot orange imparts a bright yellow color. The pretty color and delicate flavor of fresh turmeric are loved in the southern region of Thailand, where it is extensively used in curries, soups, stir-fried dishes, fried foods, snacks, and desserts.

Turmeric is much smaller than ginger; its fleshy root is composed of a fat cylindrical rhizome tapered on both ends, from the sides of which branch two opposite rows of short, slender fingerlike appendages from one to three inches in length. Growing both straight or curved, smooth or knobby and gnarly, the fingers break easily from the parent root, and are more often found in markets as unattached members.

Use the fresh root whenever possible for the recipes in this book. It has a delicate flavor that is simply exquisite—fuller, subtly more complex, and much more pleasant than the dried or powdered varieties, which can have a disagreeable medicinal smell and taste. Look for it in Southeast Asian markets, or specialty produce markets that carry a wide range of ethnic ingredients, during the warmer months of the year. If you are not able to find it fresh, substitute a fresh batch of turmeric powder, or grind your own from a dried root. Make sure the powdered kind is pure, as inferior brands frequently have a strong, acrid taste. Use approximately one-half teaspoon for each one-inch piece (or generous minced teaspoon) of fresh turmeric; often, you will need to add a little sugar to the sauce to bring forth its flavor.

The fresh rhizomes store well if kept dry in the refrigerator—wipe if they are damp, then wrap with a paper towel before placing in a zipper bag. I once was able to keep a very fresh batch for several months and, when they turned moldy and ended up in the compost pile, I was amazed to find them sprouting into beautiful plants (with large broad leaves like hostas and white flowers like hyacinths) some time later. They do have magical qualities and are known for healing scars, including their own!

Vinegars (*nahm som*): For most dishes, Thai cooks use a white vinegar distilled from coconut or grain with a 5 percent acidity. Use any unflavored white or rice vinegar of the same strength.

For certain Chinese-influenced dishes, a milder, sweeter, and more earthy black vinegar is used. Made with roasted rice and spices, it is very dark in color, almost like soy sauce. A good product is made by the Koon Chun Sauce Factory of Hong Kong, or substitute a mild balsamic vinegar.

White pepper, white peppercorns (*prik tai kao*): See *pepper*.

Yellow curry powder (*pong gkaree*): See *curry powder*.

Young ginger (*king awn*): See *ginger*

5

TECHNIQUES AND EQUIPMENT

BRIGHT COLORED LIGHTS, BLARING MUSIC, AND THE SHRILL CRY OF hawkers turn a blocked-off street in town into a festive night market. Among stalls offering carved coconut-wood bowls, seashell sculptures, and hand-painted casual wear—skewered squid grilling on charcoal boxes, whole ears of golden corn roasting on open fire, and coconut hotcakes sizzling on black-ened griddles greet throngs of local townfolk and curious tourists vacationing on the seacoast.

Further along, brilliantly lit carts bear artfully arranged palettes of glis-tening, fresh seafood on ice. On one side, eccentric cooks perform their nightly cooking demonstrations, tossing huge wokfuls of seafood with effort-less flicks of their arms, inviting leaping flames into their pans from time to time. On the other side, swirling puffs of smoke arise from charcoal grills, hissing loudly with drippings from immense tiger prawns charring to perfection. Behind them, crowded tables and rickety stools are enviably occupied, as onlookers anxiously await their turn.

A few steps beyond, mouthwatering fumes dance above crisping cakes of shelled mussels in batter, pan-frying on oversized cast-iron griddles. Those who've eaten before wandering into this lively gastronomic circus wish they hadn't. Many soon succumb to the irresistible aromas and tempting sights, settling down for a snack or a second meal of the evening.

Across the main road, long lines form on the sidewalk outside an unpretentious seafood restaurant, a favorite old haunt of this popular beach-resort town on the Gulf of Thailand. By the fish pier several blocks to the north and east, open-air restaurants sit on wooden platforms extended out to sea. Under the bewitching light of a crescent moon, patrons bask in the natural ambience of the lovely seacoast, as waves lap gently on the shore beneath and soft sea breezes cool the warm summer evening. Meanwhile, the fish, crabs, prawns, and other delights of the sea they have carefully selected from aquarium tanks and ice-covered tables are expertly prepared in bustling kitchens. Seafood, seafood, and more seafood are everywhere, cooked to order in every conceivable way to satisfy limitless customer desires.

Cooking Methods

Seafood is a very diverse food group. The enormous varieties of fish, crustaceans, and mollusks have their own special flavors and unique textures, allowing the inspired cook tremendous opportunities to apply a wide range of cooking techniques to create wonderful seafood dishes. Because most seafood requires little time to cook, quick-cooking methods prevail.

Stir-frying (*pad*): This quick-cooking method is similar to Western sautéing, in which relatively small pieces of food (usually bite-sized) are tossed about quickly in a hot pan with a small amount of oil. High heat must be maintained throughout the stir-fry for proper searing of foods to seal in their natural juices. Although stir-frying can be done in a flat skillet or large pot, it is best accomplished in a well-seasoned wok. A more detailed description of how to stir-fry effectively is included in the next section.

I do not recommend nonstick pans for stir-frying, because they do not hold heat very well and are not oil friendly. Cooking oil does not distribute over their surface, and tends to bead here and there; as a result, food is not evenly seared and flavored by it. As for electric woks, I do not regard them as woks at all. Not only does an electric wok have a nonstick surface, the heating element covers only a small area on the bottom, so the rounded contour of the pan never gets heated for effective cooking.

Because a stir-fry proceeds at a rapid pace, make sure you have all the ingredients ready before beginning. Place them in separate piles by the stove in the order that they are to go into the wok.

Unlike some styles of Chinese cooking, Thai stir-fries are seldom thickened with cornstarch or other thickeners but, instead, the sauces and seafood juices are left natural to preserve the fresh flavors of the herbs and intensity of the seasonings. Should a lot of juice cook out from seafood because insufficient heat is maintained during the stir-fry, the cooked seafood may be removed with a slotted spoon and the sauce reduced over high heat to thicken before recombining with the seafood. Stir-fried dishes, when properly done, should have just a small amount of richly colored and naturally thick sauce surrounding the pieces of seafood. If the seafood is swimming in a pool of liquid, the flavors in the dish will be diluted.

On the other hand, if your stove is an especially hot one, reduce heat or add a little cooking liquid to help insure that the seafood does not burn and leave you with a very dried-out dish. This situation, however, is rare with most American home stoves.

Deep-frying and Pan-frying (*tawd*): I have grouped these two methods together because they are similar, except for the quantity of oil used. In deep-frying, pieces of food are submerged in plenty of hot oil, whereas, in pan-frying, the seafood is fried on one side at a time in a small quantity of oil. Pan-frying differs from stir-frying in that the pieces of food are large and are turned only once rather than constantly being moved around. Both small and large pieces of food can be deep-fried.

Both frying methods can give foods a delicious crispiness, but not all fried foods are crispy. Deep-frying usually does a better job in giving that crusty, extra-crispy edge. For either form of frying, as well as stir-frying, it is important to use oil that can be heated to and maintain high temperatures without burning and breaking down. Hot oil sears the surface of food and does not penetrate it, yielding both a crispier and less greasy result. My personal preference is peanut oil (see "Oil" in chapter 4 for more information).

In any kind of frying, it is essential that the oil be well heated before adding the foods to be fried. Asians do not use thermometers to measure oil temperatures; instead, they test the hotness of the oil with a piece of food. A small piece of garlic should sizzle in a lively manner on the surface of the oil when it is dropped in, but should not burn quickly. A swirling movement in the oil and wafts of smoke rising from its surface usually signal to you that it is ready.

I find the wok to be the most efficient and safest utensil to use for both types of frying (see pages 82–83). If a flat skillet is to be used for pan-frying, a heavy pan that conducts heat well, such as one made of cast iron, is recommended. A fryer, or large, heavy pot, may be used for deep-frying, but whether pan-frying or deep-frying, a whole fish fries easiest and crispiest in a wok.

Steaming (*neung*): This moist-heat method cooks seafood on a rack or platform above boiling water in an enclosed vessel. Steaming is a popular and light way to cook seafood in Thailand and is fully described later in this chapter under "Steaming with a Stacked Metal

Steamer." Suggestions on how to rig up your own steaming vessel with utensils you may already have in your kitchen are given along with the instructions on how to use the stacked steamer.

Boiling, simmering, and poaching (*ðtom*): Seafood is cooked directly in liquid over varying temperatures: medium to high heat in boiling, low in simmering, and very low in poaching. This grouping includes soups, watery stews, and saucy dishes.

Yâm salad-making: For lack of a precise, descriptive English word, I have used the Thai terminology for this very common preparation method. Seafood is blanched swiftly in hot boiling water to barely cook (twenty seconds to one minute, depending on the type of seafood and size of the pieces), drained, and, while still warm, tossed with aromatic herbs and a hot-and-sour dressing or sauce. In restaurants, the blanching is usually done with the aid of a wire basket with a handle, so that the water can be reused to cook other batches of seafood, eventually producing a sweetly flavored base for seafood stock.

I have chosen to distinguish this method from the preceding one because of the important steps that quickly follow, giving Thai seafood salads their distinctive qualities. In fact, the sour ingredient in the dressing further cooks the seafood, and in some *yâm* (pronounced as in yummy), the seafood is cooked entirely with lime juice (like ceviche), not with heat.

Yâm is a common Thai cooking term. In fact, if you ask a Thai cook what is a good way to prepare squid, "*yâm* it" may be the answer. Besides, Thai *yâm* salads are truly yummy!

Curry-making (*gkaeng*): Although seafood is boiled or simmered in a watery sauce in many curries, I have chosen to separate it from those methods, as there are other cooking steps involved. Also, not all curries are watery; some are dry-cooked in the wok and others steamed or grilled. Furthermore, for homemade curries, the preparation of the curry paste is an integral part of the cooking process.

There are two kinds of watery curries: those that are coconut-milk based and those that are broth based. The first category involves frying the curry paste in coconut cream to release and pull together the varied flavors in the spice-and-herb mixture. To do this, coconut cream from the first pressing of finely grated, mature coconut meat, or the thickest cream from the top of an unshaken can of unsweetened coconut milk (see page 55) is heated over high heat in a pot until the coconut oil separates from it (three to five minutes). The paste is fried in the coconut oil and cream for a few minutes until it is highly aromatic and darkens in color, following which the remaining coconut milk in the can, or from the second pressing of coconut pulp steeped in water, is added to make the sauce. Only when the sauce is well-seasoned with the paste does the seafood goes in to be cooked.

For broth-based and dry-cooked curries, the curry paste is fried in a small amount of oil before broth or other ingredients are added. For more information on curries and how to work with coconut milk, see "Curries" and "Coconut milk" in chapter 4.

Curries made with homemade pastes are exceptional and worth every ounce of effort. The best pastes are made by pounding with a heavy mortar and pestle. Instructions on how to use a mortar and pestle in paste-making follows later in this chapter (see page 88).

Braising (*jian*): In braised dishes, the seafood is first seared in oil in a hot pan, following which liquid is added to finish the cooking. Braising, in short, combines pan-frying with boiling or simmering.

Grilling (*yahng, pow*): The hot, tropical climate of Thailand lends itself to outdoor cooking. With charcoal a main source of cooking fuel until recent times, grilling has emerged as one of the most popular ways of cooking. No restaurant is complete without a fired-up grill and no marketplace can exist without a vendor grilling something or another, whether it be catfish on a stick or skewered meat balls. Along the coast near the capital city, strings of open-air *talay pow* (grilled seafood) restaurants line the beaches, serving delectable, super-fresh seafood caught the same day. Just about every kind of seafood is tossed on the charcoal grill; some are served simply with a spicy dipping sauce, while others find their way into salads, curries, and nameless other dishes.

Grilling is always done over real wood coals; sometimes coconut husks and dried palm fronds are thrown in to produce extra smoke, giving the grilled foods a marvelous smoky aroma. To re-create the delectable flavors of Thai-style grilled foods, a charcoal grill or barbecue kettle is essential, along with long-handled spatulas, tongs, and basting brushes. Because charcoal grilling is messy and time-consuming, I have adapted some grilled recipes to baking and broiling in the oven, two methods not used in Thailand because few people have ovens. Of course, flavor is compromised, but for some highly flavored dishes, the smoky dimension is not crucial. Grilling on a gas grill basically produces similar results as broiling, unless pieces of charcoal or wood chips are also used.

Seafood may be grilled directly on the charcoal grill, or in a wire cage with a handle, also called a grilling basket or hinged grill. This device can be round, square, rectangular or fish-shaped. It is comprised of two wire racks hinged together on one side to hold food between them. The grilling basket is especially useful for grilling tender whole fish with skin still attached; not only does it make turning easy, it keeps the fragile fish from breaking apart should the skin stick to the charcoal grill.

Seafood can also be wrapped in banana leaves before being placed on the grill. Although the smoky dimension is reduced, the leaves add their own special fragrance, especially if they are lightly charred. The seafood is usually marinated with spices before being wrapped and, essentially, is steamed in its own juices. For a smokier flavor, partially unwrap, or cut an opening on the top of the leaf packet, toward the last few minutes of cooking.

Wok Cooking

The centuries-old wok is one of the best-designed cooking utensils of all time, and is indispensable in the Thai kitchen. Its roundness, wideness, depth, and balance not only make stovetop cooking—

particularly stir-frying, pan-frying and deep-frying—easy, but pleasurable as well. In addition, it cuts down on kitchen cleanup and, when properly cared for, its well-seasoned surface enhances the flavor of foods.

Although it was originally designed in China to cook over a cylindrical pit, the wok is easily adaptable to flat, modern cooktops. Numerous types of stands are now available to aid in altering stovetops to accept the versatile, round wok. However, for many people who did not grow up seeing a wok in daily use in their family's kitchen, there seems to be some kind of mystery shrouding it, bringing up all sorts of questions—from selection and seasoning to usage and care. Such questions are among the most asked in my cooking classes and, after years of teaching and seeing how my students have happily and successfully adopted the wok for daily use in their kitchens, I hope to be able to shed some light on the mystery in the next few pages.

Stir-frying: For stir-frying, nothing can match the wok and its companion spatula. Although a flat skillet may be used, you can toss pieces of food much more vigorously and with greater ease and satisfaction on the rounded surface of the wok, without having to worry about splattering and spilling. Food is cooked more evenly and is less likely to burn, your arm is less tired, and your stove remains much cleaner than when a flat skillet is used. Try stir-frying a big batch of leafy greens, or big chunks of crab in the shell, and you'll see what I mean.

For a successful stir-fry, always begin by heating the wok before adding anything to it. Wait until the surface literally lets off wafts of smoke—about three minutes over high heat. (You may also test the heat by sprinkling in a few drops of water—they should sizzle and turn to steam immediately.) Then, swirl in the oil to coat the surface, using the wok spatula as needed to spread it around, and wait a short while longer to heat the oil (fifteen to twenty seconds). Now you may begin your stir-fry. The rule of thumb is: Always add cold oil to a hot wok and never cold oil to a cold wok.

Preheating opens up the pores in the wok so, when oil is swirled in, they absorb some of the oil and become seasoned before each stir-fry, lessening the likelihood of food sticking to the wok's surface. If you do not have a very hot stove, preheating also ensures that as high a heat as possible is maintained throughout the stir-fry for proper searing. If oil is added to the wok before heating, it will burn and smoke before the wok is thoroughly heated, giving a false impression that the pan is hot enough to begin the stir-fry. You will also likely burn the garlic, only to find that when the bulk of the seafood is tossed in, the heat fizzles out quickly, causing the seafood to sweat out most of its juices.

When the oil is hot, add the garlic—it should sizzle, but not burn. Stir for a few seconds to flavor the oil, then follow with the seafood and other ingredients to be stir-fried. Toss frequently, making sure all the food pieces, large and small, get turned and moved around so that they cook evenly and do not burn. Listen to the sound of food cooking in your wok. The sizzling should be loud and lively. If it slows down, slow down on the stirring, as this can dissipate heat. Spread the food along the heated sides of the wok rather than lump them in the center, making use of as much of the heated surface of the wok as possible. Stir just enough to cook and brown food evenly and to prevent burning.

If you stir too much while the wok is losing heat, your seafood dishes will likely turn watery and the flavors become diluted. For an average home stove, try not to stir-fry more than one to one-and-a-half pounds of seafood at a time. It also helps if the seafood is well drained and not icy cold from the refrigerator—let it sit at room temperature for at least twenty to thirty minutes before beginning the stir-fry. Here are a few other suggestions should your stove be less than ideal in terms of heat: add the salty seasoning toward the end of cooking; if there is more than one liquid ingredient, do not add them together, but space them by fifteen to twenty seconds so that one gets to heat up and evaporate somewhat before another is added; and sprinkle liquid ingredients directly on the hot metal just above the seafood being stir-fried, so that they are heated immediately and reduced quickly to concentrate their flavors.

Stir-frying in a wok has the additional advantage of requiring less oil than a flat skillet because of its rounded bottom. While one wok can stir-fry a small or large quantity of food, different-sized skillets often are needed to cook varying quantities.

Adapting the Wok to Your Stove: Maintaining a high degree of heat is essential for stir-frying, so knowing how to adapt the wok to your stovetop is a key to success in its usage. For home cooks preparing meals for two to four people, most stovetops provide sufficient heat for successful wok cooking.

Each stovetop differs. On some gas stoves, the wok balances well enough on the grate without the need for any special stand. Though a bit wobbly, a wok with good weight and depth has a center of gravity that makes it difficult to tip over unless one is really careless. For greater stability when stir-frying on such stovetops, simply hold on to a wok handle with one hand while tossing with the other.

On other gas stoves, the grate may be removed and a wok ring fitted down onto the indentation around the burner to bring the wok as closely as possible to the heat source. (Some of my students find that the grate on their stove when turned upside down balances their wok perfectly, but this works only on certain stoves.) From my years of teaching, I have found that many people use their wok rings inefficiently. The wok is better balanced and brought closer to the flames if the wider end of the ring is placed facing up. In any event, avoid using the wok ring on top of the grate as this lifts the wok too far above the heat source and will not give good results to your stir-fry.

Wok rings come in different sizes and depths, so find one that fits the burner you plan to use for wok cooking and that is deep enough for your wok. Do not settle for the ring that comes with your wok set; if it does not fit your stove, search Asian markets for one that will. Wok rings also come either with wide-open sides or closed sides with a series of small holes around the ring. The latter type is well-suited to the electric stove as it helps to concentrate heat and direct it upward. Use a ring wide enough on its narrower end to completely surround the electric coil to assure that as much heat as possible is directed toward the wider end on which the wok sits. Heavy wire rings with open sides work best for powerful gas burners (hotter than 10,000 B.T.U.), allowing flames to leap up the sides of the wok and good air circulation to nurture the flames.

Choose a wok that is deep and well rounded, made of heavy gauge carbon or spun steel for maintaining good heat and for easy seasoning (see pages 84–85). Flat-bottom woks are now commonly available and, though they provide good balance on flat stovetops, I still prefer the age-old round bottoms. The wide, shovel-shaped wok spatula, which makes tossing such a breeze, is made to fit the rounded contours of the wok. I find it much easier to use with the round-bottom wok. Besides tossing, following a stir-fry, the spatula easily dishes out all the pieces of food, including small bits of garlic and drops of sauce, from the wok's surface, enabling me to stir-fry two or more batches of food without having to clean in between batches. This saves precious time in washing, drying, and reheating the wok when cooking dishes with compatible flavors.

With a flat-bottom wok, the introduction of a slight angle where its bottom flattens out makes tossing with the round-edged wok spatula a bit more challenging and less fun and, often, food is less evenly cooked. Particles of food caught around this edge sometimes end up overcooking or burning, making cleanup more of a chore and increasing the likelihood of scrubbing off some of the precious, hard-earned patina. This slight angle also increases the chances of scratching the area above it while turning the pieces of food with the wok spatula. Some people solve this problem by replacing the wok spatula with a wooden spoon with which to stir-fry, but tossing with a spoon is much less efficient than with the wide wok spatula, defeating part of the purpose of cooking with a wok.

Although the flat-bottom wok is specially designed for better balance on the flat coils of the electric stove, it can be a challenge to stir-fry food evenly, as its flat bottom, sitting directly on the coil, heats up much hotter than the rounded sides above it. Food can easily burn if it is not tossed quickly, and tossing is made more difficult for reasons already noted.

So, even on an electric stove, I advise my students to use a wok ring to lift the wok just a little bit above the coil. The burners of most electric stoves do put out plenty of heat; even if the wok is slightly lifted from the coils, enough heat will be conducted upward with the proper wok ring for a successful stir-fry. If a wok ring is to be used anyway, it makes sense to stay with the better-designed round-bottom wok.

Whether round bottom or flat bottom, use whatever wok you feel most comfortable with in your kitchen, and if you have been making perfect stir-fries on a flat skillet, continue doing what you have been doing.

Pan-frying and deep-frying: When pan-frying seafood, especially a whole fish, on a flat skillet, oil splatters outside the pan from time to time, as a result of the interaction of the moisture in the seafood with the hot oil. Covering often worsens matters, as condensation of steam on the lid drips more liquid into the oil. Because the skillet is low, this poses some danger of the oil in the pan catching fire. The depth, width, and rounded contour of the wok, on the other hand, keep splattering of oil outside the pan to a minimum and, when oil does splatter, it usually is far enough removed from the heat source to pose any danger. The wide surface area of the wok also makes it easier to pan-fry a whole fish, which would require a rather large flat skillet to do.

A good, deep wok is also an excellent and very safe utensil for deep-fat frying. It provides a wide surface area for the food to float around in, making it easy to turn the pieces to properly fry and evenly brown. This is particularly important with seafood, which takes little time to cook. As the pieces of seafood crisp, they can be scooped up quickly with a large wire-mesh skimmer, or fished out individually with chopsticks or a slotted spoon. Because of its rounded shape, less oil is needed to fill the wok than a straight-sided pot or fryer, and the oil is far removed from the flames so that, even if a few drops dribble over the sides, they do not endanger the remaining oil inside. Fill the wok no more than half full with oil to ensure that when there is splattering, the oil remains within the confines of the wok.

For Asians who love their fish whole, nothing works better than a wok for frying and braising whole fish. A standard fourteen-inch wok can easily accommodate a one- to one-and-a-half-pound fish and, when balanced on a wok ring, it can be easily tilted from side to side to give both ends of the fish sufficient heat to brown evenly. Turning the fish over in a wok is also much easier than in a flat skillet, as the wok spatula can simply roll it over along the rounded contours.

If the wok is well balanced on the wider end of the wok ring, when you tilt it, it will stay tilted on its own for as long as you wish, freeing your hands to do something else. This is sometimes more difficult to do if the wok has a long, heavy wooden handle or a flat bottom; for this reason and also for ease of storage, I personally prefer a wok with two short, earlike handles. If a flat-bottom wok is used to fry a whole fish, take special care if its bottom is sitting directly on a hot electric coil, as the center of the fish, which gets concentrated heat, may burn and stick to the pan before the rest of the fish is crisped. A solution is to use more oil, so that it can be ladled over the fish, and to push each end of the fish into the hot oil from time to time, though this must be done carefully so that the skin and flesh do not break apart.

For my students who love to entertain, I advise them to buy the larger sixteen-inch wok, which can fry fish large enough to feed six to eight with ease. Not only does it give two extra inches in width but a bit more depth is also gained, making it even safer to use. With a wok this size, you can cook for two just as well as for six or eight. The limitations, however, would be the size of your stove and the hotness of the burners. If little space separates the two rows of burners, a larger wok can incapacitate the other burners while you are cooking. As already mentioned, if you do not have a very hot stove, you shouldn't be cooking much more than a pound of seafood at a time.

If you are concerned about grease fires, have the wok cover, or a sack of flour nearby; should it happen, cover the wok immediately, or dump flour on the fire. *Never* try to put out a grease fire with water as this aggravates and makes matters much worse. However, I can tell you that in all my years of frying with a wok, I have never had any incidence of fire in my kitchen.

How to Season and Care for a Wok

A precious wok is one that has seen lots of use and experienced little scrubbing. A shiny, black patina covers its surface like a well-used and well-seasoned cast-iron pan. Foods do not stick to it even when cooked over high heat; moreover, their flavors are enhanced. Cleanup and care are easy, taking little time and effort.

To get your wok looking this way is not difficult if you start out with the right kind of wok. The easiest for seasoning and care is made of carbon steel (or spun steel), which has pores that open when heated to absorb oil and become sealed, and this is the kind I recommend. Widely available today in Asian markets that carry cookware, it has the added advantage of being inexpensive.

In the stores, carbon-steel woks come covered with a coating of machine oil to keep the metal from rusting, so be careful when going through the stack of woks not to get the oil all over your hands, arms, and clothing. When you are ready to season the wok you've selected, rinse thoroughly with lots of hot, soapy water to remove every trace of the machine oil. (If you have an old rusty wok stuffed somewhere in your garage from a previous attempt at wok cooking, it is most likely made of carbon steel and can be seasoned as described later. Just rinse well, scrubbing off the rust, before proceeding.)

The wok may be seasoned like any cast-iron pan, by brushing the surface with cooking oil and baking in a moderate oven for an hour. However, because of its shape and center of gravity, oil tends to flow down and gather in the center, resulting in an unevenly seasoned surface. For this reason, I prefer to do the seasoning over a burner on top of the stove.

Heat the wok for a few minutes until its entire surface is hot. Using a heatproof brush (for example, the type used for barbecuing) or a paper towel, brush or rub a thin layer of cooking oil over every inch of its surface. Use an oil with a high smoking point (peanut oil or corn oil) to minimize oil fumes. Make sure you have plenty of ventilation—turn the fan on high and open all the windows. Tilt the wok from side to side, subjecting the entire surface to intense heat to burn the oil into it. After burning a few minutes all around, turn the heat off, sop up any excess grease in the center with a paper towel, and let the pan cool completely to room temperature before beginning round two.

When the wok has cooled, turn the heat back on high, and let the wok heat for a few minutes until wafts of smoke can be seen over its surface. Turn the pan from side to side and again roast every inch of it to further burn in the first layer of oil. Then, brush or rub in another coating and proceed as before to burn this second layer into the pan. After a few minutes, turn off heat, sop up excess grease, and let pan cool.

Repeat the foregoing steps a few more times, alternating heating with cooling, each time burning in the previous layer before adding another layer. Make sure to sop up excess grease that may collect in the center after each heating to prevent a thick, gel-like coating from forming. After several coats of oil have been burned in, the wok will begin to turn dark, though the coloring may be uneven and splotchy. When the wok has developed enough of a tacky, oily surface that does not look dry when heated up, you may begin to use it for cooking.

Stir-fry only as described earlier—always heating the wok until it is smoking hot to open the pores before adding oil to seal them. Initially, bits and pieces of food may stick to the wok's surface. Avoid cooking starchy foods, which have a tendency to stick, and foods that are either acidic or require prolonged cooking by simmering with lots of liquid, as this can cook off some of the seasoning. Deep-fat frying, on the other hand, can help build up the layers of seasoning.

At the beginning, your wok will require a little more attention and care. Following each cooking session, rinse only with plain water and never use soap. If there are bits of food sticking to the surface, use a soft sponge and work the area gently—just enough to remove the food particles. Do not wipe with a towel after rinsing. Instead, dry the wok over a burner set on high heat, allowing the traces of grease from the cooking session to burn into the surface. Heat until the wok is smoking and, if the surface does not look shiny and oily, brush in a thin coating of cooking oil, letting it burn thoroughly into the metal. Sop up excess grease and let the wok cool before putting away.

After repeated use and the proper care, your wok will develop a beautiful, black patina and food will no longer stick to the surface during cooking. Even if it does, a coaxing with the wok spatula lifts it off without damaging the seasoning. By this time, you may no longer need to reseason your wok after each cleaning. Simply rinse with water and soft sponge and dry either on the stove, or turn it over on the drainboard to dry on its own. From time to time, heavy usage may deplete part of the seasoning. When this happens, reseason after cleaning as you did in its earlier days.

I pay little attention to the bottom side of my wok. I neither clean it, nor season it. Over time, it develops a thick layer of carbon from oil and food spilling over the side during cooking. This crusty layer gives the wok more heat and sometimes contributes a smoky dimension to your cooking.

A well-seasoned wok will not rust, and its blackened surface greatly enhances the flavors of food like no other nonstick pan can. It is as if it has stored memories of the many meals it has cooked and calls on this storehouse of experience to enrich the food it is now asked to cook.

Steaming with a Stacked Metal Steamer

Steaming is a healthful way to cook. Foods that are properly steamed retain their nutrition and sweet, natural flavor, requiring little or no oil. To people with limited time to cook, steam-cooking has the added benefit of being easy. Tasty food can be made with little effort as long as the ingredients used are fresh. In this book, I have included recipes for steaming many different kinds of seafood.

For steaming seafood, a stacked metal steamer is a highly recommended piece of equipment. It is made up of a pot, two deep-sided racks with holes on the bottom for steam to pass through, and a domed lid. The shape of the lid is designed to minimize the dripping of condensed steam onto the foods being cooked.

Stacked steamers are made either of aluminum or stainless steel, and are inexpensive when purchased from Asian markets that carry cookware. They come in many sizes. If you think you will be using it frequently to steam whole fish, buy a large enough steamer to accommodate the size fish you are most likely to cook for yourself and your family. My fourteen-inch steamer, for instance, can comfortably accommodate a one-and-a-half-pound whole fish.

For most steamed seafood dishes, the seafood is placed on a heatproof dish, which is in turn placed on the steamer rack. The rack fits over the pot and is covered. A couple of inches of boiling water in the bottom of the pot creates the steam to cook the seafood. To minimize sweating and condensation of steam onto the food, it is best to place the rack on the pot after the water has come to a boil, so that the cooking can start at once. For most stoves, medium-high heat produces sufficiently hot steam to cook seafood in about ten to twenty minutes. As soon as the seafood is done, immediately lift the lid and keep it off. Do not let cooked seafood sit in a covered pot after the heat has been turned off because, as the pot cools, vapor will condense and drip onto the food.

The heatproof dish on which the seafood is steamed should have a little depth to catch the sweet and tasty juices likely to steam out from the seafood. Preferably, the dish should also double as the serving dish, so that you won't need to disturb the aesthetics of the seafood arranged in a pleasing manner when it went into the steamer. This is especially important for steamed whole fish, which is delicate when cooked, and can easily break apart if an attempt is made to move it to another serving platter. The dishes I use for steamed seafood are usually platters that curve up near the edges to a depth of about an inch or a little more. Their basic flatness allows the seafood, especially fish, to lie flat on the main part of the platter while the little bit of edge holds in the sauce and juices from steaming. In Thailand, many platters for steaming are made in fish shapes and accommodate fish particularly well. Of course, whatever platters you use should fit into the steamer you have, leaving an inch of space along two sides for ease in lifting them out of the steamer after the food is cooked.

If you do not own a stacked steamer set and do not wish to invest in one just yet, you can improvise a simple makeshift steamer with equipment that you may already have in your kitchen. Use a pot wide enough to accommodate the dish that you will use for steaming. Preferably, it will have a domed lid so that steam condensing on the lid will follow the contours of the lid to the side before dripping back into the pot. A flat lid usually invites condensed steam to drip directly down onto the food, ending in an unappetizing watery result and diluted flavors.

Fill the pot with one and a half to two inches of water, and place some kind of trivet, or a heavy bowl or wide ramekin, on the bottom of the pot to serve as a platform on which to balance and lift the dish holding the food well above the water. Bring water in the pot to a boil before covering and steam as instructed.

For whole fish, because of its length, you may need to resort to a rectangular roasting pan with a lid. Proceed as described to rig it up as a steamer. Use two bowls as stands if the platter is long to better balance it, or use whatever device you may find in your kitchen that may work as a sturdy platform, such as a wok ring, for instance.

A bamboo steamer, which is best for steaming dumplings and buns, will work, too, for steaming some dishes if it is sufficiently large and deep. Do not use on a wok as you may have been advised.

Boiling water in a well-seasoned wok can easily ruin its hard-earned, shiny, black patina. Instead, balance the bamboo steamer on top of a pot of approximately the same width or just slightly narrower, or place the flat round rack with holes which may have come with your wok set on top of the pot to support the bamboo steamer.

The Mortar and Pestle and Paste-Making

Crushing the fibers of herbs releases the full range of essential oils they contain, and gives chilli sauces and curry pastes a greater breadth and depth of flavor than chopping them in a food processor can achieve. This is especially critical when working with fibrous aromatics and roots, such as lemon grass, galanga, and kaffir lime peel; they appear dry when chopped, but reduce to moist paste when pounded. Also, when these herbs are pounded together, their flavors meld into one, yielding an immensely aromatic paste in which the parts are inseparable from the whole.

To crush herbs, a mortar and pestle set is essential. In Thailand, there are several different kinds suited for particular purposes. For making curry pastes, a heavy stone mortar and pestle, carved out of granite, is the most efficient; it can reduce fibrous herbs and hard seeds in no time. The pestle and the inside surface of the mortar are polished smooth and are not rough, coarse, or porous like the kind used in Mexican cooking. Very dense and heavy, they do not chip and last for years, even when subjected to vigorous pounding daily.

Look for this dark gray, stone mortar and pestle set in a Thai or Southeast Asian market. It is available in small, medium, and large sizes and costs about sixteen to twenty-five dollars. Buy the largest size, since you can use it for big as well as small jobs. It also enables you to pound more vigorously without worrying about bits and pieces of herbs spilling all over your work area.

If you are not interested in making curry pastes and the extent of the pounding you wish to do is to make simple dipping sauces, a less substantial mortar and pestle set will suffice. You may already have a marble one in your kitchen, which is sufficient for crushing small amounts of the softer, wet ingredients like garlic and chillies. If you don't already own one, purchase a Thai-style, baked-clay mortar with hardwood pestle from a Southeast Asian market. It is inexpensive (under ten dollars) and both the mortar and the pestle are much larger than the marble set, making pounding easier and faster.

The dark brown mortar comes in two different shapes—one deeper and more bowl-shaped, the other with a noticeable molded-in stand and a wider, denser rim around the top. Because both are tall and deep, they keep the juice from the wet ingredients from splattering all over the place and, when you've finished crushing them, the lime juice, fish sauce, sugar, and whatever remaining sauce ingredients can be added right into the mortar and stirred with the pestle until the sauce is well blended.

When making a curry paste in Thailand, all the ingredients are pounded together all at once in the mortar. Often, the softer and wetter ingredients like garlic and shallots are placed in whole as they mash relatively easily. Coarse salt crystals provide some abrasion to reduce the harder and more fibrous herbs and spices, as well as release their flavors. The pounding goes on until everything in the mortar is mashed into paste and is no longer distinguishable. This can take a long time for someone inexperienced in mortar and pestle techniques.

For faster results without compromising flavor, chop or mince the ingredients ahead of time. This is where an electric chopper or processor can help out. (Lemon grass should be trimmed and sliced with a sharp knife into very thin rounds to break up the fiber that runs lengthwise.) Then, work one ingredient at a time with the mortar and pestle, starting with the dry spices. They are easily pulverized with a rolling motion of the pestle around the bottom and sides of the mortar while its surface is still dry. The dry ingredients, of course, may be ground ahead of time in a clean coffee grinder designated solely for spice-grinding. However, when grinding just a small quantity in the grinder, the spices often do not become very fine and need to be further reduced in the mortar to a fine powder.

Remove the ground spices from the mortar before proceeding with the most fibrous of the herbs. Pound one ingredient at a time, a small amount at a time, moving from the firmest and most fibrous to the softest and wettest. When each is done, remove from mortar before proceeding with the next. Herbs reduce more quickly when pounded with a sturdy, straight up-and-down motion. Develop a comfortably paced rhythm like you are beating on a drum—one that is not too fast as to tire the muscles in your arms quickly, but with enough strength so that the herbs do get crushed.

Move the herbs around with the pestle so that a single layer is pounded at a time to maximize the efficiency of the hard pestle beating against the hard surface of the mortar. When they are reduced, push them aside and move uncrushed pieces to the center to be worked, and so on. Just because the mortar is large doesn't mean that you can pound and reduce a lot of herbs at a time. For fibrous herbs, too thick a bed of them can actually take longer and require more energy from you to reduce, as the pieces cushion one another. For quicker results, pound a small amount at a time, removing the crushed herbs before adding more to be crushed. When all the ingredients have been reduced, combine them and pound together until they become a uniform, well-blended paste.

Besides the two types of mortar and pestle mentioned, I have a small, carved stone set that I use only for quick grinding of small, dry seeds, such as coriander and cumin. It works much better than the coffee grinder for pulverizing small quantities. Simply roll the pestle around the mortar, applying enough pressure to crush the seeds into powder. The small, Japanese-style, terra-cotta bowl with ridges inside, which comes with a wooden pestle, serves the same purpose, and is not meant to be used for reducing fibrous herbs to paste.

Other Helpful Equipment and Implements

My students are always checking around my kitchen to see what interesting implements and cookware I have that may make their lives simpler and, at the same time, enable them to make delicious Thai food.

Among the implements I find very useful are wire-mesh skimmers. For deep-frying, a large, wide-mesh scooper-strainer-skimmer with bamboo handle comes in handy. It scoops up crisped pieces of food easily and serves as a strainer and cooling rack as well. I like to let my crispy-fried foods drain and air-cool on the shallow, rounded basket while it sits on top of a metal bowl, for a few minutes before transferring to a serving plate. If they are drained on paper towels on a plate immediately after they are scooped out of the hot oil, the food surface that touches the plate will likely sweat and lose its crispiness. After draining and cooling on the wide-mesh strainer, you may sop up excess grease with paper towels if you wish, but if the proper oil has been used for frying, there should be hardly any remaining on the surface. If you do, use unbleached, brown paper towels, as white paper towels are laced with oil-soluble, carcinogenic dioxin. For a fried whole fish, drain on a flat-wire rack.

Besides the wide-mesh scooper, a fine wire-mesh skimmer is highly recommended for removing fine particles of food from the oil, such as chopped garlic, bits of batter, and so forth. It cleans the oil so that when the next batch of seafood is fried, these particles do not burn and make the oil taste old. This skimmer does not work well for draining foods, as its fine wire-mesh weave traps oil but, together with the wide-mesh scooper, it plays an important role in deep-frying.

To lift steamed dishes out of the steamer, a gadget which my husband has named "the picker upper" is most useful. It looks like the clamp for lifting bottles in canning, except that its two opposite, pronglike edges face inward. The prongs fit around the edges of the bowl or plate so that it can be lifted. However, this implement seems to work better with bowls that have a little bit of an outwardly edged rim to give leverage; be careful when using it to lift platters. Corningware dishes can be easily lifted when the prongs are fitted around the handles. There is also a three-pronged lifter, but it is a bit flimsy, so use it with care.

For roasting dry ingredients, such as spices, dried chillies, and shredded coconut, I find a small, cast-iron pan to be very useful, as it keeps even heat. Among modern appliances, a coffee grinder does a great job for pulverizing dry ingredients, but designate one solely for this purpose, not to be shared with coffee beans. You may also find electric choppers and miniprocessors to be helpful food-prep aids, since a fair amount of chopping is necessary to make some of the more involved, but absolutely exquisite, Thai dishes. The full-size food processor, on the other hand, I find too large for the small chopping jobs required for the recipes in this book.

For grilled dishes, a heavy stovetop grill pan comes in handy when cold, rainy days make outdoor grilling impossible. Any of the charcoal-grilled recipes may be adapted to stovetop grilling with fairly good results.

There may be other utensils and gadgets you already have in your kitchen that can simplify your Thai cooking experience. Improvise and be creative. Browsing around Asian markets, besides being fun, may yield a host of other good-to-have implements.

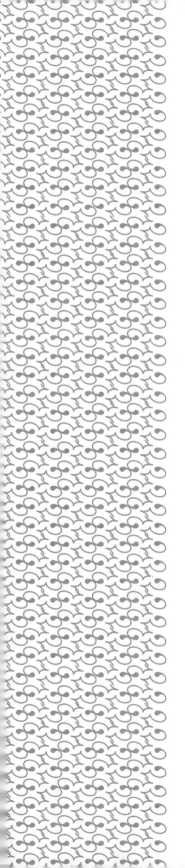

6

FISH

Hot-and-Sour, Pan-Fried Trout Soup with Roasted
Chillies and Aromatic Herbs   100

Ginger-Tamarind Fish Soup   102

Miang Bplah—Leaf-Wrapped Fish and Tasty Tidbits
with Sweet-and-Sour Sauce   104

Lime-Cooked Halibut Dressed with Roasted Chilli
Sauce, Toasted Coconut, and Peanuts   106

Crisped Catfish Salad with Sour Green Mango
and Peanuts or Cashews   108

Spicy Charcoal-Roasted Catfish Salad   110

Northeastern-Style Crispy Whole Catfish Topped
with Seasoned Thai Herbs, Chillies, and Toasted
Rice   113

Sour Tamarind Fish Chowder   116

Catfish Rounds Simmered in Turmeric-Flavored
Coconut Sauce   118

Salmon Poached in Green Curry Sauce with
Baby Eggplants and Thai Basil   120

Fish Fillets Stir-Fried in Hot-and-Spicy Coconut
Cream Sauce   122

"Drunken" Crisped Catfish Flakes   124

Wok-Tossed Salmon with Chillies and Thai Basil   126

Curried Mousse of Red Snapper in Banana Leaf Cups   127

Charcoal-Grilled Spiced Fish in Banana Leaf Packets   130

Garlic-Peppered Pompano   131

Southern-Style Turmeric Fried Fish   133

Steamed Fillet of Ling Cod with Sautéed Garlic and Ginger   136

Whole Tilapia Steamed with Ginger and Fermented Soybean Sauce   137

Pan-Fried Mackerel and Assorted Vegetables with Hot-and-Pungent
Fermented Shrimp Dipping Sauce   139

Mesquite-Grilled Mackerel Glazed with Sweet Soy Sauce   142

Flounder Simmered in Spicy Sauce   144

"Three-Flavored" Grouper or Rock Fish with Roasted Garlic
and Roasted Chillies   145

Pan-Fried Halibut Topped with Chilli-Tamarind Sauce   147

Spicy Crisped Fish with Wilted Basil and Seasonings   149

Garlic–Black Bean Pan-Fried Red Snapper   151

Pompano Steamed with Pickled Plum   153

Steamed Fillet of Sea Bass with Ginger, Green Onions,
and Sesame-Soy Sauce   154

Mom's Good and Easy Steamed Fish   156

Steamed Whole Fish with Chilli-Lime Sauce   158

Braised Whole Tilapia with Ginger and Green Onions   160

Charcoal-Roasted Striped Bass in Banana Leaf Served with
Hot-and-Sour Dipping Sauce   162

Mesquite-Grilled-and-Smoked Fish with Piquant Sour Tamarind
Sauce   164

FISH MAKE UP BY FAR THE LARGEST SEAFOOD CATEGORY. THE OCEANS, lakes, rivers, and wetlands of the world are home to countless edible species, from tiny ones that fry up to a crisp to be eaten bones and all, to huge giants of the open sea, cut up and sold in more manageable fillets and steaks for home cooking. In addition, fish is the focus of modern aquaculture more than any other kind of seafood, making many tasty varieties available year-round. The incredible range in flavors and textures possible from such an array of choices, from soft and tender to firm and meaty, allows fish to be cooked in just about any way imaginable.

Like many fish-eating cultures in the Far East, Thai people prefer to eat smaller fish (under two pounds), because they are sweeter, more delicate, and tender, especially when the flesh is cooked on the bone with skin still attached. We also like to serve them whole with head, tail, and fins still joined. These often-discarded parts in Western cuisine hold delicious soft cartilage, tender bits of luscious meat, and sweet, tasty juices when the fish is steamed, and turn scrumptiously crispy and crunchy when fried. Except for the center row of bones and the guts and gills, almost the entire fish is eaten, providing more nutrition than can be obtained from just the main flesh alone, including plenty of calcium. The skin, too, is delicious and contains beneficial omega-3 essential fatty acids. When left on, it is what makes fish fry up wonderfully crispy without the need for breading or batter. Even with many kinds of large ocean fish, the skin left from filleting is seldom thrown out, but fried into crispy pieces to sprinkle over noodles and salads, or snacked on as chips. Nothing goes to waste.

Speaking of fish skin, I am reminded of the occasion several years ago when my brother's family came from overseas to visit. My niece and nephew love sashimi, so we bought a big chunk of very fresh, sushi-grade salmon—a fish seldom available fresh back home. No sooner had I trimmed off the skin than it disappeared from under my hands to be discovered minutes later frying on the stove. The crispy strips disappeared just as quickly into hungry little mouths.

On the same visit, I took them to tour Steinhart Aquarium in San Francisco's Golden Gate Park, one of the most fascinating aquariums in the country, with innumerable species of fish from around the world. While other tourists were ooing and ahing at beautiful fish they had never before seen, my brother and sister-in-law were having a grand time "cooking" and "eating" their way from tank to tank! "This would be wonderful steamed with . . ." "That would be delicious fried up and topped with a sauce of . . ." "Is this edible, I wonder?" And on they went. Big fish, little fish, nothing escaped their attention. Needless to say, by the time we were through, we were famished and nothing could satisfy our hunger better than a seafood lunch at a favorite restaurant, followed by an expedition to the local fishmonger to pick up more to cook for dinner.

The preference of serving fish whole also speaks of the importance of symbolism in food. On special occasions and celebrations, whole fish is served to portray a picture of wholeness and prosperity. Yet another reason stems from the common knowledge that it is easiest to tell how fresh a fish is when it is still whole. Dinner guests are honored when fish is presented whole—it tells them that they are being offered the finest, as only the freshest fish holds up beautifully in cooking.

The preference for smaller fish perhaps reflects the country's dependence on easy-to-catch freshwater fish for hundreds of years. Except for the giant Mekong River catfish (*bplah beuk*), which can reach the size of a full-grown great white shark, most freshwater varieties are small. Furthermore, people generally live in harmony with nature, catching only what they can eat, leaving the larger of the species to breed and produce more abundance. With a bountiful supply of easily caught freshwater fish, most fishing off the two coasts is mainly done close to shore by small fishing boats, netting easier-to-catch smaller fish that swim near the surface. In fact, the relatively shallow and fertile waters of the Gulf of Thailand have such a rich supply of *bplah too*, a small variety of mackerel native to the waters here, that it remains one of the favorite marine fish of the Thai people. It is indeed very tasty! The presteamed, whole fish can be seen prettily arranged in twos and threes on small, round, woven bamboo trays in just about every market across the country (it is now also imported frozen to America). So commonly available is it that many rural people think it is a freshwater fish!

Although we have a preference for smaller fish and for freshwater fish, that doesn't at all mean that we don't like large, deep-sea fish. There are many exceptional species that the modern fishery industry has introduced to us in recent decades and we gladly adopt any tasty fish to styles of cooking that have been used for generations with freshwater fish. These marine fish give us more to work with in the way of flavors and textures and cooking challenges, making seafood cookery more exciting than ever. In the recipes to follow, I have adapted commonly available fish in American waters to Thai-style fish cookery. In many instances, other fish with similar qualities can be easily substituted. Freshness is most important, so rather than adhering strictly to the particular fish named in the recipes, try them out with seasonally fresh fish unique to your area.

How to Tell Freshness

It is easiest to tell how fresh fish is when it is still whole. At the local Oriental fish market I frequent, what attracts me first to a fish is its overall radiance. Its skin and scales glisten with a jewel-like luster under the lights. Next, I look at the eyes, which must be clear, shiny, and not sunken. Lifting the gill cover should reveal luminous pinkish-red gills and not dark, bloody-red, dried-out, or slimy ones. The fish should be firm to the touch, and its surface shouldn't feel slimy. When pressed gently with the finger, the flesh springs back up and doesn't leave an indentation. Above all, the fish must have a fresh smell of the sea, not a strong, fishy odor.

Exceptions are skate wings and shark, which need to be a few days old to allow the ammonia in their flesh to dissipate. If they are very fresh when bought, you will need to let them sit in the refrigerator for a few days to age to a more pleasant state. They also benefit from a two-hour soak in water containing lime juice, lemon juice, or vinegar.

If I wish for a truly fresh fish, my Chinatown fishmonger has aquarium tanks stocked with many varieties. I tell him the kind and size fish I want and make sure he nets one that is particularly lively. Whether the fish is live out of the tank, or selected from the ice-covered counter, the fishmonger first weighs and prices the fish, then scales, guts, and cleans it for me as part of the service. Most fishmongers will clean fish for you for no extra charge, so you need not worry about having to clean them. In fact, they will cut the head off for you if you so desire (Oriental fish markets resell them to Asians). The price per pound shown on tags by each type of fish is for the uncleaned weight. As a rough guide: An average one- to two-pound fish with scales loses about twenty percent of its weight after it is cleaned, but with head, tail, fins, and skin still attached. The fish size for the recipes in this book is given by the uncleaned weight.

Unless you are buying from a well-trafficked, open-counter Oriental fish market, in most cases, your ability to judge freshness will be limited by the refrigerated, glass display cases, restricting you from smelling or touching the fish. Most Western fishmongers also carry few whole fish, further reducing other indicators of freshness. For fillets and steaks, I still look for the luster in the skinned flesh and a moist, pink color, avoiding pieces that look dull and dry, and that are browning. In such cases, the reliability of the fishmonger is of utmost importance.

Because Asians love fish and consume vast quantities of them, your best bet for getting the freshest fish is to seek out an Oriental fish market—that is, if you live in a major metropolitan area with a sizeable Asian population to ensure demand and a quick turnover. Best, of course, is a fish market that carries fish live in tanks.

If you are not able to locate fresh whole fish for the recipes that call for them, frozen whole fish from a reliable source may be substituted. Some flash-frozen fish can still taste quite fresh. If such fish are also unavailable, do not skip over the recipes entirely, as fish steaks or fillets can be used in some of them with acceptable results.

How to Clean Fish

If you must clean your own fish, it really isn't all that difficult, just a bit messy. Scale the fish before gutting. Holding the fish firmly by the head or tail, scrape off the scales with a fish scaler or a dull knife held at a 45-degree angle, moving from the tail toward the head. To prevent scales from flying all over the kitchen, do this under water, submerging the fish in two or more inches of water in the sink. If the fish does not have scales, gently scrape the skin with the blunt edge of the knife to remove any sliminess.

When all the scales have been removed, make a horizontal incision with a sharp knife, from below the gills across the belly, just long enough to comfortably pull out all the entrails and oil sacs from the body cavity. Pull out the gills from inside the head, cutting them off where they are attached. Leave the head, tail, fins, and skin on for Thai-style whole-fish dishes. Rinse and drain, then rub with a thin layer of sea salt inside and out, let sit for a few minutes, and rinse thoroughly to remove all traces of slime and grime.

If you won't be cooking the fish for a few hours, drain well and place on a platter, cover with plastic wrap and refrigerate. If you won't be cooking it until the next day, salt lightly before refrigerating. Try not to keep fresh fish for much more than a day. It is best to cook it the same day it was purchased.

To Freshen Fish

If the fish you bought isn't as fresh as you would like and has a little bit of a fishy odor, you may try to freshen it. If thorough rinsing alone doesn't do the trick, sprinkle sea salt liberally over the fish, including the body cavity and under the head. Rub the salt thoroughly into the fish and let sit for about ten minutes. Then rinse in several changes of water to remove all the salt. This should eliminate the fishy odor and bring back the pink color in the flesh. Just before cooking, squeeze a little lime juice over the fish and rub evenly over its surface. Do likewise with fish steaks and fillets.

Some Cooking Tips

How to Fry a Crispy Fish Thai-style: One of the favorite ways to prepare fish is to fry it until it is thoroughly crispy—head, tail, fins, and all—but not greasy. To get it this way, the fish is fried unskinned in plenty of hot oil for longer than what is normally recommended in Western cooking, so that it is not just cooked through and still moist with juices inside the flesh, but completely dried through. When no moisture remains, oil molecules do not have any place to attach themselves to on the dried-out surface of the fish; as a result, the crisped fish is not heavy, soggy, and oily. Fish fried this way does not lose its crispiness after it comes out of the oil from juices inside being sweated out, but remains crunchy and crispy even after it cools.

Of course, the kind of oil used for frying the fish is important. It should be one that can be heated to and kept at high temperatures without burning and breaking down, such as peanut oil (my preference), corn oil, or safflower oil. The oil should be very hot before adding the fish, so that it sears the outside of the fish and does not penetrate it. This also reduces the likelihood of the fish sticking to the pan and yields cooked meat that is fluffy, rather than dense and compacted.

To help the fish cook and crisp faster, make a series of slanted 45-degree cuts about one-and-a-half inches apart through the thickness of the flesh to the level of the center bone on both sides of the fish, or score with a diagonal crisscross pattern. Make the cuts with the knife blade positioned at a 45-degree angle to the surface of the fish; the flesh overlaps the cuts so that, when it shrinks with frying, the bone is not exposed, giving a better presentation.

In brief, to deep-fry a fish, fill a wok about half full with oil, or enough to submerge at least two-thirds of the length of the fish, and heat over high heat until it is smoking hot. While waiting for the oil to heat, coat the fish thoroughly inside and out with a thin layer of flour, preferably tapioca flour or starch, which sticks better to the fish, does not get washed out in the oil, and contributes a light, crispy texture. Tapioca starch also dries the surfaces of the fish, eliminating splattering from the interaction of liquid and hot oil.

Holding the fish by the tail, gently slide it into the oil, letting go along the side of the wok as close to its surface as possible so that the oil doesn't splash up on your hand—letting go too soon is more likely to hurt you. If your stove is not a very hot one, the fish can be fried from start to finish over high or medium-high heat. For a very hot stove, reduce and fry at medium heat to keep the surface of the fish from burning before it is cooked and dried through. While frying, occasionally tilt the wok from side to side, so that the head and tail become submerged and crisped along with the midsection of the fish. This is easy to do if the wok is well-balanced on a wok ring; it is even possible to leave the wok tilted on its own in one position for a minute or two before shifting to another position (see pages 81–82). Oil may also be ladled continuously over the fish, which will cut down on the time needed to fry the second side when the fish is turned.

When the first side is well browned, well crisped, and dried through, nudge the wok spatula under the fish from its top edge and gently roll the fish over on its belly, taking care not to break any fins. Fry the second side the same way, until it is as brown and crispy as the first side. It takes a few minutes less time than the first side. For a one-and-a-half pound whole fish, the first side usually takes twelve minutes to crisp, while the second side takes about eight minutes. For smaller or flatter fish, like pompano and white perch, less time is required.

When the fish is thoroughly crisped, again nudge the wok spatula under it from its top edge. Tilt the fish up against the side of the wok above the oil for a few seconds to allow the oil to drain from the body cavity, then lift it out onto a wire rack. Let drain and cool a few minutes before transferring to a serving platter.

Not all fish should be so thoroughly fried and crisped. Use soft- to medium-firm-flesh fish, no larger than two pounds, and preferably varieties with thin fins and tails that crisp up nicely for crunching on. Delicious fried this way are snapper, rock cod, grouper, catfish, pompano, white perch, tongue sole, and other small and flat fish. Because of their size, smelts, fresh anchovies, and whole sand dabs can be fried completely immersed in oil. Firm, meaty fish with thick, dense flesh are not good fried so long, and should only be lightly crisped to retain some juices—cut the frying time by one-third to one-half.

The wok is a very safe utensil for deep-frying, so if you are afraid to fry fish in such a large quantity of oil, read the section on "Wok Cooking" in the preceding chapter and reconsider. The deliciously crunchy results produced are worth the effort.

Other Cooking Tips: To cut down on fishiness when making fish broth or soup, heat water to a rolling boil before adding the fish or fish parts, and avoid stirring until the fish is cooked. The protein of fish will dissolve into liquid if it is below the boiling point.

Save the trimmings from fish cleaning, except the guts and gills, for making seafood stock— bones with some meat still attached, skin, fish head, and tail. These can easily be strained from the broth with a wire-mesh skimmer. Add to boiling water, reduce heat, and simmer about twenty minutes. To freshen the flavor of fish stock, add a few bruised slices of ginger, a small handful of smashed cilantro root, and a few cloves of smashed garlic.

To enhance the flavor of steamed, pan-fried, or grilled fish, squeeze a little bit of lime juice over it and rub evenly over its surface just before cooking.

For whole fish dishes, whether steamed, marinated and grilled, or fried, cut a series of slanted gashes on both sides of the fish as described above. This helps the fish cook more quickly and evenly, and also allows the flesh to absorb the sauces, marinades, and seasonings. Scoring is not necessary for small fish like smelts and anchovies.

For charcoal grilling, select fish with a relatively high fat content, which yields cooked meat that is tender and not dry. Cook lean fish with other methods, such as steaming, braising, pan-frying, and currying.

How to Remove a Fish Bone from the Throat

Many Americans are afraid to eat fish cooked on the bone because they are afraid to get a fish bone stuck in their throat. This is really not a problem if you are careful, eat slowly, and chew your food well before swallowing. However, if a tiny bone should escape you and unwillingly get stuck in the throat, the best way to deal with it is to chew and swallow a big mouthful or two of plain rice, which should dislodge the bone and push it down the digestive tract. If that doesn't do it, gargle or sip slowly on fresh lime or lemon juice to soften the bone before following with the big mouthful of rice.

Fish-loving Asians are experienced in using their tongues to help sort out fish bones to pull out of the mouth before swallowing. After all, some of the tastiest parts of the fish surround the bones.

Hot-and-Sour, Pan-Fried Trout Soup
with Roasted Chillies and Aromatic Herbs
(Dtom Yâm Bplah Trout)

One 1- to 1¼-lb. trout
2½ cups unsalted seafood or chicken stock
5 stalks lemon grass
10 slices fresh galanga, about ⅛-inch thick
5 kaffir lime leaves, torn into smaller pieces
20 dried red chillies
A pinch of salt
¼ to ½ cup peanut oil, for pan-frying
3 or more Tbs. fish sauce (*nahm bplah*), to taste
¼ cup tamarind juice, the thickness of fruit concentrate
Juice of ½ lime
¼ cup short cilantro sprigs

Clean trout, keeping head and tail attached. Cut in half crosswise. Rinse and set aside to drain.

Bring stock to a rolling boil in a small pot over high heat. While waiting, trim off woody bottom tip and top third of lemon grass stalks and remove loose outer layer(s). Cut trimmed stalks at a sharp angle into four segments each and bruise pieces with a cleaver or heavy knife. Add lemon grass, galanga slices, and torn kaffir lime leaves to the boiling stock. Reduce heat and simmer 5 to 7 minutes. Keep warm.

In a dry pan, roast dried chillies with a pinch of salt over medium heat, stirring frequently until they turn dark red and are slightly charred. Let cool a few minutes before grinding half the chillies (with seeds) in a clean coffee grinder. Cut the remaining chillies into 2 to 3 segments each.

Heat a wok over high heat until it begins to smoke. Swirl in peanut oil to coat wok surface and wait one minute for the oil to heat. While waiting, pat surface of fish dry with a clean towel, including the inside of the head and body cavity. Sear fish in the hot oil 1 to 2 minutes on each side, tilting wok from side to side, so that the fish browns evenly in the hot oil.

Remove fish from wok; transfer remaining oil to a bowl and reserve for future use in frying fish. Re-heat stock to boiling. Return fish to wok and sprinkle with ground roasted chillies. Add the soup stock with all the herbs. Bring to a boil, then lower heat to a gentle simmer. Cook about two minutes.

Turn fish and season broth to desired saltiness and sourness with fish sauce, tamarind, and lime juice. Add roasted chilli pieces and simmer until fish is cooked through. Turn off heat and stir in all but 2 or 3 of the cilantro sprigs. Transfer to a soup tureen and garnish top with remaining cilantro.

Serves 3 to 4 with other dishes and rice in a multicourse family style meal.

Notes and Pointers

In my childhood, Mother frequently made *ɔtom yâm* soup with *bplah too,* a delicious, small mackerel found in plentiful supply in the brackish waters where the mighty Chao Phraya River drains into the gulf. She would pan-fry enough of them so that my brothers and I could each have our own fish. Since we all loved this fish and this soup, she took extra care to buy fish of the same size.

I have adapted this favorite soup of childhood to a common American fish—trout. My husband loves the idea, because it is a perfect soup to make on fishing trips to the mountains. The soup can be done entirely in a frying pan (one with a bit of depth to hold the broth) on a camp stove or open fire. The stock can be made right in the pan after quickly browning the fish on both sides. And, it can be served right in the frying pan, too. Dried lemon grass, galanga (use half the number of dried pieces to fresh), and kaffir lime leaves can be substituted if the fresh herbs cannot be easily transported.

Lemon grass, galanga, and kaffir lime leaves flavor the broth and are not themselves eaten, but they are kept in the soup to lend every last bit of flavor until the soup is savored. Their texture and color also make for a more interesting presentation. As with eating any fish Thai-style, the cooked flesh is scooped from the bones as desired and served in small portions along with the broth. Thai people love to eat both the skin and the tasty tidbits around the bones, head, and tail.

Ginger-Tamarind Fish Soup
(Dtom Som Bplah)

⅔ lb. fillets of any of the following: tilapia, sea perch, catfish, red snapper, or cod
2 shallots, cut in half lengthwise, then in half again crosswise
Generous ¼ cup finely slivered, peeled fresh ginger
2 green onions, split in half lengthwise, then cut into 1½-inch segments
1 jalapeno or fresno pepper (preferably red), cut into long, thin slivers, with seeds
¼ cup or more thick tamarind juice, the consistency of fruit concentrate, to taste
3 cups water
1 tsp. shrimp paste (*gkabpi*)
3 Tbs. fish sauce (*nahm bplah*), to taste
1½ to 2 Tbs. palm sugar, to taste

Cut the fish fillets into 1½-inch chunks. Set aside.

Bruise the shallot chunks with the flat side of a cleaver or heavy knife. Prepare the ginger, green onions, chilli pepper, and tamarind.

Bring 3 cups water to a boil in a medium saucepan. Dissolve shrimp paste in hot water and add shallots and tamarind juice. Return to a boil and add slivered ginger and fish pieces. Do not stir. Cook at medium heat about one minute. Season to taste with fish sauce and palm sugar and stir in chilli slivers and green onions. Cook one to two minutes longer, or until fish is cooked through. Transfer to a soup tureen and serve immediately.

Serves 3 to 5 with rice and other dishes in a family-style meal.

Notes and Pointers

In Thailand, the favored fish for this mild, gingery soup is mullet, which we call *bplah gkrabawk,* literally meaning "cylinder fish," because of its shape. Whenever I long for this soup, I am fondly reminded of the delicious version sampled at a roadside, open-air, mom-and-pop rice shop near the rural seacoast town of Chaiya. Insignificant looking like so many other rice shops that dot roads and highways in the countryside, I stumbled upon it with one of my tour groups many years ago. It was way past our lunch hour and we were very hungry, having spent more time than planned exploring the ancient, sacred shrine of Wat Phra Borom Mahathat, one of the South's three most highly revered temples, and shopping for irresistible colorful cottons and silks at the quaint but well regarded Muslim weaving village nearby.

The grandmotherly cook-owner was very sweet and friendly, and made us a scrumptious lunch in no time, the highlight being this soup and the famous salted duck eggs for which Chaiya is known throughout the kingdom. She had a basket of freshly caught young mullets, each no larger than an inch-and-a-half thick, which she cut through the bone into three two-inch lengths. The fish were so sweet and tender in the wonderfully flavored ginger-and-tamarind broth—better than any mullet I have ever tasted before or since. Everyone went for seconds without question.

One of my students once tried to make this soup with large smelts because they look like the young mullets she remembered eating at that rice shop. However, smelts made much too fishy a soup. Avoid using fish that is strong tasting or that is not very fresh, and fish with very firm flesh that may dry out if cooked a bit too long (for example, tuna or shark). Best are very fresh, mild, white-flesh fish such as those suggested.

Use a premium brand of shrimp paste (*gkabpi*)—*Pantainorasingh* and *Tra Chang* are two good ones. Shrimp paste is concentrated and may taste quite strong but, when cooked with ginger, shallots, and tamarind for a few minutes, it will blend in a delightful flavor of the sea. Lower grades of shrimp paste are usually foul smelling, while premium brands, though strongly fermented, exude a background aroma of roasted seafood. It is an essential ingredient in this soup.

Miang Bplah—Leaf-Wrapped Fish and Tasty Tidbits with Sweet-and-Sour Sauce

One 1½-lb. whole bass, tilapia, sea perch, or other white fish

Sauce:
¼ cup palm sugar
2 to 2½ Tbs. fish sauce (*nahm bplah*), to
    taste
2½ to 3 Tbs. lime juice, to taste

1 stalk lemon grass
3 Tbs. diced, peeled ginger the
    size of a small peanut
3 Tbs. diced shallot the size of a
    small peanut
2 Tbs. fresh lime cut into small
    peanut-size wedges, each with
    a little zest and some juice sacs
4 to 6 Thai chillies (*prik kee noo*),
    cut into thin rounds
¼ cup unsalted dried roasted peanuts
8 to 10 green-leaf lettuce leaves, torn into 2- to 3-
    inch pieces, or large spinach leaves from one bunch
1½ cups peanut oil, for frying

Clean the fish, cutting a small incision along the belly just large enough to remove the guts. Rinse and drain well. Using a sharp fillet knife, fillet the fish from the top edge on both sides, just sufficiently to remove the center skeleton, keeping the two fillets joined along the lower edge and still attached to both head and tail. Spread out flat and pat dry with a clean towel. Set aside on a rack with the fish flat open, skin side down, and allow the surface to dry about an hour in a well-ventilated area (or underneath an electric fan).

Make the sauce by combining the sauce ingredients in a small saucepan and heating over medium heat until the sugar is melted. Stir and simmer until thickened to the consistency of light syrup. Transfer to a small bowl and let cool. The sauce will thicken to a thick syrupy mixture when cooled.

Trim the woody bottom tip of the lemon grass and remove 2 to 3 of the fibrous, loose outer layers, leaving the more tender inner stalk. Slice very thinly into rounds to yield about 3 tablespoons. Prepare the remaining ingredients as instructed.

Heat oil in a wok over high heat until it begins to smoke. Swirl to coat a wide enough surface of the wok to accommodate the fish. Gently slide fish into oil flat open, with the skin side down. Reduce heat to medium-high (or medium if you have a very hot stove) and fry 7 to 8 minutes, until crispy and rich golden brown. Tilt the wok from side to side, from time to time, so that the head and tail can also brown in the hot oil. Turn over and fry the inside of the fish, also until crispy and dried through (5 to 6 minutes). Remove from oil and drain on a wire rack, skin side down. Sop excess grease on the top surface with a clean towel and let cool a few minutes. Reserve oil remaining in the wok for future use in frying fish.

Place fish on one side of a large serving platter. Arrange lettuce or spinach leaves and the cut-up ingredients in individual piles on the remaining area. If there is room, place the sauce in a small bowl and add to the platter. Fish may also be placed on a platter separate from the accompanying ingredients.

To eat, cut a small bite-size piece of the crisped fish, and place it on a piece of leaf along with a little bit of each of the other filling ingredients. Dribble with a small amount of sauce, fold leaf into a small packet, and stuff entire packet into your mouth. Chew the ingredients all at once for an explosion of flavors. The trick is to make the packet no larger than you can stuff into your mouth in order to get the full effect of the blending of flavors.

Notes and Pointers:

In Thai cuisine, there is a category of snack foods called *miang,* in which small tidbits of filling ingredients are wrapped for nibbling. Usually the tasty, heart-shaped, wild pepper leaf, called *bai chaploo,* is the leaf of choice, since it is broad and tough enough to wrap without breaking. It is still a rare novelty in this country, so I have substituted lettuce and spinach leaves. If there are other edible leaves you find suitable as wrappers for this finger food, do feel free to use them.

Instead of crispy fried fish, grilled or broiled fish steaks may be substituted. In fact, a similar *miang* has pan-fried, small, whole mackerel as the centerpiece (*miang bplah too*). The crunchy, crispy texture of fried fish in this recipe, however, does add an extra dimension to this fun-to-eat appetizer to accompany your cocktails. It makes an excellent dinner party dish and a conversation piece for your guests as the platter is passed around for each person to take a scrumptious bite.

Drying the surface of the fish before frying gives it an extra crispy edge. It also eliminates the possibility of oil splattering during frying and cuts down on frying time. If filleting the fish as described is not your cup of tea, try this recipe with fish fillets purchased from the market, though the result will not be quite as crispy. Snapper, cod, and catfish should work well enough, but do let the fillets sit out on a wire rack in a well-ventilated area or under an electric fan to dry before frying.

The recipe makes plenty of the sweet-and-sour sauce to serve at several different sittings. It just isn't practical to make a smaller amount; the blending of flavors tend to shift when smaller amounts are made. The sauce keeps well in the refrigerator for a few months in a sealed jar and can also be used as a dipping sauce for other fried or grilled seafood dishes.

Lime-Cooked Halibut Dressed with Roasted Chilli Sauce, Toasted Coconut, and Peanuts
(Plah Bplah Talay)

1 lb. very fresh halibut fillets
¼ cup plus 1 Tbs. fresh lime juice
½ tsp. sea salt
3 to 4 stalks lemon grass
1 cup unsweetened dried shredded coconut
½ cup roasted chilli paste (*nahm prik pow*)
1 Tbs. fish sauce (*nahm bplah*)
2 tsp. sugar
4 to 8 Thai chillies (*prik kee noo*), cut into very thin rounds, optional
2 shallots, halved lengthwise and sliced thinly crosswise, optional
½ cup chopped unsalted roasted peanuts
½ cup Thai basil leaves (*bai horapa*)
¼ cup cilantro leaves

Slice halibut into thin ¼- to ½-inch-thick slices about 1½ inches long. Combine ¼ cup lime juice with ½ tsp. sea salt and mix with the fish pieces in a shallow dish. Set aside for the fish to cook in the lime juice, turning once every few minutes to make sure all the pieces are well coated with the lime juice.

Trim lemon grass stalks, discarding woody bottom tip and 2 to 3 layers of loose outer leaves. Then cut into very thin rounds, using the bottom half of the stalks, to yield ½ cup. Toast shredded coconut in a dry pan over medium heat, stirring frequently, until fragrant and golden brown. Set aside.

In a bowl, mix roasted chilli paste, remaining lime juice, fish sauce, and sugar. Stir well. For a spicier salad, add cut-up Thai chillies and sliced shallots.

When the halibut has turned opaque and is cooked through by the lime juice (20 to 30 minutes), toss the fish and its juices with the lemon grass and chopped peanuts. Add the chilli paste mixture, toasted coconut, and basil. Stir well and transfer to a serving platter. Garnish with cilantro.

Serves 6 with other dishes and rice in a family-style meal.

Notes and Pointers:
The people of northeastern Thailand are known for their consumption of raw meats and fish. Usually these foods are heavily spiced and sour, and eaten in small quantities with lots of steamed sticky rice (see page 70). The spices and lime juice do more than just flavor, they also serve as antimicrobial agents. In this recipe, the halibut is not cooked with heat but with the acidity of lime juice, much like ceviche. The texture is soft, tender, and smooth, unlike the firm and flaky result frying, broiling,

or grilling produces. The mild flavor of the fish is enlivened by herbs and enriched with the toasted flavors of coconut and peanuts.

Besides halibut, other ocean fish may be used, such as red snapper or sea bass. Although northeasterners primarily consume freshwater fish, making this dish with fish caught in the wild from rivers or lakes is not recommended due to the risk of contamination by parasites from animal waste that may have washed into natural freshwater sources. Best to stick to deep-sea fish or fish farm-raised under stringent conditions.

If you prefer not to eat raw fish, blanch sliced fish in boiling water for 30 seconds to 1 minute, or until it turns opaque but not yet flaky. Drain well, toss with the lime juice, and proceed as above. Sea bass would be a better choice for this alternative, as it is a firmer fish and holds together better in cooking.

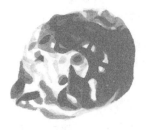

Crisped Catfish Salad with Sour Green Mango and Peanuts or Cashews

(Yâm Bplah Doog Foo)

1 lb. fillets of catfish
5 cloves garlic, chopped
6 to 10 fresh Thai chillies (*prik kee noo*), cut into thin rounds
2 to 3 Tbs. fish sauce (*nahm bplah*), to taste
Juice of 1 to 2 limes (about 2½ to 3 Tbs.), to taste
1 Tbs. plus 1 tsp. granulated sugar, to taste
3 cups peanut oil for deep-frying
2 Tbs. raw peanuts or raw cashews
6 small dried red Thai chillies (*prik kee noo haeng*)
1 to 2 shallots, quartered lengthwise and sliced very thinly crosswise
½ cup sour green mango, peeled and julienned into thin 1- to 1½-inch strips
    (or substitute a peeled tart green apple—toss julienned apple with 1 Tbs.
    lime juice)
A few lettuce leaves
A few short mint and cilantro sprigs

Broil catfish fillets over high heat until they are browned and cooked a little bit on the dry side (6 to 10 minutes on each side, depending on the thickness of the fillets). Set aside to cool.

In a large mortar, pound chopped garlic and fresh Thai chillies to a paste. Add fish sauce, lime juice, and sugar, and stir well to dissolve. Adjust the flavors so that the sauce is equally salty and sour and slightly sweet (use 1 tsp. less sugar if using green apple). Let sit for the flavors to mingle and marry.

Heat ½ cup peanut oil in a wok. Fry peanuts or cashews over a gentle low to medium flame so that they brown slowly and evenly and cook all the way through. When golden brown, strain from oil with a wire mesh skimmer. Let cool. Add dried chillies and fry over medium heat until they turn dark red. Remove from oil and drain.

When catfish has cooled sufficiently to handle, fluff the cooked flesh into very small flakes with a fork. Reheat oil in the wok over high heat and add to it the remaining oil. When hot enough to sizzle a small piece of fish, stir in fish flakes and fry over medium heat, separating pieces with a fork so that they do not stick together in one big lump. When fish flakes turn a rich golden brown and are thoroughly crispy, strain from oil with a fine wire-mesh skimmer, let cool a few minutes, and drain.

Transfer crisped fish to a lettuce-lined serving plate. Top with sliced shallots and julienned green mango (or apple). Spoon hot-and-sour sauce evenly over the salad, sprinkle with fried peanuts (or cashews), and garnish with mint and cilantro sprigs. Arrange the fried dried chillies along the side for those who wish a stronger bite. Serve immediately while fish is still crispy.

Serves 4 to 6 with other dishes and rice in a family-style meal.

Notes and Pointers:

Fish salads are very popular in Thailand, and one of the favorites is this delightful combination of crisped catfish flakes and sour green mango, robustly flavored with an intense chilli-lime sauce and punctuated with the rich taste and crunchy texture of fried nuts.

Crisping cooked, flaked fish is a common way to prepare catfish. The crisped flakes, known as *bplah doog foo* (literally "fluffy catfish"), appear in a variety of dishes, not just in this hot-and-sour salad. A personal favorite is an incendiary, endorphin-releasing stir-fry of the crisped flakes with plenty of garlic, chillies, lemon grass, and holy basil (see page 124). Normally *bplah doog foo* is made with charcoal-roasted, whole catfish, which adds a wonderful smoky aroma. Frequently, the head and tail of the fish are also fried until crispy and arranged on the serving platter with the crisped flakes piled in between to convey the appearance of a whole fish. The skin, too, is used, as this fries the crispiest; to many Thais, fish skin is one of the best parts of the fish and is never thrown away.

In this recipe, I have simplified the traditional way of making crisped catfish flakes by substituting catfish fillets which, in much of America, are more readily available than whole catfish with head, tail, and skin still joined. They are cooked by broiling in the oven, though this sacrifices the smoky dimension in the name of simplicity. If you like the smoky taste of charcoal-grilled fish, do take the trouble to cook the fillets over medium-hot charcoals.

If you would like to replicate the flavors of this fish salad as closely as possible to what you've had in Thailand's best restaurants, start with a whole catfish, roasting it over medium-hot charcoals in a grilling basket, turning frequently, until the fish is well cooked and the skin lightly charred and dried out. Flake the cooked flesh and cut the skin into small pieces and fry in hot oil until crispy. For best results, use an immature, sour, green mango. Tips on selection are given on page 60.

Spicy Charcoal-Roasted Catfish Salad
(Lahp Bplah Doog)

One 1- to 1¼-lb. whole catfish
8 cloves garlic
1 whole shallot
½ tsp. coriander seeds
¼ tsp. cumin seeds
6 to 12 dried red Thai chillies (*prik kee noo haeng*)
Pinch of salt
1 stalk lemon grass
2 tsp. chopped fresh or frozen galanga
2 tsp. shrimp paste (*gkabpi*)
1 small piece of banana leaf or aluminum foil
5 fresh Thai chillies (*prik kee noo*), cut into very thin rounds
3 to 4 Tbs. lime juice, to taste
2 to 3 Tbs. fish sauce (*nahm bplah*), to taste
1 shallot, halved lengthwise and sliced very thinly crosswise
3 to 4 Tbs. coarsely chopped mint leaves
2 to 3 Tbs. coarsely chopped cilantro leaves
1 green onion (white and half of green parts), cut into very thin rounds
2 to 3 Tbs. roasted rice powder
A few sprigs of mint and sawleaf coriander, and 5 to 6 dried Thai chillies fried till
    dark red in ¼ cup oil (optional), for garnish
An assortment of raw and lightly steamed vegetables and herbs to accompany
    the spicy catfish, such as: cabbage, lettuce, cucumber, green or long beans, Thai
    eggplant, and sprigs of basil, mint, and sawleaf coriander

Clean catfish, keeping head, tail, and skin attached. Roast catfish over medium charcoals in a grilling basket, turning frequently until it is thoroughly cooked and a little on the dry side, with the skin dark brown, slightly charred, and dried. When cool enough to handle, remove the cooked flesh and skin from the bones with a fork and fluff into very fine flakes to yield about 1 cup.

Cut root tip off garlic cloves and shallot, leaving skin on. Place in a 450° F oven, and let roast about 10 minutes until softened (shallot will take an extra 5 to 10 minutes, depending on its size). They may also be roasted in a dry pan on the stove over medium-high heat, or over hot charcoals at the same time as the catfish, turning frequently, until softened. Peel off and discard skin.

In a dry pan, roast coriander and cumin seeds separately over medium heat until both are dark brown and very aromatic. Next, roast dried red chillies with a pinch of salt, turning frequently until they are dark red and partially charred. Grind the two roasted seeds together to a fine powder in a mortar and pestle or spice grinder. Then, grind roasted dried chillies; keep separate.

Trim the woody bottom tip of lemon grass and peel off 2 to 3 of the loose, fibrous outer layers. Cut into very thin rounds, starting from the bottom end, to yield 2 tablespoons. Roast in a dry pan over medium heat until aromatic. Likewise, roast chopped galanga until fragrant. Wrap shrimp paste in a small piece of banana leaf or foil and roast directly over the flame of a burner, holding the leaf packet with a pair of tongs, until the leaf is charred on the outside and the aroma of the shrimp paste comes through. The shrimp paste may also be roasted over charcoal.

Pound roasted lemon grass, galanga, roasted garlic and shallot, and *gkabpi* to a paste with a heavy mortar and pestle. Blend in ground roasted seeds. Add cut fresh chillies, lime juice, and fish sauce to taste. Stir in 1 to 3 teaspoons of ground roasted dried chillies to spice the sauce to the heat level desired. Stir well.

Mix flaked roasted catfish with the sauce, sliced shallot, chopped mint, cilantro and green onion, and roasted rice powder. Mix well.

Transfer to a serving plate and garnish with mint sprigs, sawleaf coriander, and fried dried Thai chillies. Arrange accompanying vegetables along the side to eat along with the spicy catfish.

Serves 5 to 6 with steamed sticky rice (see page 70), or regular rice, in a multicourse Thai-style meal.

Notes and Pointers:

Like migrating birds, my husband and I spend part of each winter in Thailand when the weather there is nicest. Whenever we are there, we without fail lunch and dine several times at the neighborhood restaurant near my parents' home in the Thonglor residential district. One of Michael's favorites, the place is appropriately named My Choice. The ambience is not particularly interesting, but the food is consistently fabulous. Ordering is always an excruciating challenge, as there are so many dishes my husband absolutely loves but, if he had to select his top ten favorites from the menu, the northeastern-style roasted catfish salad or *lahb* would have to be among them. This recipe is my attempt to duplicate as closely as possible the complex range of flavors that make My Choice's salad so remarkably delicious, and one of the best I have tasted outside the northeastern region.

Like most northeastern dishes, this salad is meant to be very intense—very hot, salty, and sour. Only a small amount of the highly spiced catfish is eaten along with a forest of raw or lightly cooked vegetables, plenty of aromatic and bitter herbs, and, of course, heaping servings of steamed sticky rice. As such, the fish takes on a role somewhat like the one salad dressings, spicy dips, or condiments take in Western cuisines.

(continued on next page)

The roasted flavors in *labb* make it very different from the simpler hot-and-sour salads in other regions. Because roasting the ingredients adds to the preparation time, many of them can be done ahead of time and stored for a day or two until you are ready to make and serve the dish. For spicy food lovers, it is well worth the time and effort. Since doubling the recipe doesn't double the amount of work, as it takes just about the same amount of time to roast eight or sixteen cloves of garlic and so on, make plenty to serve a group of your friends. Because it is highly spiced, the salad keeps well in the refrigerator for a few days and makes a wonderful leftover.

If roasting catfish over a charcoal grill seems too much work, simplify the recipe by broiling catfish fillets in the oven. Of course, the salad made this way will lack the delicious smoky flavor of charcoal-roasted catfish, but is an acceptable compromise.

Try this recipe with other kinds of fish that flake easily when cooked, or with shelled, steamed clams and mussels, or grilled prawns and scallops—leave them whole.

Northeastern-Style Crispy Whole Catfish Topped with Seasoned Thai Herbs, Chillies, and Toasted Rice

(Lahb Bplah Doog Tawd Gkrawb)

One 1-lb. catfish with head, tail, and skin attached
3 to 5 dried red Thai chillies (*prik kee noo haeng*)
2 to 6 fresh Thai chillies (*prik kee noo*), cut into very thin rounds
Juice of 1 lime (about 2 Tbs.), to taste
1 tsp. Maggi or Gold Mountain seasoning sauce, to taste
1 to 2 Tbs. fish sauce (*nahm bplah*), to taste
2 to 3 tsp. sugar, to taste
1 small stalk lemon grass
2 to 3 cups peanut oil, for deep-frying
2 to 3 Tbs. tapioca starch
1 shallot, quartered lengthwise and sliced very thinly crosswise
1 green onion, cut into very thin rounds (use both the white and most of the
    green parts)
1 Tbs. coarsely chopped cilantro
1 Tbs. coarsely chopped fresh mint leaves
2 Tbs. roasted rice powder
A few mint and cilantro sprigs, for garnish

Clean fish, removing guts and gills, but keeping head, tail, fins, and skin attached. Make sure there are no oil sacs remaining inside the body cavity, as these tend to pop during frying. Cut a series of slanted gashes at a 45-degree angle to the depth of the center bone, about an inch apart from head to tail on both sides. Rinse and drain. Let sit at room temperature at least twenty minutes before cooking.

Roast dried chillies in a dry pan over medium heat, stirring frequently, until they turn evenly dark red and are slightly charred. Cool before grinding to a fine powder in a clean spice or coffee grinder. Place in a sauce bowl along with the cut-up fresh chillies. Add lime juice, Maggi (or Gold Mountain) seasoning sauce, fish sauce, and sugar. Stir well to dissolve sugar and blend the flavors. Adjust to desired combination. The sauce should be intense—very hot, equally salty and sour, with a slight hint of sweetness. Set aside.

Trim and discard woody bottom tip and fibrous outer layers of lemon grass, and slice stalk into very thin rounds, from the root end to about two inches below where the grass blades fan out. Prepare remaining ingredients.

(continued on next page)

Heat oil in a wok over high heat until it is smoking hot. Coat catfish thoroughly with a thin layer of tapioca starch, including the head, tail, fins, and body cavity. When oil is ready, hold fish by the tail and gently slide into the hot oil. There should be enough oil to submerge about two-thirds of the fish.

Fry over medium-high heat for 8 to 10 minutes on each side, or until fish is golden brown, crispy all around from the top of its head to the tip of its tail, and dried through. While frying, tilt the wok from side to side so that both head and tail get to sizzle and brown in the hot oil, or ladle hot oil continuously over them.

When it is thoroughly crispy, nudge the wok spatula under the fish from its top edge and tilt it up for 10 to 15 seconds against the side of the wok above the oil to let excess oil drain from the body cavity. Transfer to a wire rack and let cool a few minutes. Remove oil from the wok, reserving it for future use in frying fish.

Just before serving, toss lemon grass, shallot, green onion, cilantro, and mint with the limy chilli sauce and roasted rice powder. Place fish on a serving platter and spread seasoned herbs evenly over its surface, spilling half onto the platter so that servings on the second side can get some seasonings, too. Garnish with cilantro and mint sprigs.

Serve immediately, while fish is still crispy, with steamed sticky rice (see page 70), or regular rice.

Serves 3 to 4 along with other dishes in a family-style meal.

Notes and Pointers:

This recipe is an adaptation of the absolutely divine fish I had the good fortune to devour in a homey garden restaurant just outside the northern entrance to Kao Yai National Park, northeast of Bangkok. A few friends and I were visiting the park and had just scheduled a wildlife safari with park officials for later that night. We looked for the restaurant closest to where we were staying for an early dinner. The sign *Gkrua Loong Choob* ("Uncle Choob's Kitchen") appealed to us, and though the restaurant appeared deserted on that quiet weekday evening, we were warmly greeted and welcomed into the comfortable outdoor dining terrace. Beautifully presented dishes were soon laid out in front of us on the bamboo table—a hearty country meal, fueling us for the cold, windy ride later in the back of a pick-up truck in search of wildlife sightings.

The fish used was *bplah chon,* a delicious freshwater fish that loves to slither about in muddy *klong* (canal or waterway) and rice-field puddles. It is frequently referred to in English as "mud fish," or "serpent-head fish" for obvious reasons. Unfortunately, this tasty fish common in the Thai countryside is not available fresh in American fish markets, so I have substituted catfish, another slippery creature that thrives in abundance in Thailand's wet lowlands.

The roasted rice powder adds a delightful roasted aroma so characteristic of very spicy, northeastern-style salads called *lahb.* See instructions on how to make your own supply on page 68.

Since catfish skin fries to such a wonderful crispiness without being oily tasting, I can't understand why so-called pan-ready catfish available in American markets are already skinned. To fry these skinned fish to a crisp will require breading—dip in egg and roll in bread crumbs and fry over a slightly lower heat, so that they are dried through before they brown. Or substitute ⅔ lb. catfish fillets, coating them well with tapioca starch and completely submerging them in the hot oil to fry evenly. They will not fry as crispy and light tasting as when the skin is still attached.

For a variation, use the seasoned herb mixture to top grilled or broiled fish. It's very good over grilled salmon, halibut, and tuna.

Sour Tamarind Fish Chowder
(Gkaeng Som Bplah)

1 to 1¼ lbs. fillets of catfish, tilapia, cod, snapper, or other similar white-flesh fish

4 cups water or unsalted seafood stock

2 cups string beans, cut into 1 ½-inch segments

2 cups bite-size cauliflower pieces or cabbage

1 to 1½-inch section fresh young ginger (or less, if mature ginger), minced

4 to 5 Tbs. fish sauce (nahm bplah), to taste

½ cup tamarind juice the thickness of fruit concentrate, to desired sourness

2 to 3 Tbs. palm or coconut sugar, to taste

2 green onions, split in half lengthwise and cut into 1½-inch segments

2 red jalapeno or serrano peppers, finely slivered with seeds

¼ to ½ cup short cilantro sprigs

Chilli paste ingredients:

8 to 12 bright-red, dried chillies, seeded and soaked to soften, then chopped finely

1 to 2 Tbs. minced cilantro root (or substitute stem sections)

½ tsp. white peppercorns, finely ground

6 large cloves of garlic, chopped

3 shallots, chopped

½ Tbs. shrimp paste (gkabpi)

First, make the chilli paste. Using a heavy mortar and pestle, reduce ingredients to a smooth well-blended paste. For quicker results, pound ingredients separately a little at a time, then combine and pound together to blend.

Cut fish fillets into 1½- to 2-inch chunks. Set aside.

Bring 4 cups water or stock to a boil in a medium soup pot. Dissolve the paste in it, and add string beans. Simmer 2 to 3 minutes, then add cauliflower and minced ginger. Season with fish sauce, tamarind juice, and palm sugar to the desired salty-sour-and-sweet combination. This soupy curry is usually made equally sweet, sour, and salty.

When the vegetables are almost tender, bring broth to a rolling boil over high heat. Add fish pieces, green onions, and slivered chillies (if extra hotness is desired). Return to a boil and cook 1 to 2 minutes, or until fish is just cooked through. Transfer to a serving bowl and garnish with cilantro.

Serves 6 to 8 with rice and other dishes in a family-style meal.

Notes and Pointers:

I have named this soupy concoction a chowder but, in Thailand, it really is served more like a spicy curry, to be eaten with plenty of rice. (The Thai word *gkaeng* is used interchangeably to refer to both soups and curries.) Hence, it is usually described as *sour fish curry* on Thai menus—a curry that is not coconut-milk-based like the majority of popular Thai curries. However, if you enjoy its flavors and would like to serve it as a soup, simply tone down the heat level by cutting back on the chillies. The vegetables, ginger, chillies, and tamarind, among other things, make this a healthy soup with warming qualities and plenty of vitamin C.

In many parts of rural Thailand, *gkaeng som* is commonly made with *bplah chon*, a favorite freshwater fish. The fish is deep-fried either whole or in chunks with bone in, until crispy, before it is added to the spicy broth along with vegetables, which frequently include stringy water mimosa and cabbage. It is often served on a fish-shaped metal dish placed over a stand holding hot charcoal. Diners participate by adding more vegetables and broth as desired, serving themselves as they cook.

Catfish Rounds Simmered in Turmeric-Flavored Coconut Sauce

(Dtom Kem Gkati Bplah Doog)

One 1½- to 2-lb. catfish with head, tail and skin attached
Two 14-oz. cans unsweetened coconut milk, about 3½ cups
5 pieces fresh turmeric, each about 1½ inches long
2 stalks lemon grass
5 small red shallots, or 2 to 3 brown shallots
1-inch piece fresh galanga
2 tsp. sea salt
1 tsp. sugar
2½ to 3 Tbs. fish sauce (*nahm bplah*)

Clean catfish and rinse well. Using a sharp knife, cut off the head, but do not discard. Cut the rest of the fish through the bone into steaks about 1-inch thick. Leave tail with about 1½ inches of flesh attached. Set aside.

Pour coconut milk into a large saucepan. Peel turmeric and smash well with the flat side of a cleaver or heavy knife to bruise; add to the pot. Trim off the woody bottom tip and top third of the lemon grass stalks. Pull out and discard loose outer leaves. Cut trimmed stalks into two segments, and smash to bruise. Peel shallots, leaving red shallots whole; if using the larger brown shallots, cut each in half. Bruise. Slice galanga into very thin pieces. Add lemon grass, shallots, and galanga to the pot, along with salt and sugar.

Heat over medium heat and slowly bring to a boil, stirring occasionally. Add fish head and cook for 5 minutes to flavor the broth. Then follow with the remaining fish pieces. Return to a boil and add fish sauce. Cook over low to medium heat uncovered, enough so that sauce simmers slowly. Turn catfish pieces gently from time to time for even cooking until they are cooked through, about 10 to 15 minutes.

Serve warm with rice and other dishes in a family-style meal. Serves 6.

Notes and Pointers:

In the southern region of Thailand, plentiful coconut milk and fresh turmeric are frequently combined to cook various kinds of fish and vegetables. Neither a spicy curry nor a soup, this rich, savory dish has subtle flavors and is a good accompaniment to highly spiced dishes in a meal, helping douse the fire burning in the mouth and on the lips. The flavor of the coconut milk is important in this dish, so use a good-quality brand, or make your own from fresh coconut. Fresh turmeric, too, is essential (see page 72 for more about this rhizome) but, if you must substitute, use 3 teaspoons of the powdered kind and add an extra ½ teaspoon of sugar to the recipe; the sauce, however, will not be nearly as good.

When tasting the sauce during cooking, make sure it is saltier than "to taste," so that it will not be bland when served over plain, unflavored steamed rice. After all, the Thai name for this dish literally means "salty, boiled catfish in coconut milk" (*∂tom* means boil, *kem* means salty, *gkati* means coconut milk). Like curries, this dish tastes even better when made a day ahead of time. The flavors of the herbs are more pronounced and better blended and the catfish tastes less fishy. Catfish when cooked with the bone in and skin on will stay firm and does not easily fall apart when rewarmed the next day. The head, tail, bones, and skin add depth of flavor to the sauce, as well as thicken it.

Whole catfish already cut into chunks are sometimes available from Southeast Asian markets, saving you from the challenging experience of having to chop the fish through the bone. If fresh catfish with skin still attached is not available where you live, substitute with the skinned pan-ready catfish. Though the head and tail have been trimmed off, it works better than fillets, since some bones remain to flavor the broth. You may use other fish cut through the bone into steaks.

Salmon Poached in Green Curry Sauce with Baby Eggplants and Thai Basil
(Gkaeng Kiow Wahn Bplah Salmon)

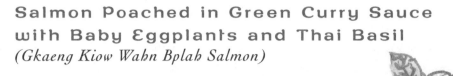

1 lb. very fresh, farm-raised salmon fillets, cut into 1½-inch chunks
2 cups or one 14-oz. can unsweetened coconut milk
2 to 4 Tbs. green curry paste
½ lb. small round Thai eggplants, cut into halves or quarters
½ cup pea eggplants or shelled fresh peas
Fish sauce (*nahm bplah*), to taste
1 to 2 tsp. palm or coconut sugar, to taste
2 kaffir lime leaves
½ to 1 cup fresh Thai sweet basil leaves and flower buds
   (*bai horapa*)
1 to 2 slivered jalapeno or serrano peppers with seeds, as desired
   for added heat

If using canned coconut milk, do not shake before opening, so that the cream remains on top. Spoon ½ cup of this thick cream into a medium saucepan placed on a burner over medium to medium-high heat. Reduce until cream is smooth and bubbly and oil begins to separate (3 to 4 minutes). Add curry paste and, with frequent stirring, fry it in the cream until the aromas and flavors are released (about 3 minutes). Pour in remaining milk and stir to make a smooth sauce.

Bring to a boil and add Thai eggplants and pea eggplants (if using). Return to a boil, then reduce heat so that eggplants gently simmer in the sauce uncovered. Cook for 10 to 12 minutes, or until the eggplants begin to soften. Add kaffir lime leaves and peas (if substituting for the pea eggplants) and season to taste with fish sauce, which may not be needed with some brands of curry pastes that are already salted. Add palm or coconut sugar to balance and enhance the spice and herb flavors and sweeten the sauce to your liking.

Simmer a few minutes longer to cook eggplants to the tenderness you prefer. In the meantime, arrange salmon chunks inside a warmed serving dish with a lid that is just wide enough to accommodate a single layer of fish.

When eggplants are tender, stir basil and chillies (if you wish the curry to be hotter) into the sauce until wilted (½ to 1 minute), increase heat to high and bring curry sauce to a rolling boil. Immediately spoon eggplants and sauce over the salmon. Cover for 5 minutes. Serve while still warm with fluffy steamed rice.

Serves 6 with other dishes in a multicourse family-style meal.

Notes and Pointers:

Green curry is a much-loved staple food of Thailand, and is frequently made with dumplings prepared from ground fish or shrimp. Rich, but light at the same time, the refreshingly herbal sauce—made with a paste mixture of hot green chillies, lemon grass, galanga ginger, zest of kaffir lime, cilantro roots, garlic, shallots, coriander seeds, cumin, and shrimp paste in a coconut milk base—goes exceedingly well with a wide variety of seafood. In this recipe, I have paired the classic sauce with my favorite American fish—salmon. This fish has a wonderful texture when it is undercooked and still pink, melting like smooth, rich cream in the mouth.

If you prefer your salmon more cooked and flaky, use a heatproof serving dish placed on top of a burner on the lowest heat setting, pour the sauce over the fish in the dish and cover. Let the very low heat cook the fish chunks until they are done to your liking (five to ten minutes). Do not stir while it is cooking. Serve the fish in the dish as transferring to another serving dish may make the pieces fall apart into small flakes.

You may also try poaching a small, whole salmon, or a section of a larger one. Use a poaching pot with a rack that lifts the fish slightly from the bottom. Make plenty of curry sauce—enough to cover the fish. If you wish a lighter sauce, dilute each two cups of coconut milk with one-half to one cup of water. Make the sauce as instructed with the desired dilution, cooking the eggplants only lightly, then pour over the fish in the pot and simmer at the lowest heat until the fish is cooked to your liking.

Be careful when using salmon caught in the wild. If it is from freshwater sources, there is a risk of contamination by parasites from animal waste washed into the water. Better to cook such salmon well rather than on the underdone side.

Many of my cooking students especially like the version we cook in class with shrimp and fillet of Dover sole cut into similar-size chunks as the salmon in the recipe. Because it stays firm and does not flake as easily, the sole may be added directly to the saucepot as soon as the eggplants are tender. Cook over high heat for one minute, then stir in the shrimp, basil, and chillies. Cook another half to one minute, or until the shrimp has turned pink and the basil wilted. Transfer to a serving dish and serve immediately.

Try also with a mixture of shrimp, scallops, and squid, or any of these by themselves, adding them directly to the curry pot with the basil and chillies and cooking until they are just cooked through, usually not much more than half to one minute if the sauce is well heated to a gentle boil before they go in.

Of course, the packaged curry paste and coconut milk you use make a world of difference in how your curry turns out. Recommended brands are given in the discussion of ingredients in chapter 4. If the small, tomato-shaped Thai eggplants are not available, substitute other kinds of eggplant and adjust cooking times to suit the particular variety.

Fish Fillets Stir-Fried in Hot-and-Spicy Coconut Cream Sauce
(Pad Ped Bplah)

1 cup rich coconut cream (preferably *Mae Ploy* or *Chao Koh* brand—spoon the thickest cream from the top of an unshaken can of unsweetened coconut milk)

3 Tbs. fish sauce (*nahm bplah*), to taste

2 tsp. palm or coconut sugar, to taste

1½ lb. fillets of catfish, sturgeon, halibut, shark, monkfish, or other medium- to firm-flesh fish, cut into 1- to 1½-inch chunks

2 to 3 Tbs. finely slivered rhizome (*gkrachai*)

6 kaffir lime leaves, finely slivered

¼ cup inch-long sprigs of green peppercorns

1 cup Thai basil leaves and flower buds (*bai horapa*)

2 red serrano, jalapeno, or fresno peppers, cut into large, lengthwise slivers

Chilli paste

7 dried red chillies, seeded, soaked to soften, then chopped

2 tsp. coriander seeds, toasted and ground finely

½ tsp. cumin seeds, toasted and ground finely

10 white peppercorns, freshly and finely ground

5 to 10 fresh red Thai chillies (*prik kee noo*), cut into thin rounds with seeds

Bottom half of 1 stalk of lemon grass, trimmed, cut into thin rounds, then minced (about 2 Tbs.)

1 Tbs. minced galanga

1 tsp. minced kaffir lime peel (soak dried peel to soften before using)

6 to 8 cloves garlic, chopped

2 shallots, chopped

Using a heavy stone mortar and pestle, pound the chilli paste ingredients a little at a time, reducing them to a fine paste. Then combine and pound together to produce a well-blended paste.

Heat a wok until its surface is very hot. Add the coconut cream and, when it is warmed through to a smooth consistency, spoon out 2 tablespoons and reserve. Reduce remaining cream over medium-high-to-high heat for a few minutes to thicken and separate oil from cream. Add the chilli paste and fry a few minutes, stirring constantly until paste darkens and becomes very aromatic. Season with fish sauce and palm sugar.

Toss in the fish chunks and stir-fry 1 to 2 minutes over high heat. When most of the pieces have lost their raw pink color on the outside, add the slivered *gkrachai* and kaffir lime leaves and sprigs of green peppercorns. Continue to stir-fry another one-half to one minute before stirring in the basil and slivered red peppers. Toss until basil is wilted and the fish is cooked through. Avoid overcooking, so that fish pieces do not flake and fall apart. Transfer to a serving dish and dribble reserved coconut cream over the top.

Serve this very spicy fish with lots of plain steamed rice; chew the herbs along with the fish and mouthfuls of rice.

Serves 6 in a multicourse family-style meal.

Notes and Pointers:

Watching this very popular dish being made along sidewalk, cook-to-order, seafood stalls is as exhilarating as eating it! Flames leap from powerful gas burners as skilled cooks dramatically toss seafood about in sizzling woks. Rising fumes fill the air, tickling throats with spicy aromas. In a matter of a few short minutes, your order is delivered piping hot to your rickety table, shared with anxious others gathered to sample the exquisite flavors of street cooking.

One bite of the spicy fish takes a few mouthfuls of rice to tame. Sweat drips down foreheads, noses start to sniffle, and ears and faces turn red. But defeat is not easily admitted as more rice is dished onto emptying plates. More please; it's so addicting and so very good!

Of course, this dry red curry dish is not just a food to be found along sidewalks, but is served daily in most restaurants across the kingdom—some more invigorating than others. A strongly flavored red curry paste is used, so if you don't want to go to the trouble of pounding the paste yourself, substitute store-bought red curry paste. However, the result will not be half as good as with this freshly made chilli paste, specially balanced for seafood.

This recipe is also excellent with eel and Dover sole. Besides fish, just about any seafood that can be stir-fried is great tossed in the wok with the spicy cream sauce. Try shrimp, shelled mussels, squid or cuttlefish, scallops, or a combination of different kinds of seafood.

"Drunken" Crisped Catfish Flakes
(Bplah Doog Foo Pad Kee Mao)

1 lb. catfish fillets
¼ cup finely chopped, shelled raw shrimp
1 large head garlic, chopped
12 to 15 Thai chillies, cut into very thin rounds
2 cups holy basil leaves (*bai gkaprow*)
1 small stalk lemon grass
1 cup peanut oil
1 to 1 ½ Tbs. fish sauce (*nahm bplah*), to taste
1 to 2 Tbs. water, rice wine, or brandy
½ tsp. sugar

Broil fish over high heat until both sides are browned and fish is cooked through, flaky, and a little on the dry side (6-8 minutes on each side, depending on the thickness of the fillets). Flake fish into tiny flakes with a fork, spread on a plate, and let sit to dry out.

Prepare shrimp, garlic, Thai chillies, and holy basil. Trim and discard woody bottom tip of lemon grass and 2 to 3 of the loose outer layers. If the stalk is thick, remove another layer so that what remains is the tender inner stalk. Slice into very thin rounds, using the bottom half of the stalk, to yield about 1 tablespoon.

Heat peanut oil in a wok until it begins to smoke. Stir in half the catfish flakes and fry over medium to high heat for several minutes until they turn golden brown and crispy. Stir frequently and separate the pieces with a fork so that they do not stick together in one big lump. Strain from oil with a fine wire-mesh skimmer and let cool a few minutes on the skimmer or a fine wire-mesh strainer. Fry the remaining half.

When all the catfish flakes have been crisped, remove oil from the wok, save for about 2 tablespoons; reserve the rest for future use in frying fish or stir-frying seafood dishes. Add garlic and sauté over medium-high heat until it begins to turn golden. Add shrimp. Stir to break into small bits as shrimp cooks.

When most of the shrimp has turned pink, add Thai chillies and basil. Stir to mix for 10 to 15 seconds, then reduce heat to medium and add fish sauce, water (or wine or brandy), and sugar. Stir and cook until basil has almost completely wilted. Add lemon grass and toss another 15 to 20 seconds. The mixture should be moist with a little bit of sauce and not completely dried out.

Return crisped catfish to the wok and toss quickly with herbs and seasonings. Transfer to a serving plate and serve immediately.

Serves 4 to 6 with other dishes and rice in a family-style meal.

Notes and Pointers:

Although "drunken" is in its name, it is not the fish that is drunk, but the opportunity it gives to the partaker. Loaded with garlic, chillies, and holy basil, its intensity makes a little bit go a long way to flavoring a plateful of rice, and helping you down enough beer to get you drunk! Though not necessary, adding the wine or brandy during cooking gives the fish an extra fragrance.

Crisping catfish in small, cooked flakes is a common way to prepare catfish. Frequently, the crisped flakes are made into salads with shredded, sour green mango (see page 108). The flakes are also delightful coated with spicy flavorings as is done in this dish and many others in creative Bangkok restaurants. Try making a thick, almost dry, curry sauce to toss the flakes in for another scrumptious way to serve catfish. Or sprinkle the flakes over salads and thick dipping sauces for extra flavor and texture.

Wok-Tossed Salmon with Chillies and Thai Basil

(Bplah Salmon Pad Gkaprow)

2 Tbs. peanut oil for stir-frying

4 cloves garlic, finely chopped

2 to 3 shallots, thinly sliced

1 lb. salmon fillets, cut into 1- to 1 ½-inch chunks

3 to 6 Thai chillies (*prik kee noo*), cut into very thin rounds

2 jalapeno or fresno peppers (preferably red), cut lengthwise
   into ¼-inch slivers with seeds

2 fresh kaffir lime leaves, very finely slivered, optional

2 tsp. black soy sauce (semisweet kind)

1 cup fresh holy basil (*bai gkaprow*), or Thai sweet basil (*bai
   horapa*), leave leaves whole, flower buds may also be used

2 Tbs. fish sauce (*nahm bplah*), to taste

2 dashes of ground white pepper

Heat a well-seasoned wok over high heat until its entire surface is smoking hot. Swirl in oil to coat the wok surface and wait 20 to 30 seconds for oil to heat. Stir in garlic and shallots. Sauté 20 to 30 seconds to flavor oil, then toss in salmon chunks. Stir-fry 30 seconds, or until the outer surfaces of fish begin to change color. Stir in the two kinds of chillies and slivered kaffir lime leaves (if using) and sprinkle black soy sauce over the mixture. Stir and follow one-half minute later with basil and fish sauce. Continue to stir-fry until basil is wilted and fish is cooked to your liking.

Sprinkle with white pepper. Toss and transfer to a serving dish.

Serves 3 to 4 with steamed jasmine rice and other dishes in a family-style meal.

Notes and Pointers:

Quick and easy stir-fried dishes with basil and chillies, called *pad gkaprow,* are very common in Thailand. The sweet floral bouquet of two basils—holy basil and tropical sweet basil—are well-loved and big handfuls of them are added, in whole leaves and short tender sprigs, to flavor meat, poultry, and seafood dishes. Since my husband and I love salmon, I have adapted the simple Thai way of stir-frying with basil to this fish. In fact, my husband so loves salmon prepared this way that it has become one of the staple dishes in our home.

Be careful not to overcook salmon, as it will flake apart and no longer stay in chunks. Personally, I like to undercook this fish a bit so that it retains its sweetness and has that special tender texture that feels as if it would melt in the mouth. Try this easy stir-fry with other kinds of medium- to firm-flesh fish and with shrimp, scallops, squid, or a combination of different kinds of seafood.

Curried Mousse of Red Snapper
in Banana Leaf Cups

(Haw Moek Bplah)

4 cups unsweetened coconut cream

4 to 6 Tbs. red curry paste

1 to 2 Tbs. fish sauce *(nahm bplah),* to taste (some brands of curry paste are already heavily salted)

3 to 4 tsp. palm or coconut sugar, to taste

1-lb. package of banana leaves

1½ lbs. fillets of red snapper

8 to 10 kaffir lime leaves, cut into very fine slivers

1½ to 2 cups fresh Thai sweet basil leaves and flower buds *(bai horapa)*

2 to 3 red serrano or jalapeno peppers, cut into fine inch-long slivers

1 Tbs. rice flour

⅔ cup coconut milk (remaining lighter milk in the bottom of the cans may be used)

3 eggs, beaten

If using canned coconut milk, you will need 2 to 3 cans (depending on the brand) to yield the 4 cups of coconut cream. (The 19 oz. *Mae Ploy* brand has the most cream of all the brands.) Do not shake cans before opening, as the cream will already be at the top. Simply spoon the thickest cream from the top of the cans and use for this recipe. On warm days, you may wish to refrigerate the cans to allow the cream to harden, making it easier to separate from the watery parts. If you are making your own coconut milk, use the thick cream from the first pressing of coconut pulp.

Heat ⅔ cup coconut cream in a medium saucepan over medium-high heat. Reduce for a few minutes until bubbly, and oil begins to separate. Add red curry paste and fry in the cream to release the herb and spice flavors. Stir well to mix paste with cream. When aromatic (3 to 5 minutes), add remaining cream. Season with fish sauce and palm or coconut sugar and simmer until mixture is smooth and well blended. (The curry sauce should be spicier, saltier, and sweeter than to taste, as its intensity will be diluted later on with the addition of the fish and eggs.) Set aside to cool to room temperature.

Make banana leaf cups by cutting leaves into circles, using a 6-inch round bowl as a guide. Invert the bowl on a section of leaf and cut around the edge of the bowl with the pointed end of a sharp knife. Cut 20 to 24 circles, avoiding sections of leaves that are split. Gently rinse to remove any sap on the surface, taking care not to tear them.

Using two circles for each cup, place dull sides (bottom side of banana leaves, usually lighter in color) of the two leaf circles together, crossing the leaf ribs so that the cup does not tear easily. Make a puckered fold about 1-inch deep and staple with a small stapler, or use a short wooden pick (see illustration). Go to the opposite point of the circle and staple another fold. Then make two more folds in between these first two folds, so that you end up stapling four equally spaced points round the circle, forming the four sides of the cup.

(continued on next page)

Cut snapper fillets into small, bite-size pieces, or chop coarsely. Place in a large mixing bowl and set aside. Prepare the kaffir lime leaves, basil (leave leaves whole, flower buds may also be used), and red peppers.

Mix rice flour with ⅔ cup coconut milk (the remaining light milk in the cans may be used for this step) and heat in a small saucepan over low to medium heat, stirring frequently until mixture thickens to a smooth, white cream. Set aside.

When curry sauce has cooled to room temperature, add to fish one-third at a time, stirring vigorously with a wooden spoon following each addition, to help the fish absorb the sauce. The mixture will thicken as you beat it. Add more sauce, and continue to beat until all the sauce has been added, and the mixture has become very thick and rich. Add ⅔ of the slivered kaffir lime leaves, reserving the rest for decoration. Select and set aside a dozen of the prettiest basil leaves and toss remainder into the curry mixture.

Beat eggs well and fold into the mixture. Wipe the inside of the banana leaf cups dry and fill with curried fish mixture, making sure each cup gets an equal amount of fish, herbs, and sauce.

Decorate top of each cup by first spooning a small dab of thickened white cream onto the center. Press a basil leaf onto the white background, topping with a few slivers of red pepper and kaffir lime leaf. Place filled cups on steamer racks and steam over medium-high heat for 15 minutes. Don't stack two racks to steam at the same time as cups on the bottom rack will tend to collect condensed steam dripping from the top rack, while those on the top rack will not get sufficient heat to cook; steam each rack separately.

As soon as the heat is turned off, lift the lid to prevent cooling steam from condensing into the cups. Remove cups from the steamer rack onto a serving platter.

Serves 8 to 10 in a family-style meal with other dishes and plain steamed rice.

Notes and Pointers:

Haw moek is a common way to prepare a fish curry and is traditionally steamed in banana leaf cups. The cups are not edible, but impart a special aroma. Nowadays, city restaurants are taking shortcuts by doing away with the leaf cups to save on labor. Aluminum foil has, unfortunately, become a frequent replacement. Other restaurants steam the curry on *kanom krok* pans (similar to Ebelskiver pans, with rounded indentations on the flat pans), which permit a pretty presentation when served on the usually terra-cotta pans with individual lids for each of the cakelike curried mousses. By the beaches in the south, resort restaurants steam the curry in bowls, then serve them inside young coconuts with tops chopped open and juice removed. The soft flesh of the coconut can be spooned out and eaten along with the curry.

Market vendors still prepare *haw moek* inside banana leaf cups. Traditional *haw moek* is not really a mousse, as chunks of fish cut through the bone are cooked in a custardlike, red curry sauce. Normally, a vegetable is included on the bottom of the cup, making it a complete dish on its own. *Haw moek* is not only made with various kinds of fish, but is frequently a combination of seafood, including squid, shrimp, shelled mussels, and even chunks of unshelled crab. There's also a mussel *haw moek*, in which the curried mixture is either steamed or baked on open mussel shells (*haw moek hoi malaeng poo,* see page 266).

If banana leaves are not available in markets near you, or if making the cups is a bit daunting, the curried mixture may also be steamed in small custard cups. Of course, the flavor will not be quite the same. Or, do as some of my students do: Line a soufflé dish with banana leaf, spoon in the entire fish mixture and decorate the top in any way you wish to impress your dinner guests. Steam until the custard is set and the fish cooked through on a steamer rack of a stacked steamer (about 30 minutes).

This dish can be made ahead of time and reheated by steaming or microwaving. If fully spiced, it keeps for up to a week in the refrigerator and, like most curries, tastes better after it has had the chance to sit for a while after cooking for the flavors to mingle and marry. The custard will also be firmer and less watery after it has completely cooled before reheating.

Charcoal-Grilled Spiced Fish
in Banana Leaf Packets
(Aep Bplah)

¾ lb. delicate to medium-firm, white fish fillets
6 kaffir lime leaves, finely slivered
6 sawleaf coriander (or substitute with parsley), coarsely chopped
2 Tbs. fish sauce *(nahm bplah)*, to taste
Banana leaves for wrapping

Chilli Paste
5 to 6 serrano peppers (preferably red), chopped
   with seeds
2 Tbs. chopped, trimmed lemon grass
1 Tbs. chopped, fresh turmeric
1 tsp. chopped, peeled ginger
2 shallots, chopped
10 cloves garlic, about 2 Tbs., chopped
2 tsp. shrimp paste *(gkabpi)*

Cut fish into thin strips about 1½ inches long and set aside.

In a heavy stone mortar, pound chilli paste ingredients a little at a time until they are all reduced to a well-blended paste.

Coat fish pieces with chilli paste and blend in slivered kaffir lime leaves, chopped sawleaf coriander (or parsley), and fish sauce. Divide into four equal portions.

Cut banana leaves into rectangles about 8" by 10". Layer two together and spoon a portion of the spiced fish onto the center, spreading it in a rectangle. Fold the two shorter sides over and use toothpicks to pin the two ends together. Trim excess leaf on both ends with scissors.

Grill over medium-hot charcoals for 3 to 4 minutes on each side, or until fish is cooked through. Transfer to a serving plate and open up leaf packets, trimming excess leaf around the edges to make a lovely presentation.

Serves 2 to 4 with rice and other dishes in a family-style meal.

Notes and Pointers:

Since the northern region of Thailand is landlocked, this spicy regional specialty is made with fillets of freshwater fish. The recipe is also good with many kinds of ocean fish, including halibut and cod. Try also with small shrimp or a combination of different kinds of shellfish.

Garlic-Peppered Pompano
(Bplah Jeramed Tawd Gkratiem Priktai)

One 1-lb. whole pompano or pomfret (or butterfish, white or sea perch, tilapia,
    gouramy, smelts, sole, or other small, flat fish)
4 cloves garlic, minced
½ tsp. fine sea salt
1 tsp. finely ground white pepper
1 cup peanut oil for frying fish
1 to 2 Tbs. tapioca starch, or substitute
    unbleached white flour or cornstarch
1 large head garlic, chopped (or about ⅓ cup)
2 tsp. fish sauce (nahm bplah)
A few short cilantro sprigs

Chilli-lime fish sauce
3 to 5 Thai chillies (prik kee noo), cut into thin
    rounds
2 Tbs. fish sauce (nahm bplah)
1 Tbs. lime juice
½ tsp. granulated sugar

Prepare chilli-lime fish sauce by combining all ingredients.

Clean fish, removing guts and gills, but keeping the head, tail, and fins attached. Rinse and drain. Holding a knife at a 45-degree angle, cut slanted gashes to bone level on both sides of the fish about an inch apart, or score in a crisscross diamond pattern.

Pound 4 cloves minced garlic with a mortar and pestle until it is completely reduced to paste. Rub onto the surface of fish, along with salt and white pepper. Set aside for 15 to 20 minutes.

Heat oil in a wok over high heat until it begins to smoke. While waiting, brush garlic from the fish and coat fish thoroughly with a thin layer of tapioca starch, including the inside of the body cavity and under the cheeks. When oil is hot, swirl to coat a large area of the wok surface. Gently slide fish into oil headfirst. Reduce heat to medium-high (or medium if you have a very hot stove) and fry for 8 to 10 minutes on each side, until it is a rich golden brown, crispy all around from head to tail, and dried through. During frying, tilt the wok from side to side so that both head and tail are submerged and evenly fried in the oil.

Transfer to a wire rack or large wire-mesh strainer to cool. Add the head of chopped garlic to the oil and fry over high heat until golden brown and crispy. Drain from oil with a fine wire-mesh skimmer.

(continued on next page)

Remove remaining oil from the wok and reserve for future use in cooking fish. Return crisped garlic to the wok over high heat, and sprinkle in 2 teaspoons fish sauce. Stir quickly and, when it has dried up, turn off the heat.

Arrange fish on a serving plate and top with crispy garlic pieces. Garnish with cilantro. Serve with chilli-lime fish sauce on the side for those who wish a chilli bite.

Serves 2 to 3 with rice and other dishes in a multicourse family-style meal. Crunch on the head, tail, and fins for a delicious source of calcium!

Notes and Pointers:

Fried fish is one of the most important staples of the Thai diet, eaten with plain steamed rice and flavored with fish sauce spiced with Thai chillies and a little lime juice. In my childhood, I loved mixing the steamed rice on my plate thoroughly with small bites of fried fish, crispy garlic, and the fish sauce mixture. An easy and very satisfying one-dish meal, better than any fried rice!

In Thailand, garlic comes in small heads and cloves, but the skin surrounding the cloves is very thin and fries up to a crisp. You may wish to save the tiny cloves from the middle of each head—cloves that are usually a nuisance to peel and are often thrown away. Just smash the unpeeled cloves whole with a cleaver and use instead of the larger cloves of chopped garlic. Use a big handful for this recipe.

Small, flat fishes like pompano have soft bones. The crispy head, tail, and fins are wonderful and very safe to eat—rich, tasty, and a good source of natural calcium. In fact, just about every part of a pompano except for the center skeleton can be chewed up and eaten easily.

Besides whole fish, steaks of larger fish may also be pan-fried until the surface is lightly crisped, then topped with the fried garlic. On one of my traveling adventures to the southwestern coast of Thailand, a tour member caught a barracuda while trolling around an island. We had plenty to fry that night to feed our group of twelve. Lots of heads of chopped garlic smothered the fabulously fresh, crisp-fried fish. Grouper is another frequent treat on the islands, frying up to a delicious crusty crispiness.

If you are able to get soft-shell crab where you live, it is excellent for this garlicky recipe. Also try oysters but, since they have a fair amount of juice inside them and shouldn't be cooked too long, dredge in a mixture of ⅔ unbleached white flour and ⅓ tapioca starch before frying. Tapioca starch by itself would produce a gooey result because of the moisture in the oysters.

For crispy garlic-peppered shrimp, see page 191.

Southern-Style Turmeric Fried Fish
(Bplah Tawd Kamin)

One 1½-lb. fresh whole fish with head and tail still attached, or 1 lb. fish steaks
2 pieces fresh turmeric, about 1½ to 2 Tbs. chopped
8 cloves garlic, chopped
1 tsp. sea salt
1 tsp. white peppercorns, freshly ground

Hot-and-Sour Dipping Sauce
8 to 10 Thai chillies (*prik kee noo*), thinly sliced in rounds
1 to 2 shallots, halved lengthwise and thinly sliced crosswise
¼ cup white vinegar
3 to 4 Tbs. fish sauce (*nahm bplah*), to taste
2 to 3 tsp. sugar, to taste

2 to 3 cups peanut oil, for frying
2 to 3 Tbs. tapioca starch
Sliced cucumbers, tomatoes, pineapple, and/or orange to line serving platter,
   optional

If using whole fish, gut, scale, and clean, keeping head, tail, fins, and skin attached. Holding a knife at a 45-degree angle, cut slanted diagonal gashes to bone level about an inch apart on both sides of the fish. Rinse and drain well.

Scrape skin from turmeric and chop finely. Place in a mortar along with the chopped garlic, sea salt, and freshly ground white pepper. Pound to mix and blend ingredients into a coarse paste. Rub paste evenly over the fish, including body cavity, head, and tail, or thoroughly over both sides of the fish steaks. Set aside to marinate for at least one-half hour. Fish should be at room temperature before frying.

Mix all the ingredients for the hot-and-sour dipping sauce. Stir well and let sit for at least one-half hour before serving so that the flavors can mingle and marry.

Heat peanut oil in a large wok. There should be enough oil to submerge at least ⅔ of the fish during frying. Allow oil to heat until it is smoking hot. While waiting, brush chopped garlic and turmeric pieces from fish, reserving for later. Coat fish with a thin layer of tapioca starch, including the inside of the body cavity, the head, and tail, to reduce splattering during frying, and add a crispier texture to the fried fish.

(continued on next page)

Fry fish 10 to 12 minutes on each side, or until fish has dried through and is thoroughly crispy (less time for fish steaks; cooking time will depend on thickness of steaks and type of fish). If you have a very hot stove, fry at medium heat; otherwise, use medium-high to high heat. While frying, tilt the wok occasionally from side to side to submerge head and tail in the hot oil. When the fish is well-browned and crispy all around, from head to tail, add marinade to oil and fry with fish until chopped pieces of garlic and turmeric are golden brown and crispy. Turn off heat.

Holding the wok spatula under the fish from its top edge, tilt it up on one side of the wok above the oil to let excess oil drain from the body cavity, then transfer to a serving platter. Using a fine wire-mesh skimmer, scoop the crispy bits of fried marinade from the oil, drain well, and spread over the fish.

Serve with hot-and-sour dipping sauce and, if you wish, sliced cucumbers, tomatoes, pineapple, and/or orange arranged on the side of the serving platter. Crunch on the crispy parts around the fins, head, body cavity, and tail for a delicious source of calcium. Strain oil and reserve for future use in frying fish.

Serves 3 to 4 with other dishes and rice in a family-style meal.

Notes and Pointers:

Influenced by a sizeable Muslim population, whose ancestors migrated into the region from the Indian subcontinent over the past two thousand years, southern Thai cuisine is laced with a mix of spices and herbs more familiar to Indian cooking. Among them, turmeric is highly favored and used generously in a wide variety of dishes. However, instead of the bright, golden yellow powder, the fresh rhizome with its depth and subtleties of flavor is preferred.

If you ever travel to the southern provinces of Thailand, you'll see large mounds of turmeric piled on mats on the ground in most large, open-air marketplaces. Covered by a tan skin much like its cousin, ginger, tinges of the small rhizome's bright-orange flesh eagerly show through the thin skin. Unfortunately, this prolifically grown root in southern Thailand is still hard to find in America's Asian markets. If you see any at a local Southeast Asian or Indian market, do not hesitate to pick up a few pieces. Gourmet produce markets with an international bent may also carry the rhizomes from time to time, usually during the warm summer months, when they are dug. They keep well if they are wrapped in a paper towel and stored inside a sealed plastic bag, lasting for several months in the refrigerator. You may also plant them in a container—they grow into beautiful plants with large, broad leaves, providing you with fresh turmeric whenever you need it.

While garlic and pepper coat fried fish in other regions, in southern cooking, turmeric is also added. Just about any fish that is delicious fried can be made southern style. It is best to use fresh turmeric for its exquisite flavor but, if you must, substitute a fresh batch of turmeric powder. Use 2 teaspoons, pounding it in with the garlic.

I am partial to catfish fried this way, after sampling the superb turmeric catfish at my favorite restaurant in southern Thailand. Located in a shady grove next to a rubber plantation outside the town of Krabi, Reun Mai ("Wooden House") excels in just about every dish it produces. This recipe is also good with sea perch, tilapia, mullet, red snapper, cod, grouper, and pompano. The cooking time given is for thicker fish like catfish and grouper. Adjust downward for flatter and smaller fish. For fish in round steaks, try halibut, king mackerel, and barracuda, or any fish that you like pan-fried; fry over high heat until cooked through, browned, and lightly crisped on the surface.

Steamed Fillet of Ling Cod with Sautéed Garlic and Ginger

(Bplah Neung Gkratiem Jiow)

¾ lb. large fillet of ling cod
¼ cup peanut oil
1 large head chopped garlic (about ¼ cup)
2-inch piece fresh ginger, peeled and cut into fine slivers
    (about ¼ cup)
2 red serrano peppers, cut into fine slivers, including seeds
1 Tbs. fish sauce (nahm bplah)
1 Tbs. light soy sauce, or Gold Mountain seasoning sauce
½ to 1 tsp. granulated sugar

Cut fillet in half crosswise. Arrange the two pieces in a single layer in a heatproof serving dish that fits on the rack of a stacked steamer. The dish should have a depth of at least an inch to catch juices that may steam out from the fish.

Heat oil in a wok over high heat until it begins to smoke. Reduce heat to medium, and add the garlic. Stir a few seconds and add the ginger. Stirring, fry until golden. Turn off heat and strain garlic and ginger from oil with a fine wire-mesh skimmer. Reserve oil for future use in stir-frying.

Spread garlic and ginger evenly over the fish. Top with slivered red chillies. Mix fish sauce, light soy sauce or seasoning sauce, and sugar, stirring to dissolve sugar. Spoon evenly over fish.

Bring 1½ to 2 inches of water to a boil in the steamer pot before stacking rack holding the fish dish over the pot. Cover and steam over high heat for about 12 minutes, or until fish is cooked through.

Turn off heat and immediately lift the cover so that condensed steam under the lid does not drip onto the fish. Carefully lift dish from the steamer rack after the burst of steam has dissipated.

Serves 2 to 3 with rice and other dishes in a family-style meal.

Notes and Pointers:

Garlic is the most used herb in Thai cooking, lending its flavor to just about every savory dish, from mild to very spicy. Sometimes it is in the foreground, though oftentimes, it stands in the background as a firm foundation. In this simple recipe, it is the primary ingredient, paired with ginger. Browning the garlic and ginger in oil beforehand changes their character, adding a toasted aroma to the steamed fish.

For an easy and mild dish, use only very fresh fish. Try also with flounder (large fillet of Dover or petrale sole), haddock, snapper, halibut, trout, and other delicate to medium-firm, mild to moderately flavored fish.

Whole Tilapia Steamed with Ginger and Fermented Soybean Sauce
(Bplah Nin Neung Dtow Jiow)

One ¾- to 1-lb. whole tilapia
4 Tbs. peanut oil
1 to 2 Tbs. tapioca starch (or cornstarch)
2 large cloves garlic, chopped
2 Tbs. finely slivered, peeled fresh ginger
2 Tbs. fermented soybean sauce (dtow jiow)
¼ cup water
1 tsp. sugar
Sprinkling of ground white pepper

Clean tilapia, removing the scales and guts but leaving head, tail, and fins attached. Rinse and drain well. Cut 2 to 3 slanted gashes to bone level on both sides of the fish about 1½ inches apart.

Heat a wok over high heat until its surface is smoking hot. Swirl the oil into the wok, coating a large enough surface area to accommodate the fish. Rub a thin coating of tapioca starch (or cornstarch) over fish, including head, tail, and body cavity. Gently slide the fish into the hot oil. Lightly brown a minute or two on both sides, moving the wok from side to side so that its entire length is seared. When turning, flip the fish over on its belly to avoid damaging the top fin.

Transfer fish to a heatproof serving plate with some depth to catch juices that may steam out from the fish. The plate should fit on the rack of a stacked steamer. Remove all but 1 tablespoon of oil remaining in the wok and reduce heat to medium. Sauté chopped garlic and slivered ginger for 10 to 15 seconds, then spoon in fermented soybean sauce. Add ¼ cup of water, stir, and let cook a couple of minutes. Balance the saltiness of soybean sauce with sugar to your liking. Simmer a short while longer before spooning sauce evenly over the surface of the fish.

Set the plate with fish on the steamer rack and place rack over steamer pot after water in the pot has come to a rolling boil. Steam covered over high heat for about 10 minutes, or until fish is cooked through. Check by inserting a fork into the thickest part of fish—fish is done when flesh gives way easily to the fork until it touches the center bone. Turn off heat, immediately uncover, and let steam dissipate before lifting the plate from steamer. Sprinkle white pepper over fish and serve while still warm.

Serves 2 to 3 with rice and other dishes in a family-style meal.

(continued on next page)

Notes and Pointers:

This Chinese-influenced, steamed fish is saltily flavored with fermented soybean sauce. Before she was able to eat spicy foods, my niece had a special fondness for fish steamed this way and frequently requested that I make it for her whenever she came to spend her summer break. Sometimes, when I was lazy, I simply shook the sauce straight from the narrow-necked bottle onto the lightly browned fish and steamed, without fussing with the other ingredients. That suited her fine as long as the fish was catfish fillets.

Of course, a good-quality fermented soybean sauce is crucial to produce a tasty result. Many brands are way too salty. Use the Healthy Boy brand from Thailand or Yeo's from Malaysia if you are able to find them. If you have no choice but the darker, more concentrated "yellow bean" sauce with the dragonfly logo, add more sugar and water to dilute its intense saltiness, and definitely cook a bit longer with the garlic and ginger.

Pan-Fried Mackerel and Assorted Vegetables with Hot-and-Pungent Fermented Shrimp Dipping Sauce
(Nahm Prik Bplah Too)

3 small mackerel, approximately 1½ lb. total
¼ to ½ tsp. fine sea salt
2 to 3 Tbs. dried shrimp
3 Tbs. good-quality shrimp paste (*gkabpi*)
Small piece of banana leaf or aluminum foil
10 cloves chopped garlic (about 2 generous Tbs.)
12-15 Thai chillies (*prik kee noo*), cut into thin rounds
Juice of 2 limes (about 4 to 5 Tbs.), to taste
3½ to 4 tsp. granulated or palm sugar, to taste

Assorted vegetables
10 green or long beans
4 to 6 cups morning glory
1 medium-size bitter melon
4 to 5 round Thai eggplants
1 to 2 long Asian eggplant
12 small okra

2 tsp. sea salt
1 beaten egg with a pinch of salt added
¼ to ½ cup oil, for pan-frying
1 to 2 Tbs. tapioca starch

Clean mackerel, rinse well, and drain. Rub evenly with a little salt, and let sit at least twenty minutes at room temperature before frying.

In a small, dry pan, roast dried shrimp over medium heat for several minutes, stirring frequently, until they have browned and become brittle and very fragrant. Cool a few minutes, then pound into a coarse powder with a mortar and wooden pestle. Transfer to a small sauce dish.

Wrap shrimp paste in a piece of banana leaf or aluminum foil and roast over the flames of a gas burner, holding the packet with a pair of tongs (or place directly on the heated coil of an electric burner). Turn frequently until leaf is charred and the aroma of shrimp paste is pronounced (5 or more minutes). Cool a few minutes, then peel back charred leaf or foil.

(continued on next page)

Pan-Fried Mackerel and Assorted Vegetables (cont.)

Pound garlic and half the chillies in the mortar until pasty. Add roasted shrimp paste and powdered roasted dried shrimp and pound together to blend. Add lime juice, sugar, and remaining chillies, stir well, and adjust flavors to make a sauce that is intensely hot, salty, and sour, with a slight sweetness. (If it is not salty enough, add a little fish sauce; since most shrimp pastes are already highly salted, it usually is not necessary.) Set aside for the flavors to mingle and marry.

Prepare vegetables. Trim and cut long or green beans into 2-inch segments. Snap morning glory into shorter stem-with-leaf segments. Cut bitter melon in half lengthwise, scoop out the seeds, and slice crosswise into ¼-inch pieces. Score round Thai eggplants deeply into quarters without cutting through. Slice the long eggplant at a sharp angle into ¼-inch ovals. Leave okra whole.

Bring 1½ quarts water to a boil in a medium saucepan. Add 2 teaspoons sea salt. One vegetable at a time, blanch green or long beans, morning glory, bitter melon, and okra until they are vibrant green and lightly cooked. Remove with a slotted spoon and drain. Leave Thai eggplants raw. Dip oval eggplant pieces in beaten egg one piece at a time, and pan-fry in a small amount of oil in a flat skillet until browned on both sides and softened. Arrange vegetables in separate piles on a serving platter.

Heat oil in a wok or skillet over high heat until it begins to smoke. Swirl to coat wok surface. Pat mackerel dry all over, including the body cavity, and dust lightly with tapioca starch. Fry in the hot oil for 3 to 5 minutes on each side (depending on size of fish), or until they are browned and cooked through. Transfer to a serving plate.

Serve the lightly cooked and raw vegetables and pan-fried fish with the fermented shrimp dipping sauce and plenty of plain, steamed rice.

Serves 6 to 8 in a multicourse, family-style meal.

Notes and Pointers:

If there is such a thing as a national dish in a country with such an overwhelming abundance of extraordinary foods, this combination of Thailand's favorite marine fish, *bplah too* (a small, short-bodied mackerel) and favorite *nahm prik* (pungent chilli dipping sauce) would have to be it. Despite its humble, peasant origins, this fish and dip is very popular among both poor and rich, though some of the more class conscious might limit their indulgence to the privacy of their home.

The very pungent shrimpy sauce may be an acquired taste to newcomers to the cuisine, but hardcore spicy food lovers who delight in strong, exotic flavors should have no trouble developing a taste for this treasured Thai combination. Of course, the key to a first-rate sauce lies in the quality of the shrimp paste which, after all, is the primary ingredient. Don't settle for just any *gkabpi* to make this sauce, but search for one with a fine, roasted aroma and not a strong, rotten stench. Among brands I've seen in America's Asian markets, *Pantainorasingh* and *Tra Chang* are among the best.

Imported, frozen, steamed *bplah too* in round, woven bamboo trays wrapped in plastic are available from some Southeast Asian markets, usually labeled *scomber*. The full-grown size of this mackerel native to the gulf of Thailand is no longer than ten inches. The precooked fish have usually been salted, so you need not salt or dust them with flour before pan-frying, should you find them to use for this recipe. Choose only plump ones with a silvery gray color. Since they're already cooked, fry only enough to brown and warm through. Even in Thailand, *bplah too* is most often sold precooked, to keep this perishable fish fresh tasting. Since the skin of fresh mackerel is fragile and has the tendency to stick, steaming ahead of time also firms the skin, making it less likely to peel off during frying.

Other vegetables may be used instead of the ones shown, the more exotic of which are described in chapter 4.

Mesquite-Grilled Mackerel Glazed with Sweet Soy Sauce

(Bplah Saba Yahng Si-ew)

One 1-lb. mackerel
3 Tbs. dark soy sauce
1 Tbs. black soy sauce (semisweet kind)
1 Tbs. oyster sauce
1 Tbs. rice wine or sake
1 tsp. pure sesame oil
½ tsp. ground white pepper
1½ to 2 tsp. granulated sugar
Pickled ginger and pickled garlic, as desired

Gut and clean fish, cutting off head and tail. Rinse and drain well. Score the fish about ¾-inch apart on both sides in a crisscross diamond pattern. Pat surface and body cavity dry with a clean towel.

Mix the two kinds of soy sauces, oyster sauce, rice wine or sake, sesame oil, white pepper, and sugar and marinate the fish in the mixture for one-half hour or more.

Place mackerel in a grilling basket with a handle, and grill over medium-hot mesquite charcoals for 6 to 8 minutes on each side, or until the fish is cooked through, turning occasionally. Baste with remaining marinade with each turn.

When fish is cooked through, transfer to a serving platter. If any marinade is left, heat in a small saucepan to boiling. Reduce for 30 seconds to 1 minute over medium heat, and spoon over the mackerel. Serve as you wish with pickled ginger and pickled garlic.

Serves 2 to 3 with rice and other dishes in a family-style meal.

Notes and Pointers:

Thailand's boom years brought an influx of Japanese businesspeople, investors, and tourists into the country. To serve their needs, restaurants serving Japanese cuisine mushroomed in big cities, and established restaurants started adding Japanese dishes to their menu. Some dishes became so popular among locals that they found their way into mainstream Thai menus. Of course, some changed character as Thai chefs added their own twists.

Because Thai people are already quite fond of the taste of their own local variety mackerel (*bplah too*), the Japanese-style mackerel (*bplah saba*) caught on easily, and is now commonly seen grilling on the streets and in the markets of coastal towns. Whenever my husband and I vacation in the southern towns of Songkla and Trang, we never miss ordering this grilled fish from our favorite restaurants. These two towns do not particularly see that many Japanese businesspeople or tourists, but they do make wonderful renditions of this Japanese-style grilled fish.

Use whatever kind of fresh or fresh-frozen mackerel you are able to find, or try the marinade in this recipe with tuna, albacore, shark, swordfish, or mahi mahi.

Flounder Simmered in Spicy Sauce
(Bplah Dtom Saep)

1 lb. large fillet of flounder or Dover sole
8 whole white peppercorns
6 cloves garlic, chopped
6 to 10 Thai chillies (*prik kee noo*), cut into ¼-inch rounds
3 shallots, chopped
1 Tbs. palm sugar
1 cup water
1 Tbs. finely slivered, peeled fresh ginger
1 Tbs. peanut oil
2 to 3 Tbs. fish sauce (*nahm bplah*), to taste
2 to 3 short cilantro sprigs, for garnish

Rinse fish and drain well. Cut fillet in half. In a mortar and pestle, pulverize peppercorns. Add garlic and chillies and pound together till pasty. Add chopped shallots, and continue to pound to make a coarse, well-blended paste.

Spoon palm sugar into a wok and add 1 teaspoon water. Heat over low to medium heat, and stir until the sugar has turned dark reddish brown but not burned. Add remaining water and crushed ingredients. Bring to a boil over high heat, stirring to dissolve palm sugar.

Add ginger, oil, and fish sauce. Stir to mix, then follow with the fish. Return to a boil before lowering heat to a level at which the sauce simmers gently. After 5 minutes, turn fish over and continue to cook uncovered until it is cooked through and sauce has thickened. If a lot of sauce remains, remove fish from the wok onto a serving dish. Increase heat to high and reduce sauce by one-third to one-half. Spoon over fish and garnish with cilantro sprigs.

Serves 3 to 4 with other dishes and rice in a family-style meal.

Notes and Pointers:
Inspired by the simple, spicy dishes in everyday cooking in the northeastern region, this light but fiery dish can be made with a minimum of effort. It can be served soupy, or the sauce can be reduced as suggested, to thicken and concentrate flavors. Like many spicy Thai dishes, it makes good leftovers.

Try this recipe also with red snapper, rock cod, or halibut steaks. Sauce is also excellent for poaching seabass and swordfish.

"Three-Flavored" Grouper or Rock Fish with Roasted Garlic and Roasted Chillies

(Bplah Gkow Tawd Sahm Roet)

One 1½-lb. whole grouper or rock fish
⅓ tsp. fine sea salt
⅛ tsp. ground white pepper
2 large heads garlic
10 to 15 large dried red chillies
2 pinches of salt
5 to 8 fresh Thai chillies (*prik kee noo*), cut into
     thin rounds
2 Tbs. fish sauce (*nahm bplah*), to taste
1 Tbs. lime juice
2 Tbs. thick tamarind juice, the consistency of fruit concentrate,
     or to taste
3 Tbs. palm sugar, or to taste
1½ to 2 cups peanut oil
1 to 2 Tbs. tapioca starch or cornstarch
Fresh red chilli, finely slivered, for garnish
Cilantro sprigs, for garnish

Scale, gut and clean fish, keeping head, tail, and fins attached. Rinse and drain well. Holding a knife with the blade at a 45-degree angle to the surface of the fish, cut slanted gashes to bone level on both sides of the fish, about 1½ inches apart. Rub fish all over, including body cavity, with a little salt and white pepper. Set aside at room temperature at least 20 minutes before cooking.

Preheat oven to 450° F. Separate the garlic into individual cloves; cut off the root tip of each clove, leaving the peel on. Roast for about 10 minutes, or until softened (but not mushy) and slightly charred. Peel; if the cloves are large and fat, cut in half lengthwise.

In a dry pan, roast dried chillies with a couple of pinches of salt over medium heat, stirring frequently, until chillies are dark red and lightly charred. Cut off stem tips and soak in tepid water for 15 minutes to one-half hour. When they have softened, drain and cut into rounds about ⅛ to ¼ inch thick. In a small bowl, combine fish sauce, lime juice, tamarind juice, and palm sugar. Stir well to dissolve palm sugar. Taste and adjust to desired combination of salty, sour, and sweet flavors, keeping in mind that the sauce will be slightly sweeter when the palm sugar is thoroughly melted during cooking.

Heat oil in a wok until it begins to smoke. While waiting, coat fish thoroughly with tapioca starch, including head, tail, fins, and body cavity. When the oil is hot enough to sizzle a piece of garlic, swirl to

(continued on next page)

coat a wide area of the wok surface. Holding fish by the tail, gently slide it head first into the oil. There should be enough oil to submerge at least two-thirds of the fish. Fry over medium-high heat (medium if you have a very hot stove), tilting the wok occasionally from side to side so that both the head and tail sizzle in the hot oil. Fry the first side until it is a rich golden brown color, crispy from head to tail, and dried through (about 10 minutes). Nudging the wok spatula under the fish from the top edge, gently flip it over on its belly and fry the second side, also to a crisp. Transfer to a wire rack or shallow wire-mesh strainer to drain.

Remove all but 3 tablespoons oil from the wok, reserving the rest for future use in frying fish or cooking seafood dishes. Increase heat to high and add roasted garlic, roasted chillies, and fresh Thai chillies. Sauté for 20 to 30 seconds. Add sweet and sour seasonings. Stir well, and heat to boiling to meld all the flavors. Taste and adjust as needed. The sauce should be equally salty, sour, and sweet.

Arrange fish on a serving platter and top with the sweet-and-sour, roasted garlic and roasted chilli sauce. Garnish with slivered red chilli and cilantro. Serve immediately, while fish is still crispy.

Serves 3 to 4 with rice and other dishes in a family-style meal. Crunch on the crispy fins, tail, and head for a delicious source of calcium!

Notes and Pointers:

In the language of Thai cuisine, "three-flavored fish" (*bplah sahm roet*) describes fried fish topped with a sauce that is salty, sweet, and sour. Of course, the thick, reddish sauce is also hot with chillies. Dishes with this name appear on the menus of most Thai seafood restaurants, but can taste quite different, as different chefs add their own special touches.

This recipe is inspired by an outstanding version made by one of my favorite restaurants on the Gulf of Thailand. Named after the chef-owner, Sunee is one of those simple, inconspicuous, open-air, seafood eateries that dot the long peninsula leading to the southern region. Nothing fancy, just worn, scratched tables with stools under flapping tarps overlooking a quiet stretch of shoreline. The most fabulous food, though, comes out from the kitchen, and I have never had anything there less than superb. Sunee loads on the garlic and chillies in her "three-flavored fish," but the heat is tempered by the sweetness of the tangy sauce. She uses grouper, fresh from the sea, though my husband has found that the sauce is also excellent with an ugly, mean-looking, mottled yellow, dark China cod, which he once bought from the local fish market to try with my recipe. It fries up extra crunchy crispy. Try this recipe also with other kinds of rock fish, red snapper, and any fish willing to fry up wonderfully crispy.

Pan-Fried Halibut Topped with Chilli-Tamarind Sauce
(Bplah Rad Prik)

1 lb. halibut steak(s)

¼ tsp. sea salt

⅛ tsp. ground white pepper

8 cloves garlic, minced

4 fresh jalapeno or fresno peppers, preferably red, minced with seeds

2 shallots, minced

1-inch section fresh galanga (or substitute with peeled fresh ginger), minced

1 Tbs. minced cilantro roots or bottom stems

10 white peppercorns, finely ground

¼ to ½ cup peanut oil

2 to 3 Tbs. tapioca starch or cornstarch

2 to 3 Tbs. fish sauce (nahm bplah), to taste

1 Tbs. palm sugar or more, to taste

½ cup tamarind juice (1-inch chunk wet tamarind dissolved in about ½ cup of water, pulp removed), or to taste

½ cup Thai sweet basil (bai horapa) leaves, flower buds may also be used

A few sprigs of cilantro or Thai sweet basil (bai horapa), for garnish

Rinse fish and drain. Rub evenly with a thin coating of salt and white pepper. If the fish has been refrigerated, let it sit at room temperature for at least 20 minutes before frying.

Mince garlic, red chilli peppers, shallots, galanga, and cilantro roots or stems. Do not seed the chillies unless you wish the sauce to be mild. For a medium-hot dish, remove the seeds from half the chillies. Using a large, heavy mortar and pestle, pulverize the peppercorns. Add the minced aromatics, stir to mix, and pound for a few minutes to blend.

Heat oil in a frying pan or wok. Coat fish with a thin layer of tapioca starch and fry in the oil until browned on both sides and cooked through to your liking (about 6 to 8 minutes on each side). Cooking time will depend on thickness of fish steak(s). Transfer to a serving platter.

Remove all but 2 tablespoons of remaining oil from the pan. Add chilli mixture and sauté over medium-high heat until the flavors and aromas are released (about 3 minutes). Make sure the fan over the stove is turned on, as chilli fumes may irritate the throat. Season with fish sauce, palm sugar, and tamarind juice as desired. The sauce should be equally salty and sour, with sweetness in the background. The consistency should be that of a thick salsa; if it seems too dry, thin it with 2 to 3 tablespoons of water. Cook another minute or two to blend the flavors; stir in basil leaves and cook just enough to wilt.

(continued on next page)

Pan-Fried Halibut Topped with Chilli-Tamarind Sauce (cont.)

Spread sauce evenly over fish and garnish with sprigs of cilantro or Thai sweet basil.

Serve hot with plain steamed rice and other dishes. Serves 3 to 4 in a family-style meal.

Notes and Pointers:

Like "three-flavored fish," this common dish of seafood restaurants can have many different incarnations, although the same name, meaning "fish smothered with chilli sauce," appears from menu to menu. I have combined in this recipe the strong points from several scrumptious renditions I've had at seaside restaurants on the beautiful southwestern coast where I frequently vacation.

The tangy chilli sauce usually tops crispy fried fish, which is what you'd get if you ordered *bplah rad prik* in Thailand. I frequently smother the sauce over crisped whole snapper, but it really is good over fish cooked other ways, too, such as grilled, broiled, baked, poached, and steamed. My friends love it over charcoal-grilled salmon and one once told me the fresh abalone he pried from a rock on a diving trip was excellent dipped in it.

Spicy Crisped Fish
with Wilted Basil and Seasonings
(Bplah Rad Prik Horapa)

One 1-lb. fresh whole fish—cod, red snapper, bass, perch, sheepshead, sea bream,
    or other similar fish
1 Tbs. minced garlic
5 to 8 Thai chillies (*prik kee noo*), preferably red, cut into ¼-inch rounds, including
    seeds
1 orange or red serrano pepper, cut into thin rounds with seeds
1 cup peanut oil, for frying
A squeeze or two of lime juice
1 to 2 Tbs. tapioca starch (or cornstarch)
1½ to 2 Tbs. fish sauce (*nahm bplah*), to taste
1 tsp. granulated sugar, or to taste
½ cup (packed) Thai basil leaves (*bai horapa*)
1 Tbs. water or unsalted stock
1 serrano or jalapeno pepper, preferably orange or red, cut into small slivers
Basil sprig, for garnish

Scale, gut, and clean fish, leaving head and tail attached. Rinse and drain well. Cut slanted gashes to bone level an inch apart on both sides of fish. Let sit at room temperature at least 20 minutes before cooking.

Pound garlic, Thai chillies, and serrano rounds with a mortar and pestle to reduce them to a coarse paste.

Heat oil in a wok until it begins to smoke. While waiting for it to heat, pat surface of fish dry, and squeeze just enough lime juice to lightly coat its surface. Then, coat with a thin layer of tapioca starch (or cornstarch), from head to tail, under the cheeks, and inside the body cavity.

When oil is hot enough to sizzle a small piece of garlic, swirl to coat a wide area of the wok surface. Holding the fish by the tail, gently slide it into the oil. If you have a very hot stove, reduce heat to medium or medium-high. Fry fish, tilting wok from side to side, from time to time, so that the entire fish is evenly fried in the oil. Fry about 7 to 10 minutes on each side (frying time depends on thickness of fish used), or until fish is a rich golden brown and evenly crispy.

Transfer to a wire rack to drain. Remove all but 1 tablespoon oil remaining in the wok, reserving the rest for future use in frying fish. Stir in the chilli–garlic mixture and sauté over medium heat for 20 to 30 seconds, until aromatic and flavors are blended. Add fish sauce and sugar, then basil. Stir a few sec-

(continued on next page)

onds, then add a tablespoon of water or stock. Increase heat to high and continue to toss basil with seasonings until it is wilted but bright green. There should be a small amount of sauce surrounding the basil and chillies—just enough to lightly coat the fish. (Too much sauce will turn the crispy fish soggy.) If the sauce has dried, add another 1 to 2 tablespoons water and cook a few seconds longer to blend with the seasonings. Stir in slivered chillies and turn off heat.

Spoon out half the mixture and spread remainder over an area of the wok large enough to accommodate the fish. Return fish to wok, placing it on the area of the wok containing the flavorings. Spread reserved half of the mixture over the top side of the fish. Transfer to a serving plate and garnish with a basil sprig.

The fish is intensely hot and salty, and is not meant to be eaten by itself. Serve with plenty of steamed rice.

Serves 2 to 3 with rice in a multicourse family-style meal. Crunch on the crispy fins, head, and tail for a delicious source of natural calcium.

Notes and Pointers:

When my mother was hospitalized a couple of years ago, my husband and I spent most of our time keeping her company in her homey private room. On the first day, we were amazed by the quality of the food on the tray the nurse brought for her first meal there. Every one of the three dishes accompanying the rice not only looked delicious but exuded wonderful aromas as well, making us both very hungry.

We soon discovered that the same three dishes were being served in the hospital cafeteria, along with numerous other great-looking entrees. No wonder the cafeteria was so crowded, and choices so difficult to make. After much indecisive lingering, our hunger dictated that we should point to four different items and be content. One of them was a small, whole fish so perfectly seasoned with chillies, fish sauce, and basil that, by itself, our stomachs were more than satisfied, but everything else was superb, too.

Though fried fish with chillies and basil is a common, everyday food, it was the intricate balance of flavor that made our dining experience at the hospital so memorable. Needless to say, we ate almost all our meals there, and even after Mother returned home from the hospital, we made sure follow-up appointments were made near the lunch hour so that we might enjoy yet another meal.

Besides whole fish, try this recipe with fish cut into steaks, such as halibut, grouper, snapper, and barracuda. Or, instead of pan-fried fish, the chilli–basil seasonings can also be smeared onto grilled fish steaks.

Garlic–Black Bean Pan-Fried Red Snapper
(Bplah Gkapong Daeng Jian Dtow See)

1 lb. red snapper fillets
1 head garlic, finely chopped
1- to 1½-inch piece fresh ginger, and finely chopped
2 tsp. chopped cilantro roots or bottom stems
3 Tbs. dried salted black beans
1 Tbs. dark soy sauce
2 tsp. sugar
2 Tbs. rice wine
½ cup peanut oil
½ to 1 tsp. ground dried red chillies, or coarsely ground peppercorns
A few sprigs of cilantro

If the snapper fillets are large, cut them in half crosswise. In all, there should be approximately 6 pieces of fish. Set aside at room temperature for at least 20 minutes before cooking.

Prepare the garlic, ginger, and cilantro roots (or stems). Chop salted black beans to a crumbly texture, without any whole beans remaining. Mix the soy sauce, sugar, and rice wine.

Heat oil in a wok or skillet over high heat until it is hot enough to sizzle a small piece of garlic. Pat snapper fillets dry with a towel, and fry in the hot oil for 1½ to 2 minutes on each side, or until they are lightly browned but not cooked through. Gently transfer to a plate without breaking the fillets. Fry in two separate batches if your wok or skillet is not very large.

Remove oil from the wok or skillet, reserving for future use in cooking fish. Wipe the pan clean and reheat over medium heat with 2 tablespoons reserved oil. Add garlic, ginger, and cilantro roots or stems, stirring frequently until aromatic. Add soy sauce mixture. Sprinkle in ground chillies or peppercorns as desired. Stir well and cook for ½ to 1 minute, or until the seasonings are well blended. Remove half the mixture from the wok and spread remaining half over enough of the cooking surface to accommodate the fish pieces. (Or you may wish to do the remaining cooking in two batches if your pan is not very big, in which case, remove three-fourths of the seasoning mixture.)

Place fish in a single layer over the seasonings, along with any juices which may have sweated out on the plate. Spread reserved seasoning mixture evenly over the top of the fish pieces. Cook over medium to medium-high heat for 1 to 2 minutes, then turn, and cook the other side, keeping the pieces well coated with the seasonings as much as possible. When fish is cooked through, transfer to a serving platter and spread whatever seasonings remain in the pan over the fish pieces. Garnish with cilantro.

Serves 5 to 6 with other dishes and rice in a family-style meal.

(continued on next page)

Garlic–Black Bean Pan-Fried Red Snapper (cont.)

Notes and Pointers:

Salted black beans are really a Chinese ingredient, but they have a pungent taste that is liked by people who love strong flavors, Thais included. I always keep a bag around in my pantry in case I need to improvise when time does not permit me to run down to the local Southeast Asian market. In fact, this recipe was born out of such improvisation.

I had forgotten to transport two pounds of fresh red snapper fillets to a cooking class I taught in Napa valley, two hours from my home. While the fish was originally destined for a red curried mousse, when I returned home following the class, I neither had red curry paste left, nor the energy to do anything fancy with it. The salted black beans came to the rescue and, not long after, a huge plate of blackened snapper appeared on the dinner table. My husband and a visiting friend were both delighted and insisted that I write down the recipe and include it in this book. After all, it was born out of a Thai cooking class.

Because it is salty, not much is needed to accompany it beyond a plate of rice. Whatever is left-over keeps well for many days in the refrigerator. Besides snapper, improvise with other similar fish fillets readily available.

Pompano Steamed with Pickled Plum

(Bplah Jeramed Neung Buay)

One 1-lb. fresh pompano or white pomfret
3 pickled salted plums
2 tsp. light soy sauce
2 tsp. pickled plum brine
1 tsp. granulated sugar
¼ cup pork cut into very thin matchstick-size
    strips
2 Tbs. finely slivered young ginger
1 red serrano, jalapeno, or fresno pepper, finely
    slivered with seeds
¼ cup Chinese celery leaves and tender stems

Gut and clean fish and rinse well. Cut slanted gashes to bone level on both sides of fish about 1½ inches apart. Place on a heatproof serving dish that fits on the rack of a stacked steamer. The dish should have some depth to catch juices that may steam out of the fish.

Pit pickled plums and cut and mash into small pieces in a small bowl. In another bowl, mix the light soy sauce, pickled plum brine, and sugar. Stir well to dissolve sugar before blending in the pickled plums. Add pork strips and stir well to coat all the pieces with the seasonings. Spread pork mixture evenly over fish and top with slivered ginger and red pepper.

Bring 2 inches of water to a boil on the bottom of a steamer pot. Place the dish with the fish on a steamer rack, and place over the pot and cover. Steam over high heat for 15 minutes, or until the fish is cooked through. Garnish with Chinese celery.

Serves 2 to 3 with other dishes and rice in a family-style meal.

Notes and Pointers:

Highly prized, both pompano and its Asian counterpart, white pomfret, possess a delicacy of flavor that is most pleasing to the palate. In this recipe, their rich and exquisite flavor is undisguised and enhanced by the sour plums. Serve this mild and delicate fish with other more heavily spiced dishes to give your tongue a gentle resting place.

If you do not eat red meat, use dried shitake or dried Chinese mushrooms, instead of pork. Soak in hot water to soften (about ½ hour), then slice caps into thin strips. Though best with pompano and pomfret, try this recipe with other very fresh fish with good flavor, such as trout, butterfish, shad, perch, striped bass, and sheepshead.

Steamed Fillet of Sea Bass with Ginger, Green Onions, and Sesame-Soy Sauce

(Bplah Hihma Neung Si-ew)

1 lb. fillet of Chilean sea bass, about 1- to 1-½ inches thick
1- to 1½-inch piece ginger
6 cloves garlic
2 green onions
¼ cup soy sauce
1 tsp. pure sesame oil
½ to 1 tsp. powdered dried red chilli
½ tsp. rice vinegar
1½ to 2 tsp. sugar, to taste

Place fish in a 2- to 3-inch deep heatproof serving dish that fits inside the rack of a stacked steamer. If you do not have a steamer, use a pot large and deep enough to accommodate the dish for steaming.

Peel ginger and slice into thin pieces. Stack several pieces at a time and cut into fine slivers. Peel the garlic cloves and slice into thin oval pieces. Arrange both evenly over fish.

Cut green onions into 2-inch segments, using the white and half the green parts. Then cut each segment lengthwise into fine slivers. Set aside.

In a small bowl, combine soy sauce, sesame oil, powdered chilli, vinegar, and sugar. Stir to blend. Spoon over fish without dislodging garlic and ginger.

Bring 2 inches of water to a boil in a steamer pot before placing the dish holding the fish on a rack above it. Or, if using a large pot, fill with 1½ inches of water and place a trivet, inverted bowl, or a vegetable steamer rack (with handle removed) inside the pot to lift the dish holding the fish from the bottom of the pot. Bring to a boil, cover, and steam over medium-high heat for about 10 minutes. (Steaming time will depend on thickness of fillet.)

Reduce heat to low, lift the cover, and wait for the hot burst of steam to dissipate before sprinkling slivered green onions over the top of fish. Replace cover, return heat to medium-high, and steam 1 to 2 minutes, or until the fish is cooked through and green onions wilted.

Serves 4 to 5 with plain steamed rice and other dishes in a family-style meal.

Notes and Pointers:

Most steamed fish dishes in Thai cuisine have origins in the cooking of ethnic Chinese, who settled in the region generations ago. Steaming is a method of cooking in which the Chinese excel. Many seafood restaurants in Bangkok are owned and operated by Chinese Thais, offering a wide range of dishes, from those unmistakably Thai with the fullness of herb and spice flavors to milder, steamed dishes with a definitely Chinese touch. A common steamed fish dish is a simple one combining the goodness of a fine quality soy sauce with the exquisite flavor of very fresh fish.

While the soy sauce used is usually a delicately flavored, light soy sauce, in this recipe, I have paired full-flavored dark soy sauce with the rich flavor and creamy texture of Chilean sea bass. For best results, use a top-quality, naturally brewed soy sauce. My personal preference is the Super Special Soy Sauce with the Kimlan label, imported from Taiwan.

Since this recipe is so easy to make and produces both an exceptionally delicious and impressive-looking dish, it is one that you may wish to keep in mind when you have limited time to cook, yet wish to entertain special guests in your home. In fact, that's what I frequently do, and my husband doesn't mind a bit, because he absolutely loves sea bass cooked this way.

If Chilean sea bass isn't within your budget, try this recipe with halibut, red sea perch, rock cod, or snapper, whether in fillets or in steaks. Fresh crab (in unshelled chunks) is also good steamed this way.

Mom's Good and Easy Steamed Fish
(Bplah Neung)

One 1-lb. very fresh whole fish—white or sea perch, striped bass, rock cod, red
    snapper, red grouper, sheepshead, porgy, or bream
¼ tsp. fine sea salt
6 cloves garlic, peeled and sliced into thin ovals
6 to 10 Thai chillies (*prik kee noo*), cut into thin rounds
1 Tbs. finely slivered, peeled fresh ginger
1 green onion, cut into thin rounds (use white and half of green)
3 to 4 Tbs. peanut oil
1 to 2 Tbs. light soy sauce, or fish sauce (*nahm bplah*)
½ to 1 tsp. sugar
Juice of ½ to 1 lime, to taste

Clean fish, removing the guts, gills, and scales. Rinse and drain. Cut 2 slanted gashes to bone level on both sides of fish, about 1½ inches apart. Sprinkle with a thin layer of salt and rub evenly over fish, including body cavity and gashes. Set aside.

Heat a wok over high heat until its surface is smoking hot. Swirl in oil to coat its surface and wait 15 to 20 seconds for it to heat. Gently slide fish into the wok and fry 1 to 2 minutes on each side, enough to lightly brown. Transfer to a shallow, heatproof serving dish that fits on the rack of a stacked steamer. Arrange garlic, chillies, and ginger evenly over fish. Sprinkle with light soy sauce or fish sauce and sugar. Spoon 1 to 2 tablespoons of hot oil remaining in the wok over the top. The oil should be hot enough to sizzle the garlic pieces.

Bring 1½ to 2 inches of water to a boil in the steamer pot before placing the rack with the fish over it. Cover and steam over high heat for about 8 minutes. Lift lid and sprinkle green onion pieces over fish. Cover and steam another minute. Turn off heat and immediately lift the lid to prevent steam from condensing onto the fish. Remove from steamer, squeeze lime juice over the top, and serve while still hot.

Serves 2 to 3 with rice and other dishes in a family-style meal.

Notes and Pointers:

My mother is a great cook. During her prime cooking years, she could duplicate just about any restaurant dish she had sampled and make it better. She also improved on old family recipes, and created many of her own signature dishes. Friends knew of her cooking talents and frequently came to visit close to mealtimes. But both my parents are generous and would graciously invite our uninvited guests to dine with us. Mother would quickly whip up another dish or two, improvising with whatever she could find in the kitchen and refrigerator to put together very tasty, impromptu masterpieces.

We always had fish in one form or another in the refrigerator. After all, fish is a staple food in our home, as it is in most Thai homes. This recipe is one of the frequent dishes she would make when she was short on time. As many times as I have watched her make it, mine just never comes out quite as good. But these days, she is no longer cooking and I am proud when she tells me that I make a darn good steamed fish.

Steamed Whole Fish with Chilli-Lime Sauce
(Bplah Neung Manao)

One 1- to 1½-lb. very fresh whole fish—sea perch, striped bass, trout, gouramy,
    pompano, rock cod, red snapper, porgy, bream, or other similar fish
Bottom half of two stalks of lemon grass
10 large cloves garlic, chopped
15 to 20 green and red Thai chillies (*prik kee noo*), cut into very thin rounds
1 Tbs. chopped cilantro roots, or 1½ Tbs. chopped stems
2 to 3 Tbs. fish sauce (*nahm bplah*)
¼ cup lime juice (about 1½ to 2 limes)
1 tsp. granulated sugar
¼ cup unsalted chicken broth
1 green onion, cut into thin rounds (use white and most of green parts)

Scale, gut, and clean the fish. Rinse and drain. Cut slanted gashes to bone level on both sides of fish 1½ inches apart.

Trim off woody bottom tip and top half of lemon grass stalks and remove loose outer layers. Bruise with the side of a cleaver or knife handle. Stuff into body cavity of fish. Arrange fish on a heatproof serving dish about 2 inches deep, that fits on the rack of a stacked steamer, or improvise a makeshift steamer large enough to accommodate the fish (see page 86).

Mix chopped garlic, chillies, and cilantro roots or stems with chicken broth. Add fish sauce, lime juice, and sugar to make a hot, salty, and limy sauce. Spoon and spread evenly over fish.

Bring 1½ to 2 inches of water to a boil in the steamer pot before placing the rack holding the fish dish over the pot. Cover and steam over medium-high heat for 12 to 14 minutes. Lift lid and sprinkle with the green onions. Cover and steam 1 to 2 minutes longer, or until fish is cooked through. Serve while fish is still hot.

Serves 3 to 4 with rice and other dishes in a family-style meal.

Notes and Pointers:

This is the most popular of Thai steamed whole fish dishes, enjoyed by people both in coastal provinces and inland. The hot lime sauce flavors freshwater fish as often as marine fish. Sometimes partially presteamed fish is actually simmered in the sauce and served on a fish-shaped metal dish over a charcoal burner. Just about any tender, mild to moderately flavored fish that steams well without drying can be prepared this way.

Some people prefer the fresh flavor of Thai chillies, so instead of steaming the fish with the sauce, the fish is steamed directly on a steamer rack lined with a section of banana leaf. After it is cooked, it is gently transferred to a serving platter and topped with the sauce. When done this way, the color of the chillies looks fresher and the lime juice is sharper in flavor. If you do take this alternative route, skip the green onions.

Braised Whole Tilapia
with Ginger and Green Onions
(Bplah Nin Jian King Dton Hawm)

One 1½-lb. whole tilapia
3 Tbs. dark soy sauce
3 Tbs. rice wine
1½ Tbs. Chinese black vinegar
3 tsp. sugar
⅓ cup peanut oil
¼ cup plus 2 Tbs. finely slivered, peeled fresh ginger
4 green onions, cut into very thin rounds (both white and most of green)

Clean fish, rinse, and drain. Cut 2 to 3 slanted gashes to bone level on both sides of the fish, about 1½ inches apart.

In a small bowl, mix soy sauce, rice wine, black vinegar, and sugar until well blended.

Heat a wok, or a skillet large enough to contain fish, over high heat until it is hot enough to quickly evaporate a drop of water. Swirl in oil to coat the wok surface; for a flat skillet, fill with about ¼ inch of oil. When oil is hot, pat fish dry and gently slide into the pan. Fry 1½ to 2 minutes, tilting the wok from side to side to allow the hot oil to evenly brown the fish from head to tail. Gently flip the fish over on its belly and brown the second side 1½ minutes.

Reduce heat to medium and remove fish from pan. Spoon out all but 1 to 2 tablespoons of the oil. Toss in slivered ginger and sauté until golden brown. Spread ginger over enough of the wok surface to accommodate the fish, and place fish over the ginger. Sprinkle with half the green onions and spoon half the sauce over the fish. Cook over medium to medium-high heat for 2 to 3 minutes, or until the sauce is mostly dried up, tilting the wok from side to side as necessary so that both ends are braised in the sauce. Turn the fish, and sprinkle with remaining green onions and sauce. Cook another 2 to 3 minutes.

Check fish for doneness; the thickest part just below the head should be flaky down to the bone and no longer pink. If the fish is not cooked through and the sauce has dried up, add 1 to 2 tablespoons of water and cook another 1 to 2 minutes.

Carefully transfer to a serving platter. Spoon remaining pieces of ginger and green onions over the top.

Serves 3 to 4 with rice and other dishes in a family-style meal.

Notes and Pointers:

This is an old family recipe from a Chinese ancestry. My mother made it from time to time while I was growing up. It was one of those simple, mild dishes that made fish taste so delicate and delicious to a child, enough to make me empty my plate of rice every time it was served. But then, mother's cooking was so good I seldom had problems finishing my rice.

Tilapia braised in this sauce really does taste delicate, as does perch, cod, striped bass, and other mild, medium- to medium-firm, white flesh fish.

Charcoal-Roasted Striped Bass in Banana Leaf Served with Hot-and-Sour Dipping Sauce
(Bplah Pow)

One 1½-lb. whole striped bass
A squeeze or two of lime juice
½ tsp. white peppercorns
6 to 8 cloves garlic
1 Tbs. chopped cilantro roots plus 1 Tbs. chopped cilantro stems; if roots are not
    available, use 2 to 3 Tbs. chopped stems
1 Tbs. Thai oyster sauce
2 Tbs. light soy sauce, or fish sauce (*nahm bplah*)
2 to 3 tsp. peanut oil
Banana leaf, large enough to wrap around fish once or twice
Aluminum foil
Slices of tomato, cucumber, or pineapple, to line serving platter
Hot-and-Sour Fermented Soybean Dipping Sauce (recipe follows)

Clean fish, removing scales, guts, and gills. Rinse and drain well. Rub a small amount of lime juice evenly all over fish. Set aside.

Pulverize white peppercorns in a heavy stone mortar. Add garlic, cilantro roots and stems, and pound to form a paste. Mix with oyster sauce and light soy sauce (or fish sauce). Coat fish evenly with the peppery mixture, including the body cavity. Allow to marinate for about one-half hour.

Clean surface of a banana leaf. Brush oil to liberally coat one side of the leaf. Place fish with marinade over the leaf and wrap it around once or twice. Then wrap with aluminum foil, sealing the edges.

Roast directly over medium-hot charcoals, turning fish from time to time until it is cooked through, about 15 minutes. Remove foil and most of the banana leaf, except the small section on which the fish rests. Place on a serving platter and arrange slices of tomato, cucumber, and/or pineapple along the edge. Serve with dipping sauce.

Serves 3 to 4 with rice and other dishes in a family-style meal.

Hot-and-Sour Fermented Soybean Dipping Sauce
4 to 8 Thai chillies (*prik kee noo*), cut into thin rounds
4 to 5 cloves garlic, chopped (or about 1 Tbs.)
1 tsp. chopped cilantro root or bottom stems
1 Tbs. fermented soybean sauce
Juice of 1 to 2 limes (about 3 Tbs.), to taste
1 to 2 tsp. granulated sugar, to taste

Pound chopped chillies, garlic, and cilantro root or stems in a mortar and pestle until pasty. Add fermented soybean sauce and mash well to reduce any whole beans into paste. Transfer to a sauce dish and add lime juice and sugar to taste. Adjust flavors so that the sauce is equally salty and sour, with a light touch of sweetness. Let sit at least 15 minutes to allow the flavors to mingle and marry.

Notes and Pointers:

Although the fish is grilled over charcoal, it actually is steamed in its own juices inside the banana leaves. For a smoky dimension, unwrap the package during the last few minutes of cooking and cover the barbecue kettle to keep in the smoke. A few moistened wood chips added at this time will help create stronger smoke.

This method of grilling fish is suitable for tender, lean fish, which shouldn't be grilled directly on the coals as the flesh will dry out and lose flavor. Fatty fish are more suitable for direct grilling, but would not fare as well with this method. Try this recipe with delicate to medium-firm, mild to moderately flavored fish.

Mesquite-Grilled-and-Smoked Fish with Piquant Sour Tamarind Sauce
(Bplah Roem Kwan)

One 1½-lb. whole fish, preferably a variety with relatively high fat content
½ tsp. sea salt
Mesquite charcoal and wood chips

Piquant Sour Tamarind Sauce:
¼ cup tamarind juice, the thickness of fruit concentrate
1 tsp. sea salt
1 Tbs. sugar
5 to 8 Thai chillies (*prik kee noo*), cut into thin rounds
2 Tbs. chopped garlic
1 small shallot, quartered lengthwise, and sliced very thinly crosswise
1 tsp. lime juice

Scale and clean fish, removing guts and gills. Rinse and drain well. Cut a series of slanted gashes to bone level about an inch apart on both sides of the fish. Rub all over with salt and set aside.

Prepare a barbecue kettle with a lid for grilling. Soak a handful of mesquite wood chips. Start mesquite coals and, when they are thoroughly red and starting to gray with ashes, spread them along the edges of the kettle so that the fish can be grilled in the center away from the hot coals (indirect method). Drain the soaked chips and scatter them around on top of the coals. Place the fish in the center of the grill and cover. Make sure the venting holes on the bottom of the kettle and on the cover are fully opened so that the coals do not die out. Turn fish every 5 minutes and cook until it is smoked and cooked through (about 25 minutes).

While fish is grilling, make the sauce. Combine tamarind juice, salt, and sugar in a small saucepan and heat over low to medium heat to boiling. Stir well to dissolve salt and sugar and blend them with the tamarind. Remove from heat and let cool a few minutes. Pound chillies and garlic to a paste with a mortar and pestle. Add to partially cooled sauce along with sliced shallot and a teaspoon of lime juice. Stir well, and transfer to a sauce bowl to serve alongside the grilled fish.

Serves 3 to 4 with rice and other dishes in a family-style meal.

Notes and Pointers:
In Thailand, a frequently used fuel for smoking fish is the dried outer husk of coconut. It produces plenty of smoke without being very hot; therefore, fish cooks slowly and picks up a wonderful

smoky flavor. Now that coconut husk is not available to me where I live, mesquite charcoal and mesquite wood chips are doing an excellent job in producing the strong smoky taste I so love with grilled fish. If you are not able to find mesquite wood chips where you live, substitute with other kinds of wood chips that produce good smoke. If the chips are very dry, soaking them before using will make them smolder rather than burn up quickly on top of the hot charcoal.

7

CRUSTACEANS

Roasted Chilli Paste   175

Homemade Shrimp Chips   177

Crispy Shrimp-and-Crab Toast with Sesame Seeds, Served with Sweet-and-Sour Plum Sauce   179

Dancing Shrimp   181

Country-Style Hot-and-Sour Prawn Soup with Aromatic Herbs and Oyster Mushrooms   182

Hot-and-Sour Shrimp Salad with Roasted Chilli Sauce, Lemon Grass, and Mint   184

Charcoal-Grilled Prawn Salad   186

Savory Shrimp Cakes, Served with Sweet-and-Sour Cucumber Relish   188

Crispy Garlic-and-Pepper-Encrusted Shrimp   191

Steamed Tiger Prawns   193

Spicy *Prik King* Shrimp   194

Choo Chee Red Curry Shrimp with Kaffir Lime Leaves and Basil   196

Charcoal-Grilled Jumbo Prawns or Lobster Tails Topped with Sour Tamarind Sauce   198

Spicy Southern-Style Stir-Fried Shrimp with *Sadtaw* or Fava Beans   199

Shrimp Cooked in Turmeric Coconut Sauce   201

Tiger Prawns Steamed with Garlic and Thai Chillies   202

Hot-and-Sour Lemon-Grass Tiger Prawns   203

Southern-Style Spicy Tamarind Prawns with Crisped Shallots and Garlic   205

Cashew Shrimp   207

"Five-Flavored" Shrimp with Toasted Sesame Seeds   209

Prawns and Bean Thread in Clay Pot   211

Charcoal-Grilled Prawns, "Sweet Fish Sauce," and *Sadao* or Neem Leaves   213

Fried Crab Cakes   215

Stuffed Crab Shells with Hot Pickled Garlic Sauce   216

Steamed or Grilled Dungeness Crab Served with Chilli-Lime Dipping Sauce   218

Stir-Fried Crab with Yellow Curry Sauce   219

Wok-Tossed Crab in the Shell with Green Onions   221

Black-Peppered Crab with Roasted Spices   223

Wok-Tossed Shelled Crab with Chillies, Garlic, and Crisped Holy Basil   225

Crab Fried Rice   227

Huge river prawns so fresh their lustrous shells still sparkle in lovely shades of blue never fail to grab the attention of first-time visitors to the kingdom as they step through the gate of Bangkok's riverside restaurants. Behind the ice-covered tables on which they are displayed, charcoal grills let off mouth-watering fumes as chosen specimens sizzle to pink excellence. How can such tantalizing queens of crustaceans be resisted?

Meanwhile, along idyllic stretches of beach on a pearl of an island, other tourists stand awed in front of seafood counters in open-air restaurants. On the ice lie monstrous spiny lobsters in speckled, blue-gray armor, so fresh they might just lunge out at any second at suspected prey. Alongside are mounds of enormous tiger prawns and neatly arranged rows of spotted crabs in dazzling rainbow colors. Those seafood lovers, deprived of such luscious beauties of the sea where they live, momentarily imagine that they must be in crustacean heaven!

Crustaceans make up the second largest seafood category in Thailand, not only in terms of number of varieties and quantities consumed, but also in the widely varied ways in which they can be prepared. Aquatic invertebrates protected by hard shells, they include shrimp, prawns, lobsters, and crabs, from both marine and freshwater sources. The hardness of their shells vary from species to species, as well as in different stages of the growth cycle, as they shed and replace their shells to allow their bodies to grow.

Although the words "shrimp" and "prawns" are synonymous and can refer to the same creature, I have chosen to use them both to roughly distinguish the smaller shrimp from the larger prawns, however hazy the dividing line may be. It just doesn't sound right to call a tiger prawn "tiger shrimp," or a jumbo prawn "jumbo shrimp." In the Thai language, shrimp, prawns, and lobsters are all *gkoong*—*gkoong lek* (*lek* means small) for shrimp, *gkoong yai* (*yai* means big) for prawns, and *gkoong mungkawn* (*mungkawn* means dragon) for lobsters. More frequently, we refer to these crustaceans by their particular variety's name and the size is implied.

Except for crayfish, most Americans know of crustaceans as saltwater creatures. In the wet, tropical environment of Thailand's inland areas, crustaceans also abound and can range in size from miniscule shrimp—scooped up by the netful to be stirred whole into batters and deep-fried into crunchy shrimp cakes, or tossed live with spicy lime sauces to be served as salads—to giant river prawns weighing as much as two pounds or more. Freshwater crabs are plentiful, too, but most are small and caught for salting and pickling to be used as a flavoring ingredient in such nationally renowned dishes as green papaya salad and salted crab-coconut dip for vegetables (recipe, page 47).

How to Select and Tell Freshness

Shrimp and Prawns: Unless you live along one of America's coasts, most shrimp and prawns available to you most likely have been frozen before. Flash-frozen seafood products can still be good, but make sure they have not been sitting in market freezers for too long, or have not been previously defrosted and refrozen. When selecting frozen bags, avoid those with frost inside the packages; also check carefully that there are no signs of freezer burn on the crustaceans themselves. Uncooked shrimp and prawns should not have a pronounced pinkish cast, which may suggest freezer burn.

Unfrozen shrimp and prawns from seafood markets should have a shiny luster on their shells to indicate freshness. Their flesh is held tightly inside firm, intact shells. White shrimp should have clear shells, revealing the light brownish color of the flesh, and should not have brown, black, or dry spots. Choose tiger prawns with shiny striped shells that are bluish-gray or light brownish-gray in color. Of course, whatever kind they are they should smell mildly of the sea, and not have a fishy or ammoniac smell. For Thai-style cooking, do not use precooked shrimp unless fresh and frozen raw shrimp aren't available. Also avoid preshelled raw shrimp, which often are not very fresh and have lost some flavor.

Many Asian markets that carry frozen seafood products will have shrimp and prawns in varying sizes, packaged in frozen blocks of four to five pounds, or loose-packed in two-pound bags. Marked on the boxes or bags are the sizes, given in the approximate number of the crustaceans per pound, and an indication of whether they come with or without heads, if that isn't already clearly visible. For example, if marked "26–30," this means *one* pound has about twenty-six to thirty prawns with heads or without heads. Small, headless sizes include "41–50" and "36–40," and medium, "31–35" and "26–30." These are the most common sizes used for everyday Thai-style dishes. Larger prawns are also available, ranging from two per pound and up, although most of the imported, large prawns from Asian waters will have heads still attached. Asians, Thais included, love the rich-tasting fluids, roe, and bits of meat inside the heads.

If the stores near you seldom carry jumbo sizes, substitute small to medium shrimp in recipes that call for larger prawns or lobsters. Adjust cooking times accordingly.

Crabs and Lobsters: Whenever possible, buy crabs and lobsters still alive and kicking. Many fishmongers have tanks filled with live crustaceans, but their availability is usually seasonal. Select a lively one with all its limbs still intact and with a good weight for its size. Its eyes and legs should move when approached by net, hand, or tongs. Male crabs generally have more meat than females; the latter wear a larger apron (flap) on the bottom side for holding eggs. For most Thai dishes, flavor is best if these crustaceans are raw before they are tossed into the wok with herbs and spices, into seafood soups, or on the charcoal grill.

After living so many years in the San Francisco Bay Area, my preference for the delectable Dungeness crab probably shows through in the recipes. Of course, you need not use them. Feel free to use other kinds of fresh crabs available where you live. Adjust the cooking times to suit the size of the crabs. Cook until they are just cooked through with flesh still moist and sweet.

If you live inland, where it just isn't possible to find live crabs or lobsters, substitute frozen cooked crustaceans if they are available, or adapt the recipes to cook with shrimp and other shellfish.

How to Clean and Prepare for Cooking

Shrimp and Prawns: Peel back the shell, starting from the legs and unwrapping it around. The question of whether to leave the tail on is a matter of aesthetics. Shrimp and prawns look prettier and larger when cooked, if their tails and the section of shell closest to the tails are left on. However, because the meat inside this part of the shell is often not eaten and wasted, I have devised a way to keep the tail looking pretty without the shell, to satisfy those people who prefer to eat these crustaceans completely shell-less.

After peeling the shell back to the end, gently squeeze down on the upper parts of the tail, fanning it out as you do, to loosen the little bit of flesh that attaches the tail shell to the shrimp. Then, pull from the very tip of the tail, removing the tail shell. What you will end up with is a complete shrimp with a nude tail that, when cooked, is better looking than one with truncated rear end. Of course, this may take a little bit of practice to learn just the right amount of pressure to apply and just the right places to squeeze to turn out shrimp with lovely shell-less tails and a tiny bit of extra meat to eat.

After the shell has been completely removed, butterfly the shrimp and prawns by cutting deeply (just short of cutting through) up the middle of the back opposite from where the legs were attached, and about three-quarters of the way toward the tail. Use a sharp knife to make a clean cut. Remove any black veins. Most imported farm-raised shrimp and prawns have clean veins that are barely visible because they have been weaned from food for a certain number of hours before being harvested. Butterflying helps shrimp and prawns cook more quickly and evenly.

Some of my students use a gadget that supposedly deveins and shells the shrimp all at once. I tried it but do not like it because it shreds the flesh of the shrimp rather than making a clean cut as a sharp knife would.

When cooking larger prawns Thai-style, the shells are left on to hold in their sweet juices, so that the outer parts of the flesh do not dry out before the center is cooked. This is especially important if the prawns are to be grilled. Butterfly them in their shell by cutting the shell up the middle of the back with a pair of scissors, then follow with a sharp knife as described.

The recipes that follow give the amount of shrimp or prawns to use in their headless, uncleaned weight. Depending on the size, they lose approximately fifteen to twenty percent of their weight after they're shelled.

Crabs and Lobsters: If you are squeamish about killing and cleaning live crabs, most specialty fish markets will take care of it for you. Just ask someone behind the counter to clean it after you've selected the liveliest one from the tank. He will pull the crab open, remove the gills, cut it down the middle into two halves if you wish, and rinse it thoroughly. Make sure he gives you the back shell, which holds the rich-tasting butter that can enhance the flavors of stir-fried crab, or that can be saved to make crab fried rice.

If you have to deal with the live crab yourself, you might stun it first by dipping in boiling water for a minute, before trying to pull it apart and cutting it up (do likewise with lobster). For best flavor in stir-fried dishes, the crab or lobster should be raw when it is tossed into the wok so that its flesh absorbs the seasonings as it cooks. For recipes using cooked crabmeat, I still prefer to start out with a live crab if it's available and cook and shell it myself, unless you can be sure that the cooked crab from the market is truly fresh. Store-bought, shelled, cooked crabmeat is not only expensive, but often not very fresh.

Instead of cooking in hot boiling water, which washes out some of the flavor into the water, I steam the crab in my stacked metal steamer (see page 85). First, bring two to three inches of water to a boil in the steamer pot. Place a steamer rack over the pot and the crab in the rack with its back shell faced down; if the crab has already been pulled apart and cleaned by the fishmonger, put the body of the crab with the exposed flesh faced down on its inverted shell. Cover tightly with a lid (if the crab is still alive, place an inverted mortar or other heavy weight on top of the pot) and steam over high heat. A one-and-a-half-pound Dungeness crab cooks in twelve to fifteen minutes, and smaller blue crabs take only about half the time. Steaming retains the sweetness of the crab and most of its tasty juices, some of which will be contained in the bowl-like back shell. If the recipe does not require the flavorful crab juice, save for soup stocks or stir-fried seafood dishes that require cooking liquid.

How Long to Keep

Since fresh crustaceans are very perishable, they should be cooked and eaten as quickly as possible after they are purchased, preferably the same day. This is imperative for fresh crabs and lobsters, unless they are still alive. Keep shrimp and prawns refrigerated no longer than a couple of days. If you wish to keep them a little bit longer, shell them and salt lightly—rinse off the salt before cooking. If they are frozen when bought, do not keep them in the freezer for much longer than a month, and defrost on the day that they will be cooked. Avoid refreezing without first cooking them.

After cooking with lots of garlic, chillies, and spices, the crustaceans can keep longer than if they are cooked plain without seasonings. The antiseptic qualities of herbs and spices preserve them for up to a week in the refrigerator—that is, if they are very fresh when they are cooked.

How to Freshen Shrimp and Prawns

Because most shrimp and prawns have been through a lot before they find their way to your home—having been caught, packed, frozen, transported over long distances, hauled from packer to distributor to retail store, from one freezing unit to another, then finally defrosted and left on ice before someone comes along and buys them—they usually are a bit exhausted, dehydrated, or maybe a little freezer burned, and can benefit from a rejuvenating saltwater bath. Place them in a bowl and add sea salt and water to barely cover. For each pound, use one generous teaspoon of sea salt and one-half cup of water. Mix with your hand for a few seconds to dissolve the salt and gently massage the shrimp. Set aside for five to ten minutes. The water will quickly turn gray and murky. Rinse thoroughly in plenty of cool water to remove all the salt. Drain well. For stir-fried dishes, make sure they are not wet when you are ready to cook; if they are, pat dry with a clean towel.

Soaking the shrimp in their own element—sea-salted water—helps perk them up, giving them a fresher smell and, when cooked, a crisp, succulent texture. Some that really have been dehydrated by prolonged freezing may even grow in size.

Some Cooking Tips

Do not overcook crustaceans, as they will dry out and harden, losing their tender, succulent texture and sweet, tasty juices. It is better to lightly under-cook as surrounding steam will continue to cook them after they have been removed from the heat.

Small to medium shrimp and prawns cook very quickly in boiling liquid. When blanching for a seafood salad, add to the water after it has come to a boil and cook over high heat only twenty to thirty seconds. Drain immediately. Shrimp will continue to cook until they are tossed in with herbs and the hot-and-sour chilli sauce, which cooks them further. In soups, bring the broth to a rolling boil over high heat before adding them. Stir and turn off heat after twenty seconds. Serve immediately, as the shrimp and prawns will continue to cook in the hot broth.

Stir-frying, although done over high heat, does not cook the crustaceans as quickly as when they are completely immersed in boiling liquids. Only the surfaces touching the hot metal in the pan are subjected to the high heat, so toss frequently to ensure that they are evenly seared. Butterflying them before cooking makes it easier to tell when they are cooked—just check the inside of the cut to see if it has turned pink and opaque. I usually dish them out of the wok when the very end of the cut is still a little translucent, as they will continue to cook after they are removed from the pan. Cooking times depend both on the size of the pieces and the heat of your stove but, roughly, medium prawns should be ready in about two minutes.

Shrimp/prawn shells make a wonderful soup stock, so don't throw away. If you won't be using them right away, rinse, drain, and store in a zipper bag in the freezer. When making stock, cover with water and bring to a boil. Reduce heat and simmer fifteen to twenty minutes. You need not add salt or anything else to the stock if it is to be used for a Thai-style seafood soup that will be flavored with fish sauce and plenty of herbs.

If you are blanching several kinds of seafood for a seafood salad, use just enough water to cook them, fishing them out with a wire-mesh scooper and saving the flavored water to make seafood stock. Water from steaming crabs and lobsters may also be saved for stock. The liquid keeps for a few days in the refrigerator; discard when it picks up a strong fishy odor. If you wish to keep it longer, freeze it.

Save the back shells of small blue crabs for stuffing or to use as containers for serving seafood. Scrub and clean well and let dry before storing.

Roasted Chilli Paste
(Nahm Prik Pow)

1½ cups thinly sliced shallots (about 8 to 10 heads)
1 cup thinly sliced garlic (about 30 to 40 cloves, or 3 to 4 heads)
¾ cup peanut oil
25 to 30 dried red chillies (½ to ¾ cup)
¼ tsp. salt
½ cup dried shrimp
1½ Tbs. shrimp paste (*gkabpi*)
Small piece of banana leaf or aluminum foil
2½ to 3 Tbs. tamarind juice, consistency of fruit concentrate
1 to 2 Tbs. fish sauce (*nahm bplah*), to taste
⅓ to ½ cup palm sugar, to taste
2 Tbs. water

Spread sliced shallots and garlic in a single layer on a platter or cookie sheet and allow to dry out for several hours or a day in a well-ventilated room. To hasten the drying process, place under an electric fan, in the sun, in a slightly warm oven, or in a dehydrator.

When they are sufficiently dried, fry shallots in peanut oil in a wok over medium heat, stirring occasionally until they turn golden. Continue to fry, stirring constantly until the pieces evenly turn medium brown. Strain from oil with a fine wire-mesh skimmer. Add dried garlic to oil and fry, stirring frequently until golden brown. Strain from oil and drain thoroughly. Leave remaining oil in the wok for later use.

In a dry cast-iron pan, roast dried red chillies with salt over medium heat, stirring frequently until they are dark red. (Salt reduces chilli fumes.) Remove from pan, wipe pan clean, and roast dried shrimp, stirring frequently until they are fragrant and lightly browned. Let both chillies and dried shrimp cool before grinding to a fine powder in a clean coffee grinder or spice mill.

Wrap shrimp paste in a small piece of banana leaf or aluminum foil and roast for a few minutes directly in the flame of a gas burner, holding the packet with a pair of tongs (or place directly on a hot electric coil). Turn frequently until leaf is well charred and the aroma of the shrimp paste strongly comes through. Let cool.

When fried garlic and shallots have cooled, grind each separately in a food processor or clean coffee grinder. Transfer to a heavy stone mortar and pound each by itself until completely reduced. Then, combine the two with ground chillies and dried shrimp. Mix well and pound together (in two or three batches if your mortar is small) until all ingredients are of one texture. Cut roasted shrimp paste into small chunks and add to the mixture. Continue to pound until well blended.

(continued on next page)

Combine 2½ tablespoons tamarind juice, I tablespoon fish sauce, ⅓ cup palm sugar, and 2 tablespoons water in a small dish and set aside.

Reheat wok with remaining oil. Add chilli mixture and fry over medium heat until fragrant. Stir in the seasoning mixture. Reduce heat to the lowest setting and slowly "roast" the mixture, with frequent stirring, until flavors have become fully integrated and mixture thickened to a dark, burnt red color. Taste and make adjustments as necessary by adding a bit more fish sauce, palm sugar, and/or tamarind to the desired combination. The paste should be noticeably sweet.

Transfer to a clean jar. Cover when cool and store in the refrigerator.

Use this homemade chilli paste in recipes calling for *nahm prik pow* (roasted chilli paste), or serve as a condiment for rice, as a jam for toast and crackers, or as a spread for fried pork rinds and shrimp chips.

Makes about 2 cups. Keeps for several months.

Notes and Pointers:

Shrimp-based, roasted chilli paste is an important flavoring ingredient in Thai cooking and, although it is available in several brands from Southeast Asian markets, nothing compares to the full-flavored paste this recipe yields. After you have made yourself a jar, stir-fry shrimp, squid, scallops, clams, fish, and whatever seafood you desire with it (recipes, pages 106, 249); or spoon some in to flavor hot-and-sour soups (page 100) and limy dressings for seafood salads (page 249).

The garlic and shallots may also be fried without predrying. Because shallots contain a fair amount of juice, it is important that they are fried over low heat for a prolonged period of time so that they dry out before they begin to brown. This may take 20 minutes or longer. As for garlic, it can be fried at medium heat and will brown and crisp much faster.

Crispy fried garlic and shallots are also available in plastic bags or small containers in many Asian markets. To substitute these packaged products for the fresh aromatics, use ¾ cup of each. Though these substitutes save time, they generally do not produce as fresh tasting a paste.

Spicy Seafood Sizzling Hot Plate,
page 278.

Wok-Tossed Mussels in the Shell with Lemon Grass and Basil,
page 272.

Baked Oysters with Salted Black Beans and Pickled Garlic,
page 256.

*Charcoal-Roasted Striped Bass in Banana Leaf Served
with Hot-and-Sour Dipping Sauce, page 162.*

Hot-and-Sour Lemon Grass Tiger Prawns,
page 203.

*"Three-Flavored" Grouper or Rock Fish with Roasted Garlic
and Roasted Chillies, page 145.*

Stir-Fried Crab with Yellow Curry Sauce,
page 219.

Crispy Garlic-and-Pepper-
Encrusted Shrimp,
page 191.

Charcoal-Grilled Prawn Salad,
page 186.

Sizzling Stir-Fried Squid with Chillies and Fragrant Herbs,
page 246.

*Hot-and-Sour, Pan-Fried Trout Soup with Roasted Chillies
and Aromatic Herbs, page 100.*

Choo Chee *Red Curry Shrimp with Kaffir Lime Leaves
and Basil, page 196.*

Wok-Tossed Salmon with Chillies and Thai Basil,
page 126.

Shrimp Cooked in Turmeric Coconut Sauce,
page 201.

*Marinated Mesquite-Grilled Scallops
Served with Sweet-and-Tangy Dipping
Sauce, page 260.*

Detail

Homemade Shrimp Chips
(Kao Gkriep Gkoong)

½ lb. fresh shrimp
2 tsp. white peppercorns, ground finely
1 tablespoon minced garlic
1½ cups tapioca starch
1½ tsp. sea salt
1 tsp. turmeric powder
¼ cup water
3 cups of peanut oil, for deep-frying

Shell shrimp and reduce to a fine smooth paste in a food processor.

Place ground peppercorns in a heavy stone mortar and run the pestle over it to make sure it is completely reduced to dust. Add the garlic and pound into a fine, well-blended paste. Add shrimp and continue to pound until none of the ingredients are distinguishable.

In a medium bowl, combine the tapioca starch, salt, and turmeric. Add the peppery shrimp mixture and knead into the flour. Gradually add water, just enough to work into a dough. *Use as little water as possible* to prevent dough from becoming gooey when cooked, making it difficult to slice into very thin chips. Do not fluff the flour, but compress the moistened bits into a compacted dough. Knead well. Divide the dough into two rounds. Roll each with the palms of your hands to form a log about 1½ inches in diameter.

Fill a steamer pot with 2 inches of water and bring to a boil. Line a steamer rack with enough parchment paper to hold the 2 logs; take care not to cover up all the holes. Place logs 2 inches apart on the paper and place the rack over the steamer pot. Cover rack with a clean towel, leaving a small opening in one corner to allow steam to escape, then secure with lid. The cloth prevents condensed steam from dripping onto the dough. Steam over medium-high heat for 30 minutes.

Remove steamed logs from steamer rack as soon as the heat is turned off, by lifting the edges of the parchment paper. Let cool on a wire rack for half an hour, or until surface dries, before removing the parchment paper and letting the other side dry.

When surface has completely dried, wrap in plastic wrap and freeze for an hour or two, or long enough for the logs to harden sufficiently for easy slicing. The logs may also be completely frozen and defrosted about one-half hour to one hour before slicing. Slice as thinly as possible, shaving with a sharp knife into rounds no thicker than ¹⁄₁₆ inch. (If they are too thick, the chips will not puff well and will be chewy and hard, not crispy.) Arrange on a wire rack positioned over a baking sheet and place in the oven at the lowest setting (around 150° F). Let dry for 2 hours or more, or until chips have completely hardened and turned brittle.

(continued on next page)

Puff and crisp dried chips by frying in plenty of hot oil in a wok over medium to medium-high heat. The oil should be hot enough for chips to puff quickly but not turn dark and burn swiftly. Do not use too low a heat, as chips will not puff to their full potential and end up being hard, not crunchy. Drop only a few at a time into the oil, as they really do puff up to many times their size and take up a lot of wok space.

The chips are done when they stop puffing and are fried to a pleasant golden brown with an orangish tint. Use a pair of chopsticks or a large wire-mesh scooper with bamboo handle to remove them from the oil.

Dried chips store well in an airtight jar or zipper bag in a cool place in the pantry. They taste best when fried just before serving.

Serves 8 to 10 as an appetizer or snack.

Notes and Pointers:

During my growing-up years, my family took frequent vacations on the seacoast. On the way, we would stop to pick up snacks to nibble on in the car and over the weekend on the beach.

Without fail, shrimp chips would be among the provisions. They came in huge bags but, whenever one was opened, it emptied quickly.

Today, I still stop to pick up bags of chips on drives down the southern peninsula. The best are puffed from chips made under the *Manora* label, with origins in the seacoast province of Songkla in the deep south. In fact, cooking students who traveled with me on my homegrown cultural tours so loved the very shrimpy and peppery chips they couldn't resist picking up a bag or two of the unpuffed chips to take home with them. One bag, when puffed, can easily fill a large, kitchen garbage bag.

Not only snacked on in Thailand, shrimp chips are very well liked in most Pacific Rim countries. Many Chinese markets in this country carry boxes of dried chips that are colored white, pink, purple, and yellow, but I find them totally uninteresting as they have little, if any, shrimp flavor at all. They also do not have much of a crunch and get soggy easily. Superior are the *krupruk* chips from Indonesia, which are naturally colored like *Manora* chips, with the orangey tint of cooked shrimp, enhanced with a little turmeric. They have a more substantial, long-lasting crunch, though *Manora* still comes out ahead with its spicy pepperiness. Unfortunately, *Manora* chips are not available except at a few specialty Thai markets in this country.

With this recipe, you can now come closer to experiencing the shrimpy shrimp chips you've had on your travels to Southeast Asia without much effort. Make yourself a big supply, as the dried chips keep well. While you are at it, make extras to give away to family and friends for the holidays. Whenever you have a craving for the crunchy chips, just drop a small handful into hot oil and watch them mysteriously puff up. Making them, though, is no mystery.

Crispy Shrimp-and-Crab Toast with Sesame Seeds, Served with Sweet-and-Sour Plum Sauce

(Kanom Bpahng Nah Gkoong Sai Bpoo)

⅔ of a sourdough baguette
¾ lb. fresh shrimp
¾ cup shelled, cooked crabmeat
15 white peppercorns, finely ground
4 large cloves garlic, minced
2 to 3 tsp. minced cilantro roots or bottom stems (not leaves)
½ tsp. sea salt
1 tsp. sugar
2 to 3 tsp. fish sauce (*nahm bplah*), to taste
1 egg, beaten
2 Tbs. sesame seeds
2 cups peanut oil, for deep frying
Cilantro leaves and finely slivered red chilli pepper, for garnish
Cucumber slices and pickled ginger
Spicy sweet-and-sour plum sauce (recipe follows), or your favorite bottled hot
    chilli sauce

Cut baguette into slices ¼- to ⅓-inch thin. Arrange on a baking sheet and dry in a warm oven (200° F) about 20 minutes, or until they are completely dried out. Set aside.

Shell shrimp (no need to butterfly and devein) and reduce to paste in a food processor. Mix with flaked, cooked crabmeat in a mixing bowl. Using a heavy mortar and pestle, pulverize the peppercorns as finely as possible. Add minced garlic and cilantro roots/stems and pound to make a fine paste. Spoon paste into the bowl, along with salt, sugar, fish sauce, and beaten egg. Mix well with shrimp and crab.

Spread shrimp mixture over baguette slices, mounding about twice the thickness of the bread, and rounding it along the edges. Lightly sprinkle with sesame seeds, and gently press to stick to the spread.

Heat oil in a wok or skillet until it is hot. Fry over medium heat spread side down 1½ to 2 minutes, or until golden brown. If the bread side has not browned, turn over to brown for just a few seconds. Remove from oil; drain and cool briefly on a wire rack with toast lying either on its side or with bread side up.

Top each piece of toast with a small cilantro leaf and sliver of red chilli. Arrange on a serving platter bordered with cucumber slices and pickled ginger. Serve while still warm and crispy with spicy plum sauce (recipe below) or your favorite bottled chilli sauce.

Serves 10 to 12 as an appetizer or snack.

(continued on next page)

Spicy Sweet-and-Sour Plum Dipping Sauce

2 red serrano or jalapeno peppers, or substitute with 1 tsp. ground dried red
  chillies
3 pickled salted plums
⅓ cup granulated sugar
3 Tbs. white vinegar

Seed the fresh peppers and chop, then reduce to paste with a mortar and pestle. Pit the plums and mash the pulp with the chilli paste. Transfer to a small saucepan and add sugar and vinegar. Heat over low to medium heat, stirring until sugar is melted. Simmer a few minutes, or until mixture is smooth and has thickened to the consistency of light syrup. Transfer to a sauce dish and cool before serving.

Notes and Pointers:

A small, nondescript, mom-and-pop cafe in the southern seaport town of Songkla spills over onto the sidewalk on weekends as crowds gather for breakfast before setting out for bargains in the bustling Sunday bazaar nearby. Among numerous eclectic offerings is the very popular pork toast — a seasoned mixture of chopped pork piled over white bread and deep-fried. A bit rich for breakfast, but memorable.

Such savory toasts served as snacks, appetizers, or breakfast by small cafes, streetside food stalls, and restaurants are usually made with pork, or a mixture of pork and shrimp, and white sandwich bread. To create a lighter version, I have replaced both filling and bread, and added my own fusion twist in this recipe. A seasoned mixture of shrimp and crab goes over thin slices of toasted sourdough baguette — the pride and joy of bakeries in the San Francisco Bay Area. In fact, the baguette does yield an end result much crispier and lighter than the more oil-absorbent white bread.

The crunchy toasts with savory filling make a wonderful party food. To save on last-minute preparation, the shrimp-and-crab mixture may be prepared a day ahead and stored in the refrigerator. Spread on dried pieces of baguette the afternoon of your party and fry shortly before serving. Because the shrimp will shrink when it is cooked, make sure to mound plenty on each piece of baguette.

Instead of the spicy plum sauce, cucumber slices, and pickled ginger, the toasts may also be served with a cucumber relish, like the one for shrimp cakes on page 189.

Dancing Shrimp
(Gkoong Dten)

¾ lb. medium, very fresh, sushi-grade ocean shrimp
10 to 15 small Thai chillies (*prik kee noo*), cut into thin rounds
12 cloves garlic, chopped
2 to 3 Tbs. fish sauce (*nahm bplah*), to taste
Juice of 2 limes, or 3 to 4 Tbs.
1 to 2 tsp. granulated sugar, to taste
1 green onion (white part only), chopped
2 Tbs. coarsely chopped cilantro
½ cup mint leaves (leave small leaves whole, tear large ones into
    small pieces)

Shell and butterfly shrimp. Keep raw, or sear quickly over red hot coals to partially cook. Arrange on a serving platter.

Crush the chillies and garlic together with a heavy mortar and pestle to make a coarse paste. Add fish sauce and lime juice. Stir in a small amount of sugar to blend and intensify the sour flavor without making the sauce sweet. Stir well to blend.

Spoon sauce over shrimp and sprinkle with chopped green onion, cilantro, and mint leaves.

Serves 3 to 4 as an appetizer in a multicourse family-style meal.

Notes and Pointers:
Truly live *dancing shrimp* served at various locales along the Maekong River are made with miniature freshwater shrimp. But, to be safe, it is best to use ocean shrimp to avoid the risk of contamination from animal waste that may have washed into freshwater sources. With all the chillies and garlic, it could very well be that microbes are killed off, as purported by some who love the live shrimp dancing down their throats.

If the shrimp are soaked in the incendiary sauce long enough, the lime juice will cook them and turn them pink, but their texture will remain lusciously tender and their sweet, natural flavor will be retained.

Country-Style Hot-and-Sour Prawn Soup with Aromatic Herbs and Oyster Mushrooms
(Dtom Yâm Gkoong)

½ lb. medium to large tiger prawns

3 stalks fresh lemon grass

8 to 10 thin slices fresh galanga, or 3 dried pieces

4 fresh or dried kaffir lime leaves

3 cups water, or unsalted seafood stock

3 to 4 Tbs. fish sauce (*nahm bplah*), to the desired saltiness

6 to 10 dried red chillies

Pinch of salt

6 to 10 whole Thai chillies (*prik kee noo*), stem removed and bruised; or
    substitute 2 to 3 sliced jalapeno or serrano peppers with seeds

½ a small onion, halved again lengthwise and sliced crosswise ¼-inch thick

2 Tbs. roasted chilli paste (*nahm prik pow*)

3 Tbs. tamarind juice the thickness of fruit concentrate

⅓ to ½ lb. fresh oyster mushrooms, leave small caps whole and cut large ones
    into pieces of similar size to the small caps (use stems also); or substitute
    brown mushrooms, sliced ¼-inch thick

1 firm medium tomato, cut into bite-size wedges, optional

2 green onions, cut into thin rounds (use most of green part also)

½ cup cilantro leaves or short cilantro sprigs

Juice of 1 to 2 limes, to the desired sourness

Shell, devein, and butterfly prawns, saving shells for stock. Give them a saltwater bath to freshen (page 173), then rinse well in several changes of water and drain.

Trim and discard woody bottom tip of lemon grass stalks and the loose outer layer(s). Cut stalks at a sharp slanted angle an inch apart all the way to about two inches below where the grass blades fan out. Smash pieces with the side of a cleaver, or handle of a heavy knife, to bruise, releasing the aromatic oils. Place in a soup pot along with galanga slices, kaffir lime leaves, shrimp shells, and 3 cups water or mild stock. Bring to a boil, reduce heat, and simmer, covered, 20 to 30 minutes. Add fish sauce to desired saltiness.

Roast dried chillies in a small pan with a pinch of salt over medium heat, stirring frequently, until they are dark red and lightly charred. Cut crosswise into 2 to 3 segments each and set aside.

When stock is ready, strain out the herbs and shrimp shells. Add roasted chillies, bruised fresh Thai chillies (or substitute), and sliced onion. Simmer a few minutes, then add roasted chilli paste, tamarind juice, and mushrooms. Increase heat to high and return stock to a rolling boil. Add prawns and tomato wedges (if using), and green onions. After 20 to 30 seconds, turn off heat, stir in cilantro and lime juice to desired sourness. Serve immediately. Do not overcook prawns.

Serves 5 to 6 with other dishes and rice in a family-style meal.

Notes and Pointers:

Whether made with prawns, as in this recipe, or with fish or a combination of seafood, *ðtom yâm* is the quintessential Thai hot-and-sour soup, well-loved not only by Thais but also by people who have discovered Thai cuisine. Practically oil-less, the spicy and limy concoction is light and herbal, with warming and cleansing qualities that make it healthy to eat, in addition to being very satisfying to the palate and tummy.

As with many popular Thai dishes, *ðtom yâm* has many incarnations. Some are light in color and almost clear; others are so laden with chillies and chilli paste that a film of red floats on top of the broth. I have called this rendition of the soup "country-style," since it is deeper in color and heartier in flavor than the clearer versions. The roasted chillies, roasted chilli paste, and tamarind, not always used in *ðtom yâm*, give the broth a richer color and a greater depth of flavor. If homemade roasted chilli paste (recipe, page 175) is used, the soup is even more flavorful.

This recipe is great with a combination of seafood—fish, shrimp, squid, scallops, mussels, and chunks of crab in the shell. Make a big pot of broth, add the seafood in the order of cooking times required, and enjoy a sweat-inducing Thai-style bouillabaisse.

Hot-and-Sour Shrimp Salad with Roasted Chilli Sauce, Lemon Grass, and Mint
(Plah Gkoong)

½ lb. medium shrimp
4 to 6 Thai chillies, cut into thin rounds
1½ to 2 tsp. roasted chilli paste (nahm prik pow)
1 to 2 Tbs. fish sauce (nahm bplah), to taste
1½ to 2 Tbs. lime juice, to taste
1 to 2 tsp. granulated sugar, to taste
1 stalk lemon grass
1 shallot, halved lengthwise and sliced thinly crosswise
1 to 2 Tbs. coarsely chopped cilantro, sawleaf coriander, or parsley
3 to 4 Tbs. coarsely chopped mint leaves
3 cups boiling water
A couple of mint sprigs, for garnish

Shell, devein, and butterfly shrimp. Give them a saltwater bath to freshen (see page 173). Then rinse thoroughly with plenty of water and drain.

Mix Thai chillies with roasted chilli paste, fish sauce, lime juice, and sugar. Taste and adjust to the desired hot, sour, sweet, and salty combination. The sauce should be intense in all respects.

Trim and discard woody bottom tip of lemon grass and 2 to 3 of the loose, fibrous, outer layers. Slice stalk from the bottom end into very thin rounds, to yield roughly 3 tablespoons. Place in a mixing bowl with sliced shallot, coarsely chopped cilantro, and mint leaves.

Blanch shrimp in boiling water for 20 seconds, or until they turn pink on the outside but are not completely cooked through. Drain. The shrimp will be further cooked by the lime juice in the sauce.

Toss shrimp while still warm with herbs and the chilli–lime sauce. Stir well to coat shrimp. Transfer to a serving plate and garnish with mint sprigs.

Serves 2 to 3 with rice and other dishes in a family-style meal.

Notes and Pointers:

Hot-and-sour salads lie at the heart of Thai cuisine. There are so many different ways to make them and, even though they are essentially hot with chillies and sour with lime juice, the balance of flavor can be such that each is distinctly unique. In this book, I have included several of these spicy and limy salads—from fish to crustaceans to mollusks.

In this recipe, the sauce combines a subtle roasted dimension from the roasted chilli paste, with the heat of fresh chillies and the sharp sour of lime juice. Undercooking the shrimp helps them retain their natural sweetness and gives them a tender, moist texture. For a special, refreshing touch, slice a sour tangerine and toss with the shrimp, herbs, and sauce.

For a variation using jumbo-size prawns: Butterfly the prawns in their shell and grill over hot coals until they turn pink, are slightly charred, but remain a little undercooked. Arrange on a serving platter. Toss the herbs with the sauce and spread on top of the grilled prawns. Likewise, the seasoned herbs can be used on grilled lobster.

Try this recipe with squid, scallops, shelled mussels and clams, and bite-sized chunks of firm fish, or a combination of seafood. It is delicious with sea bass.

Charcoal-Grilled Prawn Salad

(Yâm Gkoong Pow)

1 lb. large prawns (12 to 16 per lb.), or crayfish
2 tsp. sea salt dissolved in 1 cup water
4 to 8 red Thai chillies (*prik kee noo*), cut into ¼-inch rounds
2 red serrano, jalapeno, or fresno peppers, cut into ¼-inch rounds with seeds
5 cloves garlic, minced (about 1 Tbs.)
3 Tbs. fish sauce (*nahm bplah*), or to taste
Juice of 1 to 2 limes, or 3 to 4 Tbs., to taste
2 to 3 tsp. granulated sugar, to taste
2 stalks lemon grass
2 to 3 shallots, halved lengthwise and thinly sliced crosswise
2 green onions (use white and half of green parts), cut into ⅛-inch rounds
½ cup mint leaves, torn into small pieces
Green leaf lettuce to line serving platter
1 small tomato, sliced into rounds
A few cilantro sprigs

Place prawns in a bowl and add salted water. Let sit about five minutes, then rinse thoroughly with plenty of fresh water to remove all the salt. With scissors, snip the shells of the prawns up the center of the back, opposite from the legs, about three-quarters of the way toward the tail. Using a sharp knife, butterfly the prawns in their shells, cutting deeply along the length of the back where the shells are cut. Remove any dark veins, but leave the shells on.

Start the charcoal grill. While waiting for the coals to get hot, prepare the remaining ingredients.

Crush the two kinds of chillies and garlic with a mortar and pestle to make a coarse paste. Add fish sauce, lime juice, and sugar. Stir well. Taste and adjust flavors so that the sauce is intensely hot, sour, and salty, with a little sweetness at the back of the tongue.

Trim and discard woody bottom tip and top third of lemon grass stalks, and peel off 2 to 3 of the loose, fibrous outer layers. Cut into very thin rounds and place in a mixing bowl with prepared shallots, green onions, and mint leaves.

Grill prawns over medium-hot coals for 2 to 4 minutes (cooking time depends on size of prawns), turning once or twice, until shells are pink and slightly charred and flesh a little undercooked. Prawns will be further cooked by lime juice in the dressing. Undercooking preserves the prawns' natural sweet flavor and gives them a tender, succulent texture. Grilling in the shell keeps them from drying out.

Toss grilled prawns with the limy chilli dressing, making sure they are all well coated. Add the herbs and toss lightly to mix. Arrange on a serving platter lined with lettuce leaves, encircled along the edges with the tomato slices. Garnish with cilantro sprigs.

Serves 4 to 5 with rice and other dishes in a family-style meal.

notes and Pointers:

Oil-less, aromatic, hot-and-sour salads are a favorite food in Thailand and, along the coast, lightly grilled fresh seafood makes a wonderful companion to the chilli-lime dressings and herbs so characteristic of Thai cuisine.

The smoky flavor of large, charcoal-grilled prawns adds a special dimension to this recipe — inspired by a specialty of the house at Kun Lin restaurant at Don Hoi Lod, a quiet stretch of the gulf coast a couple of hours' drive southwest of Bangkok. Here, under the shade of enormous trees along a mangrove swamp, cooled by soft sea breezes even on the hottest days of summer, and entertained by wild monkeys and talkative myna birds, lazy crowds nibble away on deliciously fresh seafood and sip on local rice whiskey. My husband and I happened upon this very special place with extraordinary food and captivating ambience on an exploration trip to this often passed-by stretch of coast, and ended up becoming regular customers, the distance notwithstanding.

Savory Shrimp Cakes, Served with Sweet-and-Sour Cucumber Relish

(Tawd Mân Gkoong)

1½ lb. fresh shrimp, shelled
4 to 8 dried red chillies, seeded and soaked to soften
1 tsp. minced kaffir lime peel (soak dried kaffir lime peel about ½ hour to soften before using)
6 cloves garlic, chopped
2 Tbs. minced cilantro roots, or substitute bottom stems
2 shallots, chopped
¼ tsp. white peppercorns, freshly ground
3 to 4 Tbs. fish sauce (*nahm bplah*), to taste
1 egg, beaten
10 string beans, trimmed and cut crosswise into very thin rounds
3 to 4 cups peanut oil, for deep frying
Sweet-and-sour cucumber relish (recipe follows)

Grind shrimp in a food processor as finely as possible, reducing to a sticky, gray paste. It is not necessary to devein or butterfly shrimp beforehand. Set aside.

When dried chillies have softened (about 20 to 30 minutes in tap water), chop finely and pound to a paste in a heavy stone mortar. Remove from mortar and pound remaining chopped and minced ingredients, one at a time, from kaffir lime peel to shallots, so that each is reduced to paste. Finally, combine all the reduced ingredients with ground white pepper and pound to form a well-blended paste.

Spoon one-third of ground shrimp and one-third of chilli paste into the mortar and pound to blend flavorings into shrimp. Repeat in two separate batches with the remaining shrimp and chilli paste. Combine and add fish sauce, egg, and string beans. Mix well.

Heat peanut oil in a wok over medium-high heat until it is sizzling hot—test with a small piece of garlic. Wet one hand in a bowlful of water, scoop up a small amount of shrimp mixture with your fingers, form with your thumb into a round flat patty about 1½- to 2-inches wide by ½-inch thick, and drop gently into the hot oil. To drop the patty, turn your hand upside down near the surface of the wok just above the oil and use your thumb to gently nudge the sticky patty from your fingers. Drop the patty as closely to the oil as possible to avoid splashing. Rewet hand before making the next patty to prevent the shrimp mixture from sticking to your fingers. Because the mixture is very sticky, do not make the patties ahead of time, but make them one at a time as you drop them into hot oil.

When the surface of the oil is filled with floating patties, stop making them and allow those in the wok to brown. Fry a few minutes, turning occasionally, until they are evenly browned. Remove from oil and drain on a rack or wire-mesh strainer. The patties puff up while frying but deflate when cooled. Continue making patties to fill the surface of the wok and frying them until all the paste is used.

Serve warm with the cucumber relish.

Serves 8 as an appetizer in a multicourse family-style meal.

Sweet-and-Sour Cucumber Relish
¼ cup white vinegar
1 Tbs. fresh lime juice
2 Tbs. fish sauce (*nahm bplah*), to taste
3 or more Tbs. granulated sugar, to desired sweetness
2 red jalapeno, serrano, or fresno peppers (do not remove seeds), chopped and
    pounded to a paste
2 large cloves garlic, chopped and pounded to a paste
2 medium pickling cucumbers, halved lengthwise and sliced thinly
2 shallots, halved lengthwise and sliced thinly crosswise
2 Tbs. coarsely chopped cilantro leaves
2 to 3 Tbs. coarsely chopped unsalted roasted peanuts

Combine the vinegar, lime juice, fish sauce, and sugar. Add the pounded hot peppers and garlic. Stir well. Adjust the flavors of the sauce to the desired sour, salty, and sweet combination.

Toss the cucumbers and shallots with the sauce and cilantro. Just before serving, sprinkle with chopped peanuts.

Notes and Pointers:
Fried fish cakes are among the most beloved of Thai snacks and appetizers. Huge wokfuls of them can be seen frying along sidewalks and in open-air markets across the country. They also appear on the menu of just about every respectable Thai restaurant in major cities around the world. However, because finely ground fish is not available in most areas and making the cakes from scratch with fresh fish is a rather laborious process, I have replaced ground fish with shrimp in this recipe. Shrimp already has the elasticity of texture that is desired and reduces easily to a sticky paste, eliminating the need to pound and knead as is required of fish in order to cook up "bouncy" chewy rather than flaky.

The cakes made from this recipe are not the same as the shrimp cakes offered on menus in Thailand's seafood restaurants, which are not spicy, but enriched with chopped pork fat and served with a sweet plum sauce. These are lighter and spiced more like traditional fish cakes, but with an unmistaken shrimp flavor that many of my students prefer, and like fish cakes, are served with a sweet-and-sour cucumber relish.

(continued on next page)

If you live in a major metropolitan area with large, well-stocked Asian markets, you may be able to find fresh or frozen ground fish for making fish cakes. Buy only if it looks truly fresh (pinkish rather than brownish) and not ground from fish the store couldn't sell the day before. Make sure it doesn't contain any additives like m.s.g. or preservatives. There are a few kinds of frozen ground fish imported from Asia. The best for making Thai-style fish cakes are king mackerel and featherback fish. However, they usually still need to be worked to develop elasticity. To do this, pound the fish with a heavy stone mortar and pestle, or knead vigorously until it becomes very sticky and pasty. It helps if the fish is pounded or kneaded when it is very cold, and a small amount of salt is gradually added.

If you wish to make fish cakes from fresh fish, use fillets of a lean, white-flesh fish, preferably from small fish with less developed muscles. Rinse well to remove traces of blood and fat that may be on the fish's surface. Chop as finely as possible in the processor, or put through a meat grinder. Then pound to further reduce to an indistinguishable paste before kneading to develop the elasticity.

In Thailand, the finest fish for making fish cakes is a beautiful, silvery flat fish called *bplah gkrai*, known in English as "featherback fish." Its body curves up from a small, flattened head to form a prominent rounded back, which then gracefully tapers toward the tail. The tail wraps around the lower edge, becoming one long fin extending across its belly. A series of lovely spots emanate from the tail in a row just above the long lower fin. When it swims, it looks light and airy, like a feather. The flesh of this freshwater fish scrapes from its bones easily and reduces quickly to a sticky paste. Fried cakes made from this fish (*tawd mân bplah gkrai*) are exceptionally good, both in flavor and texture, and are prized in fine city restaurants.

For this recipe, if you can't find either fresh or dried kaffir lime peel, substitute a mixture of equal parts minced kaffir lime leaves and grated lime zest. Pound together with a mortar and pestle to blend the two aromatics.

As a shortcut, instead of making the simple chilli paste, store-bought red curry paste may be substituted (use 2 to 4 tablespoons) but, because of its more intense flavors, some of the delicious flavor of the shrimp itself is lost.

For the cucumber relish, if you can't find fresh red hot peppers, substitute 6 dried red chillies. Remove seeds and soak pods to soften in tap water. Then chop and pound in a mortar to a paste.

Crispy Garlic-and-Pepper-Encrusted Shrimp

(Gkoong Tawɘ Gkratiem Priktai)

1 lb. small to medium shrimp
3 cups peanut oil, for deep-frying
2 Tbs. white peppercorns, coarsely ground
10 or more large cloves garlic, chopped
2 Tbs. tapioca starch
1 to 2 Tbs. fish sauce (*nahm bplah*)
Lettuce leaves, to line serving platter
2 small tomatoes, sliced into rounds

Drain shrimp well after rinsing. Do not remove the shells. Let sit at room temperature at least 20 minutes before cooking.

Heat oil in a wok over high heat. When oil is hot and just before you are ready to fry, toss shrimp with coarsely ground pepper, chopped garlic, tapioca starch, and fish sauce. Use your hand to mix, so that you can feel and make sure all the shrimp are coated with a thin layer of tapioca starch, and the white pepper and garlic are distributed evenly. Tapioca starch will help the garlic and pepper stick to the shrimp during frying.

Test to make sure oil is hot enough by dropping in a small piece of garlic. It should sizzle vigorously on top of the oil, but not burn in a matter of seconds—reduce heat if it does. Fry one-half of the shrimp at a time. Shrimp should sizzle and turn golden, along with the loose garlic pieces, in a few minutes. Use a fork or a pair of chopsticks to separate those shrimp that are sticking to each other because of the stickiness of the flour.

Fry about 3 minutes, or until the garlic is a rich golden brown and the shrimp are crispy. Remove from oil with a slotted spoon or wire-mesh scooper and use a fine wire-mesh skimmer to remove all the garlic pieces remaining in the oil. Drain and air-cool a few minutes on a wide-mesh strainer or basket placed over a bowl. Air-cooling keeps the shrimp crispy for longer.

Before frying the second batch of shrimp, test the hotness of the oil again with a piece of garlic. After you have finished frying, let oil cool in the wok or in a heatproof bowl, then store for future use. Because the oil picks up a shrimpy, garlicky, and peppery flavor, it can be used with good results for stir-frying vegetables or seafood.

Serve while still warm on a platter lined with lettuce and tomato slices. Eat the shrimp shell, tail and all.

Serves 6 to 8 as an appetizer, or as a dish in a multicourse family-style meal.

(continued on next page)

Notes and Pointers:

One of the favorite easy dishes I teach in my classes, this crispy shrimp, though deep-fried, will not taste greasy if the right kind of oil is used and the proper temperature is maintained during cooking. In fact, after you have completed frying both batches of shrimp, notice how very little of the peanut oil has been used. Peanut oil is excellent for frying because it can hold high temperatures without breaking down. When well heated before frying, the oil sears the outside of the shrimp and does not penetrate them. Of course, frying with shell on further keeps the oil from penetrating the shrimp.

Avoid draining on paper towels right after removing the shrimp from the oil, because the surface that contacts the plate may lose its crispiness, as it cannot breathe and will, therefore, "sweat" out the juices remaining inside. Draining on a wire-mesh strainer or a wire rack allows the surface to cool quickly and retain its crispiness.

Many of my students were initially not too sure about eating shrimp shells, but they were easily convinced after they tried their first. The more adventurous even take my advice and seek out shrimp with heads still attached, for an extra crunch. In fact, if you already love crunching on those crispy shrimp heads that come with your *amaebi* sushi in Japanese restaurants, you will want to get shrimp with heads on. In addition to the delightful texture, the shells are a good source of natural calcium. Besides, not having to shell the shrimp saves a lot of time for people with limited time to cook.

If you have a strong psychological block against eating shrimp shells, this recipe can also be made with shelled shrimp. Skip the tapioca starch (it will turn gooey on the moist surface of the shrimp), and fry only about 30 seconds to 1 minute, or until shrimp turn pink. Let the garlic fry a little longer, if necessary, to crisp and brown, then scoop it up and pile it on the shrimp. Without shells, the shrimp will tend to taste a bit oilier and their surface will not crisp. If you wish a crispy coating, dip them in egg and roll in bread crumbs before frying.

Steamed Tiger Prawns

(Gkoong Neung Si-ew)

½ lb. large tiger prawns
6 to 8 cloves garlic, finely chopped
2 to 3 tsp. minced cilantro roots or bottom stems
1 Tbs. light soy sauce
1 Tbs. Thai oyster sauce
1 tsp. sesame oil
1 green onion
¼ tsp. ground white pepper

Shell prawns and butterfly, removing any black veins. Give them a saltwater bath to freshen (page 173). Rinse and drain well. Arrange single layer on a heatproof serving dish with a little depth that fits on the rack of a stacked steamer.

Combine chopped garlic and cilantro roots/stems in a small bowl. Add soy sauce, oyster sauce, and sesame oil. Mix well. Spoon and spread evenly over prawns.

Bring 1½ to 2 inches of water to a boil in the steamer pot before placing the rack holding the plate of prawns over the pot. Cover and steam over high heat for 7 to 10 minutes (depending on the size of the prawns), or until the prawns are just cooked through.

In the meantime, prepare the green onion. Trim and discard the loose green leaves. Split the stalk in half lengthwise, then cut into inch-long segments. Cut each segment lengthwise into fine matchstick slivers.

When prawns are done, immediately lift the lid so that condensed steam does not drip onto prawns. Let hot steam dissipate before lifting the dish from the steamer rack. A fair amount of very tasty juice will have steamed out from the prawns.

Liberally sprinkle with white pepper and garnish top with green onion slivers.

Serves 2 to 3 with rice and other dishes in a family-style meal.

Notes and Pointers:

Preparing a Thai meal can sometimes be a chore, because of all the cutting and chopping required. So, in menu planning for a dinner party, it is prudent to include one or two easy dishes, especially if you don't have time to make some of the dishes the day before. Not only is this recipe very easy, its mildness makes it a good accompaniment to other very hot and spicy dishes in a multicourse meal.

Spicy *Prik King* Shrimp
(Gkoong Paд Prik King)

1 lb. medium shrimp
Homemade *prik king* chilli paste (recipe follows)
2 Tbs. dried shrimp, chopped or coarsely ground
3 Tbs. peanut oil
2 to 4 Tbs. water
1 Tbs. fish sauce (*nahm bplah*), or to taste
2 to 3 tsp. palm or coconut sugar, to
     taste
2 to 3 Tbs. unsalted roasted peanuts,
     chopped or coarsely ground
6 kaffir lime leaves, cut into fine inch-long
     slivers
1 red jalapeno, serrano, or fresno pepper,
     finely slivered with seeds
⅛ to ¼ tsp. ground white pepper
1 cup lightly steamed green beans cut
     into 1½-inch segments
Prik king chilli paste (recipe follows)

Shell and butterfly shrimp. Rinse and drain well.

Heat a wok over high heat until it is smoking hot. Swirl in 2 tablespoons oil to coat the wok surface and wait 15 to 20 seconds for it to heat. Sear shrimp quickly for 1 to 2 minutes, until they turn pink on the outside but are only partially cooked through. Remove from wok.

Swirl another tablespoon of oil into wok and wait a few seconds for it to heat. Spoon in chilli mixture and fry over medium heat for one-half minute. Add 2 tablespoons water and continue to fry, with stirring, until the mixture has darkened and become very aromatic (about 3 minutes). Season to taste with fish sauce and palm sugar.

If the mixture has completely dried out and is likely to burn, add another 1 to 2 tablespoons water, and stir into the mixture. Increase heat to high and wait a few seconds before tossing in shrimp. Stir-fry with seasonings 15 to 20 seconds. Add the chopped peanuts, ¾ of the slivered kaffir lime leaves, and half the slivered red chilli. Stir well. Sprinkle liberally with ground white pepper. Stir again and, when shrimp are cooked through, transfer to a serving dish and garnish top with remaining chilli and kaffir lime leaf slivers. Arrange steamed green beans along the edges.

Serves 5 to 6 with steamed rice and other dishes in a family-style meal.

Prik King **Chilli Paste**

6 to 10 large dried red chillies, roasted and ground
½ tsp. sea salt
1-inch section fresh or frozen galanga, chopped
1 stalk lemon grass, trimmed and cut into very thin rounds
2 tsp. chopped cilantro roots or bottom stems
1 tsp. minced kaffir lime peel (soak dried peel to soften before using)
1 head garlic, chopped
2 shallots, chopped
1 tsp. shrimp paste (*gkabpi*)

Using a large mortar and pestle, make the chilli paste. Pound ingredients individually, a little at a time, until each is reduced to paste. Combine and pound together to make a well-blended mixture. Add the chopped dried shrimp, mix, and pound quickly to blend.

Notes and Pointers:

Prik king (literally, "chilli ginger") is a kind of chilli paste that is used to make a dry, highly seasoned dish, either with meats like pork, firm vegetables like long beans or green beans, and certain kinds of seafood like shrimp and fish. Of course, dried red chillies and galanga (also known as Thai ginger) are two indispensable ingredients in the chilli paste.

With fish, either fillets or whole fish may be used. Cut fillets into bite-size chunks, coat with a little tapioca starch, and deep-fry until golden brown and crispy. Then, stir-fry with the seasonings, as with the shrimp in this recipe. For whole fish, coat also with a thin layer of tapioca starch and deep-fry in plenty of oil until golden brown and crispy around the edges. Make the seasoning mixture; reduce heat to medium, and spoon half of it from the wok. Spread the remaining half over a large enough area of the wok to accommodate the fish. Sprinkle with a little water, place fish over the seasonings, and top with the reserved half of the seasoning mixture. Cook 1 to 2 minutes, sprinkle the top of the fish with a little water, then flip and cook the second side another 1 to 2 minutes.

Try this recipe with charcoal-grilled jumbo prawns or lobster. Make the seasoning mixture and spread over the grilled prawns or lobster.

Choo Chee Red Curry Shrimp
with Kaffir Lime Leaves and Basil
(Choo Chee Gkoong)

1 lb. medium shrimp
3 orange or red serrano, jalapeno, or fresno peppers
1 cup rich unsweetened coconut cream (preferably *Mae Ploy* or *Chao Koh*
    brand—spoon the thickest cream off the top of an unshaken can of coconut
    milk)
2 to 3 Tbs. red curry paste
Fish sauce (*nahm bplah*), as needed (some packaged curry pastes are already
    heavily salted)
2 tsp. palm sugar, or to taste
8 kaffir lime leaves, very finely slivered
½ to 1 cup Thai basil leaves (*bai horapa*)
1 to 2 short sprigs of Thai basil (*bai horapa*) with purple flower buds, for garnish

Shell, devein, and butterfly the shrimp; give them a saltwater bath to freshen (page 173). Rinse and drain well, and let sit at room temperature for 20 minutes before cooking.

Cut two of the three red peppers into thin rounds, including seeds, and pound with a mortar and pestle to a coarse paste. Cut other pepper with seeds into fine inch-long slivers.

Heat ⅔ cup coconut cream in a wok or skillet over high heat. When it has warmed to a smooth consistency, spoon out 1 tablespoon and reserve. Reduce remaining cream for a few minutes until it is thick and bubbly and the oil begins to separate from the cream. Add curry paste, mushing it into the cream and fry, with stirring, over medium-high heat for a few minutes, until it is aromatic and darker in color, and the mixture is very thick.

Increase heat to high and add the remaining ⅓ cup coconut cream, stirring to make a thick, well-blended sauce. Season to taste with fish sauce and palm sugar. Stir well to melt sugar and blend seasonings. Toss in shrimp and cook in the sauce, stirring frequently. When most of them have lost their raw pink color on the outside, stir in the crushed chillies and kaffir lime leaves. Stir-fry 10 to 15 seconds before adding basil and slivered chilli. Stir well to wilt basil and, when shrimp are just cooked through, turn off heat.

Transfer to a serving dish and dribble reserved tablespoon of coconut cream over shrimp. Garnish with a sprig or two of basil.

Serves 4 to 5 with rice and other dishes in a family-style meal.

Notes and Pointers:

My mother has a soft spot in her heart for *choo chee* curries—those red hot curries with a rich, thick sauce cooked in a pan so hot that it pops and sizzles, making a swishy sound, like *choo chee*. Just enough of the concentrated sauce coats the pieces of seafood cooked with it, or is spooned over seafood cooked separately. Although excellent with shrimp and prawns, America's favorite seafood, Mother is first and foremost a fish lover and, now that she is advanced in years and no longer cooks, she, without fail, orders *choo chee* fish whenever we take her out to dine at her favorite restaurants.

So, after you've tried this recipe and enjoyed enough *choo chee* with shrimp, make the spicy and aromatic sauce to spoon over crispy fried fish. Mother's favorite fish for *choo chee* is a small, flat fish called *bplah neua awn* ("soft-flesh fish"), which fries to a delightfully crunchy crispiness and can be eaten almost entirely, bones and all. When it comes to eating crispy fish fins, heads, and bones, Mom beats us all. People from her generation know no waste and, from her, I've learned that food is sacred, and a life that has been sacrificed to keep us nourished should not be dishonored by throwing out any of its parts. Watching her enjoy every small bit of her crispy fish, even at a ripe old age, is a heartwarming sight.

To make the sauce, follow the instructions to the end, simply skipping the shrimp. Try the sauce over crispy fried, whole small or flat fish, such as pompano, butterfish, sole, white perch, smelts, and anchovies. For instructions on frying crispy fish Thai-style, see page 77. The sauce is also good over pan-fried or grilled mackerel. Or, if you prefer, smother over grilled halibut, salmon, albacore, tuna, mahi mahi, jumbo prawns, lobster, or whatever else you like to toss on your charcoal grill. Top with the coconut cream and garnish with basil sprigs. For strong-tasting fish, about 2 tablespoons of fine inch-long slivers of fresh rhizome (*gkrachai*) can be added to the sauce at the same time as the basil and cooked until both are wilted.

Besides cooking with shrimp, as in this recipe, substitute squid, scallops, shelled clams, and mussels, or a combination of shellfish and mollusks. For an easy but truly exceptional homemade *choo chee* curry, try the recipe on page 262.

Charcoal-Grilled Jumbo Prawns or Lobster Tails Topped with Sour Tamarind Sauce

(Gkoong Pow Rahd Sawd Makahm Bpiak)

1½ lb. jumbo prawns, or lobster tails
1 Tbs. peanut oil
1 Tbs. finely chopped garlic
1 Tbs. chopped cilantro roots or stems, pounded to a
   paste
1 Tbs. *Sriracha* bottled hot chilli sauce
3 Tbs. tamarind juice, the thickness of fruit concentrate
1½ to 2 Tbs. palm sugar, to taste
1 to 2 Tbs. fish sauce (*nahm bplah*), to taste
4 to 6 lettuce leaves
2 serrano or jalapeno peppers, preferably red, cut into small slivers
A few cilantro sprigs, for garnish

With scissors, snip the shells of the prawns up the center of the back three-quarters of the way toward the tail. Using a sharp knife, butterfly the prawns in their shells, cutting deeply without cutting through. Remove any dark veins, but leave the shells on. Rinse and drain. For lobster tails, cut a slit down the middle of the back to expose the flesh.

Grill prawns or lobster tails over medium-hot charcoals, turning occasionally, until they are just cooked through (4 to 8 minutes, depending on the size of the prawns or lobster tails). Do not overcook.

Heat oil in a small pan and sauté garlic and cilantro roots/stems over medium heat until aromatic. Add *Sriracha* chilli sauce and tamarind juice, and season to taste with palm sugar and fish sauce. Stir well to blend. Reduce heat, and simmer until the sauce has thickened to the consistency of light syrup.

Arrange prawns opened like a butterfly, or lobster tails with the exposed flesh facing up, on a lettuce-lined serving platter. Spoon tamarind sauce over them, and garnish top with slivered chillies and cilantro.

Serves 5 to 6 with rice and other dishes in a family-style meal.

Notes and Pointers:

For an easy barbecue, make the tamarind sauce in this recipe in advance, so that you have time to visit with friends while grilling the prawns. The sweet-and-sour sauce can also be spooned over grilled scallops, or use it as a dip for crisp fried foods.

Spicy Southern-Style Stir-Fried Shrimp with *Sadtaw* or Fava Beans

(Gkoong Pad Sadtaw)

8 to 10 cloves garlic, chopped
2 serrano peppers, preferably red or orange, chopped with seeds
6 to 10 Thai chillies (*prik kee noo*), preferably red, chopped
2 tsp. shrimp paste (*gkabpi*)
2 Tbs. peanut oil
½ cup shelled *sadtaw*, or substitute with fava beans
¾ lb. medium shrimp, shelled and butterflied
2 Tbs. lime juice
2 tsp. palm sugar
2 to 3 tsp. fish sauce (*nahm bplah*), to taste
3 to 4 short sprigs of green peppercorns, optional
3 kaffir lime leaves, torn into small pieces
1 red jalapeno or fresno pepper, cut into bite-size slivers with seeds
¼ cup thick coconut cream (if from a can, warm through until smooth)

Pound garlic, both kinds of chopped chillies, and shrimp paste together with a mortar and pestle to make a coarse paste.

Heat a wok over high heat until it begins to smoke. Swirl in oil to coat surface and wait a few seconds for it to heat. Add chilli paste and sauté until fragrant. Add *sadtaw* or fava beans and stir-fry 20 to 30 seconds. Follow with the shrimp and continue to stir-fry over high heat until most of the shrimp have started to turn pink.

Season to taste with lime juice, palm sugar, and fish sauce, and add the green peppercorn sprigs, kaffir lime leaves, pepper slivers, and coconut cream. Stir well and, when shrimp are cooked through, transfer to a serving plate.

Serves 3 to 4 with rice and other dishes in a family-style meal.

Notes and Pointers:

Sadtaw is a prized vegetable in the southern region of Thailand. It actually is not a vegetable, but the young beanlike seeds of a large tree in long, flat and wavy, oversized, bright green seedpods. Each seedpod yields only a small handful of seeds. Bunches of these colorful seedpods can be seen hanging from stalls in just about every open-air marketplace in the southern provinces, as well as in fruit and vegetable stands along major roads. Because it is fairly expensive and a delicacy, it is used sparingly, even in the dishes in which it is featured. Only a few bites of the tasty seeds with shrimp in a

(continued on next page)

spicy sauce are enough to satisfy a craving. The sauce in this recipe is a truly southern combination of flavors—very pungent and meant to be eaten with plenty of rice.

I have suggested substituting fava beans for the *sadtaw* because they are approximately the same size and color, with a slight bitter taste. Lima beans and broad beans may also be used; adjust the cooking times as needed to tenderize them.

Shrimp Cooked in Turmeric Coconut Sauce
(Gkoong Dtom Gkati Kamin)

1 large stalk lemon grass
1 cup coconut milk
2 tsp. chopped, peeled fresh turmeric, pounded to a paste
4 Thai chillies (*prik kee noo*), stem removed and crushed whole
1½ to 2 Tbs. tamarind juice, the consistency of fruit concentrate
1 tsp. palm sugar
¾ to 1 tsp. fine sea salt
¾ lb. medium shrimp, shelled and butterflied
1 shallot, finely chopped
3 serrano peppers, preferably orange or red, cut into thin slivers, including seeds
4 kaffir lime leaves, cut into very fine, inch-long slivers

Trim and discard woody bottom tip of lemon grass and remove 2 to 3 of the fibrous outer layers. Slice the less fibrous inner stalk at a sharp angle into very thin, long oval pieces (should yield approximately 3 tablespoons).

Heat coconut milk in a saucepan over medium heat until it begins to boil. Add turmeric paste, lemon grass, and crushed Thai chillies. Reduce heat and simmer a few minutes. Season to taste with tamarind, palm sugar, and sea salt.

Increase heat to high and add shrimp, chopped shallot, and ⅔ of the slivered chillies. Stir well and, when shrimp are cooked through, turn off heat. Stir in half the kaffir lime leaf slivers and transfer to a serving dish. Top with the remaining slivered kaffir lime leaves and slivered chillies.

Serves 3 to 4 with rice and other dishes in a family-style meal.

Notes and Pointers:

This southern-influenced recipe is adapted from a delightful dish I once had at Bai Dtong ("Banana Leaf") Restaurant in Bangkok. It is easy to make and presents well. Fresh turmeric imparts a pleasing color and flavor to the creamy coconut sauce, while the tender pieces of the lemon grass's inner core punctuate each bite with a contrasting texture. Its mildness makes it perfect for accompanying spice-laden dishes, cooling and cleaning the tongue with its creaminess before other spicy bites are taken.

This dish, however, is not half as good if you substitute powdered turmeric. Much of the delicate and rich flavor of the fresh rhizome is lost through drying, and it turns bitter and medicinal. It's worth the time and trouble to search for the fresh root; find it in Southeast Asian markets and gourmet specialty produce stores with an international bent. See page 72 for more information on this rhizome.

Tiger Prawns Steamed with Garlic and Thai Chillies
(Gkoong Neung Gkratiem)

½ lb. medium to large tiger prawns
10 cloves garlic
5 to 6 red and green Thai chillies (*prik kee noo*)
1 Tbs. fish sauce (*nahm bplah*)
1 Tbs. Thai oyster sauce
A squeeze of lime, optional
A handful of short cilantro sprigs

Shell and butterfly prawns, removing any black veins. Give them a saltwater bath to freshen them (page 173). Rinse well and drain.

Chop half the garlic cloves and slice the other half into thin pieces. Chop Thai chillies. Combine chopped garlic and chopped chillies in a mortar and pound to a paste. Add fish sauce and oyster sauce, and stir well.

Arrange prawns in a single layer, with the butterflied edges spread out, on a shallow heatproof serving dish that fits on the rack of a stacked steamer. The dish should have about an inch of depth to catch juices that may steam out from the prawns. Spread garlic-chilli sauce evenly over them, then top with garlic slices.

Bring 1½ to 2 inches of water to a boil in the bottom of the steamer pot before placing the rack holding the dish of prawns over the pot. Cover and steam over high heat 8 to 10 minutes (depending on the size of the prawns), or until prawns are just cooked through. Immediately lift the lid off the steamer so that condensed steam does not drip onto prawns. Remove the steamer rack from the pot, letting the hot steam dissipate before lifting the plate carefully out from the rack. A fair amount of very tasty juices will have steamed out from the prawns.

Squeeze a light sprinkle of lime juice over the prawns, if desired, garnish with cilantro sprigs, and serve while still warm.

Serves 2 to 3 with rice and other dishes in a multicourse family-style meal.

Notes and Pointers:
Light, but spicy hot, this easy dish can satisfy your craving for spicy foods without taking much of your time. Because it is oil-less, it has the additional benefit of being high protein and low in calories.

In fancy Bangkok restaurants, large prawns are usually butterflied in their shells and steamed with their shells still on (oftentimes, heads still on, too). This not only keeps the prawns sweet, moist, and tasty, but the shells add extra flavor to the juices released onto the dish. Steaming whole also makes an impressive presentation. Spoon the juices over rice to eat along with the prawns.

Hot-and-Sour Lemon Grass Tiger Prawns
(Gkoong Dtom Yâm Haeng)

2 lb. large tiger prawns with heads (about 10 to 15 per pound in size), or
    substitute smaller headless prawns
2 heads garlic
6 shallots
3 stalks lemon grass
8 to 10 dried red chillies
Pinch of salt
8 to 12 Thai chillies (*prik kee noo*), stems removed and bruised whole
8 kaffir lime leaves, cut into fine inch-long slivers
Juice of 2 to 3 limes, to taste
4 to 5 Tbs. fish sauce (*nahm bplah*), to taste
1 to 2 Tbs. palm sugar, to taste
¼ cup short cilantro sprigs
¼ cup or more peanut oil, for stir-frying

With scissors, cut the shells of the prawns up the center of the back opposite from the legs to about one-half inch from the tail. Using a sharp knife, butterfly the prawns in their shells, cutting deeply without cutting through. Remove any black veins, but leave shells and heads on. Rinse and drain, and let sit at room temperature for at least 20 minutes before cooking.

Break one of the heads of garlic into individual cloves. Cut root tip off each clove, leaving skin on. Do likewise with 3 shallots. Place them on a tray and roast in a hot oven (450°F) until softened, about 10 minutes for garlic, 15 to 20 minutes for shallots. (Cutting the tip keeps the garlic and shallots from popping and splattering the oven.) Chop the other head of garlic and 3 shallots and set aside.

Trim and discard the woody bottom tip of lemon grass stalks. Remove one or two layers of the more fibrous outer leaves. Cut remaining inner stalk into thin rounds, then chop coarsely. Set aside in a covered bowl to prevent drying out.

Place dried chillies in a dry pan with a pinch of salt and roast over medium heat, until they are dark red and slightly charred, stirring frequently. Let cool before grinding in a spice grinder to a fine powder. When roasted garlic and shallots are ready, peel their skin and mash them in a mortar and pestle with the powdered chillies, to form a well-blended paste. Set aside. Prepare the remaining ingredients as instructed.

Heat a wok over high heat until it is smoking hot. Swirl in 3 tablespoons oil to coat wok surface, and wait 15 to 20 seconds for it to heat. Toss in prawns and sear them in the hot wok for 1 to 2 minutes. When most of the shells have turned pink, remove from wok. Add another 2 to 3 Tbs. of oil and heat

(continued on next page)

15 to 20 seconds. Sauté chopped garlic and shallots for 15 to 20 seconds, before adding mashed, roasted paste. Sauté a short while longer, then stir in chopped lemon grass, slivered kaffir lime leaves, and crushed whole Thai chillies. Stir-fry another 30 seconds to 1 minute.

When the mixture is well blended and fragrant with herbs, season to taste with fish sauce, palm sugar, and lime juice. Reduce liquid so that the mixture is thick and almost dry. Toss the prawns back in and stir-fry with the lemon grass mixture for 1 to 2 minutes, or until they are just cooked through. Transfer to a serving platter and garnish top with cilantro.

Serves 8 with rice and other dishes in a shared family-style meal.

Notes and Pointers:

This recipe is a dry version of the well-known hot-and-sour soup or *ðtom yâm*. In fact, that's exactly what the Thai name means: dry *ðtom yâm* prawns (*gkoong* means prawns, *ħaeng* means dry). Every time I make these prawns, I am reminded of my first trip to the beautiful seacoast of Krabi many, many years ago. The coastline was enchanting, decorated with dramatic limestone karsts, and the islands offshore were idyllic, fringed with dazzling white-sand beaches and lively coral gardens. To make a paradise complete, the food was divine at the secluded resort with charming, island-style huts.

I will always remember the magical tiger prawns—so gorgeously fresh their eyes still twinkled as they lay on the ice beckoning me to pick them out for the chef to cook. He masterfully prepared and dressed the chosen ones in the most fitting clothes and delivered them to my table cloaked in an alluring veil of spicy fragrance. One bite and I thought I must be in heaven!

The magnificent sunset coast in all its glory captured my heart, and I have returned every year since. Much has changed and chefs have come and gone, but the food is still memorable. Without fail, the first meal on every visit would include the very special hot-and-sour prawns for old time's sake.

Southern-Style Spicy Tamarind Prawns with Crisped Shallots and Garlic

(Gkoong Yai Pad Som Makahm Bpiak)

1 lb. large prawns (about 16 to 20 per pound)
¼ cup peanut oil
2 large shallots, halved lengthwise and sliced crosswise ⅛-inch thick
8 cloves garlic, chopped
4 large dried red chillies, each cut into 2 to 3 pieces
¼ cup chopped onion
2 jalapeno or serrano peppers, chopped with seeds
⅓ cup tamarind juice, the thickness of fruit concentrate
2 Tbs. fish sauce (nahm bplah), to taste
1 Tbs. *Sriracha* hot chilli sauce
1 Tbs. Maggi or Gold Mountain seasoning sauce
1 Tbs. palm or coconut sugar, to taste
Lettuce to line serving platter
1 red jalapeno pepper, cut into long, fine slivers
1 green onion (dense part only), cut into 1½-inch lengths, then split into thin
   matchstick-size slivers
A few cilantro sprigs, for garnish

Shell, devein, and butterfly prawns; give them a saltwater bath to freshen them (see page 173). Rinse and drain well. Let sit at room temperature for at least 20 minutes before stir-frying.

Heat oil in a small skillet for 2 to 3 minutes. Add sliced shallots and fry over low to medium heat, stirring occasionally, until the pieces are evenly browned and crisped (about 20 to 25 minutes). Drain from oil by pouring over a fine wire-mesh strainer balanced on a bowl. Wipe skillet clean of any shallot remnants and return oil to skillet. Fry the garlic over medium-high heat until golden brown. Drain as described, reserving oil for stir-frying.

Heat a wok over high heat until its entire surface is smoking hot. Swirl in 2 tablespoons reserved oil to coat the wok surface. Wait a few seconds for it to heat. Add dried chilli pieces and fry quickly until they are dark red. Remove from oil with the wire-mesh skimmer. Toss chopped onion and chillies into the wok and sauté until softened and aromatic. Add tamarind juice, fish sauce, *Sriracha* hot chilli sauce, Maggi or Gold Mountain sauce, and palm sugar. Stir well to blend, and heat to a sizzling boil.

Add prawns and, with frequent stirring, cook over high heat until sauce is thick and prawns are cooked to your liking (2 to 4 minutes, depending on their size). Turn off heat and add fried shallots, garlic, and dried chillies. Toss well.

(continued on next page)

Southern-Style Spicy Tamarind Prawns (cont.)

Transfer to a lettuce-lined serving platter. Garnish with slivered red chilli, green onion, and cilantro sprigs.

Serves 6 with other dishes and rice in a family-style meal.

Notes and Pointers:

Though tamarind is a souring agent used throughout Thailand, it is particularly favored in the south where it is combined with abundant fresh tiger prawns, either farm-raised or fished from the extensive coastal areas of the peninsula, to produce a dish distinctly identified with the region's seafood offerings. The prawns are mildly spiced with a tangy tamarind taste.

Though the recipe is for large prawns, it is equally good with smaller shrimp. Adjust the cooking time accordingly. Try it also with squid or a combination of shrimp and squid. Make sure the squid is well drained before stir-frying; squeeze gently to remove all water trapped in the rings, so that it does not dilute the sauce. Scallops are also wonderful cooked in this sauce, but dry them well with a towel before adding to the wok.

For more on how to properly crisp shallots, see page 69. To save yourself the work of crisping shallots and garlic, use packaged products available in small containers or bags from Southeast Asian markets—use 2 to 3 tablespoons shallots, and 2 tablespoons garlic. However, they generally do not taste as fresh.

Cashew Shrimp
(Gkoong Pad Med Mamuang Himapahn)

½ lb. fresh medium shrimp

Marinade
1 ½ tsp. tapioca starch
1 tsp. fish sauce (*nahm bplah*), or light soy sauce
1 tsp. black soy sauce (semisweet kind)
1 tsp. peanut oil

⅓ cup peanut oil
⅓ cup raw whole cashews
8 large dried red chillies, cut in half crosswise
6 large cloves garlic, chopped
½ small onion, thinly sliced or diced
1 Tbs. Thai oyster sauce
¼ tsp. coarsely ground white peppercorns
1 green onion, split in half lengthwise and cut crosswise into 1 ½-inch segments

Shell, devein, and butterfly shrimp. Give them a saltwater bath to freshen them (page 173), then rinse in several changes of water to remove all the salt. Drain well.

Add all marinade ingredients to shrimp and use your hand to mix them with the shrimp, feeling to make sure tapioca starch evenly coats the shrimp, and is not lumped around just a few of them. Set aside, unrefrigerated, for at least 20 minutes before cooking.

Heat oil in a wok over medium heat for a couple of minutes. Fry cashews over low to medium heat for 5 minutes or more, stirring frequently, so that they slowly sizzle to an even, rich golden brown. Browning the nuts slowly allows them to cook all the way through, leaching out the nut oils and giving them a good crunchy texture when cooled. Avoid browning quickly at too high a heat, as partially cooked nuts can become soggy when tossed with the shrimp and seasonings. When ready, remove from oil with a slotted spoon. Cool for a few minutes.

Remove the oil from the wok, except for about 1 ½ tablespoons. Add dried red chillies and fry over medium heat until dark red. Scoop them from the oil with a slotted spoon. Increase heat to high and add garlic. Lightly brown for 20 to 30 seconds. Follow with the onion and sauté until softened and translucent. Toss in shrimp and marinade and, with constant stirring, stir-fry until most of them have turned pink on the outside.

(continued on next page)

Cashew Shrimp (cont.)

Sprinkle in oyster sauce and white pepper and return chillies to the wok. Continue to stir-fry until shrimp are cooked through. Turn off heat, and add green onions and cashews. Toss quickly to mix. Transfer to a serving dish and serve immediately.

Serves 3 to 4 with other dishes and rice in a family-style meal.

Notes and Pointers:

Cashews are a main agricultural crop in many of the southern provinces, particularly on the western portion of the peninsula. The lovely broad-leaf trees grace long stretches of lush coastal highway and, in February and March, colorful, pear-shaped fruits about the size of a large plum dangle from their arching branches. Protruding from underneath each of the bright red or bright yellow fruits is a hard brown nut. Soon, stalls sprout along the highway selling large bagfuls of the shelled, raw or roasted nuts. They are very fresh tasting, unlike the kind you get in cans or jars in American supermarkets.

For this recipe, always start with raw cashews and fry them as needed. Do not substitute packaged roasted nuts. When freshly fried over low heat until they are cooked through, the nuts develop an especially rich and fragrant flavor.

Besides shrimp, try this recipe with scallops and bite-size chunks of meaty fish, such as tuna, swordfish, sturgeon, and monkfish. When using fish, skip the tapioca starch in the marinade.

"Five-Flavored" Shrimp with Toasted Sesame Seeds
(Gkoong Hah Roet)

1 lb. medium shrimp
2 Tbs. sesame seeds
5 to 10 dried red chillies, to desired hotness
Pinch or two of salt
¼ cup peanut oil
2 to 3 shallots, sliced into rounds ⅛-inch thick
¼ cup tamarind juice, the thickness of fruit concentrate
1 tsp. white vinegar
2 Tbs. fish sauce (*nahm bplah*), or to taste
2 to 3 Tbs. granulated sugar, to taste
1 large head garlic, chopped
A few cilantro sprigs, for garnish

Shell, devein, and butterfly shrimp. Give them a saltwater bath to refresh and improve their texture (page 173), then rinse in several changes of water to remove all the salt. Drain and let shrimp sit at room temperature for at least 20 minutes before cooking.

Toast sesame seeds in a small, dry pan over medium heat, stirring frequently, until they are golden brown and aromatic. Transfer to a small dish. Wipe pan clean and return to stove. Roast dried red chillies with salt, stirring frequently, until they turn dark red and are slightly charred. Let cool before grinding in a clean coffee grinder.

Wipe pan, and reheat with the oil. Fry sliced shallots over low to medium heat, browning them slowly, so that they dry and turn crispy (20 minutes or longer, depending on the shallots). In the meantime, mix the tamarind juice, vinegar, fish sauce, and sugar in a small saucepan and reduce over medium heat, stirring frequently, to thicken to the consistency of light syrup. Remove from heat and stir in ground, roasted dried chillies to desired hotness.

When shallots have browned and turned crispy, remove from oil with a fine wire-mesh skimmer. Increase heat to high and fry garlic to golden brown. Likewise strain from oil. Reserve oil for future stir-frying.

Heat a wok over high heat until its surface is smoking hot. Swirl in 2 tablespoons of reserved oil to coat the surface, and wait 15 to 20 seconds for it to heat. Toss in shrimp and stir-fry quickly, until they turn pink on the outside. Add thickened sauce and continue to stir-fry until shrimp are cooked through. Turn off heat. Toss in fried garlic and shallots and toasted sesame seeds, and transfer to a serving plate. Garnish with cilantro sprigs.

Serves 4 to 6 with other dishes and rice in a family-style meal.

(continued on next page)

Notes and Pointers:

"Five-flavored" shrimp or prawns appear regularly on the menus of large, specialty seafood restaurants. All five flavors are present in about equal degrees—hot, sour, sweet, salty, and bitter. The bitter taste is provided by the crisped and browned garlic and shallots.

In restaurants, the five-flavored sauce is usually served over crispy fried prawns. The prawns are deep-fried in the shell with the heads, tails, and legs still attached. Coated first with tapioca starch, they are dropped into a wok with plenty of hot oil and fried over high heat until thoroughly crispy (about 3 minutes). They are then arranged on a serving platter with a bowl of the sauce on the side. Dipped in the tamarind sauce, every bit of the prawns are eaten—the heads, tails, and shells are an excellent source of natural calcium. If you wish to serve the prawns this way, make the sauce as instructed. Let cool a few minutes, then stir in the fried shallots and garlic and the toasted sesame seeds.

If you are short on time, packaged crisped shallots may be substituted. They are available in small containers at many Asian markets. Shake the container to make sure the pieces are crispy, not soggy. They should make a rattling sound. Fried garlic is also available packaged but, since it doesn't take long to brown chopped garlic, it is much better to make it yourself for that fresh garlic taste.

Prawns and Bean Thread in Clay Pot
(Gkoong Ohb Woon Sen)

1 lb. medium to large tiger prawns

1 tsp. peanut oil

8 to 10 large, ¼-inch-thick slices unpeeled, fresh ginger, bruised with side of
    cleaver

10 cloves garlic, smashed whole with side of cleaver

12 cilantro roots, cleaned and smashed with side of cleaver (or substitute a
    handful of bottom stems)

2 tsp. white or black peppercorns, cracked

2 green onions, both white and green parts, cut into inch-long pieces

2 small (1.7 oz.) or 1 medium (3.5 oz.) packages bean thread noodles (*woon sen*),
    soaked in tap water 5 to 10 minutes to soften

1 Tbs. fish sauce (*nahm bplah*)

1 Tbs. black soy sauce (semisweet kind)

4 Tbs. Thai oyster sauce

¾ cup mild chicken or seafood stock

A few cilantro sprigs, for garnish

Shell prawns, but leave tails on; butterfly and remove any dark veins. Give the shelled prawns a salt-water bath to freshen them (page 173), then rinse several times to remove all the salt. Drain well and let sit at room temperature at least 20 minutes before cooking.

Oil the bottom of a clay pot with peanut oil, and spread ginger slices over it. Follow with garlic, cilantro roots (or stems), pepper, and green onions. Layer drained, softened bean thread noodles over them, and sprinkle with a mixture of fish sauce and black soy sauce. Arrange prawns over noodles, and coat evenly with oyster sauce.

In a small saucepan, heat chicken or seafood stock to boiling. Pour in gently along the side of the clay pot, so that the oyster sauce is not washed off the prawns. Cover with lid and place clay pot over medium heat. Bring to a boil and cook 5 to 8 minutes, or until prawns are just cooked and succulent.

Serve hot in the clay pot, garnished with cilantro sprigs.

Serves 6 with rice and other dishes in a family-style meal.

Notes and Pointers:

Children love this dish, not just because it is mild, but because it has noodles—a food that is always a hit with them. Before she learned to like prawns, my niece frequently asked grandma to make her a big potful but, "skip the prawns," she would say. Little did she know then that the noodles wouldn't be very good if not for the sweet and tasty juices dripping down from the crustaceans.

(continued on next page)

My mother would gladly oblige, since the dish was so easy to make, especially when the prawns were always cooked with the shell and head on to keep them succulent and tender and add flavor to the drippings. Adults devoured the prawns happily while the children got their fill of slippery noodles.

Seafood restaurants also feature crab cooked this way. Use 1½ to 2 pounds of very fresh raw crabs. Chop the main body portion into halves for small crabs, or quarters for a large crab, and lightly crack the shell of the legs and claws. Place crab pieces over the herbs on the bottom of the clay pot. Add half the hot broth, cover, and place over a burner set at medium heat for 7 to 8 minutes. In the meantime, toss the softened bean thread noodles with the remaining broth and seasonings. Add to the clay pot and stir in with the crab pieces. Continue to cook another 5 to 8 minutes, or until crab is cooked through and the noodles softened.

Instead of oiling the bottom of the clay pot, restaurants normally line it with strips of pork fat; to enrich the flavor of the noodles, a small amount of oil is mixed in with the seasoning mixture, or the noodles are first quickly tossed in a hot wok with oil and the seasonings before adding to the clay pot. This recipe yields a lighter version, which I prefer.

If you don't have a clay pot, you may substitute a deep Corningware dish with lid. However, clay pots are really inexpensive in Asian markets and make an impressive presentation. Since they are breakable, most restaurants in Thailand have switched to less interesting metal pots shaped like the traditional clay pots.

Charcoal-Grilled Prawns, "Sweet Fish Sauce," and *Sadao* or Neem Leaves

(Sadao Nahm Bplah Wahn Gkoong Pow)

1½ lb. large prawns, or lobster
2 shallots, sliced ⅛-inch thick crosswise
¼ cup peanut oil
5 dried red Thai chillies (*prik kee noo haeng*)
5 large dried red chillies
2 Tbs. chopped garlic
½ cup tamarind juice, the consistency of fruit concentrate
2 Tbs. fish sauce (*nahm bplah*), or to taste
¼ cup plus 2 Tbs. palm sugar, or to taste
2 Tbs. ground dried shrimp
2 Tbs. chopped, unsalted, dry-roasted peanuts
A few cilantro leaves
Handful of cilantro sprigs
1 bunch blanched neem leaves and flower buds (*sadao*), or substitute bitter salad greens

Using scissors, cut the shells of the prawns up the middle of the back opposite to the legs to about half an inch from the tail. Then, with a sharp knife, butterfly the prawns in their shells to where the shell is cut. Remove any black veins, but keep the shells on. Rinse and drain.

In a small pan, fry shallots over low to medium heat in peanut oil, stirring occasionally, until they are a rich, golden brown and crispy (25 minutes, or longer if the shallots are very juicy). Drain from oil with a fine wire-mesh skimmer. Next, fry the two kinds of dried chillies until they are dark red. Remove from oil and drain. Fry the chopped garlic in the same oil over high heat until it turns golden brown. Drain from oil with the fine wire-mesh skimmer.

Combine tamarind, fish sauce, and palm sugar in a small saucepan over medium heat and stir until sugar is melted. Simmer, stirring frequently, until thickened to the consistency of very light syrup. Mix in ground dried shrimp. Taste and adjust the flavors so that the sauce is equally sweet, sour, and salty. Turn off heat and let cool.

Grill the prawns or lobster over medium-hot wood coals until they are just cooked through (or slightly undercooked for a more succulent, moist, and sweet flavor). Just before serving, crumble the

(continued on next page)

crisp-fried chillies into little pieces and stir into the sauce, along with chopped peanuts, crisped shallots, and garlic. Top with a few cilantro leaves.

Arrange grilled prawns on a serving platter lined on one side with cilantro sprigs and blanched neem leaves and flower buds (or bitter salad greens) and serve with the sweet tamarind sauce.

Serves 6 with rice and other dishes in a family-style meal.

Notes and Pointers:

Thai people are very fond of nibbling on the tender leaves and flower buds of bitter *sadao* (neem leaves) together with either charcoal-grilled catfish or large river prawns and *nahm bplah wahn* ("sweet fish sauce"). In spite of its name, fish sauce isn't really the primary flavor in the sweet, sour, and salty sauce, enriched with the roasted flavors of chillies and peanuts. The sauce and grilled fish or prawns temper *sadao*'s bitterness, and actually make the combination taste very nice and rich in the mouth. Since neem trees produce tender shoots and flower buds during months near the end of the rainy season, and in the cool season, this dish is extremely popular and consumed in great quantities whenever the leaves and buds appear in the markets. It has become one of those national dishes that constitute the core of everyday country cooking.

Although the tasty sauce is good on its own with the grilled seafood, to many Thais, it is inseparable from the bitter *sadao,* for any mention of *nahm bplah wahn* would conjure up an image of the herb. But, for the American palate unaccustomed to the bitter flavor, not having the herb is no great loss. For me personally, I find chewing on strong-tasting herbs along with the sweet sauce really does make the prawns taste much more interesting. Substitute bitter salad greens and nibble along with the sauce and see if this is something you can get used to. If you can, the next time you are in Thailand during the cool season, try some *sadao*. You might just fall for it like Thai people have.

In areas of the country where sizeable populations of Southeast Asians have settled, you may be able to find *sadao* in frozen packages in the ethnic markets. It is vibrantly rich green in color, though freezing most likely will have darkened it. Tiny buds top the tender shoots, which, in turn, are attached in a clump to a single, short, stout woody stalk. Blanching the *sadao* in lightly salted water reduces its bitterness, so that you can taste its other qualities. It is said that if the herb is blanched with the water drained from rinsing rice, the bitterness will be further reduced, and its flavor enhanced without losing out on any of its highly nutritious properties, which studies have shown to be stress-reducing, protective against colds and flus, healthy for the heart, and beneficial in the prevention of tumors and cancer.

To simplify the recipe, use good-quality, store-bought, packaged crisped shallots and garlic instead of making your own. Use 3 tablespoons fried shallots and 2 tablespoons fried garlic.

Fried Crab Cakes
(Tawd Mân Bpoo)

1 egg
10 cloves garlic, minced
1 tsp. ground white pepper
¼ tsp. ground cinnamon
⅛ tsp. ground cumin
2 tsp. Thai oyster sauce
1 Tbs. fish sauce (*nahm bplah*), or to taste
1 Tbs. unbleached white flour
1 tsp. granulated sugar
⅔ lb. shelled, cooked crabmeat
⅓ lb. ground pork
⅓ lb. fresh shrimp, shelled and very finely chopped
6 string beans, cut into very thin rounds
3 to 4 cups peanut oil, for deep-frying
1 cucumber, sliced into ⅛-inch rounds
Sriracha bottled chilli sauce, or sweet-and-sour plum sauce (page 180)

Mix egg, garlic, white pepper, cinnamon, cumin, oyster sauce, fish sauce, flour, and sugar. Beat until well blended. Add crabmeat, ground pork, and chopped shrimp. Knead until well blended and sticky. Add the string beans and stir well.

Heat oil in a wok over high heat until it begins to smoke. While waiting, form the crab mixture into balls about 1½ inches in diameter, then flatten into ½-inch-thick, round patties. Drop into the hot oil and fry over medium heat for 2 to 3 minutes, turning occasionally, until patties are a rich, golden brown. Fry in two or three batches, so that there is room for the patties to float in the oil to brown evenly.

Remove from oil with a wire-mesh scooper, and drain well. Arrange on a platter surrounded by cucumber slices. Serve with *Sriracha* hot sauce or a sweet-and-sour plum sauce.

Serves 6 to 8 as an appetizer in a multicourse family-style meal.

Notes and Pointers:
If you are a crab lover, you probably already have a crab cake recipe that you make frequently. If you are ready for a change, here is another recipe to try.

Stuffed Crab Shells
with Hot Pickled Garlic Sauce
(Bpoo Jah)

¼ tsp. white peppercorns, freshly ground
1 Tbs. cilantro roots or stem sections, finely
   chopped
6 cloves garlic, chopped
1 tsp. chopped fresh ginger
1½ cups shelled, cooked crabmeat
½ cup ground pork
½ cup finely chopped raw shrimp
2 chopped shallots, or 4 green onions
   (dense part of stalks), chopped
2 Tbs. tapioca starch or cornstarch
2 to 3 Tbs. fish sauce (*nahm bplah*), to taste
2 large eggs
1 cooked, salted, duck egg yolk, optional (see notes)
5 to 6 blue crab shells, cleaned, or substitute mussel shells
2 Tbs. cilantro leaves
2 red jalapeno or fresno peppers, thinly slivered
3 to 4 cups peanut oil, for deep-frying
Hot pickled garlic sauce (recipe follows), or *Sriracha* bottled hot chilli sauce

Pound white pepper, cilantro roots/stems, garlic, and ginger with a heavy mortar and pestle, reducing them to form a well-blended paste. Mix paste with crabmeat, ground pork, chopped shrimp, shallots (or green onions), tapioca starch, fish sauce, and one beaten egg. If using salted egg yolk, cut the cooked egg yolk into small chunks, and add to the mixture. Mix well.

Fill crab shells, mounding slightly, and smooth down the surface. Place on a steamer rack and steam 12 to 15 minutes to cook. (If using smaller shells, like mussel shells, steam 6 to 8 minutes.) Let cool.

Beat the other egg. Brush the top of the stuffing of each shell with egg and deep-fry in hot oil, stuffing side down, until golden brown. Remove from oil and drain. Slowly dribble remaining beaten egg into the hot oil, and fry into golden-brown egg shreds. Scoop out with a fine wire-mesh skimmer and drain. Arrange the stuffed shells on a serving platter, sprinkle fried egg shreds over them, and garnish with cilantro leaves and slivered chillies. Serve with pickled garlic sauce, or *Sriracha* bottled hot chilli sauce.

Serves 5 to 6 as an appetizer in a multicourse family-style meal.

Hot Pickled Garlic Sauce

10 to 15 Thai chillies (*prik kee noo*), stems removed, bruised and left whole
2 to 3 heads Thai pickled garlic, separated into cloves, and bruised
Juice of 1 lime
1 Tbs. pickled garlic brine
1 to 2 Tbs. fish sauce (*nahm bplah*), to taste

Place the chillies and pickled garlic in a sauce bowl. Add lime juice and pickled garlic brine. Add enough fish sauce to desired saltiness. Sauce tastes better when allowed to sit at least one hour, or overnight.

Notes and Pointers:

The name of this recipe literally means "dearie crab" or "darling crab." I really don't know how it got its name, but I imagine it has to do with kids and the curiosity they have in the odd crustacean. *Jah*, which is translated as "dearie," is a tender and cute expression often used to address small children (the word is placed following their nicknames), or for them to address something smaller than themselves, such as the crab. The small, blue crab shells are somewhat cute, I suppose.

Since it's probably easier for you to save mussel shells than small crab shells, they make excellent substitutes. Besides, you can serve more people at a dinner party, since the stuffing can fill more mussel shells than crab shells. The mussel shells are also a perfect size for hors d'oeuvres.

Salted duck eggs are available from any Chinese or Southeast Asian market, but the quality can vary quite a bit from batch to batch. They aren't quite like what we have back home, which are really very good without being very salty, especially if they come from the coastal area around Chaiya on the southern peninsula. This lovely rural countryside is known throughout the country for its incomparable salted duck eggs with rich red yolks. Even my husband is impressed and, whenever we drive by on our journeys south, we always stop to pick up a few boxes from roadside stalls. Many people say the salted eggs here are superior because the ducks are fed ground-up oyster shells along with their feed.

Restaurants usually press a piece of the firm, golden yolk on top and in the center of the stuffing to give an appealing presentation. If you decide to use the yolk, hard-boil the salted duck egg like you would a regular egg, then shell and remove the cooked yolk. In this recipe, it is cut up and tossed in with the crab mixture, but you may also keep the pieces separate to top the stuffing.

For the sauce, use pickled garlic imported from Thailand, which is packed in a flavorful, sweet-and-sour brine.

Steamed or Grilled Dungeness Crab
Served with Chilli-Lime Dipping Sauce
(Bpoo Neung/Bpoo Pow Gkap Nahm Jim)

1 large Dungeness crab, or 2 lbs. smaller crabs
4 to 8 red and green fresh Thai chillies (*prik kee noo*), cut into thin rounds
6 to 8 cloves garlic, chopped
2 to 3 tsp. minced cilantro root, or bottom stems
2 Tbs. fish sauce (*nahm bplah*), to taste
Juice of 1 to 2 limes, or about 3 Tbs.
2 to 3 tsp. sugar, to taste

Steam crab on a steamer rack placed over a steamer pot filled with about 2 inches boiling water. Steam over high heat for 12 to 15 minutes, or until crab is cooked through. Or, grill the crab over medium-hot charcoals until it is cooked through.

While crab is cooking, make the dipping sauce. Pound Thai chillies, garlic, and cilantro root together in a mortar until pasty. Add fish sauce, lime juice, and sugar. Stir well to melt the sugar and blend the flavors. Taste and adjust the flavors so that the sauce is equally sour and salty, lightly sweet, and to the hotness you desire. Let sit for the ingredients to mingle and marry.

After crab is cooked, cool it enough to handle before breaking into smaller sections. Pull open the shell, remove the gills, and split the main body into half and each half in two. Crack shells of the claws and legs. Arrange crab on a serving platter and serve with dipping sauce.

Serves 2 to 3 with rice and other dishes in a family-style meal.

Notes and Pointers:

Eating crabs in the San Francisco Bay Area, where I have transplanted myself, is a real treat, as the large Dungeness crab is easy to eat and loaded with meat. But I grew up on the other side of the Pacific, where crabs do not grow quite as big in the tropical waters, but are plentiful along the wide expanses of seacoast and in adjacent wetlands. In my childhood, my family frequently vacationed along the eastern shores of the gulf; on our way home, we would always stop to pick up bundles of crabs from roadside vendors for a crab feast that evening to end our memorable stay by the sea.

Back home, a lot of crabs are cooked and eaten very simply by steaming or boiling like they are cooked here, then cracked and shelled at the dinner table, and dipped in sauces. Instead of the rich garlic butter or heavy mayonnaise sauces, we prefer a light, oil-less, hot-and-sour chilli sauce that does not compromise the delicate, sweet flavor of fresh crab. Try the dipping sauce in this recipe the next time you have cracked crab for dinner—as a low-cal alternative to garlic butter.

Stir-fried Crab with Yellow Curry Sauce
(Bpoo Pad Pong Gkaree)

1 large, fresh, uncooked Dungeness crab, or 2 to 2½ lbs. smaller crabs
2 eggs
1 cup coconut milk or milk
2 Tbs. roasted chilli paste (*nahm prik pow*)
4 Tbs. Thai oyster sauce
3 Tbs. peanut oil
8 cloves garlic, chopped
1 small onion, quartered and sliced ¼-inch crosswise
4 jalapeno peppers, preferably red, cut lengthwise into 6 to 8 slivers each with seeds
4 tsp. yellow curry powder
1 cup Asian or Chinese celery leaves and inch-long tender stems
4 green onions, white and green parts, split in half lengthwise, and cut into
   1½-inch segments
½ tsp. ground white pepper
2 to 3 Tbs. fish sauce (*nahm bplah*), or light soy sauce, to taste

Pry crab(s) open, remove gills, and rinse. Chop off claws and legs and separate each into two pieces at the joints. Crack shell with the blunt edge of a cleaver, or use a nutcracker. Cut the body in half down the middle, then each half into 2 to 3 pieces for large crabs. (Steam the back shell and save the creamy crab butter inside for making fried rice, or add to sauce mixture that follows.) Set aside at room temperature, so that it is not icy cold when you begin the stir-fry.

Beat eggs and mix them with the coconut milk or milk, roasted chilli paste, and oyster sauce. (If using canned coconut milk, stir or heat just enough to dissolve the coagulated cream to a smooth consistency. Cool before mixing with other ingredients.)

Heat a wok over high heat until its surface is smoking hot. Swirl in oil and wait 15 to 20 seconds for it to heat before tossing in chopped garlic and sliced onion. Sauté 20 to 30 seconds, then toss in crab pieces. Stir-fry for 1 to 2 minutes, or until most of the shell has turned pink. Add chillies and sprinkle evenly with curry powder. Toss and cook another minute.

Stir milk-and-egg mixture and pour over the crab pieces. Cover the wok and let the mixture come to a boil. Turn crab pieces, cover, and cook 1 to 2 minutes. Add the Chinese celery and green onions, sprinkle with white pepper, and toss crabs again. Season with fish sauce or light soy sauce to taste, and cook crabs until they are cooked through and sauce has thickened.

Serves 3 to 4 with rice in a multicourse family-style meal.

(continued on next page)

Notes and Pointers:

Yellow curry powder is seldom used to make curries in Thailand. Instead, it is preferred as a flavoring ingredient in some stir-fried dishes and in marinades for grilling. In this common stir-fry, served throughout Thailand, a fragrant Madras yellow curry powder is combined with roasted chilli paste to produce a sweet and mildly spiced sauce to flavor crabs. If a homemade roasted chilli paste is used (page 175), the sauce will have a greater depth of flavor.

For any stir-fried crab dish, use only fresh raw crabs that have not been cooked. As the cracked pieces are tossed in the wok with the seasonings, they gradually absorb the sauce as they cook, staying moist and succulent, and becoming imbued with all the flavors of the seasonings. Previously cooked crabs will dry out when cooked again in the stir-fry; their cooked flesh also will not absorb the sauce the same way that raw flesh does.

The sauce in this recipe can also be used to top pan-fried, crispy fried, or grilled fish. Simply cook all the ingredients as instructed, skipping the crab, and spoon sauce over the fish. Or, try the stir-fry with large prawns, squid, and scallops.

Wok-Tossed Crab in the Shell with Green Onions

(Bpoo Pad Hom)

1 large Dungeness crab, or about 2 to 2½ lbs. smaller crabs
1 stalk lemon grass
3 Tbs. peanut oil, for stir-frying
6 cloves garlic, chopped
1 chopped shallot, or ¼ cup chopped yellow onion
1 Tbs. minced, peeled fresh ginger
1 tsp. sugar
2 Tbs. fish sauce (*nahm bplah*), or to taste
2 Tbs. water or stock
4 green onions, split in half lengthwise and cut into 2-inch lengths (both white
   and most of green parts)
2 orange or red serrano or jalapeno peppers, cut into large slivers with seeds
¼ tsp. ground white pepper
2 Tbs. rice wine
A few sprigs of cilantro, for garnish

Pry crab(s) open, remove gills, and rinse. Chop off claws and legs, and separate each into two pieces at the joints. Crack shell with the blunt edge of a cleaver, or use nutcracker. Cut the body in half down the middle, and each half into 2 to 3 pieces for large crabs. (Steam the back shell and save the creamy crab butter inside it for making fried rice.) Set aside at room temperature, so that it is not icy cold when you begin the stir-fry.

Trim and discard woody bottom tip of the lemon grass stalk, and remove the loose outer layer(s). Crush trimmed stalk with a cleaver or mallet, then cut at a sharp slanted angle ¼-inch apart, to make pieces about an inch long.

Heat a wok over high heat until it begins to smoke. Swirl in oil to coat wok surface, and wait 15 to 20 seconds for oil to heat. Add garlic, chopped shallot/onion, ginger, and lemon grass. Stir for about 30 seconds, then toss in crab. Stir-fry 1 to 2 minutes, or until most of shell has turned pink. Sprinkle with sugar, fish sauce, and 2 tablespoons water or stock.

Continue to stir-fry another 1 to 2 minutes, then toss in green onions and chillies. Stir and cook a minute longer. Sprinkle in white pepper and rice wine. Stir to mix, then cover wok for one-half to one minute, or until the crab pieces are cooked through. Transfer to a serving plate and garnish with cilantro.

Serves 3 to 4 with other dishes and rice in a family-style meal.

(continued on next page)

Notes and Pointers:

The light seasonings in this easy stir-fry add subtle flavors to enhance the delicate flavor of crab. Always use a raw crab for stir-frying, so that the flesh absorbs the seasonings as it cooks, and stays moist and succulent.

Cooking times vary according to the kind, size, and thickness of the crab(s). At any time during stir-frying, if the mixture in the wok looks too dry, and might burn, sprinkle in a tablespoon or two of water or stock. In the finished dish, the crab pieces are coated with the flavorings with very little sauce.

Dancing Shrimp

Black-Peppered Crab with Roasted Spices

(Bpoo Pad Priktai Dâm Gkap Kreuang Tehd)

2 lbs. crabs: blue, Dungeness, or other medium to large crab
1 tsp. cumin seeds
2 tsp. coriander seeds
10 dried red chillies
Pinch or two of salt
3 Tbs. peanut oil
10 cloves garlic, finely chopped
1 to 1½ Tbs. coarsely ground black peppercorns
½ cup mild seafood or chicken stock
2 Tbs. Thai oyster sauce
2 Tbs. fish sauce (*nahm bplah*), to taste
1 Tbs. granulated sugar
2 green onions, cut into thin rounds (use white and half of green parts)
2 orange or red serrano, jalapeno, or fresno peppers, cut in half lengthwise, then
   sliced at a diagonal ¼-inch thick, with seeds

Pry crab(s) open, remove gills, and rinse. For blue crabs or other smaller crabs, chop down the middle of the body, leaving legs and claws attached. For Dungeness or large crabs, chop claws and legs off and separate each into two pieces at the joints. Then, chop down the middle of the body and further chop each half into 2 to 3 pieces. Lightly crack shell of legs and claws, enough so that sauce can seep in during cooking.

In a small, dry pan, roast the cumin and coriander seeds separately over medium heat, until they are aromatic and evenly darkened. Pulverize with a mortar and pestle, or use a clean coffee grinder. Using the same pan, roast the dried red chillies with the salt, stirring often, until they are dark red and slightly charred. Grind to a fine powder and measure out 1 teaspoon for this recipe.

Heat a wok over high heat until it begins to smoke. Swirl in oil to coat wok surface and wait a few seconds for it to heat. Add the garlic, sauté 15 to 20 seconds, until golden and aromatic. Follow with the black pepper, cumin, coriander, and ground dried red chillies. Stir a few seconds before tossing in crab pieces. Stir-fry about 1 minute and, when most of the shells are turning pink, add stock. Bring to a boil and season with oyster sauce, fish sauce, and sugar. Cover and cook for 2 to 4 minutes (depending on size of crabs) over medium-high heat, lifting lid every 30 seconds or so to stir and turn crabs. Toss in green onions and chilli slivers and continue to stir-fry, uncovered, until crab pieces are cooked through.

Serves 4 to 6 with rice and other dishes in a family-style meal.

(continued on next page)

Notes and Pointers:

While most stir-fried crabs in the shell are relatively mild dishes, this recipe is packed with a strong spiciness and an aromatic, roasted fragrance. Serve with plenty of rice. Crack the crab and eat as you go, with mouthfuls of rice to temper the heat.

If you like the intense flavors in this recipe, try cooking other crustaceans this way, too, such as large prawns and lobster tails.

Wok-Tossed Shelled Crab with Chillies, Garlic, and Crisped Holy Basil

(Neua Bpoo Pad Gkaprow Gkrawb)

2 cups peanut oil, for frying
2 cups holy basil leaves (*bai gkaprow*)
10 cloves garlic, chopped
8 to 12 Thai chillies (*prik kee noo*), cut into thin rounds, then crushed with mortar
   and pestle
1½ cups shelled crabmeat
1 to 1½ Tbs. fish sauce (*nahm bplah*), to taste
½ to 1 tsp. granulated sugar, to taste

Heat oil in a wok over high heat until it begins to smoke. Stir in holy basil and fry until the leaves dry and turn crispy and dark green (1 to 2 minutes). Remove from oil with a large wire-mesh skimmer with bamboo handle.

Clean oil with a fine wire-mesh skimmer. Remove all but 2 tablespoons from the wok, reserving the rest for future use in frying or stir-frying. Increase heat to high, and add garlic, stir 10 to 15 seconds, then add Thai chillies. Stir a few more seconds before adding the crab. Stir-fry for one-half minute, then season to taste with fish sauce and sugar. Continue to stir-fry until crab has dried.

Turn off heat and add two-thirds of the crisped basil. Toss quickly to mix with crab and seasonings. Transfer to a serving dish; arrange the remaining crisped basil around the dish and serve immediately, while basil is still crispy.

Serve this hot and spicy dish with plenty of plain steamed rice.

Serves 4 to 6 in a multicourse family-style meal.

Notes and Pointers:

The inspiration for this quick-and-easy stir-fry came from one of my favorite restaurants on the Gulf of Thailand. Situated along a quiet stretch of shoreline in the small squid-fishing village of Pranburi Marina, Sunee is an unassuming, open-air restaurant run by a friendly family who really knows seafood. Every dish I have eaten here has been absolutely delicious! Although the area is a little out of the way—awkwardly located four hours' drive south of Bangkok, and without any special attractions to speak of other than a long row of smelly, though photogenic, squid-drying racks—I make a special effort to come here for lunch at least once every year. The problem of eating here is that there are so many favorites that placing an order is a major challenge. To partially solve this problem, I often invite a group of friends to come along and share as many dishes as we can manage to eat.

(continued on next page)

If you ever happen to be on the main highway going south at an opportune time, do take a detour and drive the fourteen kilometers from the provincial town of Pranburi toward the coast. Sunee is located next to a long dock, from which tons of squid are unloaded from fishing boats early every morning. Besides this crab stir-fry, a must on your first visit is *meuk daed diow*, or "single sun squid" — squid that have been dried for one day in the hot sun, then refrigerated and fried the next day. It's exceptional!

A 2-pound Dungeness crab yields approximately 1½ cups of shelled crabmeat. Since I live on the West Coast, this is my crab of choice to use for this stir-fry, but you may use any kind of crab.

If you are not able to find fresh holy basil, substitute Thai sweet basil, but it is holy basil that makes this dish extra special to me.

After frying the basil, the oil becomes infused with a rich basil flavor, so save it for stir-frying dishes that can benefit from its fragrance.

Crab Fried Rice
(*Kao Pad Bpoo*)

3 to 4 Tbs. peanut oil
6 cloves garlic, chopped
2 Tbs. crab paste (page 48), or use crab butter from inside the shell of a crab
3 cups cooled, cooked rice with grains loosened
I cup cooked crabmeat
2 eggs
2 green onions, white and green parts, thinly sliced into rounds
2 Tbs. fish sauce (*nahm bplah*), or to taste
I tsp. granulated sugar, or to taste
Juice of I lime, or to taste
Generous sprinkling of ground white pepper
½ cup short cilantro sprigs
I medium pickling cucumber, halved lengthwise, and sliced ⅛-inch thick at a
   sharp, slanted angle
4 small wedges of lime

Thai chillies in fish sauce (*Prik nahm bplah*)
10 to 15 Thai chillies (*prik kee noo*), sliced into thin rounds
¼ cup fish sauce (*nahm bplah*)

Heat a wok over high heat until it is smoking hot. Swirl in oil to coat the wok surface, and wait a few seconds for it to heat. Add garlic. Brown lightly and add crab paste (if using). Stir a few seconds, then add rice, making sure grains are loosened beforehand and not lumped together. Toss rice for one minute to coat evenly with oil and crab paste. Then, add crab meat and crab butter (if using instead of crab paste). Stir well into rice. Stir-fry 1 to 2 minutes, or until rice appears to be warmed through and glistening.

Push rice up one side of the wok to clear a small area. Crack eggs onto this area, breaking the yolks. Let set, turning the eggs and rice occasionally, so that neither burns. When eggs are set, cut them with the spatula into small chunks and toss in with the rice. Add green onions and season rice to taste with fish sauce, sugar, and lime juice. Sprinkle liberally with ground white pepper. Toss well.

Spoon onto individual plates, garnish with cilantro, a wedge of lime, and arrange sliced cucumbers on the side. Mix Thai chillies with fish sauce in a sauce dish and serve alongside for those who wish a saltier and hotter bite.

Serves 3 to 4.

(continued on next page)

Crab Fried Rice (cont.)

Notes and Pointers:

In my home, making fried rice is a way of using up leftover rice, and an easy way to throw together a one-dish lunch in a hurry. Usually, all sorts of other leftovers and remnants of vegetables, herbs, and sauces are tossed into the wok as well and stir-fried with the rice, a little oil, and seasonings. But, when it comes to crab fried rice, the process elevates into something quite special, what with the price of crabs as high as it is. I plan for it, since I do not like store-bought cooked crabmeat, which usually is not very fresh, on top of being prohibitively expensive. I make a special trip to the local Chinatown seafood market and pick out the liveliest crab I can find from the tanks, take it home, and steam and shell it myself.

Fried rice is best when made with leftover rice that has been refrigerated, or with specially cooked rice a little on the firm and chewy side, that has been completely cooled. Frying warm, freshly cooked rice just out of the steamer is not advised, as the grains easily turn mushy and fall apart rather than stay firm and *al dente*. For my fried rice, I prefer using firmly cooked Thai jasmine rice, as it has that extra special chewy texture, much like sticky rice, after it is fried.

Crab paste, available in small jars from Asian markets, enriches fried rice. For more information, see page 48.

If shelling your own crab is too much work, and ready-shelled crabmeat is out of your budget, use this same recipe to make yourself shrimp fried rice or seafood fried rice with a combination of shrimp, firm fish, squid, and shelled mussels. There is a paste similar to crab paste, also available in small jars and labeled "shrimp paste in soya bean oil" (not to be confused with the fermented *gkabpi* shrimp paste), that can be used to give extra shrimp flavor. If you wish, you may also throw some vegetables into the fried rice, like shelled peas, diced carrot, and sliced pieces of snow or snap peas. For my crab and seafood fried rice, I prefer to keep it as simple as possible, with lots of fresh seafood without any distractions.

8

MOLLUSKS

Stuffed Squid Soup with Napa Cabbage
or Squash   237

Spicy Salad of Crisped Dried Cuttlefish, Shrimp,
and Cashews   239

Crispy Shrimp-and-Crab-Stuffed Squid   241

Squid Steamed with Chilli-Lime Sauce   243

Spicy Southern-Style Stir-Fried Squid   244

Sizzling Stir-Fried Squid with Chillies and
Fragrant Herbs   246

Squid Sautéed with Garlic and Lime   248

Squid Stir-Fried with Roasted Chilli Sauce and
Thai Basil   249

Marinated Charcoal-Grilled Squid   250

Clam and Mussel Coconut Lime Soup with Oyster
Mushrooms   252

Shellfish Salad with Aromatic Thai Herbs, Crisped
Shallots and Garlic, and Sweet-and-Sour Chilli
Dressing   254

Baked Oysters with Salted Black Beans and
Pickled Garlic   256

Savory Pan-Fried Mussel Cake with Wilted Bean
Sprouts   257

Marinated Mesquite-Grilled Scallops Served with Sweet-and-Tangy Dipping Sauce   260

Pan-Seared Sea Scallops Topped with *Choo Chee* Curry Sauce   262

Spicy Stir-Fried Scallops and Mussels with Homemade Chilli Paste and Thai Eggplants   264

Curried Mussels on the Half Shell with Flaked Crab   266

Steamed Mussels in Clay Pot with Aromatic Herbs   268

Clams Stir-Fried with Roasted Chilli Sauce and Basil   270

Wok-Tossed Mussels in the Shell with Lemon Grass and Basil   272

Oyster and Egg Scramble   273

Spicy "Broken Fish Trap" Soup   274

Mixed Seafood Salad with Lemon Grass, Mint, and Chilli-Lime Dressing   276

Spicy Seafood Sizzling Hot Plate   278

"Drunken" Mixed Seafood Stir-Fry with Holy Basil   280

Stir-Fried "Fish Trap"   282

ON A RECENT TRIP TO THAILAND, MY HUSBAND AND I MADE AN EXPEDI-
tion to explore the coastal province of Samut Songkram, southwest of
Bangkok, when we happened upon a fascinating floating market. It was the
morning of the twelfth day of the waxing moon, one of six days in the lunar
month when natives who live along the maze of canals and in nearby villages,
paddle, walk, and drive to a meeting place along a paved landing to buy, sell,
browse, visit friends, barter, and trade.

Among the gregarious gathering, we spotted a docked boat that had a
flurry of activity taking place around it. Soon, our noses caught the fragrant
waft of heavenly seafood being seared and charred. We eagerly joined the
crowd of hungry customers awaiting their turn, and watched with great interest the friendly vendor and local "master chef" turn out, in dramatic fashion, one batch after another of exceptional pan-fried mussel cakes on an
oversized griddle inside her wooden rowboat.

A continuous parade of colorful boats paddled by on the canal, hawking
seasonal fruits and vegetables, dried goods, and a large assortment of noodles, sweet treats, and other inviting snack foods—many of them made to order right there on the tiny boats equipped with gas and charcoal burners.
Waiting for our order to be filled, therefore, was not at all an issue; in fact, we

watched her fill countless orders—from passersby on the landing and fellow boat vendors floating by for a fulfilling morning treat—all the while chatting and laughing with friends and acquaintances. Depending on what someone's pocketbook could afford, she would add or subtract the number of mussels from the batter in special orders and charge accordingly. The heartwarming exchange of energy and of food, nurturance, good humor, and spirit made our plate of pan-fried mussels truly unforgettable, and an experience we surely will repeat for years to come.

Mussels, clams, scallops, and oysters are bivalve members of the mollusk family, their soft bodies protected by a pair of shells. In addition, there are univalve (single shell) members, also called gastropods, such as snails, periwinkle, conch, and abalone; and cephalopods (squid, cuttlefish, and octopus), which have no external shell, but an internal plasticlike cartilage or, in the case of cuttlefish, a white chalky bone.

The type of mussels found in Thailand's waters is a succulent, green-shelled variety with bright reddish flesh when raw, and the most common and well-liked clam is small but thin-shelled, holding plenty of sweetly luscious meat. Called *hoi lai* (*hoi* means shellfish, and *lai* means pattern or design), its gray-tan shell has pretty, irregular, diamondlike markings in deeper grayish brown. In fact, an artistic Canadian woman who traveled on one of my homegrown tours was so taken by the simple beauty that she selected a pair to take home to make herself some earrings. The puzzled waiter intently watched her wipe the shells after she cherished the delicious contents and not long after, he returned from the kitchen with a bagful of carefully washed and scrubbed shells for the lovely lady!

In addition to these two widely consumed shellfish, there are numerous other varieties, ranging from the tiny clams that kids love to dig along beaches, which are pickled in fish sauce to serve with rice porridge for breakfast, to giant sea clams with colorful lips, often seen tucked among coral reefs. The latter, plus conch and small, warm-water abalone are delicacies seldom seen in markets or restaurants. Scallops and oysters are also delicacies and are not found in great quantities in Thailand's waters. On the other hand, squid and cuttlefish are among the most abundant creatures that swim the warm tropical seas, providing an endless supply of inexpensive food to cook in many different ways.

Like fish and crustaceans, mollusks are not only delicious but are a nutritious food. They are rich in protein and minerals, especially iron, zinc, copper, iodine, and potassium, and low in fat and calories.

How to Select and Tell Freshness

Shellfish: Buy shellfish only from reliable sources, as they are inedible if they have been contaminated by toxins from polluted waters, or by pathogenic bacteria or toxin-producing algae that can cause food poisoning. Reputable seafood markets carry mollusks that are farm-raised in licensed, regularly inspected areas rather than harvested from the wild. If you wish to gather your own, check with the local fishery department to make sure the waters are not contaminated. Toxic algae usually bloom during the hot summer months, so avoid these months unless you can be assured by the authorities.

Select mussels, clams, and oysters with their shells tightly shut to ensure that they are still alive. Since some may open their shells to breathe, press the shells together with your fingers, and if they close and remain closed, they are still alive.

Fresh oysters are also sold already shelled in glass jars. They should look shiny, and the liquid surrounding them should be clear, not milky.

Clams and mussels that are either shelled or on the half-shell are available already cooked from some seafood markets, and Asian stores that carry frozen seafood products. If they are frozen, make sure there is no frost in the packages to indicate that they haven't been sitting around in the freezer too long. If they are not frozen, use your nose to guide you. They should have a mild, fresh smell, not a fishy or ammonialike odor.

Because scallops are very perishable, they are usually shelled and washed as soon as they are caught and immediately frozen or covered with ice. Fresh scallops should be white, firm, and moist, with only a faint scent of the sea. Frozen scallop products are permitted by government regulations to contain up to twenty-five percent water. Drain well after defrosting and blot dry with a clean towel to avoid diluting stir-fries and marinades with excess water held in their flesh.

Squid and Cuttlefish: Squid is more slender, pointier in shape, and has thinner flesh than cuttlefish and, instead of a cuttle bone, is supported by an internal plasticlike quill. Otherwise, the two cephalopods look very much alike with tube- or baglike bodies and tentacles extending from the head.

I prefer to buy squid before they are cleaned, because it is easier to tell how fresh they are. Most have been frozen before, since they spoil quickly. Large fishing vessels that go out to sea for days at a time are equipped with refrigeration facilities to freeze the squid soon after they are caught. What looks like fresh squid in supermarkets and seafood markets is often defrosted, frozen squid.

Choose ones with a shiny luster on clean, unbroken skin. They should look or feel firm rather than limp and soggy and, of course, smell mild and fresh. In Asian markets, squid is frequently available in frozen three-pound boxes. Some of these boxes have cellophane windows, or are unsealed, so that they can be opened to check the contents inside. Select a box with clean and plump, neatly arranged squid. I like those with body tubes about four to five inches long.

If only cleaned squid are available, they should still have a translucent quality to them rather than a dull, opaque white. Precleaned squid do not come with tentacles, which is another reason to buy them whole and uncleaned. The crisp texture of the tentacles is special to squid lovers. Since the quantity of squid to use in the recipes to follow is given by their uncleaned weight, figure on using twenty to twenty-five percent less of precleaned squid.

Because an industrial machine has been used to clean them, precleaned squid are not always very clean, and broken guts trapped inside their tubelike bodies can make them taste old. Go through each of them, and remove any remains found inside.

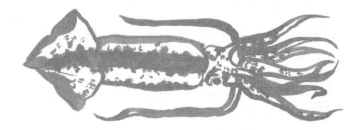

Cuttlefish are almost never available fresh or in whole, uncleaned form in this country. Their flesh is much thicker and meatier than squid. Some Asian markets carry them in frozen bags in two sizes. The small baby size, about two inches long, is very tender. A slightly larger size (three to four inches) is firmer and meatier, but can still cook up quite tender. Both are excellent, and may be used in any of the squid dishes. Both also come already cleaned and skinned in white pieces without tentacles.

How to Clean and Prepare for Cooking

Shellfish: Scrub the shells of mussels and clams under water to remove any mud, sand, and crusty particles. Discard any with broken shells or shells that are open and will not close when pressed together. Pull or cut off the beard from mussels if they have them—this stringy vegetative growth is actually produced by the mussels' own secretions as a means to attach themselves together in clusters to rocks, sandbanks, and other objects. For soups or brothy dishes, the beard may be left on to add extra flavor to the liquids.

If they are sandy or are heavy, suggesting that there may be sand inside the shells, soak in salted water for an hour or more to induce them to spit out the sand. Use three to four tablespoons of sea salt per quart of cool water. After soaking, rinse thoroughly in several changes of cool water.

Squid and Cuttlefish: There are different ways to clean squid, but basically what needs to be done includes removing all the guts from inside the tubelike body, cutting the tentacles from the head, and peeling off the skin. Thin-flesh squid is usually kept in tubes to be cut into rounds. Larger, thicker-flesh squid may also be cut down the middle of the belly and opened up into a flat piece to be sliced into smaller, bite-size pieces that curl up when cooked.

To avoid having to stick my fingers into the tube to pull out all the guts, I use a knife to push out the insides, including the quill. In order to do this easily, the head must be pulled off the squid rather than cut off. Hold the squid loosely and firmly yank the head to dislodge it. Along with the head comes a trail of guts, and what remains inside is now loosened. Cut in between the eyes and tentacles (do not cut too closely to the tentacles so that they stay in one piece) and discard the part with the eyes and entrails. If there is a hard round ball, or a part of one, attached to the cut end of the tentacles, pull it out and discard. This is the beak of the squid through which it feeds, or what I call "squid lips."

Now lay the body with the lighter-colored belly facing up and the flippers on the opposite side, flat on the cutting board. Using a sharp knife, gently scrape the skin off the bottom tip. Then, holding the knife at an angle of at least 45 degrees or sharper, apply pressure, without cutting into the squid, to push and scrape from the bottom tip to the other end, removing both the skin and the remaining entrails all in one movement of the hand. Then, hold down on the tip of the quill with the knife and pull the body back to remove it. The skin on the second side can be easily peeled off with the fingers, or scraped off with the knife. Be careful not to pull off the flippers.

This method may take a little practice but, once you get a sense of how firmly to pull the head, how to angle your knife, and how much pressure to apply to push and scrape, you will find that it is very quick and easy. Holding the knife at an angle prevents you from cutting the squid, while pushing with sufficient pressure from the very tip ensures that everything comes out.

Once you have a clean tube inside out, cut into one-inch rounds and keep fresh in cold salted water until fifteen to twenty minutes before you are ready to cook them. Then, drain and rinse in fresh water to remove the salt. Drain well before cooking.

To remove remnants of broken guts from precleaned squid, use a knife as above to push out the remains. If they have a fishy smell, soak in salted water to freshen.

Cuttlefish have thicker flesh and can be scored for an impressive presentation when they are cooked. Score the outer surface with a sharp knife in a diagonal crisscross pattern, making deep cuts one-sixteenth to one-eighth of an inch apart without cutting through. After scoring, cut the cuttlefish into bite-size pieces. When cooked, the pieces will curl up, revealing a lovely design. If the scoring is done with the knife blade held at a 45-degree angle to the surface of the squid, a beautiful pine-cone effect will be achieved. Scoring takes time but is well worth the effort to impress your dinner guests. The frozen cuttlefish mentioned in the above section really are a delight to eat and, although firmer and meatier than squid, they seldom become tough and chewy when cooked.

How to Store

Fresh mussels and clams should be cooked while still alive. They keep for up to three days if they are stored properly in the refrigerator. Never leave them enclosed in a plastic bag, as they will suffocate. Instead, put them in a bowl and cover with a damp loose-weave cloth. They may also be stored in a small amount of salted water, but don't completely submerge them. Change the water daily. Clean when you are ready to cook them, discarding any that have died.

Live, unshelled oysters keep a few days longer. Place them with the deeper shell down, and cover with a damp cloth in the refrigerator. Never store in water. Shelled oysters in their own juice stay fresh for a few days. Do not use if the juice has turned milky.

Shelled scallops keep a couple of days if they are very fresh when bought. Do not store in water, as this will draw out their delicious, sweet juices. Cover or place in a plastic bag to keep them from drying out, and store in the coolest spot in the refrigerator.

Squid should be cleaned the day they are bought or defrosted. If not, their flesh will become discolored and develop a fishy odor. After they are cleaned, store in a little salted water to keep them from drying out, but cook within a day if possible. After they're cooked, especially with plenty of garlic, chillies, and fish sauce, they stay good for several days.

Avoid refreezing previously frozen mollusks unless they have been cooked.

Some Cooking Tips

Like crustaceans, mollusks cook quickly. Take care not to overcook, as they can shrivel and become tough, especially clams and squid, and lose their delicate texture and sweet flavor. Cook fresh mussels and clams only until their shells open, not much longer. Any that don't open after sufficient cooking should be discarded, as they have probably died before going into the pan.

Squid and cuttlefish are tender when they are just lightly cooked. They're ready when they lose their translucence, turn opaque white, and curl along the edges. In boiling water, this takes only about thirty seconds. If they are toughened by overcooking, simmering another ten to fifteen minutes will turn them tender again, but it will be a different kind of tender. Their delightful crisp texture will be lost; moreover, they will have shrunk considerably.

Scallops have a delicate texture that can be lost by overcooking. Undercook them slightly so that they are smooth and succulent, rather than flaky and stringy.

Clams, mussels, and oysters hold very flavorful and sweet juices inside their shells. When shelling them raw or after they have been lightly steamed, make sure to save the tasty juices for soup stocks, or to use as cooking liquid in seafood dishes. The water from steaming, too, may be saved. Use these liquids within a few days before they turn fishy and old tasting, or freeze for longer storage.

When stir-frying clams and mussels in the shell, cooking liquids are not necessary as they will spit out their own sweet juices when they begin to cook. Just cover the pan to surround them with heat and stir occasionally until their shells open.

Defrosted frozen squid and scallops can add a lot of unwanted liquid to a stir-fry, so make sure they are well drained before tossing them into the wok. If their surface is wet, pat dry with a clean towel.

The tube-shaped body of squid makes it perfect for stuffing. However, it does shrink when cooked, sometimes by as much as half, so stuff lightly and only fill partially. Buy large squid for ease in stuffing.

Stuffed Squid Soup
with Napa Cabbage or Squash
(Gkaeng Cheud Bplah Meuk Yad Sai)

1 lb. pork soup bones
5 cups water
1 lb. medium to large squid
¼ tsp. white peppercorns, freshly ground
2 large cloves garlic, finely chopped
1 Tbs. chopped cilantro roots, or substitute bottom stems
⅓ lb. shrimp
¼ lb. ground pork
2 to 3 Tbs. fish sauce (*nahm bplah*), to taste
4 cloves chopped garlic
2 to 3 tsp. peanut oil
1½ cups oyster mushrooms or brown mushrooms
2 tsp. preserved Tianjin vegetables (*dtahng chai*), optional
1 tsp. sea salt
4 cups Napa cabbage cut into bite-size pieces, or use cabbage, bok choy, or
    summer squash
2 green onions, split in half lengthwise and cut into 1-inch segments (white and
    most of green parts)
¼ cup cilantro sprigs
½ tsp. ground white pepper

Place soup bones in a large pot with 5 cups water. Bring to a slow boil over medium heat, then reduce heat to the lowest setting and simmer partially covered for 40 minutes or longer. Simmering over low heat yields a clearer and sweeter soup; spoon off foam occasionally.

In the meantime, clean and skin squid. Leave in whole tubes. Rinse and drain well.

Pound white peppercorns, garlic, and cilantro roots or stems with a mortar and pestle to form a well-blended paste. Shell and chop shrimp finely; mix with the ground pork, garlic-pepper paste, and 1 tablespoon fish sauce. Mix well and stuff loosely into squid about three-fourths full—do not stuff too tightly as squid shrinks when cooked.

Brown chopped garlic in the peanut oil in the rounded bottom of a wok. Transfer to a small bowl and let cool. Leave small caps of oyster mushrooms whole and cut the larger caps into pieces of similar size, using stems also. If using brown mushrooms, slice into ¼-inch pieces.

When stock is ready, remove the bones. Flavor broth with preserved Tianjin vegetables (if using), sea salt, and fish sauce to the desired saltiness. Bring to a boil over high heat and drop stuffed squid gently

(continued on next page)

into hot broth. Return to a boil, then simmer about 5 minutes over low to medium heat. If any pork-shrimp mixture is left, form into small bite-size balls and drop into broth along with any squid tentacles. Add Napa cabbage. Cook another 5 minutes; add mushrooms. Continue to simmer a few minutes more until the vegetables are tender.

Fish stuffed squid from the broth and slice at a slanted angle into ½-inch thick ovals. Return to soup, and add green onions.

Just before serving, spoon in the browned garlic pieces with some of the oil, and stir in the cilantro and white pepper. Ladle into individual serving bowls.

Serves 8 with rice and other dishes in a family-style meal.

Notes and Pointers:

In everyday Thai-style dining, all the nonrice dishes, including soups, are served together with rice, rather than as separate courses to be eaten by themselves. During the meal, we take a bite of one dish along with rice, then switch to a bite of a second dish. The third bite might take us back to the first dish or on to the third or fourth. A small amount, enough for just one or two bites, is spooned onto our plate at a time rather than being piled high along with everything else, as in Western-style dining. In short, we nibble-eat, sharing the dishes with others dining with us, all the while making sure each and everyone gets enough of the extra special dishes in the meal.

Soups are often dished onto small, individual bowls placed alongside our dinner plates. We take a spoonful, then continue with our nibble-eating of other dishes and rice, returning to take another spoonful from time to time. Nonspicy soups like this one serve as a palate cleanser, perhaps subduing the burning sensations on the tongue and lips or clearing the way for us to taste the full range of subtle flavors in other delicately balanced dishes.

This mild and appetizing soup is sweet with the natural flavors from the seafood, pork, and vegetables. (If you are lazy, you may start out with mild chicken stock instead of making a broth from scratch with the pork bones.) The squid shrink to about half their size when the filling in them is cooked, so take care not to overstuff, as the filling shrinks less. When simmered as long as they are in this recipe, squid will be tender in a different way than when blanched quickly for a salad, while, at the same time, adding a flavor of the sea to the broth. Large squid are easier to stuff than smaller ones. It would help if their openings were large enough for small spoonfuls of filling to comfortably fit in. Try a sausage stuffing funnel or a pastry bag with a wide-open tip.

Napa cabbage really adds a lot to the broth. I like to simmer until the pieces are tender and feel as though they would melt in the mouth, as opposed to the crispness I prefer in stir-fries with this vegetable. Sometimes, I also add a small package of softened, glassy bean thread noodles to the soup for textural interest and extra bulk. They cook quickly, so stir them in during the last couple of minutes of cooking.

Spicy Salad of Crisped Dried Cuttlefish, Shrimp, and Cashews

(Yâm Sadet)

2 small dried cuttlefish (about 2 inches in length)
¼ lb. small fresh shrimp
1 stalk lemon grass
1 Tbs. coarsely chopped peeled fresh ginger
2 Tbs. coarsely chopped shallot
½ tsp. coarsely chopped fresh lime peel
1½ Tbs. lime juice
6 Thai chillies (*prik kee noo*), cut into very thin rounds
2 tsp. fish sauce (*nahm bplah*)
1 to 1½ tsp. sugar, to taste
½ cup peanut oil, for frying
½ cup raw whole cashews
6 to 8 *bai chaploo* (see Notes and Pointers), or 12 or more large spinach leaves

Tear dried cuttlefish across the body (it won't tear easily lengthwise) into small strips about the size of a cashew to yield ½ cup. If it is too tough to tear, warm first over the low flame of a burner for a minute or two, holding it with a pair of tongs and turning frequently until it is softened. Cool enough to handle, then tear.

Shell shrimp, devein, and butterfly. Rinse and drain well.

Trim and discard woody bottom tip of lemon grass and remove the loose, fibrous outer layers. Slice inner stalk from bottom end into very thin rounds to yield 2 tablespoons. Prepare the ginger, shallot, and lime peel.

Mix lime juice with Thai chillies, fish sauce, and sugar in a small sauce dish. Stir well to dissolve sugar.

Heat oil in a wok over medium heat for a couple of minutes. Add cashews and fry over low heat, so that they sizzle very slowly. Stir frequently for 5 to 7 minutes, until the nuts turn golden brown and are cooked all the way through to the core. Strain from oil with a wire-mesh scooper. Increase heat to medium and fry the dried cuttlefish for 1 to 2 minutes, until they are browned. Strain from oil. The pieces should turn crispy when they cool.

Increase heat to high. Pat surface of shrimp dry with a towel, and fry quickly in the hot oil until they turn pink (about one-half to one minute). Remove from oil and drain. Reserve the oil for future use in frying or stir-frying seafood dishes.

(continued on next page)

Arrange *bai chaploo* or spinach leaves on a serving plate. Toss the shrimp, crisped cuttlefish, and cashews with the lemon grass, ginger, shallot, lime peel, and chilli–lime sauce. Spoon over the leaves and serve immediately.

Serves 3 to 4 as an appetizer or salad in a multicourse family-style meal.

Notes and Pointers:

This salad/appetizer is a house special of my favorite restaurant in the heart of the southern region — Reun Mai ("Wooden House") on the outskirts of the town of Krabi. In a relaxed setting under the shade of a bamboo grove next to a rubber plantation, this restaurant serves some of the most memorable meals I've had in the south. Cooking students who have traveled with me love this restaurant and enjoy this unusual salad as much as I do. The strong, sharp flavors really do wake up the mouth, as well as start the gastric juices flowing in preparation to receive other wondrous food.

Do not use large cuttlefish, as they can be tough. The 2- to 3-inch size comes in small bags in Southeast Asian markets. When fried, the pieces turn crispy and chewy but are not tough. They do have a strong flavor that goes well with the other strongly flavored ingredients in the salad. If you are not able to find dried cuttlefish or do not like the flavor, substitute dried shrimp. Either fry or toast the shrimp in a dry pan until they pick up a little bit of a crispy edge.

A lighter version of this dish can be made by roasting the cashews in the oven, cooking the shrimp in hot water, and roasting the dried cuttlefish over a low flame for a few minutes until it is blistered and browned (the cuttlefish is limp when hot but turns crispy when cooled).

Bai chaploo is a thick, heart-shaped wild pepper leaf frequently used in salads to wrap chopped tidbits of ingredients. Since it is rarely available in this country, spinach is an acceptable substitute.

Crispy Shrimp-and-Crab-Stuffed Squid
(Bplah Meuk Krawb Sawd Sai Gkoong Bpoo)

2 to 2½ lbs. medium to large squid
¾ lb. fresh shrimp
6 cloves garlic, chopped
¼ tsp. white peppercorns, freshly ground
1 Tbs. chopped cilantro roots and bottom stems
2 Tbs. fish sauce (*nahm bplah*)
½ tsp. sugar
½ tsp. pure sesame oil
1 beaten egg white
1 Tbs. tapioca starch or cornstarch
1 green onion (dense part only), finely chopped
1 cup cooked crabmeat
2 to 3 cups peanut oil, for frying
1 egg
½ cup dried breadcrumbs
Lettuce, sliced cucumber, and sliced tomato, for lining serving plate
A few cilantro sprigs, for garnish
Sriracha bottled hot chilli sauce or chopped Thai chillies in fish sauce and lime
    juice (mix 5 chopped Thai chillies, 5 cloves chopped garlic, 1 to 2 Tbs. fish
    sauce, 2 Tbs. lime juice, and 1 tsp. sugar)

Clean and skin squid and leave in whole tubes; save tentacles for use in other squid dishes. Rinse and drain well. Shell the shrimp and chop finely in the food processor.

Make a paste out of the garlic, white pepper, and cilantro roots/stems by pounding with a mortar and pestle. Mix paste with fish sauce, sugar, sesame oil, egg white, and tapioca starch (or cornstarch). Stir the mixture in with the chopped shrimp until sticky and well blended. Add chopped green onion and flaked crabmeat. Blend well with shrimp.

Thoroughly dry squid inside out with a clean towel. Stuff the shrimp-crab mixture into the cavity of the squid loosely to fill about three-fourths of the tube (squid shrinks with cooking). Arrange stuffed squid on a steamer rack and steam over medium-high heat for 7 to 8 minutes. (Let water in steamer pot come to a boil before placing the rack over the pot.) Remove from heat and let drain and dry on a wire rack or on a strainer. When cool enough to handle, prick evenly with a fork.

Heat oil in a wok over high heat. Crack egg into a shallow bowl and beat lightly. Dip stuffed squid in the egg and roll in breadcrumbs to thoroughly coat. Fry in hot oil over medium heat until golden brown and crispy. Remove from oil with a wire-mesh skimmer and drain a few minutes on a wire rack.

(continued on next page)

Crispy Shrimp-and-Crab-Stuffed Squid (cont.)

Arrange squid on a serving platter lined with lettuce, sliced cucumber, and tomato. Each squid may also be sliced with a sharp knife into 3 to 4 round or oval pieces before arranging on the platter. Garnish with cilantro sprigs. Serve while still warm and crispy with bottled *Sriracha* chilli sauce and/or chopped Thai chillies in fish sauce and lime juice.

Serves 8 to 10 as an appetizer in a multicourse family-style meal.

Notes and Pointers:

Sliced rounds or ovals of stuffed squid with golden crispy edges make an attractive and tasty appetizer for a dinner party. The squid may be stuffed and steamed a day or two ahead of time and stored in the refrigerator. Fry them shortly before serving. If you desire crispier morsels, slice them into rounds or ovals before breading for frying.

The baglike tubes of squid invite stuffing but, because they are limp, it takes a little bit of practice to get the sticky shrimp mixture in. Buy large squid since they are a little easier to stuff.

There may be some splattering and bursting during frying if the squid are stuffed too tightly and not pricked with a fork. Also make sure that the surface has dried from steaming before breading for frying.

The shrimp-and-crab filling is good in its own right. If you find stuffing the squid too much of a chore, or cannot find larger squid, stuff the filling into sausage casing to make a shrimp sausage for grilling or frying. Or, make into a roll wrapped with thin rice paper, deep-fry until crispy, then slice into bite-size pieces. Serve with a sweet-and-sour chilli sauce like the one on page 254. I sometimes form the shrimp-and-crab mixture into small bite-size balls, roll them in bread crumbs, and fry until browned and crispy—makes a wonderful appetizer; or steam slightly larger balls to set, then skewer with bamboo sticks, and grill over hot charcoals for a smoky flavor. The mixture also makes a delicious filling for wontons.

Squid Steamed with Chilli-Lime Sauce
(Bplah Meuk Neung Manao)

1 lb. fresh squid, cleaned, skinned, and cut into 1-inch rounds
10 large cloves garlic, finely chopped
6 to 12 Thai chillies (*prik kee noo*), cut into very thin rounds
2 tsp. minced cilantro roots, or substitute with bottom stems
Juice of 1 to 2 limes, or about ¼ cup
2 to 3 Tbs. fish sauce (*nahm bplah*), to taste
1 to 1½ tsp. sugar, to taste

Mix chopped garlic, sliced Thai chillies, minced cilantro roots (or stems), lime juice, fish sauce, and sugar together and set aside to let flavors mingle and marry.

Drain cleaned squid pieces well. Squeeze lightly to remove any excess water. Arrange pieces on a heatproof serving dish that fits on the rack of a stacked steamer, as much as possible in a single layer. The dish should be about an inch deep to contain the sauce.

Bring 1½ to 2 inches of water on the bottom of the steamer pot to a rolling boil. Place the dish with the squid on the rack, and steam at high heat 5 to 7 minutes, or until the squid pieces have changed color and are beginning to curl along the edges. Remove from steamer and quickly drain off all the water that has steamed out of the squid or condensed from steaming (save for soup stock if you wish). Rearrange the squid pieces on the dish. Spoon the chilli-lime sauce evenly over them and return immediately to the hot steamer. Steam another 30 seconds.

Serves 3 to 4 with steamed rice in a multicourse family-style meal.

Notes and Pointers:

This light, oil-less, easy-to-digest dish is full of healthful benefits—*if* you can take the heat. Lots of garlic, chillies, and lime juice help unclog noses stuffed up from colds and supply plentiful vitamin C and antiseptic aid to help flush away the flu.

For a more appealing presentation, steam the cleaned squid whole, along with their tentacles, directly on a steamer rack until just cooked. Slice into bite-size pieces, arrange prettily, as if they are still whole, on a serving platter edged on one side with lettuce and a few slices of tomato or cucumber, and spoon the sauce over them. For a variation, two to three tablespoons of coarsely chopped pickled garlic and one to two tablespoons of coarsely chopped cilantro can be added to the sauce.

Spicy Southern-Style Stir-Fried Squid
(Pad Ped Bplah Meuk)

2½ lb. squid
1-inch section fresh ginger or *galanga,* minced
Bottom half of a lemon grass stalk, trimmed and thinly sliced into thin rounds,
    then chopped finely
3 to 6 serrano, jalapeno, or fresno peppers (preferably red), chopped with seeds
6 cloves garlic, chopped
1 Tbs. chopped cilantro roots (or substitute stem sections)
2 to 3 Tbs. peanut oil
3 shallots, halved lengthwise and thinly sliced crosswise
4 to 6 kaffir lime leaves, cut into fine inch-long slivers
2 to 3 Tbs. fish sauce (*nahm bplah*), to taste
Juice of ½ lime (about 1 Tbs.)
2 to 3 Tbs. tamarind juice, the thickness of fruit concentrate
2 to 3 tsp. palm sugar, to taste
Dash of white pepper
A small handful of cilantro leaves

Clean squid and cut into 1-inch rounds; leave tentacles whole. Drain well and squeeze gently to remove excess water trapped inside the rounds. Let them sit at room temperature for about 20 minutes.

Make a well-blended paste out of the ginger or galanga, lemon grass, chilli peppers, garlic, and cilantro roots by pounding the chopped and minced ingredients in a heavy stone mortar and pestle.

Heat a wok over high heat until it is smoking hot. Swirl in oil to coat its surface and heat 10 to 15 seconds before adding chilli paste. Fry paste in oil until aromatic. Add sliced shallots and toss for 20 seconds. Follow with squid and kaffir lime leaf slivers. Stir-fry 30 seconds to 1 minute, then season to taste with fish sauce, lime juice, tamarind, and palm sugar. Toss another 30 seconds to 1 minute, or until the squid is just cooked and still juicy and tender—do not overcook.

If the sauce is thin and watery, remove cooked squid from wok with a slotted spoon and reduce over high heat until it is thick and rich in color. Turn off heat and toss squid with the thickened sauce. Sprinkle with white pepper, stir, and transfer to a serving dish. Garnish with cilantro leaves.

Serves 6 with rice in a multicourse family-style meal.

Notes and Pointers:

There are many *pad ped* ("spicy stir-fry") dishes in Thai cuisine. Some reflect regional preferences; others are innovative creations of inspired cooks. This recipe offers a southern twist, with a tang from tamarind coming through the chilli and herbal flavors, softened by the background sweetness of palm sugar.

Try this stir-fry with shrimp, or a combination of shrimp and squid. Scallops would be good, too, as would shelled mussels combined with shrimp.

Sizzling Stir-Fried Squid
with Chillies and Fragrant Herbs
(Bplah Meuk Pad Chah)

1 lb. fresh squid
5 to 7 red and green serrano peppers, or 4 jalapeno or fresno peppers, chopped
5 to 7 cloves garlic, chopped
2½ Tbs. peanut oil
2 to 3 Tbs. fresh or frozen rhizome (*gkrachai*) , cut into very fine inch-long slivers
4 kaffir lime leaves, torn into small pieces
1 cup holy basil (*bai gkaprow*), or substitute Thai sweet basil (*bai horapa*)
1 jalapeno, serrano, or fresno pepper, cut in half lengthwise and each half at a
    slanted angle ¼-inch thick with seeds
A few short sprigs of fresh green peppercorns, optional
1 to 2 Tbs. fish sauce (*nahm bplah*), to taste
1 tsp. granulated sugar

Clean squid and cut into 1-inch rounds; leave tentacles whole. Drain well and squeeze gently to remove any water that may be trapped inside the rounds. Let sit at room temperature at least 20 minutes before cooking. If surface is still wet when you are ready to cook, pat dry with a clean towel.

Pound chillies and garlic with a mortar and pestle until pasty.

Heat a wok over high heat until it is smoking hot. Swirl in oil to coat its surface and wait 10 to 15 seconds for it to heat. Add chilli mixture and sauté until it is aromatic and the flavors are well blended. Toss in squid. Stir-fry over high heat for about 30 seconds, or until the squid begins to loose its translucence. Add slivered rhizome, kaffir lime leaves, holy basil, pepper slivers, and green peppercorn sprigs.

Stir-fry another minute and season to taste with fish sauce and sugar. Continue to stir-fry until all the squid has changed from translucent to opaque white and the pieces are curled along the edges. Transfer to a serving plate.

Serves 3 to 4 with rice and other dishes in a family-style meal.

Notes and Pointers:
Giving an English name to Thai dishes can sometimes be quite a challenge. Translating from the common Thai name doesn't always work. This stir-fry, for instance, is widely known as *pad chah*—*pad* means stir-fry and *chah* is the loud sizzling and splashing sound of food being tossed into a very hot wok. It conjures up an image of excitement in the kitchen. In addition, *pad chah* dishes are full of exuberant flavor, giving diners a joyful lift.

    This *pad chah* recipe is particularly lively. Not only is it dancing with spicy heat, but is also profusely fragrant with three luscious herbs—holy basil, *gkrachai* (rhizome), and kaffir lime leaves. My husband loves the combination and has placed the recipe among his top ten favorite seafood dishes. He even makes a pretty mean *pad chah* on days when I am too busy to cook. It's an all around winner—easy to make, enlivening, and oh so tasty.

Cuttlefish is excellent cooked this way; buy the 2-to-3-inch size available in frozen bags from Asian markets. Score them to cook into pretty patterned pieces. The recipe is also good with shrimp, scallops, and chunks of firm, meaty fish, such as sturgeon, halibut, tuna, and swordfish. I had it once with skate, which was first deep-fried in small thin slices until well crisped before tossing into the stir-fry. The pungent and perfumy qualities of *gkrachai* (rhizome) disguise the fishy odors of strong-tasting fish. Use the fresh or frozen roots; if these aren't available, use the pickled kind in jars, or dried slivers reconstituted by soaking in warm water. The latter will not soften enough to eat and are concentrated, so use only half of what is suggested.

Squid Sautéed with Garlic and Lime
(*Bplah Meuk Gkratiem Manao*)

1 lb. squid or cuttlefish
2 green onions
2 Tbs. peanut oil
1 head finely chopped garlic (about ¼ cup)
1 tsp. freshly ground white peppercorns
½ tsp. sea salt
1 Tbs. lime juice

Clean squid and cut into 1-inch rounds; leave tentacles whole. Drain well and squeeze gently to remove any water that may be trapped inside the rounds. (If using cuttlefish, score the steaks on the exterior surface with a diagonal crisscross pattern without cutting through, then cut into bite-size rectangles.) Let sit at room temperature at least 20 minutes before cooking. If the surface is still wet when you are ready to cook, pat dry with a clean towel.

Trim and discard root tip of green onions and half the green part. Slice thin rounds from white part to yield 1 tablespoon. Chop coarsely. Cut the remainder of the stalks into 1½-inch segments, then cut lengthwise into fine matchstick slivers.

Heat a wok until its surface is smoking hot. Add oil and sauté garlic over medium heat until it is faintly golden. Increase heat to high and add squid. Sauté, with frequent stirring, until squid begins to lose its translucence. Add white pepper and salt. Continue to cook until the squid is just cooked through.

Toss in chopped green onions and sprinkle with lime juice. Stir and quickly remove from heat onto a serving dish. Garnish top with green onion slivers.

Serves 3 to 4 with rice and other dishes in a family-style meal.

Notes and Pointers:

Since the local Southeast Asian market near where we live started carrying imported, frozen cuttlefish on a regular basis, this dish has become a frequent feature on our dinner table. My husband, who enjoys cooking, would alternate between this mild, peppery dish and the boldly spicy *pad chah* (page 246), making both with the tender and meaty cuttlefish. I make sure our freezer always has a bag around for a quick-and-easy meal when we run out of fresh food and don't have time to go grocery shopping.

The 2- to 3-inch cleaned cuttlefish are very tender but yet have a meaty texture. I seem to have much better luck buying cleaned cuttlefish that are fresh tasting than cleaned squid. Perhaps it is because squid are machine cleaned and subjected to a lot of water pressure in the process. They are left in tubes and not opened into steaks; frequently, broken guts are left trapped inside the tubes, which turns some of them old tasting.

Squid Stir-Fried with Roasted Chilli Sauce and Thai Basil

(Bplah Meuk Pad Prik Pow)

1 lb. fresh squid
2 Tbs. peanut oil
4 to 6 cloves garlic, chopped
2 Tbs. roasted chilli paste (*nahm prik pow*)
1 to 1½ Tbs. fish sauce (*nahm bplah*), to taste
¼ to ½ tsp. granulated sugar, to taste
1 to 2 serrano peppers, halved lengthwise and each half cut into 3
   to 4 slivers with seeds
½ cup Thai sweet basil leaves (*bai horapa*), flower buds may also be
   used

Clean squid and cut into 1-inch rounds; leave tentacles whole. Drain well and squeeze gently to remove any water that may be trapped inside the rounds. Let sit at room temperature at least 20 minutes before cooking. If surface is still wet when you are ready to cook, pat dry with a clean towel.

Heat a wok over high heat until it is smoking hot. Swirl in oil to coat wok surface and wait 10 to 15 seconds for the oil to heat. Add garlic and roasted chilli paste. Stir to soften chilli paste; mix it in with the oil, and lightly brown garlic (about 15 to 20 seconds). Toss in the squid. Stir-fry for about 1 minute, or until most of squid pieces have begun to lose their translucence. Season to taste with fish sauce and sugar. Add chilli slivers and basil, and toss until wilted and squid is just cooked through. Avoid overcooking as this can make the squid chewy and rubbery.

Serves 3 to 4 with rice and other dishes in a family-style meal.

Notes and Pointers:

This easy recipe is another good one to keep around when you feel like having Thai food but don't have a lot of time to cook. Just reach for your jar of roasted chilli paste and prepare some garlic, basil, and chillies. Clean some squid, or cut some up if you have frozen cleaned squid or cuttlefish in your freezer. Of course, the quality of the roasted chilli paste you use is key to how well the stir-fry will turn out. For sure, if you have made yourself a jar from scratch, using the recipe on page 175, the result should be most satisfying. Try also with prawns and scallops, or a combination of these two and squid.

Marinated Charcoal-Grilled Squid

(Bplah Meuk Yahng)

1½ lbs. large squid or small cuttlefish
1 Tbs. fish sauce (*nahm bplah*)
1 Tbs. soy sauce
1 Tbs. Thai oyster sauce
1 Tbs. lime juice
1 tsp. ground white pepper
2 Tbs. peanut oil
Sriracha bottled chilli sauce or a sweet-and-sour chilli sauce (such as the recipe
    on page 254)

Clean and skin squid, leaving in whole tubes; save tentacles for stir-fried seafood dishes. Rinse and drain well. Squeeze all the water out from inside the tubes. If using cuttlefish, leave in whole steaks; do not score.

Mix remaining ingredients and marinate squid or cuttlefish in the mixture for an hour or more. If squid or cuttlefish are not very large, skewer with bamboo sticks so that they are easier to turn. For cuttlefish, use two sticks, skewering horizontally across the steaks, using one stick near the top and one near the bottom of the cuttlefish's body. This helps keep them flat while grilling, as the heat will make them curl. With the grill positioned just above the coals, grill the squid/cuttlefish over hot charcoals, basting with the remaining marinade, until they are cooked through. For a smoky taste, use mesquite charcoal, or add moistened wood chips to the fuel.

Remove from skewers and slice into bite-size pieces. Serve with *Sriracha* bottled chilli sauce, or a sweet-and-sour chilli sauce like the one on page 254.

Serves 4 to 6 with other dishes in a family-style meal.

Notes and Pointers:

On a trip to the southern islands many years ago, the captain of our chartered boat stopped by a group of anchored fishing boats to make a trade—a chestful of ice for some very fresh, just-caught squid. While my tour members and I snorkeled, he and his crew gathered scraps of wood on the deserted island and built a fire near the beach to roast the squid. No sooner had we surfaced from the water, than the mouth-watering aroma of grilled seafood greeted us. A string of squid on a long stick beautifully grilled over the open fire were brought down to us at the water's edge. Hungry from the long swim around the captivating reef, we eagerly devoured them, sitting waist-deep in water, biting and tearing with our teeth. Squid ink dripped down from our hands and chins. Soon, pretty little fishes surrounded us wanting their share, too, which they got as we washed ourselves clean after a truly unforgettable meal!

With squid just fished out of the water, little is needed to improve their flavor. We are not so fortunate in everyday life, so a little help is needed. The marinade in this recipe may be simple, but it gives squid and cuttlefish an appetizing flavor and the lime juice tenderizes them as well.

Clam and Mussel Coconut Lime Soup with Oyster Mushrooms
(Dtom Kah Hoi Lai)

1 ½ lbs. manila clams
1 lb. mussels
2 cups water
2-inch section fresh or frozen galanga, thinly sliced
Bottom ⅔ of 2 lemon grass stalks, trimmed, crushed, and cut at a sharp, slanted
    angle ¼-inch apart into inch-long pieces
2 shallots, peeled and crushed whole
10 Thai chillies, stem removed and crushed whole
2 cups coconut milk, or 1 14-oz. can
4 cloves garlic, minced
2 cups sliced oyster mushrooms or substitute brown mushrooms
3 to 4 Tbs. fish sauce (*nahm bplah*), to desired saltiness
2 Tbs. tamarind juice, the thickness of fruit concentrate
2 tsp. palm sugar
2 to 3 Tbs. lime juice, to desired sourness
⅛ tsp. ground white pepper
6 kaffir lime leaves, cut into fine inch-long slivers

Rinse clams and mussels thoroughly, scrubbing off any mud, sand, or other crusty particles from their shells. Soak in cool, salted water for half an hour or more, then rinse and drain.

Bring 2 cups water to a boil in a 2-quart saucepan. Add clams, cover, and let steam until shells open. Strain from water with a slotted spoon. Likewise, steam mussels in the same water until their shells open. Strain and save the shellfish-flavored water. Remove flesh of mussels and clams from their shells, saving any juice remaining inside them, and set aside.

Measure 1 ½ cups of the cooking water, and return to pot. Add the juice saved from shelling the shellfish. Bring to a boil; add the galanga, lemon grass, and shallots. Cover and simmer over low heat about 5 minutes. Add crushed Thai chillies and simmer another 5 to 10 minutes.

Strain herbs from the broth and add coconut milk. Warm through until smooth. Add garlic and mushrooms. Bring to a slow boil over medium heat, stirring frequently to prevent cream from curdling.

Add shelled mussels and clams, and season to taste with fish sauce, tamarind, palm sugar, and lime juice. Stir in white pepper and half the kaffir lime leaf slivers. Turn off heat.

Ladle into individual serving bowls and top each with a few slivers of kaffir lime leaf.

Serves 6 to 8 with other dishes and rice in a family-style meal.

Notes and Pointers:

An adaptation of a classic Thai soup frequently made with chicken, this recipe is my version of a Thai-style chowder. Instead of shelling them, the clams and mussels may also be cooked and served in the shell in the coconut milk broth, with the herbs left in. For a richer soup, use straight coconut milk without any broth or water, simmering the herbs in it for a few minutes before adding the seasonings and the shellfish. Take care not to cook coconut milk over too high a heat and for too long a time, as this may cause the cream to curdle and the oil to separate. The soup can be made a day ahead of time and warmed before serving but, in my home, it seldom makes it into the refrigerator.

Hardly a seafood restaurant along either of Thailand's coasts is without a combination seafood coconut soup (*ðtom kah talay*) on its menu. Pieces of tasty fish, sweet and juicy mussels in the shell, succulent shrimp, tender squid, and chunks of precious crab swim in a sea of rich coconut broth flavored with herbs, chillies, and lime juice. After all, seafood and coconut milk are natural companions. What scene is more idyllic than a lovely stretch of beach, fringed with graceful coconut palms, while small boats on the calm sea beyond pull in lines and fish traps. Seafood is plentiful, and so are coconuts for making fresh coconut milk. Millions of them are picked every year, on plantations big and small, along wide expanses of the peninsula and on enchanting islands offshore. Monkeys are trained to pick them, while piecemeal workers, oblivious to the outside world, dehusk mountainous heaps with great speed and agility in the shade of the peaceful groves. The husks provide valuable fuel for grilling and smoking seafood. The rest is shredded and shipped abroad for horticultural use to replace dwindling peat-moss supplies from endangered bogs.

Shellfish Salad with Aromatic Thai Herbs, Crisped Shallots and Garlic, and Sweet-and-Sour Chilli Dressing

(Yâm Gkoong Hoi)

Sweet-and-Sour Chilli Dressing

10 to 15 Thai chillies (*prik kee noo*)
2 Tbs. vinegar
1 Tbs. tamarind juice, the thickness of fruit concentrate
Juice of 1 lime
3 Tbs. fish sauce (*nahm bplah*), to taste
2 to 3 Tbs. sugar, to taste

Shellfish Salad

½ lb. medium tiger prawns
½ lb. scallops
½ lb. shelled mussels
½ lb. small, shelled oysters
⅓ cup peanut oil
3 shallots, sliced into thin rounds
6 cloves garlic, chopped
2 stalks lemon grass
4 medium-size kaffir lime leaves
1-inch section fresh galanga or substitute fresh ginger
½ to 1 cup mint leaves (tear large leaves into smaller pieces)
½ to 1 cup cilantro leaves
6 lettuce leaves
A few cilantro or mint sprigs

First, make the dressing, so that the ingredients are given time to mingle and their flavors to blend. Chop the chillies finely; if you have a mortar and pestle, pound to a paste. Add vinegar, tamarind, lime juice, fish sauce, and sugar to the desired sweet, sour, and salty combination. Stir well and set aside.

Shell the tiger prawns, devein, and butterfly. Give them a saltwater bath to freshen them (see page 173). Drain the scallops, mussels, and oysters, and set aside.

Heat peanut oil in a small skillet. Fry shallots over low to medium heat, stirring occasionally, until evenly browned and crisped (may take 20 minutes or more). Drain from oil with a wire-mesh strainer. Reheat the oil remaining in the skillet and fry garlic over medium-high heat until golden and crispy. Drain from oil and set aside. (Save garlic and shallot flavored oil for stir-frying other seafood dishes.)

While waiting for the shallots to crisp and brown, trim and discard woody bottom tip and 2 to 3 of the loose outer layers of lemon grass stalks. Slice into very thin rounds, using the bottom two-thirds of stalks. Stack the kaffir lime leaves and, using a sharp knife, cut into very fine inch-long slivers. Trim the eyes and brown spots on the galanga and slice into very thin rounds; then layer the rounds a few at a time and shred into fine slivers to yield about ¼ cup. (If using ginger, peel before slivering.) Place all the herbs in a mixing bowl, along with mint and cilantro leaves. Toss to mix.

Bring 1½ quarts water to a boil. Blanch shellfish separately, 15 to 30 seconds, until just cooked (15 seconds for mussels, bay scallops, and oysters; 30 seconds for tiger prawns; 30 to 40 seconds for sea scallops, depending on the size). Use a wire-mesh skimmer to strain each out of the water, saving the water, if you wish, for making seafood stock. Toss all the shellfish, while still warm, with the fresh herbs. When ready to serve, add the dressing and crisped shallots and garlic. Toss well and serve on a plate lined with lettuce leaves. Garnish with a few cilantro leaves or mint sprigs.

Serves 8 with rice and other dishes in a family-style meal.

Notes and Pointers:

My husband tells me that I have good travel karma. Wherever we go, I manage to stumble unintentionally into places and people who brighten our journeys and enrich our lives. Among these people and places are some of the finest mom-and-pop eateries, which seldom see travelers from outside the region. Smiles and gentle gestures communicate more than words and the scrumptious food in these friendly, unpretentious places is imbued with the character of the generous and heartful cooks. The hearty, country food made by and shared with soulful people gratifies us in many more ways than one, and we leave with our hearts content and their smiling faces forever imbedded in our memory.

This seafood salad is made "country-style," with a depth and richness that perfectly complement the hearty flavors of shellfish.

Baked Oysters with Salted Black Beans and Pickled Garlic

(Hoi Nahnglom Ohb Dtow See)

6 to 8 large fresh oysters in the shell
1 head pickled garlic
3 Tbs. pork fat, cut into small chunks, or use 2 Tbs. peanut oil
3 Tbs. dried salted black beans, chopped into coarse crumbs
4 cloves garlic, minced
2 tsp. chopped cilantro roots or stems
1 Tbs. fresh ginger, peeled and minced

Preheat oven to 400°F.

Pry oysters open with an oyster knife. Discard top shell, leaving oysters on deeper half shell. Separate the pickled garlic into cloves, discarding the skin. Chop the cloves finely.

Render the pork fat in a small skillet or wok. Sauté chopped black beans and minced fresh garlic over medium heat in pork fat (or peanut oil) for 30 seconds. Add the cilantro roots or stems and ginger. Sauté another 30 seconds. Stir in pickled garlic and turn off heat.

Spoon black bean mixture over oysters and place oysters on a baking dish. Bake 5 to 7 minutes, or until oysters are done to your liking.

Serves 3 to 4 as an appetizer in a multicourse meal.

Notes and Pointers:

Although oysters are delicate in flavor, the pungent mix of flavorings complements them and does not overpower. I sometimes add some ground, roasted, dried chillies or coarsely ground white pepper to spice them to serve as an accompaniment to rice, rather than as an appetizer. This Chinese-influenced preparation uses pork fat to enrich the oysters, but it is not necessary if you are health conscious.

Very fresh oysters have strong muscles and are hard to open. To make it easier, heat them with the deeper shell down in a 400° F oven for about 5 minutes, then plunge into ice-cold water and drain.

Savory Pan-Fried Mussel Cake
with Wilted Bean Sprouts

(Hoi Malaeng Poo Tawd)

1½ cups shelled mussels (see notes)
½ cup tapioca starch
½ cup unbleached white flour
½ tsp. sea salt
¼ tsp. ground white pepper
1 cup limestone water, or water
4 red serrano, jalapeno, or fresno peppers, chopped with seeds
3 Tbs. white vinegar
3 Tbs. fish sauce (*nahm bplah*)
1½ to 2 Tbs. granulated sugar, to taste
½ to ¾ cup peanut oil
10 cloves garlic, chopped
6 eggs
5 cups fresh bean sprouts
3 green onions, split in half lengthwise and cut into 1½-inch segments (use white
   and most of green parts)
½ tsp. ground white pepper
½ cup cilantro sprigs
Sriracha bottled chilli sauce

Mix tapioca starch, flour, salt, ¼ tsp. ground white pepper, and limestone water in a mixing bowl and stir to make a smooth batter (yields about 1½ cups). Pound chopped red chillies with a mortar and pestle until well crushed. Add vinegar, fish sauce, and sugar. Stir well to dissolve sugar. Taste and adjust flavors to your liking; there should be about 9 tablespoons of sauce.

Heat ¼ cup oil in a wok or small pan. Fry garlic over medium heat, stirring frequently, until it is evenly golden brown. Strain garlic from oil with a fine wire-mesh skimmer. Set both garlic pieces and oil aside.

Heat a flat griddle pan (preferably well-seasoned cast iron) over high heat until it begins to smoke. Spoon in 2 tablespoons of oil (the garlic-flavored oil may be used here). In a small bowl, combine ½ cup batter with ½ cup mussels. Stir well, and empty onto hot surface of griddle. Spread mussels evenly over batter. Reduce heat to medium and fry until batter is browned and crispy on the bottom and dried on top.

Flip and fry second side for about 2 minutes, pressing cake down with a spatula from time to time. Cut cake with the spatula into 8 more manageable pieces, so that the batter around the bulging mus-

(continued on next page)

sels can be pressed down more easily to brown and crisp on the hot metal pan. Cook until pieces are well browned on both sides, dried through, and crispy on the edges.

Increase heat to high. Push pieces close together and crack two eggs over them. Break yolks with the spatula and spread eggs evenly over the pieces. Allow eggs to set a bit before turning. Continue to fry until eggs are completely dried on both sides and well browned; sprinkle with one-third of the fried garlic.

If your griddle is large, push fried mussel pieces to one side away from the main heat source. (If there is little room left on your griddle, remove mussel pieces to a plate.) Dribble in 2 to 3 teaspoons oil onto the hottest part of the griddle. Let heat a few seconds over high heat until it is smoking hot before tossing in one-third of the bean sprouts. The sprouts should sizzle loudly when they hit the pan. Stir-fry 15 to 20 seconds, then add one-third of the green onions. Stir, then spoon in one-third of the sauce (about 3 tablespoons). Continue to stir-fry over high heat until the sauce is reduced and bean sprouts wilted.

Toss fried mussel pieces quickly with bean sprouts and sauce to coat them evenly. Transfer to a serving plate, sprinkle liberally with ground white pepper and garnish with cilantro. Serve immediately with *Sriracha* chilli sauce, as desired.

Clean the griddle and cook two more batches in similar fashion; or refrigerate batter, sauce, and other ingredients to cook another day (keeps for a few days).

One batch serves 2 for a filling snack, or more as an appetizer in a multicourse family-style meal.

notes and Pointers:

Definitely not low-cal, this rich street food of night markets in coastal towns, as well as in urban areas inland, has as many incarnations as there are cooks. Some can actually be quite doughy and downright greasy, with disappointingly few mussels waiting to be discovered. On the other hand, when well made, this popular snack and one-dish meal can be very satisfying, and definitely an experience well worth repeating.

Watching the cake being made in dramatic fashion over a large, flat griddle with hot flames leaping beneath, is as much a part of the experience as savoring the finished product. However, because of the time required to make each cake to perfection from start to finish, many vendors partially make the cakes ahead of time, finishing them in a few minutes as orders are placed. The best, of course, are freshly made to order in their entirety and are well worth the wait.

In Thailand, this recipe is usually made with raw shelled mussels, which are mixed in with the batter before frying. Because it is difficult to buy raw shelled mussels in American markets and it is a lot of trouble to shell them yourself while they are still alive, cooked mussels can be substituted. However, they will not mix as well with the batter, making it more difficult to brown the second side of the cake, but it will still work if the instructions are strictly followed. The trick is to fry the mussels and batter longer than you imagine should be done. Each batch should take about 15 minutes, from start to finish, to ensure a cake with hearty flavor and a good chewy texture with a little bit of crispy edge. Keep in mind that practice makes perfect.

One pound of fresh whole mussels yields approximately 1 cup shelled flesh. Therefore, if you are not able to purchase mussels already shelled, use about 1½ pounds for this recipe. Place the whole mussels on a steamer rack and steam over high heat 2 to 3 minutes, or until the shells open. Remove the flesh from the shells.

Cooked and shelled green mussels from New Zealand, available frozen in plastic pouches from many Asian and seafood markets, may also be used for this recipe. If they are large, cut each into 2 to 3 pieces.

Limestone water is the secret ingredient, which helps give a crispy edge to the fried batter. For more information, see page 63.

Marinated Mesquite-Grilled Scallops
Served with Sweet-and-Tangy Dipping Sauce
(Hoi Shel Yahng Sohng Kreuang)

1½ lbs. large sea scallops
1 Tbs. finely chopped cilantro roots, or substitute bottom stems
8 large cloves garlic, finely chopped
2 shallots, finely chopped
2 tsp. white peppercorns, freshly ground
1 Tbs. coriander seeds, freshly ground
2 tsp. yellow curry powder
2 tsp. peanut oil
2 to 3 Tbs. fish sauce (*nahm bplah*), to taste
1 to 2 tsp. sugar, to taste
Bamboo skewers
2 Tbs. coconut milk, optional
Sweet-and-tangy dipping sauce (recipe follows)

Drain scallops well and set aside.

Using a heavy mortar and pestle, pound cilantro roots, garlic, and shallots to a paste. Add the freshly ground white pepper, coriander, and curry powder. Stir and pound to blend dry and wet ingredients. Add oil, fish sauce, and sugar to achieve the desired saltiness and sweetness. Stir well to dissolve sugar.

Pat scallops dry with a clean towel. Coat with prepared seasoning mixture and set aside to marinate for 30 minutes or longer. Skewer on bamboo sticks, saving the remaining marinade. Grill over hot mesquite charcoals, with the grill positioned very close to the coals. Add coconut milk to marinade remaining in the bowl and baste scallops during grilling. Grill about 2 minutes on each side, or until scallops are done to your liking; do not turn too frequently, so that the scallops can brown and char lightly. Baste with each turning.

Serve with the sweet-and-tangy chilli dipping sauce that follows.

Serves 5 to 6 with other dishes and rice in a family-style meal.

Sweet-and-Tangy Dipping Sauce
10 to 15 dried red chillies
3 to 4 large cloves garlic, chopped
¼ cup white vinegar
Juice of ½ to 1 lime, to taste
2 to 3 Tbs. fish sauce (*nahm bplah*), to taste
¼ to ½ cup granulated sugar, to desired sweetness
A few cilantro leaves and/or an inch section of green onion, chopped, optional

Cut stem tip off dried chillies, and place chillies in a bowl; do not remove seeds. Add tap water to cover. Soak until softened (about ½ to 1 hour), then chop finely.

Reduce garlic to a paste with a mortar and pestle. Add chopped softened chillies. Pound well to blend. Add vinegar, lime juice, fish sauce, and sugar. Stir well to dissolve sugar. Adjust flavors so that the sauce has a balance of the salty, sweet, and sour taste that you like. Let sit for at least 15 minutes, for the flavors to blend and mingle. Just before serving, add chopped cilantro and/or green onion, if you wish.

Notes and Pointers:

The marinated grilled scallops are very good even without the dipping sauce. They are peppery and aromatic, smoky and very succulent. While you're at it, make extra marinade and toss in some prawns, cuttlefish, and chunks of meaty fish, such as king mackerel, albacore, swordfish, shark, and sturgeon, to make a scrumptious seafood barbecue. For a change, or for guests who do not like seafood, massage the marinade into chicken pieces and grill up a feast.

The recipe makes more sauce than you will need for the scallops, so save the extra for the next grilling session. It keeps for a few weeks, and actually tastes better after it has aged for several days. Store in a sealed jar in the refrigerator and use on any kind of grilled or crisp-fried foods. Of course, it keeps better without the chopped cilantro and green onion, so you may wish to spoon out only what you think you'll need at each meal and add the chopped herbs only to that portion.

Pan-Seared Sea Scallops Topped with *Choo Chee* Curry Sauce
(*Gkaeng Choo Chee Hoi Shel*)

1 lb. large sea scallops
6 to 10 dried red chillies
5 red serrano peppers, or 3 red jalapeno or fresno peppers
8 to 10 cloves garlic
3 shallots
2 tsp. shrimp paste (*gkabpi*)
8 to 10 kaffir lime leaves
¾ cup coconut cream, or the thickest cream from the top of a can of
   unsweetened coconut milk (preferably *Mae Ploy* or *Chao Koh* brand)
2 Tbs. fish sauce (*nahm bplah*), or to taste
2 to 3 tsp. palm or coconut sugar, to taste
2 Tbs. peanut oil
A few sprigs of cilantro

Drain scallops well. If they have been refrigerated, leave them out at room temperature for 20 minutes before cooking.

Trim and discard stem end of dried chillies, tap the seeds out, and soak in warm water for 15 to 30 minutes to soften. Chop finely when softened. If you like an extra spicy dish, do not remove seeds from fresh chilli peppers. Chop them, and the garlic and shallots. Make a well-blended paste out of these four chopped ingredients and the shrimp paste, either by pounding with a heavy mortar and pestle or reducing them in the food processor to a fine puree.

Sliver the kaffir lime leaves by stacking 3 to 4 at a time and using a sharp knife to cut through the stack and across the leaves at a diagonal into very fine hairlike slivers about an inch long. Or cut with scissors.

Spoon coconut cream into a wok or saucepan and heat over medium-high heat. Reduce for a few minutes to thicken. Stir in chilli paste and fry for a few minutes to release and blend the flavors. Season to taste with fish sauce and palm sugar, and add two-thirds of the slivered kaffir lime leaves. Reduce mixture to a very thick consistency and a rich red color. Remove from heat and set aside.

Heat a well-seasoned cast-iron pan or heavy skillet over high heat until its surface is smoking hot. While waiting, pat scallops dry with a clean towel. Add oil to coat the surface of the heated pan and wait 30 seconds for oil to heat. Sear scallops in the hot pan over high heat for 1 to 2 minutes on each side, depending on their size, or until they are cooked to your liking.

Transfer to a serving platter and smother scallops with the curry sauce. Garnish with remaining kaffir lime leaf slivers and a few sprigs of cilantro.

Serves 4 with rice and other dishes in a family-style meal.

Notes and Pointers:

This recipe is among my husband's top ten favorite Thai dishes and, as many times as we've made and wolfed it down, we couldn't seem to get enough. Not only is the outstanding sauce superb on scallops, it can be spooned on just about any kind of pan-seared, pan-fried, broiled, or grilled seafood.

The name of the curry, *choo chee*, is an approximation of the hissing, popping, and splattering sounds that the thick sauce makes as it cooks and thickens over a hot flame. My students find it amusing and, because the curry is packed with a punch, a number of them have adopted the exclamation "Choo Chee!" to express their euphoria when savoring an exquisitely spiced dish!

This recipe is an adaptation of a traditional curry, using a more modern style of cooking—by searing food quickly in a very hot pan, so that the outside is charred or browned while the inside remains partially raw. In rural Thailand, *choo chee* curry smothers small, crisp-fried fish, rather than seared scallops, the sauce thick with chillies and herbs and very little coconut cream to temper its intense bite. It's a great way for one small fish to flavor mountains of plain steamed rice and feed a family. In the cities, milder and richer *choo chee* is served with large river prawns and shrimp, in addition to fried fish.

Choo chee is frequently made with red curry paste, which imparts a full range of strong herbal accents. Because scallops have a delicate flavor, I prefer a simpler chilli paste that doesn't distract from their fine taste. Without fibrous herbs like lemon grass and galanga, which benefit from pounding in a mortar and pestle to release their aromatic oils, the paste in this recipe can be easily made in a food processor without compromising flavor.

Use only very fresh scallops. Sear just enough to brown and char the outside; do not overcook, as this will make them dry and stringy. They should taste refreshingly sweet with a smooth, buttery texture that melts with each bite. Truly fresh scallops are particularly good when they are undercooked; don't forget that they can be eaten raw and are a staple of sushi bars.

Spicy Stir-fried Scallops and Mussels with Homemade Chilli Paste and Thai Eggplants

(Paɗ Peɗ Hoi Shel Gkap Hoi Malaeng Poo)

1 lb. fresh mussels in the shell
¾ lb. sea scallops
Homemade chilli paste (recipe follows)
2 Tbs. peanut oil
6 small round Thai eggplants, quartered
1 Tbs. fish sauce (*nahm bplah*), or to taste
1 tsp. palm sugar, or to taste
2 red and green serrano peppers, cut into small slivers with seeds
5 kaffir lime leaves, torn into small pieces
½ cup holy basil (*bai gkaprow*), or substitute Thai sweet basil (*bai horapa*)
1 to 2 short basil sprigs, for garnish

Chilli paste

5 to 8 dried red chillies, stem tip cut off, soaked to soften,
    then chopped
2 red serrano or jalapeno peppers, or 4 to 8 red Thai
    chillies, chopped
¼ tsp. sea salt
Bottom half of a stalk of lemon grass, trimmed and cut
    into thin rounds to yield about 2 Tbs.
1 tsp. chopped fresh or frozen galanga
½ tsp. chopped kaffir lime peel (soak dried peel to soften)
1 Tbs. chopped shallot
8 to 10 cloves garlic, chopped (or about 2 Tbs.)
½ tsp. shrimp paste (*gkabpi*)

Place mussels on the rack of a stacked steamer and steam over high heat until shells open. Cool and remove flesh from shell. If scallops are very large, cut in half. Drain and let sit at room temperature 20 minutes before cooking.

Make chilli paste by pounding paste ingredients a little at a time until they are reduced to a well-blended paste. Salt provides some abrasiveness to help reduce the more fibrous ingredients.

Just before you are ready to stir-fry, pat scallops and mussels dry with a clean towel. Heat a wok over high heat until it begins to smoke. Swirl in the oil to coat wok surface and wait 10 to 15 seconds for it to heat. Stir in chilli paste and sauté in oil until aromatic (about 30 seconds). Add Thai eggplants and stir-fry 30 seconds. Follow with scallops, tossing them with eggplants and chilli paste for 30 seconds to 1 minute. Add mussels. Stir well to coat with chilli mixture.

Season to taste with fish sauce and palm sugar. Add slivered chillies, kaffir lime leaves, and basil, and toss until basil is wilted. Transfer to a serving dish and garnish with a sprig or two of fresh basil.

Serves 4 to 5 with rice and other dishes in a multicourse family-style meal.

Notes and Pointers:

This recipe is yet another version of the spicy stir-fry called *pad ped*, a dry red curry made by tossing food with a pungent chilli paste and herbs in a hot wok. Unlike many that use a standard red curry paste enriched with coconut cream, this rendition is lighter, though every bit as intense, using a homemade chilli paste that's fairly easy to prepare and enhances the flavors of seafood particularly well. My cooking students find it worth every ounce of effort to make the paste from scratch, as the resulting dish is exquisitely balanced and unlike anything they've ever had in a restaurant. The paste can be made a few days ahead of time and stored in the refrigerator. Once the paste is made, the dish is really very quick to put together.

The crunchy crispness of Thai eggplants adds a delightful textural contrast to the softness of the scallops and mussels. Other kinds of eggplants cannot be easily substituted, as they do not cook up crisp. Zucchini or snap peas make better substitutes but, because they do not stay firm as long, add them to the wok 30 seconds after the scallops. Roll-cut the zucchini into bite-size chunks—cut at a 45-degree angle one-half inch from the end, roll over half way, make another angled cut, roll again, and so on. Cut the snap peas at an angle in half. Use about one cup of either.

The stir-fry can be done entirely with scallops or with mussels. Try also with shrimp, squid, cuttlefish, and firm fish fillets cut into bite-size chunks, or a combination of all the seafood mentioned. It is excellent with sturgeon, eel, and skate. Cut skate into thin slices and crisp in hot oil before tossing into the stir-fry. My local seafood market carries live sturgeon; after selecting my fish, they clean, skin, and fillet it for me. It is simply exquisite in this stir-fry! If substituting fish, use one pound of fillets for this recipe; use the same amount of shrimp and cuttlefish.

For a mixed seafood stir-fry, add the seafood needing the longest cooking time first; follow with the others in descending order of cooking time required, so that nothing is overcooked and loses its succulent texture and natural sweetness.

Curried Mussels on the Half Shell with Flaked Crab

(Haw Moek Hoi Malaeng Poo)

2 lbs. large fresh mussels
2 cups coconut cream (use thickest cream from the
   tops of 2 cans of unsweetened coconut milk)
1½ tsp. rice flour
¼ tsp. salt
1½ to 2½ Tbs. red curry paste
1 to 2 Tbs. fish sauce (*nahm bplah*), as
   needed
2 to 3 tsp. palm sugar, to taste
⅓ cup chopped Thai basil (*bai horapa*)
8 kaffir lime leaves—mince half the leaves and
   cut the other half into very fine inch-long
   slivers
1 cup shelled cooked crabmeat
2 eggs, beaten
30 to 40 cilantro leaves
2 red jalapeno or fresno peppers, cut into fine slivers about 1½ inches long

Rinse and scrub mussels to clean shells. Place on a steamer rack and steam over medium heat until shells open. Remove from steamer, pull the two halves of the shells apart, and scoop flesh out into a bowl. Select 30 to 40 of the nicest-looking half shells, rinse, and set aside to drain.

Spoon ½ cup coconut cream into a small saucepan with rice flour and salt. Stir to dissolve flour into cream. Heat over medium heat, stirring frequently, until mixture thickens to a smooth, creamy consistency. Set aside to cool.

Spoon remaining coconut cream into a saucepan, warming just enough over medium heat to melt cream to a smooth, fluid consistency. Turn off heat. Add red curry paste and palm sugar. Stir well to dissolve both into cream. Add fish sauce, as needed, to the desired level of saltiness (taste first, as some brands of curry paste are already heavily salted). If the sauce is very warm, let it cool.

Preheat oven to 400° F.

When sauce has cooled almost to room temperature, drain mussels, and add to curry sauce, along with chopped basil and minced kaffir lime leaves. Stir well. Flake crabmeat with a fork and fold into mixture along with beaten eggs.

Spoon a mussel into each half shell, along with some flaked crab and sauce to fill. Balance filled shells on a rack placed on a baking sheet and bake 10 to 12 minutes (cooking time will depend on the size of the shells).

Top each with a dab of thickened coconut cream, cilantro leaf, red pepper sliver, and a few kaffir lime leaf slivers. Arrange on a serving platter.

Serves 6 to 8 with rice in a multicourse family-style meal.

Notes and Pointers:

Great eating has always been one of the side benefits of visiting my family overseas every year. When Mother was cooking, weight gain was expected and, even now that she no longer cooks, the weight keeps inching up. There are just so many fine restaurants nearby, tempting us with their ravishing menus—some reading like inspired books. My husband so loves Thai food that, when he taught himself how to read Thai, deciphering menus was a source of great joy. Now he skips over the often poor, off-the-wall English translations, if there are any, and goes straight to the Thai script for their much more enticing descriptions.

Among the many restaurants on our rotating list is one called Lai Cram. One of their house specials is a fabulous mussel curry baked on the half shell. The presentation is impressive and the flavors even more so. This recipe, though not quite the same, since a store-bought red curry paste is used, gives you a tiny taste of the truly great foods that can be had in a country where fine eating is one of the favorite pastimes.

Baked curried mussels on the half shell make an impressive appetizer for a dinner party. They can be prepared a day ahead of time and warmed before garnishing for serving.

Steamed Mussels in Clay Pot with Aromatic Herbs

(Hoi Malaeng Poo Ohb Maw Din)

1½ lbs. fresh mussels, in the shell
2 stalks lemon grass
Ten ⅛-inch-thick slices fresh galanga
5 fresh kaffir lime leaves
4 small red shallots, or substitute 2 brown shallots
2 red serrano, jalapeno, or fresno peppers
4 Thai chillies, stem removed and crushed whole, optional
½ cup Thai sweet basil leaves (bai horapa)
1 Tbs. fish sauce (nahm bplah)
Hot chilli-lime sauce, optional (recipe, page 218)

Rinse mussels, scrubbing off any barnacles, mud, and sand. Soak in cold salted water for 30 minutes or more. Discard any opened shells that would not close when pressed between the fingers. Rinse in several changes of cool water and drain.

Trim off woody bottom tip of lemon grass stalks and discard loose outer layers. Cut stalks at a very sharp slanted angle, exposing as much of the interior as possible, into segments about 1½ inches long. Use bottom two-thirds of stalks. Crush each piece by smashing with flat side of a cleaver or a mallet. Slice galanga (no need to peel), and tear each kaffir lime leaf into 2 to 3 pieces.

Peel red shallots and crush whole with the flat side of a cleaver. If substituting larger orange-brown shallots, cut into quarters, then crush. Cut serrano, jalapeño, or fresno peppers lengthwise into large slivers with the seeds and crush Thai chillies whole.

Toss all the prepared herbs and basil with 1 tablespoon fish sauce in a mixing bowl. Add mussels and mix well. Transfer to a clay pot, cover, and place on a burner over medium heat. Let cook for 12 to 15 minutes, turning mussels halfway through, or until they have opened.

If you wish, serve with a hot chilli-lime sauce, like the one for steamed crab on page 218.

Serves 3 to 4 with rice and other dishes in a family-style meal.

Notes and Pointers:

Of all seafood, mussels are a favorite for steaming. The moist-heat cooking method preserves their lusciously succulent texture and sweet, natural flavor. All seafood-loving cultures around the world steam mussels in some way or other. While Western cuisines frequently steam them in wine or other flavored broth along with some butter, I prefer to steam them in their own juices, without using any fat or cooking liquid, surrounded only by crushed herbs that lend their flavors. The tasty sauce produced from such steaming is pure mussel and herb juice and is delicious as a broth or spooned over rice to eat along with the mussels.

Besides being very easy, this dish presents well, as the clay pot in which the mussels are cooked doubles as a lovely serving dish. Clay pots are inexpensive in Asian markets that carry cookware and are a delight to use. If you can't find one, you may substitute a deep Corningware dish with a cover or a metal pot. Since the latter heats up faster and hotter, cook at a slightly lower heat or start out with a tablespoon or two of broth to wet the bottom. The beauty of using a clay pot, though, is the even distribution of heat that it gives and, as it slowly heats, the mussels begin to sweat and become steamed in their own juices.

Clams Stir-Fried
with Roasted Chilli Sauce and Basil
(Hoi Paò Nahm Prik Pow)

2 lbs. fresh clams
2 to 3 Tbs. peanut oil
8 cloves garlic, chopped
6 to 10 Thai chillies, cut in half crosswise and bruised
2 to 3 Tbs. roasted chilli paste *(nahm prik pow)*
2 Tbs. water, or stock
1 to 2 tsp. sugar, to taste
1 packed cup Thai basil leaves *(bai horapa)*, flower buds may also be used
1 Tbs. fish sauce, as needed to taste

Rinse clams well, scrubbing off any gritty sand. Soak in cold salted water for 30 minutes to 1 hour. Discard any opened shells that do not close when pressed between the fingers. Rinse in several changes of cool water and drain.

Heat a wok over high heat until its surface begins to smoke. Swirl in oil to coat the wok surface and wait 15 to 20 seconds for it to heat. Add garlic and Thai chillies, followed a few seconds later with the roasted chilli paste and water or stock. Sprinkle in 1 teaspoon sugar. Stir well and, when ingredients in the wok look well blended, toss in clams. Stir to mix with seasonings. Stir-fry for 1 minute or so, then cover and reduce heat to medium. Stir about every 20 seconds.

When clams begin to spit water, uncover and increase heat to high and, when some of them begin to open, stir in basil. Taste sauce to see if it is salty and sweet enough. Adjust by adding fish sauce and/or sugar to taste. Continue to stir-fry until clams have fully opened. Do not overcook, as they will shrink and become tough. Transfer to a serving dish and serve while still hot.

Serves 5 to 6 with other dishes and steamed rice in a family-style meal.

Notes and Pointers:

In my childhood and youth, I was very fond of clams, particularly the kind with pretty patterned shells called *hoi lai*. They are smaller than the Manila clams sold in seafood markets here—about half the size, but their shells are much thinner and lighter, so they provide much more meat in one kilogram than the larger clams. Furthermore, their meat is sweet, tender, and very tasty. Since they can sometimes be muddy or sandy, these clams are pried opened to rinse their flesh before cooking. Their thin shells and small size make them easy to pry open with a knife blade.

Sprigs of basil are always complimentary whenever these clams are purchased at the market in Thailand. Mother frequently stir-fried big wokfuls of them with the basil and the premium roasted chilli paste made by someone she knew. No matter how big a platter of clams was set on the dinner table, each and every one of them would be picked clean by my brothers and me. In addition, the delicious sauce spooned over rice helped me polish off the mountain of grains on my plate with lip-smacking satisfaction.

Though the clams here are not quite like *hoi lai,* I still love to indulge in them from time to time, cooking them the same way the patterned clams are commonly prepared back home. A homemade roasted chilli paste (recipe, page 175) makes the wok-tossed clams extra special.

Wok-Tossed Mussels in the Shell with Lemon Grass and Basil
(Hoi Malaeng Poo Gkata)

1 lb. fresh mussels
1 stalk lemon grass
2 Tbs. peanut oil
6 cloves garlic, chopped
2 to 3 jalapeno peppers, slivered or sliced into thin rounds
    with seeds
1 Tbs. fish sauce (*nahm bplah*), or to taste
½ to 1 cup fresh Thai basil leaves (*bai horapa*), flower buds
    may also be used

Rinse mussels and scrub shells clean of grit and sand particles. Cover with cold salted water and soak about 30 minutes. Rinse and drain.

Trim and discard woody bottom tip and loose outer layers of lemon grass stalk. Cut with a sharp knife into thin rounds, using the bottom two-thirds of stalk. Prepare remaining ingredients.

Heat a wok over high heat until it is smoking hot. Swirl in oil and wait 10 to 15 seconds for it to heat. Stir in garlic and lemon grass and sauté about 15 seconds before adding chillies. Stir-fry another 10 to 15 seconds, then toss in mussels, stirring well to evenly coat them with herbs. Sprinkle with fish sauce, stir, and cover the wok. Stir every 15 seconds or so, until the mussels begin to spit and open their shells. Toss in basil and continue to cook uncovered until the shells are fully open and the basil wilted. Do not overcook, as the meat in the mussels will shrink. Transfer to a serving dish and serve with steamed rice.

Serves 4 with other dishes and rice in a family-style meal.

Notes and Pointers:

This very easy and delectable mussel stir-fry is one you will want to make frequently if you love this shellfish as much as I do. The fragrant herbs enhance their flavor and make the resulting sauce very tasty. Spoon over rice and eat along with the meat from the mussels.

This recipe is also good with clams, although I much prefer it with the succulent mussels.

Oyster and Egg Scramble

(Aw Suan)

1 cup small shelled oysters, or large oysters cut into bite-size pieces
1 Tbs. tapioca starch
1 green onion (dense part only), cut into very thin rounds
3 Tbs. peanut oil
2 eggs, beaten
1 Tbs. light soy sauce
½ tsp. ground white pepper
2 Tbs. coarsely chopped cilantro
1 red serrano, jalapeno, or fresno pepper, finely slivered
A few short cilantro sprigs
Sriracha bottled hot chilli sauce

Place oysters in a bowl along with any oyster juice. Sprinkle with tapioca flour and green onion. Stir to coat oysters evenly.

Heat a wok or skillet over high heat until its surface begins to smoke. Swirl in oil and wait 15 to 20 seconds for it to heat. Stir in beaten eggs. Scramble about 10 seconds, then add oysters. Stir-fry quickly over high heat until eggs are almost set. Season to taste with light soy sauce and sprinkle in half the white pepper. Continue to stir-fry until both eggs and oysters are cooked. Stir in chopped cilantro and transfer to a serving plate.

Sprinkle remaining white pepper over the oysters and eggs, and garnish with red chilli slivers and cilantro sprigs. Serve while still warm with *Sriracha* hot sauce as desired.

Serves 3 to 4 in a multicourse family-style meal.

Notes and Pointers:

Oysters are one of the world's most nutritious foods. They are low in fat and in calories, and are rich in vitamins (A, B$_1$, B$_2$, C, and D) and minerals (calcium, magnesium, iodine, iron, potassium, copper, zinc, phosphorus, manganese, and sulfur). They also contain essential omega-3 fatty acids that keep the heart and central nervous system healthy. In addition, oyster lovers claim that they are an aphrodisiac because of their dopamine content—a vital neurotransmitter that governs brain activity and influences sexual desire. However, since they feed by filtering water through their bodies, they can easily be contaminated by toxins and microorganisms from pollution. To be safe, always buy from a reliable source.

Because of their delicate flavor and texture, oysters are usually prepared very simply. This recipe is a common way they are served in Thailand—an easy and quick stir-fry, just enough to cook them so that their full range of flavors can be savored. If you have tried only raw oysters and don't think much of them, try this recipe and you might just change your mind. Make sure to pick up as fresh a jar of shelled oysters as possible, with very clear juice and shiny flesh.

Spicy "Broken Fish Trap" Soup
(Dtom Yâm Bpoh Dtaek)

½ lb. medium prawns, shelled and butterflied (save shells for stock)
12 fresh mussels in the shell, or use clams
⅔ lb. sea scallops
2 raw Dungeness crab claws, separated at joints and cracked, plus half the crab's
    main body, cut into 2 to 3 pieces
3 medium whole squid, cleaned and cut into 1-inch rounds
⅔ lb. firm fish fillet, cut into 1-inch chunks
Bottom half of 3 large stalks of lemon grass
6 cups unsalted seafood or chicken stock
¼ cup fish sauce (*nahm bplah*), or to desired saltiness
Ten ⅛-inch-thick slices fresh galanga
2 shallots, cut into ½-inch cubes and crushed
6 kaffir lime leaves, torn into 2 to 3 pieces each
12 to 15 Thai chillies (*prik kee noo*), stem removed and crushed whole
Juice of 1 to 2 limes, to desired sourness
1 tsp. granulated sugar, as needed to balance the sour flavor
½ to 1 cup holy basil (*bai gkaprow*), or Thai sweet basil (*bai horapa*)
¼ tsp. white peppercorns, freshly ground

Clean and prepare the various kinds of seafood. For a more succulent, crisp texture and fresher flavor, give the prawns a saltwater bath (page 173.) Scrub mussel shells to clean, soak in cool salted water for 20 to 30 minutes, then rinse and drain.

Trim off woody bottom tip of lemon grass stalks and discard loose outer layers. Cut stalks at a sharp, slanted angle into pieces about 1 to 1½ inches long. Smash with the flat side of a cleaver to bruise and release the aromatic oils.

Bring stock to a boil in a large pot. (A simple soup stock can be made by simmering shrimp shells, crab shells, fish heads and bones in water for 20 minutes.) Season with fish sauce to desired saltiness. Add lemon grass, galanga, shallots, and kaffir lime leaves. Simmer, covered, 5 to 7 minutes to flavor broth, then add Thai chillies and simmer a few minutes longer.

Increase heat to high and bring stock to a rolling boil. Stir in the crab, follow 20 seconds later with the mussels and 1 minute later with the remaining seafood. Add lime juice to the desired sourness, sugar as needed to balance, and stir in the basil and fresh-ground white pepper. If the broth is very hot, the shrimp, fish, and squid should be cooked in about half a minute. Serve immediately. Do not overcook seafood.

Serves 8 with other dishes and rice in a family-style meal.

Notes and Pointers:

Served like most soups are in Thailand, in a hot pot with a central chimney in which hot coals (or Sterno) burn, the piping hot soup is also searing with spicy heat. Awaiting in the deceptively milky waters are abundant morsels of fish, crustaceans, and mollusks as if they have all just made their escape from a broken fish trap. Thai dishes with "broken fish trap" (*bpoh ɗtaek*) in their names feature several varieties of seafood cooked together, just as fish traps lure different kinds of curious creatures into their nets.

Not only spicy hot, this soup is also herbal and limy, accented with the distinctive fragrance of holy basil. It is all at once hot, sour, and salty, but not sweet. Add only enough sugar to balance the lime juice and bring forth the herbal and seafood flavors without making the soup sweet. Back home, our sweeter and more zestful limes require no sugar when added to this soup.

Mixed Seafood Salad
with Lemon Grass, Mint,
and Chilli-Lime Dressing
(Yâm Talay)

¾ lb. fresh squid
⅔ lb. fresh medium shrimp
½ lb. fillet of sea bass
⅔ lb. sea scallops
2 stalks lemon grass
1-inch section fresh galanga, cut into very fine slivers
4 shallots, halved lengthwise and sliced thinly crosswise
½ to 1 cup fresh mint leaves, large leaves torn into smaller pieces
½ cup cilantro leaves
4 to 6 lettuce leaves, to line serving platter
Hot-and-sour chilli-lime dressing (recipe follows)

Clean and skin squid and cut into 1-inch rounds; leave tentacles whole. Shell, devein, and butterfly shrimp and give them a saltwater bath to freshen them (page 173). Cut the fish into 1-inch chunks, and drain scallops.

Trim and discard woody bottom tip and loose outer layer(s) of lemon grass stalks. Cut into very thin rounds, using the bottom two-thirds of stalks. Place in a large mixing bowl. Add the galanga and shallots to the bowl, along with the mint and cilantro leaves. Set aside.

Bring two quarts of water to a rolling boil. Using a wire-mesh basket with bamboo handle, blanch the seafood, one kind at a time, until each is just cooked through (about 20 to 30 seconds for squid and shrimp; 30 to 40 seconds for scallops; and 1 minute or more for sea bass). Cooking time will depend on the size of the pieces. Drain well, making sure there is no water trapped inside squid rounds.

Toss seafood while still warm with the herbs in the mixing bowl. Add dressing and toss to distribute. Transfer to a serving platter lined with lettuce leaves. Serve warm or at room temperature.

Serves 8 with other dishes and rice in a family-style meal.

Hot-and-Sour Chilli-Lime Dressing
10 to 20 fresh Thai chillies (*prik kee noo*), chopped
6 to 8 cloves garlic, chopped
3 to 4 Tbs. fish sauce (*nahm bplah*), to taste
Juice of 2 to 3 fresh limes, to taste
2 to 4 tsp. sugar, to taste

Pound chillies and garlic in a mortar to reduce to paste. Add fish sauce, lime juice, and sugar. Mix well and adjust to desired combination, keeping in mind that the flavors will be reduced when dressing is tossed with the bulk of the other ingredients.

Notes and Pointers:

Seafood salads are like tropical sea breezes. They have an aroma of the sea (from the seafood and fish sauce) and are hot like the hot tropical air (from the chillies, galanga, and garlic) while, at the same time, are cooling and refreshing (from the mint and cilantro leaves, lemon grass, and lime juice). Eating them transports me momentarily to the beautiful shores of memory and the enchantment of dining on wonderful seafood along a quiet stretch of beach, caressed by the soft sea breezes and the rustling sounds of swaying coconut palms.

The hot-and-sour chilli-lime dressing in this recipe is the standard one used for Thai seafood salads. It is intense just like the hot climate in the tropics and will make you sweat. But, unlike the intense tropical heat that can make you sluggish, the hotness of chillies enlivens, awakening the senses, and bringing rushes of excitement into your blood.

Instead of a mixture of seafood, turn this recipe into any kind of seafood salad you wish—hot-and-sour shrimp salad, hot-and-sour squid salad, and so on. Sea bass is superb by itself with this combination of herbs and hot, limy dressing.

Spicy Seafood Sizzling Hot Plate
(Bpoh Dtaek Gkrata Rawn)

6 whole mussels, rinsed
⅓ lb. white fish fillet, cut into bite-size chunks
6 sea scallops
6 large shrimp, shelled and butterflied
3 squid, cleaned and cut into 1-inch rounds
¼ cup shelled cooked crabmeat
2 to 3 Tbs. peanut oil
6 cloves garlic, finely chopped
2 red jalapeno, fresno, or serrano peppers, finely chopped with seeds
1 Tbs. finely chopped cilantro roots and/or bottom stems
3 to 4 Tbs. *Sriracha* bottled chilli sauce
1 Tbs. fish sauce (*nahm bplah*), to taste
2 to 3 tsp. sugar, to taste
2 Tbs. water or stock
½ cup short Thai basil sprigs (*bai horapa*)

Clean and prepare the various kinds of seafood. Let sit at room temperature at least 20 minutes before cooking. If seafood is still wet when you are ready to cook, pat dry with a clean towel.

Place a cast-iron serving platter on a burner over low heat. At the same time, heat a wok over high heat until its surface is smoking hot. Add oil and wait a few seconds for oil to heat. Sauté garlic and chilli peppers for 20 to 30 seconds. Add cilantro roots/stems, *Sriracha* chilli sauce, fish sauce, sugar, and water or stock. Cook about 1 minute to blend the flavors.

Toss in mussels. Stir-fry 30 to 40 seconds and follow with the fish and scallops. Stir another 30 seconds, then add shrimp and squid. Toss well to coat the seafood evenly with the seasonings. When the mussels start to open and shrimp are turning pink, add crabmeat and Thai basil. Turn heat under cast-iron pan to high.

If a lot of juice cooks out of the seafood, remove cooked seafood with a slotted spoon and reduce liquid to a thick, reddish brown sauce. Toss seafood back in, stir well, and turn off heat.

By this time, the cast-iron platter should be very hot. Carefully transfer it to its wooden base tray. Immediately spoon seafood and sauce onto the hot platter. The sauce should make the iron sizzle loudly and smoke and fume, making for a dramatic presentation.

Serves 4 to 6 with rice and other dishes in a family-style meal.

Notes and Pointers:

Whenever a loudly sizzling platter of food is brought to the table in an Asian restaurant, heads turn and excitement is aroused as the platter moves through the dining room. The smoke and fumes leave a trail of enticing aromas, making diners at adjacent tables wish they had been the ones who placed the order. Some wonder what magic trick the chef has wielded to make such a dramatic show.

There really is no mystery, just a very hot iron pan and sauce from a stir-fried dish. It's not even necessary to have the special rectangular iron pan with wooden base as is used in restaurants. Any cast-iron pan in your kitchen should do, with a wooden cutting board to set it on. The sizzling does more than just produce a lot of noise and fumes, it also concentrates flavors in the sauce and sears the seafood just a bit more.

"Drunken" Mixed Seafood Stir-Fry
with Holy Basil
(Pad Kee Mao Talay)

8 mussels in the shell
½ lb. halibut fillet, cut into 1½-inch chunks
⅓ lb. sea scallops
⅓ lb. medium tiger prawns, shelled and butterflied
10 to 15 fresh Thai chillies (*prik kee noo*), cut into thin rounds
12 to 15 cloves garlic, or 1 large head, chopped
1 tsp. minced cilantro roots, or substitute bottom stems
2 to 3 Tbs. peanut oil
2 shallots, thinly sliced
1 Tbs. Thai oyster sauce
1 tsp. granulated sugar
1 or more Tbs. fish sauce (*nahm bplah*), to taste
1 cup holy basil leaves (*bai gkaprow*), flower buds may also be used
1 Tbs. whole green peppercorns, optional
1 red jalapeno or fresno chilli pepper, cut into long slivers with seeds

Prepare seafood, rinse, and drain well. If seafood is still wet when you are ready to cook, pat dry with a clean towel.

Pound Thai chillies, garlic, and cilantro roots (or stems) with a mortar and pestle until pasty and well blended.

Heat a wok over high heat until it is smoking hot. Swirl in oil to coat the surface and wait 15 to 20 seconds for it to heat. Add crushed aromatics and sliced shallots, and stir until fragrant. Toss in mussels and stir-fry about 30 seconds. Follow with the fish chunks and stir-fry another 15 to 20 seconds. Then add remaining seafood.

Toss seafood frequently and, when the shrimp begins to turn pink on the outside, sprinkle in the oyster sauce, sugar, and fish sauce. Add basil, peppercorns, and slivered red chilli. Continue to stir-fry until seafood is just cooked and basil wilted. Transfer to a serving dish and serve hot with plain steamed rice.

Serves 4 to 6 with rice in a multicourse family-style meal.

Notes and Pointers:
For spicy food lovers, this is an exhilarating dish! It is meant to be at the peak of intensity, so excruciating to the lips and tongue, but so satisfying. It makes you reach for ice-cold beer to douse the

fire. As you continue to eat and drink, you might just get yourself into a drunken state—drunk with alcohol and drunk on endorphins all at the same time.

The seafood is not drunk in this recipe—no liquor is added to the stir-fry, but its name speaks of the state it may leave the diner in. In Thai, *kee mao* describes people who like to drink and get drunk, and *pad kee mao* dishes are very spicy stir-fries, flavored with loads of Thai chillies, garlic, and holy basil, which drinking Thais find fitting accompaniments to their ice-cold rice whiskey and soda. If you prefer, use just one kind of seafood instead of a mixture. My husband makes an awfully good halibut *kee mao*. You might try making a catfish *kee mao* or, if you like clams and mussels, shell them and spice them up to accompany your wine and beer.

Stir-Fried "Fish Trap"

(Pad Reua Bpoh)

⅓ lb. white fish fillet, cut into 1-inch chunks

⅓ lb. medium shrimp, shelled and butterflied

¼ lb. squid, cleaned and cut into 1-inch rounds

¼ lb. shelled, cooked crabmeat

6 to 10 Thai chillies (*prik kee noo*), cut into thin rounds

1 head garlic, chopped (or about ¼ cup)

2 tsp. chopped cilantro roots, or 1 Tbs. chopped stems

1 tsp. coarsely ground white peppercorns

3 Tbs. peanut oil

1 Tbs. Thai oyster sauce

½ to 1 cup Chinese celery leaves and young stems, or substitute with the tender leaves of regular celery, cut into 1-inch segments

1 orange or red serrano, jalapeno, or fresno pepper, cut into small slivers with seeds

2 tsp. light soy sauce

1 Tbs. fish sauce (*nahm bplah*)

1 tsp. granulated sugar

Clean and prepare seafood and drain well. Let sit at room temperature for 20 minutes before stir-frying. Just before cooking, pat fish, shrimp, and squid dry with a clean towel.

Pound Thai chillies, garlic, cilantro roots (or stems), and white peppercorns with a mortar and pestle to make a coarse paste.

Heat a wok over high heat until it is smoking hot. Swirl in oil to coat its surface and wait 10 to 15 seconds for oil to heat. Stir in chilli mixture and sauté until aromatic and flavors have blended. Spoon in oyster sauce, stir, then add fish chunks. Stir-fry 15 to 20 seconds before tossing in the shrimp.

Continue to stir-fry over high heat until most of the shrimp has started to turn pink on the outside. Add squid, celery, and pepper slivers. Stir-fry another 15 seconds before seasoning seafood mixture to taste with light soy sauce, fish sauce, and sugar. Stir well and, when all the seafood is cooked through, toss the crabmeat in with the mixture and transfer to a serving plate.

Serves 3 to 4 with other dishes and rice in a family-style meal.

Notes and Pointers:

This spicy concoction combines the hotness of chillies with that of freshly ground white peppercorns. The heat is tempered with the refreshing fragrance of celery. I have translated the Thai name for this combination seafood stir-fry as "stir-fried fish trap," meaning that whatever swims or crawls into the fish trap is game for the stir-fry. This usually includes fish, crab, squid, and shrimp.

Along the coast, small fishing boats go out daily and set up traps randomly across the sea floor. Long lengths of rope are tied to the traps and on the other end they are secured to a plastic or Styrofoam float, usually recycled plastic bottles. A flag on a bamboo pole further marks the floats. The fishermen distinguish their traps from others' by the color of their flags. They return a few hours later, pull up the traps, and see what they have caught. *Reua bpoh,* in the recipe's Thai name, really refers to these fish-trap setting fishing boats.

APPENDIX
THAI MARKETS THROUGHOUT THE UNITED STATES

Arizona
99 Ranch Market 668 N 44th Street, Phoenix, AZ 85008 (602) 275-6699

California
NORTHERN CALIFORNIA
Asian Market 5 Mary Street, San Rafael, CA 94901 (415) 459-7133

Bangkok 16 3214 16th Street, San Francisco, CA 94103 (415) 431-5838

Bangkok Grocery 1482 Fremont Boulevard, Seaside, CA 93955 (408) 394-4161

Bangkok Market 1585 Mabury Road, San Jose, CA 95133 (408) 258-5956

Chao Thai Market 1704 University Avenue, Berkeley, CA 94703 (510) 486-0515

Diablo Oriental Foods 2590 North Main Street, Walnut Creek, CA 94596
(925) 933-2590

Erawan Market 1463 University Avenue, Berkeley, CA 94702 (510) 849-9707
fax (650) 994-9896

Happy Grocery 1230 Stockton Street, San Francisco, CA 94133 (415) 677-9950

Khanh Phong Supermarket 429 Ninth Street, Oakland, CA 94067
(510) 839-9094

Lao Market 1619 International Boulevard, Oakland, CA 94606 (510) 536-5888

Phnom Penh 923 Petaluma Hill Road, Santa Rosa, CA 95404 (707) 545-7426

Thai Lao Market 2001 Story Road # 500, San Jose, CA 95122 (408) 259-7895

SOUTHERN CALIFORNIA
Bangkok Market 4757 Melrose Avenue, Los Angeles, CA 90029 (323) 662-9705
(877) 999-8424

Muang Laos Market 1 4202 National Avenue, San Diego, CA 92113
(619) 264-2294

Siam Market 27266 East Baseline Street, Highland, CA 92346 (909) 862-8060

Silom Market 5321 Hollywood Boulevard, Hollywood, CA 90027 (323) 993-9008

Thai-Lao Market 1721 West La Palma Avenue, Anaheim, CA 92801 (714) 535-2656

Thai Number One Market 5927 Cherry Avenue, Long Beach, CA 90805 (310) 422-6915

Colorado

Krung Thai Grocery 11700 East Montview Boulevard, Aurora, CO 80010 (303) 343-9450

Lek's Asian Market 112 Del Mar Circle, Aurora, CO 80011 (303) 366-2429

Oriental Food Market 1750 30th Street, Boulder, CO 80301 (303) 442-7830

Xuantrang Market 1095 South Federal Boulevard, Denver, CO 80219 (303) 936-7537

Connecticut

A DONG 160 Shield Street, West Hartford, CT 06110 (860) 953-8903, 953-3838

Viengthong Asian Market 282 Park Road, West Hartford, CT 06119 (860) 231-7513

Florida

Asia Market 9525 SW 160th Street, Miami, FL 33157 (305) 232-2728

Bangkok Minimarket 13390 SW 228th Street, Homestead, FL 33033 (305) 247-0498

Modern Thai Food, Incorporated 135 Yacht Club Way #210, Hypoluxo, FL 33462 (888) THAI-888

Thai Market 916 Harrelson Street, Fort Walton Beach, FL 32547 (904) 863-2013

Georgia

Thai Oriental Market 6467 Highway 85, Riverdale, GA 30274 (404) 997-3186

Illinois

Hoa Nam 1101 West Argyle Street, Chicago, IL 60640 (773) 275-9157

Thai Grocery 5014 North Broadway Street, Chicago, IL 60640 (773) 561-5345

Louisiana

Dong Khanh Market 3709 Westbank Expressway #H, Harvey, LA 70058 (504) 341-3639

Maryland

Maxim Gourmet Oriental Market 460 Hungerford Drive, Rockville, MD 20850 (301) 279-0110

Thai Market Incorporated 902 Thayer Avenue, Silver Spring, MD 20910 (301) 495-2779

New York

Asia Market 71½ Mulberry Street, New York, NY 10013 (212) 962-2028

Bangkok Center Grocery 104 Mosco Street (Chinatown), New York, NY 10013 (212) 349-1979

Bangkok Food Market 64-11 39th Avenue, Woodside, NY 11373 (718) 458-3685

Siam Grocery 790 Ninth Avenue, New York, NY 10019 (212) 245-4660

Udom 81A Bayard Street, New York, NY 10013 (212) 349-7662

Vasinee Food 333 North Henry Street, Brooklyn, NY 11222 (718) 349-6911

Nevada

International Market 1802 South Main Street, Las Vegas, NV 89104 (702) 386-9050

Thai Market 3297 Las Vegas Boulevard, Las Vegas, NV 89030 (702) 643-8080

Oregon

Uwajimaya 10500 SW Beaverton-Hillsdale Highway, Beaverton, OR 97005 (503) 643-4512

Texas

Hong Kong Food Market 3 13400 Veterans Memorial Drive, Houston, Texas 77014 (281) 537-5280

Hong Kong Supermarket 5708 South Gessner Drive, Houston, Texas 77036 (713) 995-1393

Siam Grocery 2636 North Fitzhugh Avenue, Dallas, TX 75204 (214) 823-8676

Washington

Uwajimaya 519 6th Avenue South, Seattle, WA 98104 (206) 624-6248

Uwajimaya 15555 NW 24th Street, Bellevue, WA 98007(425) 747-9012

Viet Wah 1032 South Jackson Street, Seattle, WA 98104 (206) 328-3557

ON-LINE RESOURCES

WHILE THERE ARE A NUMBER OF SITES PROVIDING THAI FOODS, AT THE TIME OF PRINTING THE FOUR ONLINE MARKETS listed below appear to offer the best selection of Thai ingredients. Keep in mind that when you are ordering fresh produce, you may want to order from the company nearest you.

Bangkok Market (www.bangkokmarket.com), located in Maywood, California, since its inception in 1972, was the first Thai retailer in the country and concentrates on customer satisfaction. They offer a variety of rice and noodles, spices, sauces, pastes, canned products, and utensils.

Import Food (www.importfood.com), located in Seattle, Washington, offers a convenient Thai food starter set for beginner cooks. Its full inventory consists of fresh Thai produce, canned goods, pastes and sauces, spices, noodles, rice, and carefully selected pieces of cookware.

Temple of Thai (www.templeofthai.com), located in Carroll, Iowa, promises that if you can't find what you're looking for they will assist you by e-mail. Rice and noodles, canned products, pastes, sauces, oils, spices, and pickled and preserved foods make up their selection of dry goods, while their fresh produce consists of Thai chillies, galanga root, and lemon grass. They also have a small selection of steamers, rice cookers, mortars and pestles, and pots and baskets.

Thai Grocer (www.thaigrocer.com), located in Chicago, Illinois, was the first complete Thai grocery on the internet. They stock a wide variety of canned products, sauces, pastes, herbs, spices, dried foods, rice, grains, noodles, and a full selection of equipment and utensils. They have recently added fresh Thai produce to their inventory, and they are committed to updating their selection to offer an ever-wider variety of products.

GARDEN RESOURCES

Kaffir Lime Trees

Four Winds Growers P.O. Box 3538 (F), Fremont, CA 94539 (510) 656-2591
  (http://www.fourwindsgrowers.com)

Thai Herbs and Vegetables (Seeds)

Johnny's Selected Seeds 1 Foss Hill Road, RR Box 2580, Albion, Maine 04910-9731 (207) 437-4395
  (http://www.johnnyseeds.com)

INDEX

abalone,148, 232

Aep Bplah, 130

albacore, 143, 261

anchovies, 98

    salted and dried, 41

appetizers:

    Crab Cakes, Fried, 215

    Crab Shells, Stuffed, with Hot Pickled Garlic Sauce, 216–17

    Cuttlefish, Crisped Dried, Spicy Salad of Shrimp, Cashews and, 239–40

    Miang Bplah (Leaf-Wrapped Fish and Tasty Tidbits), 104–5

    Mussel Cake, Savory Pan-Fried, with Wilted Bean Sprouts, 257–59

    Mussels on the Shell, Curried, with Flaked Crab, 266–67

    Oysters, Baked, with Salted Black Beans and Pickled Garlic, 256

    Shrimp, Crispy Garlic-and-Pepper-Encrusted, 191–92

    Shrimp, Dancing, 181

    Shrimp-and-Crab Toast with Sesame Seeds, Crispy, Served with Sweet-and-Sour Plum Sauce, 179–80

    Shrimp Cakes, Savory, Served with Sweet-and-Sour Cucumber Relish, 188–90

    Shrimp Chips, Homemade, 177–78

    Squid, Shrimp-and-Crab-Stuffed, Crispy, 241–42

aquaculture, 30–31, 93

Aw Suan, 273

Ayuthaya, 22

Baked Oysters with Salted Black Beans and Pickled Garlic, 256

bamboo steamers, 86–87

banana blossom, 48

banana leaf (leaves), 50

    Cups, Curried Mousse of Red Snapper in, 127–29

    Packets, Charcoal-Grilled Spiced Fish in, 130

    Striped Bass in, Charcoal-Roasted, Served with Hot-and-Sour Dipping Sauce, 162–63

Bangkok Market, 288

barracuda, 132, 135, 150

basil, 50–51

    Choo Chee Red Curry Shrimp with Kaffir Lime Leaves and, 196–97

Clams Stir-Fried with Roasted Chilli Sauce and, 270–71

Curried Mousse of Red Snapper in Banana Leaf Cups, 127–29

Curried Mussels on Half Shell with Flaked Crab, 266–67

"Drunken" Crisped Catfish Flakes, 124–25

Fish Fillets Stir-Fried in Hot-and Spicy Coconut Cream Sauce, 122–23

Holy, Crisped, Wok-Tossed Shelled Crab with Chillies, Garlic and, 225–26

Holy, "Drunken" Mixed Seafood Stir-Fry with, 280–81

Lime-Cooked Halibut Dressed with Roasted Chilli Sauce, Toasted Coconut, and Peanuts, 106–7

Pan-Fried Halibut Topped with Chilli-Tamarind Sauce, 147–48

Sizzling Stir–Fried Squid with Chilies and Fragrant Herbs, 246–47

Spicy "Broken Fish Trap" Soup, 274–75

Spicy Seafood Sizzling Hot Plate, 278–79

Spicy Stir-Fried Scallops and Mussels with Home-made Chilli Paste and Thai Eggplants, 264–65

Steamed Mussels in Clay Pot with Aromatic Herbs, 268–69

Thai, Salmon Poached in Green Curry Sauce with Baby Eggplants and, 120–21

Thai, Squid Stir-Fried with Roasted Chilli Sauce and, 249–50

Thai, Wok-Tossed Salmon with Chillies and, 126

Wilted, Spicy Crisped Fish with Seasonings and, 149–50

Wok-Tossed Mussels in Shell with Lemon Grass and, 272

bass, 104, 149

    sea, 107, 144, 185

    sea, in Mixed Seafood Salad with Lemon Grass, Mint, and Chilli-Lime Dressing, 276–77

    Sea, Steamed Fillet of, with Ginger, Green Onions, and Sesame-Soy Sauce, 154–55

    striped, 153, 156, 158, 161

    Striped, in Banana Leaf, Charcoal-Roasted, Served with Hot-and-Sour Dipping Sauce, 162–63

beans:

    Fava, Spicy Southern-Style Stir-Fried Shrimp with, 199–200

beans (*continued*)
    see also black bean(s), salted
  Bean Sprouts, Wilted, Savory Pan-Fried Mussel Cake
    with, 257–59
bean thread noodles, 51
  Prawns and, in Clay Pot, 211–12
bitter flavors, 17–18
bitter melon, 18, 48, 51, 139
black bean(s), salted, 68
  Baked Oysters with Pickled Garlic and, 256
  Garlic Pan-Fried Red Snapper, 151–52
black pepper(ed), 22, 66, 211
  Crab with Roasted Spices, 223–24
blanching seafood, for salad, 78, 174
boiling, 78
bplah chon, 41, 44, 114, 117
bplah daed diow, 41
bplah daek, 43–45
Bplah Doog Foo Pad Kee Mao, 124–25
Bplah Dtom Saep, 144
Bplah Gkapong Daeng Jian Dtow See, 151
Bplah Gkow Tawd Sahm Roet, 145–46
bplah gkrawb, 41–42
bplah haeng, 41–42
Bplah Hihma Neung Si-ew, 154–55
Bplah Jeramed Neung Buay, 153
Bplah Jeramed Tawd Gkratiem Priktai, 131
bplah kem, 41–43
Bplah Meuk Gkratiem Manao, 248
bplah meuk haeng, 45–46
Bplah Meuk Krawb Sawd Sai Gkoong Bpoo, 241–42
Bplah Meuk Neung Manao, 243
Bplah Meuk Pad Chah, 246–47
Bplah Meuk Pad Prik Pow, 249–50
Bplah Meuk Yahng, 250–51
Bplah Neung, 156–57
Bplah Neung Gkratiem Jiow, 136
Bplah Neung Manao, 158–59
Bplah Nin Jian King Kton Hawm, 160–61
Bplah Nin Neung Dtow Jiow, 137–38
Bplah Pow, 162–63
Bplah Rad Prik, 147–48
Bplah Rad Prik Horapa, 149–50
bplah rah, 43–45
Bplah Roem Kwan, 164–65
Bplah Saba Yahng Si-ew, 142–43
bplah salit, 41
Bplah Salmon Pad Gkaprow, 126
Bplah Tawd Kamin, 133–35
Bpoh Dtaek Gkrata Rawn, 278–79
Bpoo Jah, 216–17
bpoo kem, 46–48
Bpoo Neung, 218

Bpoo Pad Hom, 221–22
Bpoo Pad Pong Gkaree, 219–20
Bpoo Pad Priktai Dâm Gkap Kreuang Tehd, 223–24
Bpoo Pow Gkap Nahm Jim, 218
Braised Tilapia, Whole, with Ginger and Green Onions,
  160–61
braising, 79
bream, 156, 158
broccoli, Asian, 43
  with Salted Mackerel, 42–43
"Broken Fish Trap" Soup, Spicy, 274–75
broth, seafood, 99
butterfish, 131, 153

cabbage:
  Napa, Stuffed Squid Soup with, 237–38
  preserved Tianjin vegetables, 66
cakes (savory):
  Crab, Fried, 215
  Mussel, Pan-Fried, with Wilted Bean Sprouts, 257–59
  Shrimp, Served with Sweet-and-Sour Cucumber
    Relish, 188–90
cashew(s), 53
  Crispy Catfish Salad with Sour Green Mango and, 108–9
  Shrimp, 207–8
  Spicy Salad of Crisped Dried Cuttlefish, Shrimp and,
    239–40
cast-iron pans, 77, 90
catfish, 14, 94, 98, 102, 105, 116, 122, 134, 214
  Charcoal-Roasted, Salad, Spicy, 110–12
  Crisped, Salad with Sour Green Mango and Peanuts
    or Cashews, 108–9
  Flakes, "Drunken" Crisped, 124–25
  Rounds Simmered in Turmeric-Flavored Coconut
    Sauce, 118–19
  Whole, Northeastern-Style Crispy, Topped with
    Seasoned Thai Herbs, Chillies, and Toasted Rice,
    113–15
celery, Chinese, 54, 153, 219, 282
charcoal-grilled:
  Fish, Spiced, in Banana Leaf Packets, 130
  Jumbo Prawns or Lobster Tails Topped with Sour
    Tamarind Sauce, 198
  Prawns, "Sweet Fish Sauce," and *Sadao* or Neem
    Leaves, 213–14
  Prawn Salad, 186–87
  Squid, Marinated, 250–51
  see also mesquite-grilled
charcoal-roasted:
  Catfish Salad, Spicy, 110–12
  Striped Bass in Banana Leaf Served with Hot-
    and-Sour Dipping Sauce, 162–63

chilli(es), 18, 21, 22, 32, 53–54
    Dressing, Sweet-and-Sour, 254
    dried red, 53–54
    Lime Dressing, Hot-and-Sour, 276–77
    Northeastern-Style Whole Catfish Topped with
        Seasoned Thai Herbs, Toasted Rice and, 110–12
    prik kee noo, 53
    removing seeds from, 54
    roasting dried, 53
    sauce, *Sriracha*, 70
    Sizzling Stir-Fried Squid with Fragrant Herbs
        and, 246–47
    Tamarind Sauce, Pan-Fried Halibut Topped with,
        147–48
    Thai, 53
    Thai, in Fish Sauce, 227
    Wok-Tossed Salmon with Thai Basil and, 126
    Wok-Tossed Shelled Crab with Garlic, Crisped
        Holy Basil and, 225–26
chilli(es), roasted:
    Hot-and-Sour Trout Soup with Aromatic
        Herbs and, 100–101
    paste, 39–40
    Paste, Homemade, 175–76
    Sauce, Clams Stir-Fried with Basil and, 270–71
    Sauce, Hot-and-Sour Shrimp Salad with Lemon
        Grass, Mint and, 184–85
    Sauce, Lime-Cooked Halibut Dressed with Toasted
        Coconut, Peanuts and, 106–7
    Sauce, Squid Stir-Fried with Thai Basil and, 249–50
    "Three-Flavored" Grouper or Rock Fish with Roasted
        Garlic and, 145–46
chilli-lime sauces:
    Charcoal-Roasted Striped Bass in Banana Leaf,
        Served with Hot-Sour-Dipping Sauce, 162–63
    Dipping, 218
    Fish Sauce, 131
    Mixed Seafood Salad with Lemon Grass, Mint, and
        Chilli-Lime Dressing, 276–77
    Squid Steamed with, 243
    Steamed Whole Fish with, 158–59
Chilli Paste, 116, 122, 130, 264
    Prik King, 195
    Roasted, 39–40, 75–76
cholesterol, 32
choo chee, 197, 263
    Curry Sauce, Pan-Seared Sea Scallops Topped with,
        262–63
    Red Curry Shrimp with Kaffir Lime Leaves and Basil,
        196–97
Choo Chee Gkoong, 196–97
choppers, electric, 90
chowders:

Clam and Mussel Coconut Lime Soup with Oyster
    Mushrooms, 252–53
    Fish, Sour Tamarind, 116–17
cilantro, 17, 54
cilantro root, 54
clam(s), 112, 185, 197, 232–36, 272, 281
    cooking tips for, 236
    and Mussel Coconut Lime Soup with Oyster
        Mushrooms, 252–53
    selecting, 233
    Stir-Fried with Roasted Chilli Sauce and Basil,
        270–71
    storing, 235
clay pot:
    Mussels Steamed in, with Aromatic Herbs, 268–69
    Prawns and Bean Thread in, 211–12
coconut, 54–55
    Clam and Mussel Lime Soup with Oyster Mush-
        rooms, 252–53
    roasting, 55
    Sauce, Turmeric-Flavored, Catfish Rounds Simmered
        in, 118–19
    Toasted, Lime-Cooked Halibut Dressed with Roasted
        Chilli Sauce, Peanuts and, 106–7
    Turmeric Sauce, Shrimp Cooked in, 201
coconut cream, 55
    Salted Crab Sauce, 47–48
    Sauce, Hot-and-Spicy, Fish Fillets Stir-Fried in,
        122–23
coconut milk, 55–56
coconut sugar, 65–66
cod, 102, 105, 116, 130, 135, 149, 161
    China, 146
    Ling, Steamed Fillet of, with Sautéed Garlic
        and Ginger, 136
    rock, 98, 144, 155, 156, 158
coffee grinders, 90
conch, 232
cooking methods, 76–88
    boiling, simmering, and poaching, 78
    braising, 79
    curry-making, 78–79
    deep-frying and pan-frying, 77, 82–83
    frying crispy fish Thai-style, 97–98
    grilling, 79
    paste-making with mortar and pestle, 87–88
    steaming, 77–78, 85–87
    stir-frying, 76–77, 80–81, 85
    wok cooking, 79–85
    yâm salad-making, 78
cooking to taste, 19–20
coriander, sawleaf, 48, 68, 110, 130
coriander seeds, 56

corn oil, 65

country-style dishes:

Hot-and-Sour Prawn Soup with Aromatic Herbs and Oyster Mushrooms, 182–83

Shellfish Salad with Aromatic Thai Herbs, Crisped Shallots and Garlic, and Sweet-and-Sour Chilli Dressing, 254–55

crab(meat)(s), 169–74, 129, 155, 183, 212, 253

Black-Peppered, with Roasted Spices, 223–24

blue, back shells of, 174, 216

Cakes, Fried, 215

cleaning and preparing for cooking, 172–73

Dungeness, Steamed or Grilled, Served with Chilli-Lime Dipping Sauce, 218

Flaked, Curried Mussels on Half Shell with, 266–67

Fried Rice, 227–28

perishability of, 173

salted, 46–48

Salted, Coconut Cream Sauce, 47–48

selecting, 171

Shells, Stuffed, with Hot Pickled Garlic Sauce, 216–17

-and-Shrimp-Stuffed Squid, Crispy, 241–42

-and-Shrimp Toast with Sesame Seeds, Crispy, Served with Sweet-and-Sour Plum Sauce, 179–80

soft-shelled, 132

Spicy "Broken Fish Trap" Soup, 274–75

Spicy Seafood Sizzling Hot Plate, 278–79

Stir-Fried, with Yellow Curry Sauce, 219–20

Stir-Fried "Fish Trap," 282–83

Wok-Tossed, in Shell with Green Onions, 221–22

Wok-Tossed Shelled, with Chillies, Garlic, and Crisped Holy Basil, 225–26

crab butter paste, 48, 227

crispy or crisped seafood:

Catfish, Whole, Topped with Seasoned Thai Herbs, Chillies, and Toasted Rice, 113–15

Catfish Flakes, "Drunken," 124–25

Catfish Salad with Sour Green Mango and Peanuts or Cashews, 108–9

fish, frying Thai-style, 97–98

Fish, Fried, Southern-Style Turmeric, 133–35

Fish, Spicy, with Wilted Basil and Seasonings, 149–50

Fish, "Three-Flavored" Grouper or Rock, with Roasted Garlic and Roasted Chillies, 145–46

Pompano, Garlic-Peppered, 131–32

Shrimp Chips, Homemade, 177–78

Shrimp, Garlic-and-Pepper-Encrusted, 191–92

Shrimp-and-Crab Toast with Sesame Seeds, Served with Sweet-and-Sour Plum Sauce, 179–80

Squid, Shrimp-and-Crab-Stuffed, 241–42

crustaceans, 167–228

cleaning and preparing for cooking, 171–73

cooking tips for, 174

freshening, 173–74

perishability of, 173

selecting, 170–71

see also crab(meat)(s); prawn(s); shrimp

Cucumber Relish, Sweet-and-Sour, 189, 190

cumin, 56

curry(ied)(ies), 57

Choo Chee, Sauce, Pan-Seared Sea Scallops Topped with, 262–63

Choo Chee Red, Shrimp with Kaffir Lime Leaves and Basil, 196–97

cooking methods for, 56, 78–79

Fish Fillets Stir-Fried in Hot-and-Spicy Coconut Cream Sauce, 122–23

Green, Sauce, Salmon Poached in, with Baby Eggplants and Thai Basil, 120–21

Mousse of Red Snapper in Banana Leaf Cups, 127–29

Mussels on Half Shell with Flaked Crab, 266–67

pastes, 87, 88

powder, 57

Scallops and Mussels, Spicy Stir-Fried, with Home-made Chilli Paste and Thai Eggplants, 264–65

Yellow, Sauce, Stir-Fried Crab with, 219–20

cuttlefish, 123, 232–36, 247, 248, 249, 250, 261, 265

cleaning and preparing for cooking, 235

cooking tips for, 236

Crisped Dried, Spicy Salad of Shrimp, Cashews and, 239–40

dried, 45–46

selecting, 233, 234

dancing shrimp:

at food stall on Mekong River, 14–15

Homemade, 181

deep-frying, 77

wire-mesh skimmers for, 89–90

in wok, 82–83, 97–98

dipping sauces:

Chilli-Lime, 218

flavor harmony in, 18

Hot-and-Pungent Fermented Shrimp, 139–40

Hot-and-Sour, 133

Hot-and-Sour Fermented Soybean, 162–63

Piquant Sour Tamarind, 164

Salted Crab Coconut Cream Sauce, 47–48

Spicy Sweet-and-Sour Plum, 180

Sweet-and-Tangy, 260–61

dressings:

Hot-and-Sour Chilli-Lime, 276–77

Sweet-and-Sour Chilli, 254

"Drunken" Crisped Catfish Flakes, 124–25

"Drunken" Mixed Seafood Stir-Fry with Holy Basil, 280–81
Dtom Kah Hoi Lai, 252–53
Dtom Kem Gkati Bplah Doog, 118–19
Dtom Som Bplah, 102–3
Dtom Yâm Bplah Trout, 100–101
Dtom Yâm Bpoh Dtaek, 274–75
Dtom Yâm Gkoong, 182–83

eel, 123, 265
Egg and Oyster Scramble, 273
eggplants, 18, 58
    Baby, Salmon Poached in Green Curry Sauce with Thai Basil and, 120–21
    Thai, Spicy Stir-Fried Scallops and Mussels with Homemade Chilli Paste and, 264–65
equipment, 89–90
    cast-iron pans, 77, 90
    charcoal grill, 79
    coffee grinders, 90
    electric choppers and miniprocessors, 90
    grilling basket, 79
    hinged grill, 79
    mortar and pestle, 87–88
    "picker upper," 90
    steamer, stacked metal, 85–86
    stovetop grill pans, 90
    wire-mesh scoopers and skimmers, 89–90
    woks, 79–85

Fava Beans, Spicy Southern-Style Stir-Fried Shrimp with, 199–200
fish, 91–165, 183, 185, 195, 208, 220, 247, 253, 261, 263, 265
    aquaculture and, 30–31, 93
    cakes, fried, 189–90
    Charcoal-Grilled Spiced, in Banana Leaf Packets, 130
    Chowder, Sour Tamarind, 116–17
    cleaning, 96–97
    cooking tips for, 97–99
    crispy, frying, Thai-style, 97–98
    fermented or pickled, 43–45
    Fillets Stir-Fried in Hot-and-Spicy Coconut Cream Sauce, 122–23
    Flounder Simmered in Spicy Sauce, 144
    freshening, 97
    freshness of, 95–96
    freshwater, 29–31, 94
    Fried, Southern-Style Turmeric, 133–35
    Grouper or Rock Fish, "Three-Flavored," with Roasted Garlic and Roasted Chillies, 145–46

habitat destruction and, 30
Halibut, Lime-Cooked, Dressed with Roasted Chilli Sauce, Toasted Coconut, and Peanuts, 106–7
Halibut, Pan-Fried, Topped with Chilli-Tamarind Sauce, 147–48
healthful properties of, 31–32
Leaf-Wrapped, and Tasty Tidbits with Sweet-and-Sour Sauce, 104–5
Ling Cod, Steamed Fillet of, with Sautéed Garlic and Ginger, 136
Mackerel, Mesquite-Grilled, Glazed with Sweet Soy Sauce, 142–43
Mackerel and Assorted Vegetables, Pan-Fried, with Hot-and-Pungent Fermented Shrimp Dipping Sauce, 139–41
Mesquite-Grilled-and-Smoked, with Piquant Sour Tamarind Sauce, 164–65
Pompano, Garlic-Peppered, 131–32
Pompano Steamed with Pickled Plum, 153
Red Snapper, Curried Mousse of, in Banana Leaf Cups, 127–29
Red Snapper, Garlic–Black Bean Pan-Fried, 151–52
Salmon, Wok-Tossed, with Chillies and Thai Basil, 126
Salmon Poached in Green Curry Sauce with Baby Eggplants and Thai Basil, 120–21
Sea Bass, Steamed Fillet of, with Ginger, Green Onions, and Sesame-Soy Sauce, 154–55
serving whole, 93–94
skin of, 94
smaller, Thai preference for, 93, 94–95
Soup, Ginger-Tamarind, 102–3
Spicy "Broken Fish Trap" Soup, 274–75
Spicy Crisped, with Wilted Basil and Seasonings, 149–50
Spicy Seafood Sizzling Hot Plate, 278–79
Steamed, Mom's Good and Easy, 156–57
Steamed Whole, with Chilli-Lime Sauce, 158–59
Stir-Fried "Fish Trap," 282–83
Striped Bass in Banana Leaf, Charcoal-Roasted, Served with Hot-and-Sour Dipping Sauce, 162–63
sun-dried, salted, and smoke-dried, 41–43
Tilapia, Braised Whole, with Ginger and Green Onions, 160–61
Tilapia, Whole, Steamed with Ginger and Fermented Soybean Sauce, 137–38
Trout, Pan-Fried, Soup with Roasted Chillies and Aromatic Herbs, Hot-and-Sour, 100–101
whole, scoring before cooking, 99
see also specific fish
fish bones, removing from throat, 99
"fish bridges," 26–27
fishing, 25–26, 29, 94–95

fish markets, live fish in, 13–14, 96
fish sauce, 21, 34–36
    Chilli-Lime, 131
    "Sweet," Charcoal-Grilled Prawns, *Sadao* or Neem
        Leaves and, 213–14
    Thai chillies in, 227
"Fish Trap":
    Spicy "Broken," Soup, 274–75
    Stir-Fried, 282–83
"Five-Flavored" Shrimp with Toasted Sesame Seeds,
    209–10
flavors:
    harmony of, 18–19
    primary, 17–18
Flounder Simmered in Spicy Sauce, 144
food stalls, 14–15
freshwater fish, 29–31, 94
    crisped, smoke-dried, 41–42
    fermented or pickled, 43–45
    salted and partially sun-dried, 41
Fried Rice, Crab, 227–28
fried seafood:
    Crab Cakes, 215
    Crab Shells, Stuffed, with Hot Pickled Garlic Sauce,
        216–17
    Fish, Southern-Style Turmeric, 133–35
    Fish, Spicy Crisped, with Wilted Basil and
        Seasonings, 149–50
    Grouper or Rock Fish, "Three-Flavored," with
        Roasted Garlic and Roasted Chillies, 145–46
    Pompano, Garlic-Peppered, 131–32
    Shrimp, Crispy Garlic-and-Pepper-Encrusted, 191–92
    Shrimp Cakes, Savory, Served with Sweet-and-Sour
        Cucumber Relish, 188–90
    Squid, Crispy Shrimp-and-Crab-Stuffed, 241–42
    see also pan-fried seafood
frying:
    crispy fish Thai-style, 97–98
    see also deep-frying
fusion food, 21–23

galanga or galangal, 17, 58–59, 100, 101, 122, 147, 184,
    194–95, 252, 254–55, 264–65, 268, 274, 276–77
garden resources, 288
garlic, 32, 59–60
    Black Bean Pan-Fried Red Snapper, 151–52
    Crisped, Shellfish Salad with Aromatic Thai Herbs,
        Crisped Shallots, and Sweet-and-Sour Chilli
        Dressing, 254–55
    Crisped, Southern-Style Spicy Tamarind Prawns with
        Crisped Shallots and, 205–6
    fried, 59–60

oil, 59–60
    -Peppered Pompano, 131–32
    -and-Pepper-Encrusted Shrimp, Crispy, 191–92
    pickled, 60
    Pickled, Baked Oysters with Salted Black Beans and,
        256
    Pickled, Sauce, Hot, 217
    Roasted, "Three-Flavored" Grouper or Rock Fish
        with Roasted Chillies and, 145–46
    roasting, 60
    Sautéed, Steamed Fillet of Ling Cod with Ginger and,
        136
    Squid Sautéed with Lime and, 248
    Wok-Tossed Shelled Crab with Chillies, Crisped Holy
        Basil and, 225–26
ginger, 17, 60, 130, 151, 153, 156, 211, 216, 221
    Braised Whole Tilapia with Green Onions and,
        160–61
    and Dried Shrimp Salad, 38–39
    galanga or galangal, 17, 58–59
    Steamed Fillet of Ling Cod with Sautéed Garlic
        and, 136
    Steamed Fillet of Sea Bass with Green Onions,
        Sesame-Soy Sauce and, 154–55
    Tamarind Fish Soup, 102–3
    Whole Tilapia Steamed with Fermented Soybean
        Sauce and, 137–38
gkabpi, 36–38
Gkaeng Cheud Bplah Meuk Yad Sai, 237–38
Gkaeng Choo Chee Hoi Shel, 262–63
Gkaeng Kiow Wahn Bplah Salmon, 120–21
Gkaeng Som Bplah, 116–17
Gkoong Dten, 181
Gkoong Dtom Gkati Kamin, 201
Gkoong Dtom Yâm Haeng, 203
gkoong haeng, 38–39
Gkoong Hah Roet, 209–10
Gkoong Neung Gkratiem, 202
Gkoong Neung Si-ew, 193
Gkoong Obb Woon Sen, 211–12
Gkoong Pad Med Mamuang Himapahn, 207–8
Gkoong Pad Prik King, 194–95
Gkoong Pad Sadtaw, 199–200
Gkoong Pow Rahd Sawd Makahm Bpiak, 198
Gkoong Tawd Gkratiem Priktai, 191–92
Gkoong Yai Pad Som Makahm Bpiak, 205–6
gkrachai, 67
    see also rhizome
Gold Mountain seasoning sauce, 60
gouramy, 41, 44, 131, 158
green curry, 57
    Sauce, Salmon Poached in, with Baby Eggplants
        and Thai Basil, 120–21

green mango, 60–61
  Sour, Crisped Catfish Salad with Peanuts or Cashews and, 108–9
green onions, 61
  Braised Whole Tilapia with Ginger and, 160–61
  Steamed Fillet of Sea Bass with Ginger, Sesame-Soy Sauce and, 154–55
  Wok-Tossed Crab in Shell with, 221–22
green peppercorns, 66, 122, 199, 246, 280
grilled seafood:
  Catfish, Charcoal-Roasted, Salad, Spicy, 110–12
  Dungeness Crab Served with Chilli-Lime Dipping Sauce, 218
  Fish, Mesquite-Grilled-and-Smoked, with Piquant Sour Tamarind Sauce, 164–65
  Fish, Spiced, Charcoal-Grilled in Banana Leaf Packets, 130
  Mackerel, Mesquite-Grilled, Glazed with Sweet Soy Sauce, 142–43
  Prawn, Charcoal-Grilled, Salad, 186–87
  Prawns, Charcoal-Grilled, "Sweet Fish Sauce," and Sadao or Neem Leaves, 213–14
  Prawns, Jumbo, or Lobster Tails, Charcoal-Grilled, Topped with Sour Tamarind Sauce, 198
  Scallops, Mesquite-Grilled Marinated, Served with Sweet-and-Tangy Dipping Sauce, 260–61
  Squid, Marinated, Charcoal-Grilled, 250–51
  Striped Bass, Charcoal-Roasted, in Banana Leaf Served with Hot-and-Sour Dipping Sauce, 162–63
grilling, 79, 90
grouper, 98, 132, 135, 150, 156
  "Three-Flavored," with Roasted Garlic and Roasted Chillies, 145–46

haddock, 136
halibut, 115, 122, 130, 135, 136, 144, 150, 155, 247
  "Drunken" Mixed Seafood Stir-Fry with Holy Basil, 280–81
  Lime-Cooked, Dressed with Roasted Chilli Sauce, Toasted Coconut, and Peanuts, 106–7
  Pan-Fried, Topped with Chilli-Tamarind Sauce, 147–48
haw moek, 57
Haw Moek Bplah, 127–29
Haw Moek Hoi Malaeng Poo, 266–67
herbs, 17–18, 19
  crushing with mortar and pestle, 87, 88
  nutritional benefits of, 32
  see also specific herbs
Hoi Malaeng Poo Gkata, 272
Hoi Malaeng Poo Ohb Maw Din, 268–69
Hoi Malaeng Poo Tawd, 257–59

Hoi Nahnglom Ohb Dtow See, 256
Hoi Pad Nahm Prik Pow, 270–71
Hoi Shel Yahng Sohng Kreuang, 260–61
hot, spicy, and pungent flavors, 17, 18, 19
Hot-and-Pungent Fermented Shrimp Dipping Sauce, 139–40
hot-and-sour:
  Chilli-Lime Dressing, 276–77
  Dipping Sauce, 133
  Fermented Soybean Dipping Sauce, 162–63
  Lemon Grass Tiger Prawns, 203–4
  Pan-Fried Trout Soup with Roasted Chillies and Aromatic Herbs, 100–101
  Prawn Soup with Aromatic Herbs and Oyster Mushrooms, Country-Style, 182–83
  Shrimp Salad with Roasted Chilli Sauce, Lemon Grass, and Mint, 184–85
Hot Plate, Spicy Seafood Sizzling, 278–79

ice, seafood consumption and, 27, 28–29
Import Food, 288
ingredients, 49–73
  flavoring, preserved seafood as, 33–48
  variations in, 19–20

kachai, 67
kaffir lime, 17, 61–62
  leaves, 100, 120, 122, 126, 127–29, 130, 182, 194, 199, 201, 203, 244, 246, 252, 254, 262, 264, 266, 274
  Leaves, Choo Chee Red Curry Shrimp with Basil and, 196–97
  peel, 122, 188–90, 194–95, 264
  trees, 288
Ka-nah Bplah Kem, 42–43
Kanom Bpahng Nah Gkoong Sai Bpoo, 179–80
Kao Gkriep Gkoong, 177–78
Kao Pad Bpoo, 227–28

Lahb Bplah Doog Tawd Gkrawb, 113–15
Lahp Bplah Doog, 110–12
Leaf-Wrapped Fish and Tasty Tidbits with Sweet-and-Sour Sauce, 104–5
lemon grass, 17, 62–63, 100, 104, 106, 110, 113, 118, 122, 124, 130, 182, 186, 194, 201, 221, 239, 244, 252, 254, 264, 268, 274
  Hot-and-Sour Shrimp Salad with Roasted Chilli Sauce, Mint and, 184–85
  Mixed Seafood Salad with Mint, Chilli-Lime Dressing and, 276–77
  Tiger Prawns, Hot-and-Sour, 203–4

lemon grass (*continued*)
    Wok-Tossed Mussels in Shell with Basil and, 272
lime(s), 63
    Chilli Dipping Sauce, 218
    Chilli Dressing, Hot-and-Sour, 276–77
    Chilli Fish Sauce, 131
    Chilli Sauce, Squid Steamed with, 243
    Chilli Sauce, Steamed Whole Fish with, 158–59
    Clam and Mussel Coconut Soup with Oyster Mush-
        rooms, 252–53
    -Cooked Halibut Dressed with Roasted Chilli Sauce,
        Toasted Coconut, and Peanuts, 106–7
    kaffir, 17, 61–62
    kaffir, leaves, 100, 120, 122, 126, 127–29, 130, 182,
        194, 199, 201, 203, 244, 246, 252, 254, 262, 264,
        266, 268, 274
    Kaffir, Leaves, *Choo Chee* Red Curry Shrimp with Basil
        and, 196–79
    kaffir, trees, 288
    Squid Sautéed with Garlic and, 248
limestone water, 63–64
Ling Cod, Steamed Fillet of, with Sautéed Garlic and
        Ginger, 136
lobster(s), 170, 185, 195, 224
    perishability of, 173
    selecting, 171
    spiny, 169
    Tails, Charcoal-Grilled, Topped with Sour Tamarind
        Sauce, 198
Loen Bpoo Kem, 47–48

mackerel, 36, 95, 101
    and Assorted Vegetables, Pan-Fried, with Hot-and-
        Pungent Fermented Shrimp Dipping Sauce, 139–41
    king, 135, 261
    Mesquite-Grilled, Glazed with Sweet Soy Sauce, 142–43
    salted, 42
    Salted, Asian Broccoli with, 42–43
Maggi seasoning sauce, 64
mahi mahi, 143
mân bpoo, 48
mân gkoong, 48
mango, green, *see* green mango
markets, Thai, 285–87
meals:
    balance of dishes in, 19
    rice as main food in, 20
    serving Thai-style, 238
mesquite-grilled:
    Mackerel Glazed with Sweet Soy Sauce, 142–43
    Scallops, Marinated, Served with Sweet-and-Tangy
        Dipping Sauce, 260–61

-and-Smoked Fish with Piquant Sour Tamarind
        Sauce, 164–65
Miang Bplah, 104–5
miniprocessors, 90
mint, 64
    Hot-and-Sour Shrimp Salad with Roasted Chilli
        Sauce, Lemon Grass and, 184–85
    Mixed Seafood Salad with Lemon Grass, Chilli-Lime
        Dressing and, 276–77
mixed seafood dishes:
    "Drunken," Stir-Fry with Holy Basil, 280–81
    Salad with Lemon Grass, Mint, and Chilli-Lime
        Dressing, 276–77
    Shellfish Salad with Aromatic Thai Herbs, Crisped
        Shallots and Garlic, and Sweet-and-Sour Chilli
        Dressing, 254–55
    Spicy "Broken Fish Trap" Soup, 274–75
    Spicy Seafood Sizzling Hot Plate, 278–79
    Stir-Fried "Fish Trap," 282–83
mollusks, 229–83
    Clam and Mussel Coconut Lime Soup with Oyster
        Mushrooms, 252–53
    Clams Stir-Fried with Roasted Chilli Sauce and Basil,
        270–71
    cleaning and preparing for cooking, 234–35
    cooking tips for, 236
    Cuttlefish, Crisped Dried, Spicy Salad of Shrimp,
        Cashews and, 239–40
    "Drunken" Mixed Seafood Stir-Fry with Holy Basil,
        280–81
    Mixed Seafood Salad with Lemon Grass, Mint, and
        Chilli-Lime Dressing, 276–77
    Mussel Cake, Savory Pan-Fried, with Wilted Bean
        Sprouts, 257–59
    Mussels in Shell, Wok-Tossed, with Lemon Grass and
        Basil, 272
    Mussels on Half Shell, Curried, with Flaked Crab,
        266–67
    Mussels Steamed in Clay Pot with Aromatic Herbs,
        268–69
    Oyster and Egg Scramble, 273
    Oysters, Baked, with Salted Black Beans and Pickled
        Garlic, 256
    Scallops, Marinated Mesquite-Grilled, Served with
        Sweet-and-Tangy Dipping Sauce, 260–61
    Scallops and Mussels, Spicy Stir-Fried, with Home-
        made Chilli Paste and Thai Eggplants, 264–65
    Sea Scallops, Pan-Seared, Topped with *Choo Chee*
        Curry Sauce, 262–63
    selecting, 232–34
    Shellfish Salad with Aromatic Thai Herbs, Crisped
        Shallots and Garlic, and Sweet-and-Sour Chilli
        Dressing, 254–55

Spicy "Broken Fish Trap" Soup, 274–75
Spicy Seafood Sizzling Hot Plate, 278–79
Stir-Fried "Fish Trap," 282–83
storing, 235–36
see also clams, mussels, squid
Mom's Good and Easy Steamed Fish, 156–57
monkfish, 122, 208
morning glory, 64
mortar and pestle, 87–88
Mousse of Red Snapper, Curried, in Banana Leaf Cups, 127–29
mudfish, 41, 44
mullet, 102, 135
mushrooms, oyster:
    Clam and Mussel Coconut Lime Soup with, 252–53
    Country-Style Hot-and-Sour Prawn Soup with Aromatic Herbs and, 182–83
mussel(s), 112, 123, 129, 183, 185, 197, 232–36, 245
    Cake, Savory Pan-Fried, with Wilted Bean Sprouts, 257–59
    and Clam Coconut Lime Soup with Oyster Mushrooms, 252–53
    cooking tips for, 236
    "Drunken" Mixed Seafood Stir-Fry with Holy Basil, 280–81
    on Half Shell, Curried, with Flaked Crab, 266–67
    selecting, 233
    in Shell, Wok-Tossed, with Lemon Grass and Basil, 272
    Shellfish Salad with Aromatic Thai Herbs, Crisped Shallots and Garlic, and Sweet-and-Sour Chilli Dressing, 254–55
    Spicy "Broken Fish Trap" Soup, 274–75
    Spicy Seafood Sizzling Hot Plate, 278–79
    Spicy Stir-Fried Scallops and, with Homemade Chilli Paste and Thai Eggplants, 264–65
    Steamed in Clay Pot with Aromatic Herbs, 268–69
    storing, 235

nahm bplah, 34–36
nahm mân hoi, 40
nahm prik, 36
Nahm Prik Bplah Too, 139–41
nahm prik pow, 39–40
    Homemade, 175–76
Napa Cabbage, Stuffed Squid Soup with, 237–38
Neem Leaves, Charcoal-Grilled Prawns, "Sweet Fish Sauce" and, 213–14
Neua Bpoo Pad Gkaprow Gkrawb, 225–26
nonstick pans, 76
noodles, bean thread, 51
    Prawns and, in Clay Pot, 211–12

northeastern-style dishes:
    Catfish, Charcoal-Roasted, Salad, Spicy, 110–12
    Catfish, Crispy Whole, Topped with Seasoned Thai Herbs, Chillies, and Toasted Rice, 113–15
    Halibut, Lime-Cooked, Dressed with Roasted Chilli Sauce, Toasted Coconut, and Peanuts, 106–7

octopus, 232
oil, 64–65
    garlic, 59–60
omega–3 fatty acids, 32, 94
onions, green, *see* green onions
on-line resources, 288
oyster(s), 132, 232–33, 236
    Baked, with Salted Black Beans and Pickled Garlic, 256
    cooking tips for, 236
    and Egg Scramble, 273
    nutrients in, 273
    opening, 256
    selecting, 233
    Shellfish Salad with Aromatic Thai Herbs, Crisped Shallots and Garlic, and Sweet-and-Sour Chilli Dressing, 254–55
    storing, 236
oyster mushrooms:
    Clam and Mussel Coconut Lime Soup with, 252–53
    Country-Style Hot-and-Sour Prawn Soup with Aromatic Herbs and, 182–83
oyster sauce, 40

pad chah, 246
    Bplah Meuk, 246–47
pad gkaprow, 126
Pad Kee Mao Talay, 280–81
pad ped, 57
Pad Ped Bplah, 122
Pad Ped Bplah Meuk, 244–45
Pad Ped Hoi Shel Gkap Moi Malaeng Poo, 264–65
Pad Reua Bpoh, 282–83
palm sugar, 65–66
pan-fried seafood:
    Halibut Topped with Chilli-Tamarind Sauce, 147–48
    Mackerel and Assorted Vegetables with Hot-and-Pungent Fermented Shrimp Dipping Sauce, 139–41
    Mussel Cake, Savory, with Wilted Bean Sprouts, 257–59
    Red Snapper, Garlic-Black Bean, 151–52
    Trout Soup, Hot-and-Sour, with Roasted Chillies and Aromatic Herbs, 100–101
pan-frying, 77
    in wok, 82–83

Pan-Seared Sea Scallops Topped with *Choo Chee* Curry
    Sauce, 262–63
paste-making with mortar and pestle, 87–88
pea eggplant, 20, 58
peanut oil, 64–65, 77, 97
peanuts, 21, 66
    Crispy Catfish Salad with Sour Green Mango and,
        108–9
    Lime-Cooked Halibut Dressed with Roasted Chilli
        Sauce, Toasted Coconut, and Peanuts, 106–7
pepper(corn)(s), 22, 66
    Black-Peppered Crab with Roasted Spices, 223–24
    -and-Garlic-Encrusted Shrimp, Crispy, 191–92
    Garlic-Peppered Pompano, 131–32
    see also green peppercorns
perch, 98, 102, 104, 131, 135, 149, 153, 155, 156, 158,
    161
periwinkle, 232
"picker upper," 90
pilot fish, 41
Piquant Sour Tamarind Sauce, 164
Plah Bplah Talay, 106–7
Plah Gkoong, 184–85
plum, pickled salted, 67
    Dipping Sauce, Spicy Sweet-and-Sour, 180
    Pompano Steamed with, 153
Poached Salmon in Green Curry Sauce with Baby Egg-
    plants and Thai Basil, 120–21
poaching, 78
Polo, Marco, 30
polygonum, 48, 67
pomfret, 131, 153
pompano, 98, 135, 158
    Garlic-Peppered, 131–32
    Steamed with Pickled Plum, 153
porgy, 156, 158
prawn(s), 112, 169, 185, 195, 220, 224, 249, 261, 263
    and Bean Thread in Clay Pot, 211–12
    Charcoal-Grilled, Salad, 186–87
    Charcoal-Grilled, "Sweet Fish Sauce," and *Sadao* or
        Neem Leaves, 213–14
    cleaning and preparing for cooking, 171–72
    cooking tips for, 174
    "Drunken" Mixed Seafood Stir-Fry with Holy Basil,
        280–81
    freshening, 173–74
    Jumbo, Charcoal-Grilled, Topped with Sour
        Tamarind Sauce, 198.
    perishability of, 173
    selecting, 170–71
    Shellfish Salad with Aromatic Thai Herbs, Crisped
        Shallots and Garlic, and Sweet-and-Sour Chilli
        Dressing, 254–55

shrimp vs., 170
    Soup, Country-Style Hot-and-Sour, with Aromatic
        Herbs and Oyster Mushrooms, 182–83
    Southern-Style Spicy Tamarind, with Crisped Shallots
        and Garlic, 205–6
    Spicy "Broken Fish Trap" Soup, 274–75
    Tiger, Hot-and-Sour Lemon Grass, 203–4
    Tiger, Steamed, 193
    Tiger, Steamed with Garlic and Thai Chillies, 202
    see also shrimp
preserved seafood, 28, 33–48
preserved Tianjin vegetables, 66, 237
prik king:
    Chilli Paste, 195
    Shrimp, Spicy, 194–95
Prik Nahm Bplah, 227
pungent, hot, and spicy flavors, 17, 18, 19

recipes, as guidelines, 20
red curry, 57, 190
    Choo Chee, Shrimp with Kaffir Lime Leaves and Basil,
        196–97
    Fish Fillets Stir-Fried in Hot-and-Spicy Coconut
        Cream Sauce, 122–23
    Scallops and Mussels, Spicy Stir-Fried, with Home-
        made Chilli Paste and Thai Eggplants, 264–65
red snapper, 98, 102, 105, 107, 116, 135, 136, 144, 146,
    148, 149, 150, 155, 156, 158
    Curried Mousse of, in Banana Leaf Cups, 127–29
    Garlic–Black Bean Pan-Fried, 151–52
refrigeration, 28, 29
Relish, Cucumber, Sweet-and-Sour, 189, 190
rhizome, 67, 122, 197, 246–47
rice:
    Crab Fried, 227–28
    in everyday Thai-style dining, 238
    and fish diet, healthful properties of, 31–32
    as main food in Thai cuisine, 20, 29, 30
    roasted, powder, 68
    sticky, 70–71
rice flour, 67
rice wine, 67–68
Rock Fish, "Three-Flavored," with Roasted Garlic and
    Roasted Chillies, 145–46

sadao, 214
    Charcoal-Grilled Prawns, "Sweet Fish Sauce" and,
        213–14
Sadao Nahm Bplah Wahn Gkoong Pow, 213–14
Sadtaw, Spicy Southern-Style Stir-Fried Shrimp with,
    199–200
safflower oil, 65

salads:
 blanching seafood for, 174
 Catfish, Charcoal-Roasted, Spicy, 110–12
 Catfish, Crisped, with Sour Green Mango and
  Peanuts or Cashews, 108–9
 Cuttlefish, Crisped Dried, Shrimp, and Cashew,
  Spicy, 239–40
 Mixed Seafood, with Lemon Grass, Mint, and
  Chilli-Lime Dressing, 276–77
 Prawn, Charcoal-Grilled, 186–87
 Shellfish, with Aromatic Thai Herbs, Crisped
  Shallots and Garlic, and Sweet-and-Sour Chilli
  Dressing, 254–55
 Shrimp, Dried, and Ginger, 38–39
 Shrimp, Hot-and-Sour, with Roasted Chilli Sauce,
  Lemon Grass, and Mint, 184–85
 yâm salad-making method for, 78
salmon, 115, 148
 Poached in Green Curry Sauce with Baby Eggplants
  and Thai Basil, 120–21
 Wok-Tossed, with Chillies and Thai Basil, 126
salt, 68
salty flavors, 17, 18–19
sand dabs, 98
sauces:
 Chilli-Lime Fish Sauce, 131
 Hot Pickled Garlic, 217
 Piquant Sour Tamarind, 164
 Salted Crab Coconut Cream, 47–48
 Sweet-and-Sour, 104
 see also dipping sauces
Sautéed Squid, with Garlic and Lime, 248
sawleaf coriander, 48, 68, 110, 130
scallops, 112, 123, 126, 183, 185, 197, 198, 206, 208, 220,
 232, 245, 247, 249
 cooking tips for, 236
 "Drunken" Mixed Seafood Stir-Fry with Holy
  Basil, 280–81
 Marinated Mesquite-Grilled, Served with Sweet-and-
  Tangy Dipping Sauce, 260–61
 Mixed Seafood Salad with Lemon Grass, Mint,
  and Chilli-Lime Dressing, 276–77
 Sea, Pan-Seared, Topped with *Choo Chee* Curry Sauce,
  262–63
 selecting, 233
 Shellfish Salad with Aromatic Thai Herbs, Crisped
  Shallots and Garlic, and Sweet-and-Sour Chilli
  Dressing, 254–55
 Spicy "Broken Fish Trap" Soup, 274–75
 Spicy Seafood Sizzling Hot Plate, 278–79
 Spicy Stir-Fried Mussels and, with Homemade Chilli
  Paste and Thai Eggplants, 264–65
 storing, 236

sea bass, 107, 144, 185
 Mixed Seafood Salad with Lemon Grass, Mint,
  and Chilli-Lime Dressing, 276–77
 Steamed Fillet of, with Ginger, Green Onions, and
  Sesame-Soy Sauce, 154–55
sea bream, 149
seafood:
 author's use of term, 31
 healthful properties of, 31–32
 origin of word, 27, 28
 see also crustaceans; fish; mollusks
seeds, for Thai herbs and vegetables, 288
serpent-head fish, 41, 44
serving meals, in everyday Thai-style dining, 238
sesame oil, 65
sesame seeds, 68
 Toasted, "Five-Flavored" Shrimp with, 209–10
shad, 153
shallots, 68–69
 Crisped, Shellfish Salad with Aromatic Thai Herbs,
  Crisped Garlic, and Sweet-and-Sour Chilli
  Dressing, 254–55
 Crisped, Southern-Style Spicy Tamarind Prawns with
  Crisped Garlic and, 205–6
 fried, 69
 roasted, 69
Shao Hsing, 67–68
shark, 95–96, 122, 143, 261
sheepshead, 149, 153, 156
shellfish:
 cleaning and preparing for cooking, 234
 Salad with Aromatic Thai Herbs, Crisped Shallots and
  Garlic, and Sweet-and-Sour Chilli Dressing, 254–55
 selecting, 232–33
 see also clam(s), crab(meat)(s); crustaceans; mollusks;
  mussel(s); oyster(s); prawn(s); scallops; shrimp
shrimp, 121, 123, 126, 129, 130, 228, 245, 247, 253, 263,
 265
 Cakes, Savory, Served with Sweet-and-Sour
  Cucumber Relish, 188–90
 Cashew, 207–8
 Chips, Homemade, 177–78
 Choo Chee Red Curry, with Kaffir Lime Leaves and
  Basil, 196–97
 cleaning and preparing for cooking, 171–72
 Cooked in Turmeric Coconut Sauce, 201
 cooking tips for, 174
 -and-Crab-Stuffed Squid, Crispy, 241–42
 -and-Crab Toast with Sesame Seeds, Crispy, Served
  with Sweet-and-Sour Plum Sauce, 179–80
 Crispy Garlic-and-Pepper-Encrusted, 191–92
 Dancing (recipe), 181
 dancing, at food stall on Mekong River, 14–15

shrimp (*continued*)
"Five-Flavored," with Toasted Sesame Seeds, 209–10
freshening, 173–74
ground dried, 39
Mixed Seafood Salad with Lemon Grass, Mint, and Chilli-Lime Dressing, 276–77
perishability of, 173
prawns vs., 170
Salad, Hot-and-Sour, with Roasted Chilli Sauce, Lemon Grass, and Mint, 184–85
selecting, 170–71
Spicy *Prik King*, 194–95
Spicy Salad of Crisped Dried Cuttlefish, Cashews and, 239–40
Spicy Seafood Sizzling Hot Plate, 278–79
Stir-Fried, with *Sadtaw* or Fava Beans, Spicy Southern-Style, 199–200
Stir-Fried "Fish Trap," 282–83
see also prawn(s)
shrimp, dried, 38–39
Dipping Sauce, Hot-and-Pungent, 139–40
and Ginger Salad, 38–39
Roasted Chilli Paste, 175–76
shrimp butter paste, 48
shrimp paste, 36–38
Roasted Chilli Paste, 175–76
simmered seafood:
Catfish Rounds, in Turmeric-Flavored Coconut Sauce, 118–19
Flounder, in Spicy Sauce, 144
simmering, 78
"single sun" fish, 41
sizzling:
Seafood Hot Plate, Spicy, 278–79
Stir-Fried Squid with Chillies and Fragrant Herbs, 246–47
skate wings, 95–96, 247, 265
skimmers, wire-mesh, 89–90
smelts, 98, 131
snacks:
Leaf-Wrapped Fish and Tasty Tidbits with Sweet-and-Sour Sauce, 104–5
Mussel Cake, Savory Pan-Fried, with Wilted Bean Sprouts, 257–59
Shrimp-and-Crab Toast with Sesame Seeds, Crispy, Served with Sweet-and-Sour Plum Sauce, 179–80
Shrimp Cakes, Savory, Served with Sweet-and-Sour Cucumber Relish, 188–90
Shrimp Chips, Homemade, 177–78
snails, 232
snapper, *see* red snapper
sole, 98, 121, 123, 136, 144
soups, 99

"Broken Fish Trap," Spicy, 274–75
Clam and Mussel Coconut Lime, with Oyster Mushrooms, 252–53
Fish, Ginger-Tamarind, 102–3
Fish Chowder, Sour Tamarind, 116–17
Prawn, Country-Style Hot-and-Sour, with Aromatic Herbs and Oyster Mushrooms, 182–83
serving alongside dinner plates, 238
Squid, Stuffed, with Napa Cabbage or Squash, 237–38
Trout, Pan-Fried, Hot-and-Sour, with Roasted Chillies and Aromatic Herbs, 100–101
sour fish curry, 116
sour flavors, 17, 18–19
southern-style dishes:
Catfish Rounds Simmered in Turmeric-Flavored Coconut Sauce, 118–19
Fish, Turmeric Fried, 133–35
Prawns, Spicy Tamarind, with Crisped Shallots and Garlic, 205–6
Shrimp, Spicy Stir-Fried, with *Sadtaw* or Fava Beans, 199–200
Shrimp Cooked in Turmeric Coconut Sauce, 201
Squid, Spicy Stir-Fried, 244–45
soybean sauce, fermented, 69
Dipping Sauce, Hot-and-Sour, 162–63
Whole Tilapia Steamed with Ginger and, 137–39
soy sauce, 69–70
spicy, hot, and pungent flavors, 17, 18, 19
Squash, Stuffed Squid Soup with, 237–38
squid, 123, 126, 129, 183, 185, 197, 206, 220, 232–36, 245, 253, 265
cleaning and preparing for cooking, 234–35
cooking tips for, 236
dried, 45–46
Marinated Charcoal-Grilled, 250–51
Mixed Seafood Salad with Lemon Grass, Mint, and Chilli-Lime Dressing, 276–77
Sautéed with Garlic and Lime, 248
selecting, 233
Shrimp-and-Crab-Stuffed, Crispy, 241–42
Sizzling Stir-Fried, with Chillies and Fragrant Herbs, 246–47
Spicy "Broken Fish Trap" Soup, 274–75
Spicy Seafood Sizzling Hot Plate, 278–79
Spicy Southern-Style Stir-Fried, 244–45
Steamed with Chilli-Lime Sauce, 243
Stir-Fried "Fish Trap," 282–83
Stir-Fried with Roasted Chilli Sauce and Thai Basil, 249–50
storing, 236
Stuffed, Soup with Napa Cabbage or Squash, 237–38
Sriracha chilli sauce, 70

steamed seafood:
   Dungeness Crab Served with Chilli-Lime Dipping
      Sauce, 218
   Fish, Mom's Good and Easy, 156–57
   Fish, Whole, with Chilli-Lime Sauce, 158–59
   Ling Cod, Fillet of, with Sautéed Garlic and Ginger,
      136
   Mussels in Clay Pot with Aromatic Herbs, 268–69
   Pompano, with Pickled Plum, 153
   Sea Bass, Fillet of, with Ginger, Green Onions, and
      Sesame-Soy Sauce, 154–55
   Squid with Chilli-Lime Sauce, 243
   Tiger Prawns, 193
   Tiger Prawns, with Garlic and Thai Chillies, 202
   Tilapia, Whole, with Ginger and Fermented Soybean
      Sauce, 137–38
steaming, 77–78
   "picker upper" for, 90
   with stacked metal steamer, 85–87
sticky rice, 70–71
stir-fried seafood:
   Clams, with Roasted Chilli Sauce and Basil, 270–71
   Crab, Black-Peppered, with Roasted Spices,
      223–24
   Crab, Shelled, Wok-Tossed, with Chillies, Garlic, and
      Crisped Holy Basil, 225–26
   Crab in Shell, Wok-Tossed, with Green Onions,
      221–22
   Crab with Yellow Curry Sauce, 219–20
   "Drunken" Mixed Seafood, with Holy Basil, 280–81
   Fish Fillets, in Hot-and-Spicy Coconut Cream Sauce,
      122–23
   "Fish Trap," 282–83
   Mussels in Shell, Wok-Tossed, with Lemon Grass and
      Basil, 272
   Prawns, Southern-Style Spicy Tamarind, with
      Crisped Shallots and Garlic, 205–6
   Salmon, Wok-Tossed, with Chillies and Thai Basil,
      126
   Scallops and Mussels, Spicy, with Homemade Chilli
      Paste and Thai Eggplants, 264–65
   Shrimp, Cashew, 207–8
   Shrimp, "Five Flavored," with Toasted Sesame Seeds,
      209–10
   Shrimp with Saðtaw or Fava Beans, Spicy
      Southern-Style, 199–200
   Squid, Sizzling, with Chillies and Fragrant Herbs,
      246–47
   Squid, Spicy Southern-Style, 244–45
   Squid, with Roasted Chilli Sauce and Thai Basil,
      249–50
   Tiger Prawns, Hot-and-Sour Lemon Grass, 203–4
stir-frying, 76–77

clams and mussels, 236
crustaceans, 174
in wok, 80–81, 85
stock, seafood, 68, 99, 174, 236
striped bass, 153, 156, 158, 161
   Charcoal-Roasted in Banana Leaf, Served with Hot-
      and-Sour Dipping Sauce, 162–63
stuffed:
   Crab Shells with Hot Pickled Garlic Sauce, 216–17
   Shrimp-and-Crab-, Squid, Crispy, 241–42
   Squid Soup with Napa Cabbage or Squash, 237–38
sturgeon, 122, 208, 247, 261, 265
sugar, palm or coconut, 65–66
sunflower oil, 65
sweet-and-sour:
   Chilli Dressing, 254
   Cucumber Relish, 189, 190
   Plum Dipping Sauce, Spicy, 180
   Sauce, Leaf-Wrapped Fish and Tasty Tidbits
      with, 104–5
Sweet-and-Tangy Dipping Sauce, 260–61
sweet flavors, 17, 18–19
swordfish, 143, 144, 208, 247, 261

tamarind, 71
   Chilli Sauce, Pan-Fried Halibut Topped with, 147–48
   Ginger Fish Soup, 102–3
   Prawns, Southern-Style Spicy, with Crisped Shallots
      and Garlic, 205–6
   Sour, Fish Chowder, 116–17
   Sour, Sauce, Charcoal-Grilled Jumbo Prawns or
      Lobster Tails Topped with, 198
   Sour, Sauce, Piquant, 164
tapioca flour or starch, 72
Tawð Mân Bpoo, 215
Tawð Mân Gkoong, 188–90
Temple of Thai, 288
Thai cooking, 17–32
   balance of dishes in meal in, 19
   cooking methods in, 76–88
   equipment for, 87–90
   fish and rice in, 29–32
   flavor harmony in, 18–19
   freshwater fish in, 29–31
   as fusion food, 21–23
   ingredients in, 49–73
   preserved seafood as flavoring ingredients in, 33–48
   primary flavors in, 17–18
   rice as main food in, 20, 29, 30
   seafood introduced into, 27–29
   variations in ingredients and, 19–20
   wok cooking in, 79–85

Thai eggplant, 48, 58, 110, 120, 139, 264
Thai Grocer, 288
Thai markets, 285–87
"Three-Flavored" Grouper or Rock Fish with
    Roasted Garlic and Roasted Chillies, 145–46
tilapia, 44, 102, 104, 116, 131, 135
    Braised Whole, with Ginger and Green Onions,
        160–61
    Whole, Steamed with Ginger and Fermented
        Soybean Sauce, 137–38
Toast, Shrimp-and-Crab, with Sesame Seeds, Crispy,
    Served with Sweet-and-Sour Plum Sauce, 179–80
trout, 136, 153, 158
    Pan-Fried, Soup with Roasted Chillies and Aromatic
        Herbs, Hot-and-Sour, 100–101
tuna, 115, 143, 208, 247
turmeric, 72–73
    Coconut Sauce, Shrimp Cooked in, 201
    -Flavored Coconut Sauce, Catfish Rounds
        Simmered in, 118–19
    Fried Fish, Southern-Style, 133–35

vegetables:
    Assorted, Pan-Fried Mackerel and, with Hot-and-
        Pungent Fermented Shrimp Dipping Sauce,
        139–41
    with Salted Crab Coconut Cream Sauce, 47–48
vinegars, 73

water, limestone, 63–64
wire-mesh skimmers, 89–90
wok cooking, 79–85
    adapting wok to stove, 81–82
    deep-frying fish in, 98
    flat-bottom woks and, 82, 83
    pan-frying and deep-frying, 82–83
    seasoning and caring for wok, 84–85
    stir-frying, 80–81, 85
wok rings, 81–82
wok-tossed seafood:
    Crab, Shelled, with Chillies, Garlic, and Crisped Holy
        Basil, 225–26
    Crab in Shell with Green Onions, 221–22
    Mussels in Shell with Lemon Grass and
        Basil, 272
    Salmon with Chillies and Thai Basil, 126
    see also stir-fried seafood

Yâm Bplah Doog Foo, 108–9
Yâm Gkoong Haeng, 38–39
Yâm Gkoong Hoi, 254–55
Yâm Gkoong Pow, 186–87
Yâm Sadet, 239–40
yâm salad-making, 78
Yâm Talay, 276–77
yellow curry, 57
    Sauce, Stir-Fried Crab with, 219–20

ABOUT THE AUTHOR

BORN AND RAISED IN THAILAND, KASMA LOHA-UNCHIT CAME TO THE United States in 1968 to study Business Administration. Pursuing this course of life, she obtained her degree, with honors, from Arizona State University in 1972, later received her MBA from University of California at Berkeley, and worked in insurance for many years. It wasn't until the tragic death of her young husband in 1980 and her subsequent studies of Oriental medicine and professional psychology at John F. Kennedy University in Orinda, California, that she had the realization that has set her on her present path. Coming to understand that nurturing others through the sharing of food and culture had been her most important source of healing throughout her life, she abandoned her studies and began her adventures into the world of cooking and nourishing the self.

Since 1985, Kasma Loha-unchit has taught Thai cooking—just as she learned the art from her mother, a fine cook in Bangkok—in her own home-based cooking school in the San Francisco Bay Area and led cultural tours to her homeland. Thousands of Thai food aficionados from both the Bay Area and around the world have taken Kasma's classes and workshops, and many continue to return to her kitchen in Oakland for more instruction and ideas on the cooking of Thai and Southeast Asian foods. It was through their persistence and encouragement to unveil the secrets of working with Asian ingredients and techniques covered in her classes, that Kasma finally wrote her first book, *It Rains Fishes: Legends, Traditions and the Joys of Thai Cooking.*

Published by Pomegranate Artbooks in San Francisco in the summer of 1995, *It Rains Fishes* introduced the art of Thai cooking in easy-to-follow recipes woven into a rich tapestry of folklore, travel tales, and intimate stories of the Thai people and their culture. Fittingly, it received excellent reviews, garnered a wonderful amount of publicity, and ultimately won the 1996 Julia Child Award for Best International Cookbook from the International Association of Culinary Professionals.

Her second book, *Dancing Shrimp*, expounds upon the nurturing qualities of Thai food and the common spices and herbs used, while focusing on specific recipes for the plentiful seafood found throughout the country. Since Kasma continues to lead cultural and culinary tours to Thailand twice a year, it also contains many stories of her journeys, special delicacies she has found, and the traditional way of life of the Thai people.

Happily, food has nourished and fed Kasma's soul. She lives in Oakland with her husband, Michael, a writer, who encourages and supports her career by maintaining her informational Web site. She also writes a monthly column for the *San Jose Mercury News*. More information on Kasma and her school or travels can be found at www.thaifoodandtravel.com.